Paula

ISABEL ALLENDE was born in Peru of Chilean parents and now lives in California. She worked as a journalist for many years before writing the internationally bestselling novel *The House of the Spirits*. Since then she has published the equally highly acclaimed *Of Love and Shadows*, *Eva Luna*, *The Stories of Eva Luna* and *The Infinite Plan*, which won the bi-monthly *Independent* Foreign Fiction Award.

In December 1991, Isabel Allende's daughter Paula, aged 28, fell gravely ill and sank into a coma. This book was written during the interminable hours the novelist spent in the corridors of a Madrid hospital, in the hotel room where she lived for several months, and beside Paula's bed at home in California, during the summer and autumn of 1992.

'Allende's best work to date . . . she has everything it takes: the ear, the eye, the mind, the heart, the all-encompassing humanity.'
New York Times

'*Paula* is more than a memoir. It is a tender, moving and vivid record of a mother's agony at the bedside of her daughter. *Paula* begins as a long letter as a way of giving her back the life that is ebbing away . . . the result is a mesmerizing story. In flawlessly rich prose Allende shares with us her most intimate feelings . . . an emotionally charged, spellbinding memoir.'
Washington Post

'*Paula* is full of the same portentous dreams and friendly ghosts, the same unlikely events that make Allende's fiction so delightful. This true story of Allende's life is even more wonderful, spirited and humorous than its imaginary rendition in her first novel, *The House of the Spirits*.' *San Francisco Examiner*

ISABEL ALLENDE

Paula

*Translated from the Spanish
by Margaret Sayers Peden*

Quality Paperbacks Direct
London

We did not come to remain whole.
We came to lose our leaves like the trees,
The trees that are broken
And start again, drawing up from the great roots.

—ROBERT BLY

In December 1991 my daughter, Paula, fell gravely ill and soon thereafter sank into a coma. These pages were written during the interminable hours spent in the corridors of a Madrid hospital and in the hotel room where I lived for several months, as well as beside her bed in our home in California during the summer and fall of 1992.

PART ONE

December 1991
to May 1992

LISTEN, PAULA. I AM GOING TO TELL YOU A STORY, SO that when you wake up you will not feel so lost. The legend of our family begins at the end of the last century, when a robust Basque sailor disembarked on the coast of Chile with his mother's reliquary strung around his neck and his head swimming with plans for greatness. But why start so far back? It is enough to say that those who came after him were a breed of impetuous women and men with sentimental hearts and strong arms fit for hard work. Some few irascible types died frothing at the mouth, although the cause may not have been rage, as evil tongues had it, but, rather, some local pestilence. The Basque's descendants bought fertile land on the outskirts of the capital, which with time increased in value; they became more refined and constructed lordly mansions with great parks and groves; they wed their daughters to rich young men from established families; they educated their children in rigorous religious schools; and thus over the course of the years they were integrated into a proud aristocracy of landowners that prevailed for more than a century—until the whirlwind of modern times replaced them with technocrats and businessmen. My grandfather was one of the former, the good old families, but his father died young of an unexplained shotgun wound. The details of what happened that fateful night were never revealed, but it could have been a duel, or revenge, or some accident of love. In any case, his family was left without means and, because he was the oldest, my grandfather had to drop out of school and look for work to support his mother and educate his younger brothers. Much later, when he had become a wealthy man to whom others doffed their hats, he confessed to me that genteel poverty is the worst of all because it must be concealed. He was always well turned out—in his father's clothes, altered to fit, the collars starched stiff and suits well pressed to disguise the threadbare cloth. Those years of penury tempered his character; in his credo, life was strife and hard work, and an honorable man should not pass through this world without helping his neighbor. Still young, he already exhibited the concentration and integrity that were his characteristics; he was made of the same hard stone as his ancestors and, like many of them, had his feet firmly on the ground. Even so, some small part of his soul drifted toward the abyss of dreams. Which was what allowed him to fall in love with my grandmother, the youngest of a family of twelve, all eccentrically and deliciously bizarre—like Teresa, who at the end of her life began to sprout the wings of a saint and at whose death all the roses in the Parque Japonés withered overnight. Or Ambrosio, a dedicated carouser and fornicator, who was known at moments of rare generosity to remove all his clothing in the street and hand it to the poor. I grew up listening to stories about my grandmother's ability to foretell the future, read minds, converse with animals, and move objects with her gaze. Everyone says that once she moved a billiard table across a room, but the only thing I ever saw move in her presence was an insignificant sugar bowl that used to skitter erratically across the table at tea time. These gifts aroused certain misgivings, and many eligible suitors were intimidated by her, despite her charms. My grandfather, however, regarded telepathy and telekinesis as innocent diversions and in no way a serious obstacle to marriage. The only thing that concerned him was the difference in their ages. My grandmother was much younger than he, and when he first met her she was still playing with dolls and walking around clutching a grimy little pillow.

Because he was so used to seeing her as a young girl, he was unaware of his passion for her until one day she appeared in a long dress and with her hair up, and then the revelation of a love that had been gestating for years threw him into such a fit of shyness that he stopped calling. My grandmother divined his state of mind before he himself was able to undo the tangle of his own feelings and sent him a letter, the first of many she was to write him at decisive moments in their lives. This was not a perfumed billet-doux testing the waters of their relationship, but a brief note penciled on lined paper asking him straight out whether he wanted to marry her and, if so, when. Several months later they were wed. Standing before the altar, the bride was a vision from another era, adorned in ivory lace and a riot of wax orange blossoms threaded through her chignon. When my grandfather saw her, he knew he would love her obstinately till the end of his days.

To me, they were always Tata and Memé. Of their children, only my mother will figure in this story, because if I begin to tell you about all the rest of the tribe we shall never be finished, and besides, the ones who are still living are very far away. That's what happens to exiles; they are scattered to the four winds and then find it extremely difficult to get back together again. My mother was born between the two world wars, on a fine spring day in the 1920s. She was a sensitive girl, temperamentally unsuited to joining her brothers in their sweeps through the attic to catch mice they preserved in bottles of Formol. She led a sheltered life within the walls of her home and her school; she amused herself with charitable works and romantic novels, and had the reputation of being the most beautiful girl ever seen in this family of enigmatic women. From the time of puberty, she had lovesick admirers buzzing around like flies, young men her father held at bay and her mother analyzed with her tarot cards; these innocent flirtations were cut short when a talented and equivocal young man appeared and effortlessly dislodged his rivals, fulfilling his destiny and filling my mother's heart with uneasy emotions. That was your grandfather Tomás, who disappeared in a fog, and the only reason I mention him, Paula, is because some of his blood flows in your veins. This clever man with a quick mind and merciless tongue was too intelligent and free of prejudice for that provincial society, a rara avis in the Santiago of his time. It was said that he had a murky past; rumors flew that he belonged to the Masonic sect, and so was an enemy of the Church, and that he had a bastard son hidden away somewhere, but Tata could not put forward any of these arguments to dissuade his daughter because he lacked proof, and my grandfather was not a man to stain another's reputation without good reason. In those days Chile was like a mille-feuille pastry. It had more castes than India, and there was a pejorative term to set every person in his or her rightful place: *roto, pije, arribista, siútico,* and many more, working upward toward the comfortable plateau of "people like ourselves." Birth determined status. It was easy to descend in the social hierarchy, but money, fame, or talent was not sufficient to allow one to rise, that required the sustained effort of several generations. Tomás's honorable lineage was in his favor, even though in Tata's eyes he had questionable political ties. By then the name Salvador Allende, the founder of Chile's Socialist Party, was being bruited about; he preached against private property, conservative morality, and the power of the large landowners. Tomás was the cousin of that young deputy.

Look, Paula, this is Tata's picture. This man with the severe features, clear eyes, rimless eyeglasses, and black beret is your great-grandfather. In the picture he is seated, hands on his cane, and beside him, leaning against his right knee, is a little girl of three in her party dress, a pint-size charmer staring into the camera with liquid eyes. That's *you.* My mother and I are standing behind you, the chair masking the fact that I was carrying your brother Nicolás. The old man is facing the camera, and you can see his proud bearing, the calm dignity of the self-made man who has marched straight down the road of life and expects nothing more. I remember him as always being old—although almost without wrinkles except for the two deep furrows at the corners of his mouth—with a lion's mane of snow-white hair and an abrupt laugh filled with yellow teeth. At the end of his days it was painful for him to move, but he always struggled to his feet to say hello and goodbye to the ladies and, hobbling along on his cane, escort them to the garden gate as they left. I loved his hands, twisted oak branches, strong and gnarled, his inevitable silk neckerchief, and his odor of English

Creolin-and-lavender soap. With inexhaustible good humor, he tried to instill in his descendants his stoic philosophy: he believed discomfort was healthful and that central heating sapped the strength; he insisted on simple food—no sauces or pot-au-feu— and he thought it bad taste to have too good a time. Every morning he took a cold shower, a custom no one in the family imitated, and one that when he resembled nothing more than a geriatric beetle he fulfilled, old but undaunted, seated in a chair beneath the icy blast. He spoke in ringing aphorisms and answered direct questions with a different question, so that even though I knew his character to the core, I know very little about his ideology. Look carefully at Mother, Paula. In this picture she is in her early forties, and at the peak of her beauty. That short skirt and beehive hair were all the rage. She's laughing, and her large eyes are two green lines punctuated by the sharp arch of black eyebrows. That was the happiest period of her life, when she had finished raising her children, was still in love, and the world seemed secure.

I wish I could show you a photograph of my father, but they were all burned more than forty years ago.

Where are you wandering, Paula? How will you be when you wake up? Will you be the same woman, or will we be like strangers and have to learn to know one another all over again? Will you have your memory, or will I need to sit patiently and relate the entire story of your twenty-eight years and my forty-nine?

"May God watch over your daughter," don Manuel told me, barely able to whisper. He's the one in the bed next to yours, an elderly peasant who has undergone several operations on his stomach but has not given up fighting for health and life. "May God watch over your daughter" was also what a young woman with a baby in her arms said yesterday. She had heard about you and come to the hospital to offer me hope. She suffered an attack of porphyria two years ago and was in a coma for more than a month. It was a year before she was normal again and she will have to be careful for the rest of her life, but she is working now, and she married and had a baby. She assured me that being in a coma is like a sleep without dreams, a mysterious parenthesis. "Don't cry anymore, Señora," she said, "your daughter doesn't feel a thing; she will walk out of here and never remember what happened." Every morning I prowl the corridors of the sixth floor looking for the specialist, in hopes of learning something new. He holds your life in his hands, and I don't trust him. He wafts through like a breeze, distracted and rushed, offering me worrisome explanations about enzymes and copies of articles about your illness that I try to read but do not understand. He seems more interested in the statistics from his computer and formulas from his laboratory than in your poor body lying crucified on this bed. He tells me—without meeting my eyes—"That's how it is with this condition; some recover quickly after the crisis, while others spend weeks in intensive therapy. It used to be that the patients simply died, but now we can keep them alive until their metabolism resumes functioning." Well, if that's how it is, all we can do is wait and be strong. If you can take it, Paula, so can I.

When you wake up we will have months, maybe years, to piece together the broken fragments of your past; better yet, we can invent memories that fit your fantasies. For the time being, I will tell you about myself and the other members of this family we both belong to, but don't ask me to be precise, because inevitably errors will creep in. I have forgotten a lot, and some of the facts are twisted. There are places, dates, and names I don't remember; on the other hand, I never forget a good story. Sitting here by your side, watching the screen with the luminous lines measuring your heartbeats, I try to use my grandmother's magic to communicate with you. If she were here she could carry my messages to you and help me hold you in this world. Have you begun some strange trek through the sand dunes of the unconscious? What good are all these words if you can't hear me? Or these pages you may never read? My life is created as I narrate, and my memory grows stronger with writing; what I do not put in words on a page will be erased by time.

Today is January 8, 1992. On a day like today, eleven years ago in Caracas, I began a letter that would be my goodbye to my grand-father, who was dying, leaving a hard-fought century behind him. His strong body had not failed, but long ago he had made his prepa-rations to follow Memé, who was beckoning to him from the other side. I could not return to Chile, and he so detested the telephone that it didn't seem right to call, but I wanted to tell him not to worry, that nothing would be lost of the treasury of anecdotes he had told me through the years of our comradeship; I had forgotten nothing. Soon he died, but the story I had begun to tell had enmeshed me, and I couldn't stop. Other voices were speaking through me; I was writing in a trance, with the sensation of unwinding a ball of yarn, driven by the same urgency I feel as I write now. At the end of a year the pages had grown to five hundred, filling a canvas bag, and I realized that this was no longer a letter. Timidly, I announced to my family that I had written a book. "What's the title?" my mother asked. We made a list of possibilities but could not agree on any, and finally it was you, Paula, who tossed a coin in the air to decide it. Thus was born and baptized my first novel, *The House of the Spirits,* and I was initiated into the ineradicable vice of telling stories. That book saved my life. Writing is a long process of introspection; it is a voyage toward the darkest caverns of consciousness, a long, slow meditation. I write feeling my way in silence, and along the way discover particles of truth, small crystals that fit in the palm of one hand and justify my passage through this world. I also began my second novel on an eighth of January, and since have not dared change that auspicious date, partly out of superstition, but also for reasons of discipline. I have begun all my books on a January 8.

When some months ago I finished my most recent novel, *The Infinite Plan,* I began preparing for today. I had everything in my mind—theme, title, first sentence—but I shall not write that story yet. Since you fell ill I have had no strength for anything but you, Paula. You have been sleeping for a month now. I don't know how to reach you; I call and call but your name is lost in the nooks and crannies of this hospital. My soul is choking in sand. Sadness is a sterile desert. I don't know how to pray. I cannot string together two thoughts, much less immerse myself in creating a new book. I plunge into these pages in an irrational attempt to overcome my terror. I think that perhaps if I give form to this devastation I shall be able to help you, and myself, and that the meticulous exercise of writing can be our salvation. Eleven years ago I wrote a letter to my grandfather to say goodbye to him in death. On this January 8, 1992, I am writing you, Paula, to bring you back to life.

My mother was a radiant young woman of eighteen when Tata took the family to Europe on a monumental journey that in those days was made only once in a lifetime: Chile lies at the bottom of the world. He intended to place his daughter in an English school to be "finished," hoping that in the process she would forget her love for Tomás, but Hitler wrecked those plans; the Second World War burst out with cataclysmic force, surprising them on the Côte d'Azur. With incredible difficulty, moving against the streams of people escaping on foot, horseback, or any available vehicle, they managed to reach Antwerp and board the last Chilean ship to set sail from the docks. The decks and lifeboats had been commandeered by dozens of families of fleeing Jews who had left their belongings—in some cases, fortunes—in the hands of unscrupulous consuls who sold them visas in exchange for gold. Unable to obtain staterooms, they traveled like cattle, sleeping in the open and going hungry because of food rationing. Through that arduous crossing, Memé consoled women weeping over the loss of their homes and the uncertainty of the future, while Tata negotiated food from the kitchen and blankets from the sailors to distribute among the refugees. In appreciation, one of them, a furrier by trade, gave Memé a luxurious coat of gray astrakhan. For several weeks they sailed through waters infested with enemy submarines, blacking out lights by night and praying by day, until they had left the Atlantic behind and safely reached Chile. As the boat docked in the port of Valparaíso, the first sight that met their eyes was the unmistakable figure of Tomás in a white linen suit and Panama hat. At that moment, Tata realized the futility of opposing the mysterious dictates of destiny and so, grudgingly, gave his consent for the wedding. The ceremony was held at home, with the participation of the papal nuncio and various personages from the official world. The bride wore a sober satin gown and a defiant expression. I don't know how the groom looked, because the photograph has been cropped; we can see nothing of him but one arm. As he led his daughter to the large room where an altar of cascading roses had been erected, Tata paused at the foot of the stairway.

"There is still time to change your mind," he said. "Don't marry him, Daughter, think better of it. Just give me a sign and I will run this mob out of here and send the banquet to the orphanage." My mother replied with an icy stare.

Just as my grandmother had been warned by the spirits in one of her sessions, my parents' marriage was a disaster from the very beginning. Once again, my mother boarded a ship, this time for Peru, where Tomás had been named secretary at the Chilean embassy. She took with her a collection of heavy trunks containing her bridal trousseau and a mountain of gifts, so much china, crystal, and silver that even now, a half-century later, we keep running into them in unexpected corners. Fifty years of diplomatic assignments in many latitudes, divorce, and long exile have not rid the family of this flotsam. I greatly fear, Paula, that among other ghastly prizes you will inherit a lamp that is still in my mother's possession, a baroque chaos of nymphs and plump cherubs. Your house is monastically spare, and your meager closet contains nothing but four blouses and two pairs of slacks. I wonder what you do with the things I keep giving you? You're like Memé, whose feet had scarcely touched solid ground before she removed the astrakhan coat and draped it over a beggarwoman's shoulders. My mother spent the first two days of her honeymoon so nauseated by the tossing Pacific Ocean that she was unable to leave her stateroom; then, just as she felt a little better and could go outside to drink in the fresh air, her husband was felled by a toothache. While she strolled around the decks, indifferent to the covetous stares of officers and sailors, he lay moaning in his bunk. At sunset the vast horizon was flooded with shades of orange and at night a scandal of stars invited love, but suffering was more powerful than romance. Three interminable days had to pass before the patient allowed the ship's physician to intervene with his forceps and ease the torment. Only then did the swelling subside, and husband and wife could begin married life. The next night they appeared together in the dining room as guests at the captain's table. After a formal toast to the newlyweds, the appetizer was served: prawns arranged in goblets carved of ice. In a gesture of flirtatious intimacy, my mother reached across and speared a bit of seafood from her husband's plate, unfortunately flicking a minute drop of cocktail sauce onto his necktie. Tomás seized a knife to scrape away the offensive spot, but merely spread the stain. To the astonishment of his fellow guests and the mortification of his wife, the diplomat dipped his fingers into his dish, scooped up a handful of crustaceans, and smeared them over his chest, desecrating shirt, suit, and the unsoiled portion of his tie; then, after passing his hands over his slicked-down hair, he rose to his feet, bowed slightly, and strode off to his stateroom, where he stayed for the remainder of the voyage, deep in a sullen silence. Despite these mishaps, I was conceived on that sea voyage.

Nothing had prepared my mother for motherhood. In those days, such matters were discussed in whispers before unwed girls, and Memé had given no thought to advising her about the libidinous preoccupations of the birds and the flowers because her soul floated on different planes, more intrigued with the translucence of apparitions than the gross realities of this world. Nevertheless, as soon as my mother sensed she was pregnant, she knew it would be a girl. She named her Isabel and established a dialogue that continues to the present day. Clinging to the creature developing in her womb, she tried to compensate for the loneliness of a woman who has chosen badly in love. She talked to me aloud, startling everyone who saw her carrying on as if hallucinating, and I suppose that I heard her and answered, although I have no memory of the intrauterine phase of my life.

My father had a taste for splendor. Ostentation had always been looked upon as a vice in Chile, where sobriety is a sign of refinement. In contrast, in Lima, the city of viceroys, swagger and swash is considered stylish. Tomás installed himself in a house incommensurate with his position as second secretary in the embassy, surrounded himself with Indian servants, ordered a luxurious automobile from Detroit, and squandered money on parties, gaming, and yacht clubs, without anyone's being able to explain how he could afford such extravagances. In a short time he had managed to establish relations with the most illustrious members of Lima's political and social circles, had discovered the weaknesses of each, and, through his contacts, heard a number of indiscreet confidences, even a few state secrets. He became the indispensable element in

Lima's revels. At the height of the war, he obtained the best whiskey, the purest cocaine, and the most obliging party girls; all doors opened to him. While he climbed the ladder of his career, his wife felt as if she was a prisoner with no hope for escape, joined at twenty to an evasive man on whom she was totally dependent. She languished in the humid summer heat, writing interminable pages to her mother; their correspondence was a conversation between the deaf, crossing at sea and buried in the bottom of mailbags. Nevertheless, as melancholy letters stacked up on her desk, Memé became convinced of her daughter's disenchantment. She interrupted the spiritist sessions with her three esoteric friends from the White Sisterhood, packed her prophetic deck of cards in her suitcase, and set off for Lima in a light biplane, one of the few that carried passengers, since during times of war planes were reserved for military purposes. She arrived just in time for my birth. As her own children had been born at home with the aid of her husband and a midwife, she was bewildered by the modern methods of the clinic. With one jab of a needle, they rendered her daughter senseless, depriving her of any chance to participate in events, and as soon as the baby was born transferred it to an aseptic nursery. Much later, when the fog of the anesthesia had lifted, they informed my mother that she had given birth to a baby girl, but that in accord with regulations she could have her only during the time she was nursing.

"She's a freak, that's why they won't let me see her!"

"She's a precious little thing!" my grandmother replied, trying to sound a note of conviction, although she herself had not yet actually seen me: through the glass, she had spied a blanket-wrapped bundle, something that to her eyes did not look entirely human.

While I screamed with hunger on a different floor, my mother thrashed about, prepared to reclaim her daughter by force, should that be necessary. A doctor came, diagnosed hysteria, and administered a second injection that knocked her out for another twelve hours. By then my grandmother was convinced that they were in the anteroom to hell, and as soon as her daughter was conscious, she splashed cold water on her face and helped her get dressed.

"We have to get out of here. Put on your clothes and we'll stroll out arm in arm like two ladies who've come to visit."

"For God's sake, Mama, we can't go without the baby!"

"Of course we can't!" exclaimed my grandmother, who probably had overlooked that detail.

The two women walked purposefully into the room where the newborn babies were sequestered, picked one out, and hastily exited, without raising an alarm. They could tell the sex, because the infant had a rose-colored ribbon around its wrist, and though there wasn't enough time to be certain that it was theirs, that wasn't vital anyway, all babies are more or less alike at that age. It is possible that in their haste they traded me for another baby, and that somewhere there is a woman with spinach-colored eyes and a gift for clairvoyance who is taking my place. Once safely home, they stripped me bare to be sure I was whole, and discovered a small birthmark in the shape of a sun at the base of my spine. "That's a good sign," Memé assured my mother. "We won't have to worry about her, she'll grow up healthy and blessed with good fortune." I was born in August, under the sign of Leo, sex, female, and, if I was not switched in the clinic, I have three-quarters Spanish-Basque blood, one-quarter French, and a tot of Araucan or Mapuche Indian, like everyone else in my land. Despite my birth in Lima, I am Chilean. I come from a "long petal of sea and wine and snow," as Pablo Neruda described my country, and you're from there, too, Paula, even though you bear the indelible stamp of the Caribbean where you spent the years of your childhood. It may be difficult for you to understand the mentality of those of us from the south. In Chile we are influenced by the eternal presence of the mountains that separate us from the rest of the continent, and by a sense of precariousness inevitable in a region of geological and political catastrophes. Everything trembles beneath our feet; we know no security. If anyone asks us how we are, we answer, "About the same," or "All right, I guess." We move from one uncertainty to another; we pick our way through a twilight region. Nothing is precise. We do not like confrontations, we prefer to negotiate. When circumstances push us to extremes, our worst instincts are awakened and history takes a tragic turn, because the same men who seem mild-mannered in their everyday lives can, if offered impunity and the right pretext, turn into bloodthirsty beasts. In normal times, however, Chileans are sober, circumspect, and formal, and suffer an acute fear of attracting attention, which to them is synonymous with looking ridiculous. For that very reason, I have been an embarrassment to my family.

And where was Tomás while his wife was giving birth and his mother-in-law effecting the discreet kidnapping of her first grandchild? I have no idea. My father is a great lacuna in my life. He went away so early, and vanished so completely, that I have no memory of him at all. My mother lived with him for four years, including two long separations—but sufficient time to bring three children into the world. She was so fertile that she became pregnant if a pair of men's undershorts was waved anywhere within a radius of a half kilometer, a predisposition I inherited, although, to my good fortune, the age of The Pill arrived in time for me. With each birth her husband disappeared—as he did at the sign of any major difficulty—and then, once the emergency was over, returned, beaming, with some extravagant present. She watched the proliferation of paintings on the walls and Chinese porcelains on the shelves, totally mystified at where all the money was coming from. It was impossible to explain such luxuries when others at the consulate could scarcely make ends meet, but when she asked him, my father gave her the runaround—just as he did when she asked about his nocturnal absences, his mysterious trips, and his shady friendships. My mother had two children, and was about to give birth to the third, when the whole house of cards of her innocence came tumbling down. Lima awoke one morning to rumors of a scandal that escaped the newspapers but filtered into every salon. It had to do with an elderly millionaire who used to lend his apartment to special friends for clandestine trysts. In the bedroom, lost among pieces of antique furniture and Persian tapestries, hung a false mirror in a heavy baroque frame—actually, a window. On the other side, the master of the house liked to sit with a select group of guests, well supplied with liquor and drugs, eager to enjoy the antics of the current, usually unsuspecting, couple in the bed. That night a high-ranking politician was among the invited. When the curtain was drawn for the voyeurs to spy on the unwary lovers, the first surprise was that they were two males; the second was that one of them, decked out in a corset and lace garters, was the eldest son of the politician, a young lawyer destined for a brilliant career. In his humiliation, the father lost control; he kicked out the mirror, threw himself on his son to tear off the women's frippery, and, had he not been restrained, might have murdered him. A few hours later every circle in Lima was humming with the particulars of the event, adding more and more scabrous details with each telling. It was suspected that it was not a chance incident, that someone had planned the scene out of pure malice. Frightened, Tomás disappeared without a word. My mother did not hear of the scandal until several days later; she was isolated by the demands of her series of pregnancies, and also by a desire to escape the creditors who were clamoring for payment. Tired of waiting for their wages, the servants had deserted; only Margara remained, a Chilean employee with a hermetic face and heart of stone who had served the family since the beginning of time. It was in these straits that my mother felt the pangs of imminent birth. She gritted her teeth and prepared to have the baby under the most primitive circumstances. I was almost three, and my brother Pancho was barely walking. That night, huddled together in the corridor, we heard my mother's moans and witnessed Margara scurrying back and forth with towels and kettles of hot water. Juan came into the world at midnight, tiny and wrinkled, a hairless wisp of a mouse, barely breathing. It was soon obvious that he couldn't swallow; he had some knot in his throat that wouldn't let food pass. Although my mother's breasts were bursting with milk, he was destined to perish of hunger, but Margara was determined to keep him alive, at first by squeezing drops from milk-soaked cotton, then later using a wooden spoon to force a thick pap down his throat.

For years, morbid explanations for my father's disappearance rattled around in my head. I asked about him until finally I gave up, recognizing that there is a conspiracy of silence around him. Those who knew him describe him to me as a very intelligent man, and stop there. When I was young, I imagined him as a criminal, and later, when I learned about sexual perversions, I attributed all of them to him, but the facts suggest that nothing so dramatic colored his past; he merely had a cowardly soul. One day he found himself trapped by his lies; events were out of control, so he ran away. He left the Foreign Service and never again saw my mother or any of his family or friends. He simply vanished in smoke. I visualized him—partly in jest, of course—fleeing toward Machu Picchu disguised as a Peruvian Indian woman, wearing a wig with long black braids and layers of many-colored skirts. "Don't ever say that again!" my mother screamed when I told her my fantasy. "Where do you get such crazy ideas?" Whatever happened, he disappeared without a trace, although obviously he did not hie himself off to the thin, clear air of the Andes to live unnoticed in some Aymara village; he just descended a rung in the immutable scale of Chile's social classes and became invisible. He must have returned to Santiago and walked the streets of the city center but as he did not frequent the same social milieu it was as if he had died. I never again saw my paternal grandmother or any of my father's family—except for Salvador Allende, who out of a strong sense of loyalty kept in close touch with us. Nor did I see my father again, or hear his name spoken aloud. I know absolutely nothing about his physical appearance, so it is ironic that one day I was called to identify his body in the morgue—but that came much later. I'm sorry, Paula, that this character must disappear at this point, because villains always are the most delicious part of a story.

My mother, who had been brought up in a world of privilege in which women were excluded from money matters, entrenched herself in her house, wiped away the tears of abandonment, and found consolation in the fact that for a time, at least, she would not starve; she had the treasure of the silver trays, which she could pawn one by one to pay the bills. She was alone in a strange land with three children, surrounded by the trappings of wealth but without a cent in her pocketbook and too proud to ask for help. The embassy, nonetheless, was alert, and learned immediately that Tomás had disappeared, leaving his family in bankruptcy. The honor of the nation was at stake; they could not allow the name of a Chilean official to be dragged through the mud, much less permit his wife and children to be put out into the street by creditors. So the consul was sent to call on the family, with instructions to help them return to Chile with the greatest possible discretion. You guessed right, Paula, that man was your Tío Ramón, your grandfather, a prince, and the direct descendant of Jesus Christ. He himself tells that he was one of the ugliest men of his generation, but I think he is exaggerating. We can't call him handsome, but what he lacks in good looks he more than makes up for in intelligence and charm. Besides, the years have lent him an air of great dignity. At the time he was sent to our aid, Tío Ramón was bone thin, had a greenish tint to his skin, a walrus mustache, and Mephistophelian eyebrows; he was the father of four children and a practicing Catholic, and not a spot on the mythic character he would become after he had shed his skin like a snake. Margara opened the door to this visitor and led him to the bedroom of her señora, who received him lying in bed surrounded by her children, still slightly battered by the youngest's birth but glowing with striking beauty and youthful ebullience. The consul, who had scarcely known his colleague's wife—he had always seen her pregnant, and with a remote air that did not invite closer contact—stood near the door, sinking into a swamp of emotions. As he questioned her about the intricacies of her situation and explained the plan to send her back to Chile, he was tormented by a stampede of wild bulls in the area of his chest. Calculating that there was no more fascinating woman alive, and failing to understand how her husband could have abandoned her—he would give his life for her—he sighed at the crushing injustice of having met her too late. She looked at him for a long moment, and finally agreed:

"All right, I will return to my father's house."

"In a few days a ship is leaving Callao for Vuh-Valparaíso. I'll try to obtain passages," he stammered.

"I shall be traveling with my three children, Margara, and the dog. I don't know whether my baby will survive the trip, this little one is very weak," and although her eyes were shining with tears, she refused to allow herself to cry.

In a flash, Ramón's wife and his children filed before his eyes, followed by his father pointing an accusing finger, and his uncle, the bishop, holding a crucifix shooting rays of damnation. He saw himself excommunicated from the Church and disgraced in the Foreign Service, but he could think of nothing but this woman's perfect face. He felt as if he had been blown off his feet by a hurricane. He took two steps toward the bed. In those two steps, his future was decided.

"From now on, I will look after you and your children. . . . Forever."

Forever. What is that, Paula? I have lost count of the days in this white building where echoes reign and it is never night. The boundaries of reality have been blurred; life is a labyrinth of facing mirrors and deformed images. A month ago, at this very hour, I was a different woman. I have a photograph from that day. I am at a party launching the publication in Spain of my most recent novel. I am wearing a silver necklace and bracelets and an aubergine-colored dress. My nails are manicured and my smile confident. I am a century younger than I am today. I don't know that woman; in four weeks, sorrow has transformed me. As I stood at a microphone describing the circumstances that led me to write *The Infinite Plan,* my agent pushed her way through the crowd and whispered in my ear that you had been taken to the hospital. I had a jolting presentiment that something fundamental had happened to change our lives. We had been together the day before, and you were very ill. When I landed in Madrid, I was surprised that you weren't at the airport to greet me, as you always have been. I dropped my suitcases at the hotel and, still reeling from the long flight from California, rushed to your house, where I found you vomiting and burning with fever. You had just returned from a spiritual retreat with the nuns from the school where you work forty hours a week as a volunteer helping underprivileged children, and you told me it had been an intense and saddening experience. You were beset with doubts, your faith was fragile.

"I go looking everywhere for God, but He slips away from me, Mama."

"God can wait for a while. Right now it's more urgent to look for a doctor. What's the matter with you, Paula?"

"Porphyria," you replied without hesitation. Since learning several years earlier you had inherited the condition, you had taken very good care of yourself, and regularly consulted one of the few specialists in Spain. When Ernesto found you so weak, he took you to the emergency room; they diagnosed flu, and sent you back home. That night your husband told me that for weeks, even months, you had been tense and tired. As we sat and discussed what we thought was depression, you were suffering behind the closed door of your bedroom; the porphyria was poisoning you, and neither of us saw it. I don't know how I went on with my obligations; my mind was on you, and in a break between interviews I ran to the telephone to call. The minute I heard you were worse, I canceled the rest of my tour and flew to the hospital. I ran up the six flights of stairs and located your room in this monstrous building. I found you lying in bed, ashen, with a disoriented expression on your face. One glance was enough to realize how ill you were.

"Why are you crying?" you asked in an unrecognizable voice.

"Because I'm afraid. I love you, Paula."

"I love you, too, Mama."

That was the last thing you said to me, Paula. Instants later you were delirious, babbling numbers, with your eyes fixed on the ceiling. Ernesto and I sat beside your bed all night, in a daze, taking turns in the one available chair, while in other beds in the room an elderly patient was dying, a demented woman was screaming, and an undernourished Gypsy girl with signs of a recent beating tried to sleep. At dawn I convinced your husband to go rest, he was exhausted from being up several nights. He kissed you goodbye and left. An hour later the true horror was unleashed: a spine-chilling vomit of blood followed by convulsions. Your tense body arched upward, shuddering in violent spasms that lifted you from the bed. Your arms trembled and your fingers contracted as if you were trying to hold on to something. Your eyes were filled with terror, your face congested, and saliva ran from your mouth. I threw my body on yours to hold you down, and screamed at the top of my lungs for help. The room filled with people in white, and I was dragged out of the room by force. I remember finding myself kneeling on the floor, then being slapped. "Be quiet, Señora; you must be calm or you will have to leave." A male nurse was shaking me. "Your daughter is better now, you can go in." I tried to stand but my knees buckled. Someone helped me to your bed and then left. I was alone with you and with the patients in the other beds, who were watching in silence, each deep in her own private hell. Your color was ghostly, your eyes were rolled back, dried blood threaded from your lips, and you were cold. I waited, calling you by all the names I had given you as a little girl, but you were far away in another world. I tried to get you to drink a little water. When I shook you, you looked at me with glassy, dilated eyes, staring through me toward another horizon, and then suddenly you were as still as death, not breathing. Somehow I called for help, and immediately tried to give you mouth-to-mouth resuscitation, but fear made me clumsy. I did everything badly. I blew air into your mouth erratically, any way at all, five or six times, and then I noticed your heart had stopped beating, and began to pound your chest with my fists. Help arrived seconds later, and the last thing I saw was your bed hurtling toward the elevator at the end of the corridor. From that moment life stopped for you. And for me. Together we crossed a mysterious threshold and entered a zone of inky darkness.

"Her condition is critical," the physician on call in the intensive care unit told me.

"Should I call her father in Chile?" I asked. "It will take him more than twenty hours to get here."

"Yes."

People began to come by: Ernesto's relatives, and friends and nuns from your school. Someone notified the members of the family scattered through Chile, Venezuela, and the United States. Shortly afterward, your husband arrived, calm and gentle, more concerned about others' feelings than his own, but he looked very fatigued. They allowed him to see you for a few minutes, and when he came back he informed us that you were hooked up to a respirator and being given a blood transfusion. "It isn't as bad as they say," he told us. "I feel Paula's strong heart beating close to mine," a phrase that at the moment seemed to have little meaning but now that I know him I can better understand. We spent that day and the next night in the waiting room. At times I drifted into an exhausted sleep, but when I opened my eyes I found Ernesto always in the same position, unmoving, waiting.

"I'm terrified, Ernesto," I admitted toward dawn.

"There's nothing we can do. Paula is in God's hands."

"You find that easier to accept than I do, because at least you have your faith."

"It's as painful to me as to you, but I have less fear of death and more hope for life," he replied, putting his arms around me. I buried my face in his jacket, breathing his young male scent, racked by an atavistic fear.

As it grew light, my mother and Michael arrived from Chile, along with Willie, from California. Your father was very pale. He had boarded the airplane in Santiago convinced that he would find you dead. The flight must have seemed an eternity. Devastated, I hugged my mother, and realized that although she may have shrunken with the years, she still radiates an aura of protection. Beside her, Willie is a giant, yet when I wanted a chest to lay my head upon, my mother's seemed more ample and comforting than his. We went into the intensive care room and found you conscious, and improved over the previous day. The doctors had begun to replace the sodium in your body—which you were losing in alarming amounts—and the transfusion had revived you. That illusion, however, lasted only a few hours; soon afterward, you became very agitated, and with the massive dose of sedatives they used to treat it you descended into the deep coma from which you have not awakened to this day.

"Your poor daughter, she doesn't deserve this. I'm old, why can't I die in her place?" don Manuel wonders from time to time, his voice barely audible.

It is so difficult to write these pages, Paula, to retrace the steps of this painful journey, verify details, imagine how things might have been if you had fallen into more capable hands, if they had not immobilized you with drugs, if . . . , if . . . . How can I shake this guilt? When you mentioned the porphyria I thought you were exaggerating and, instead of seeking further help, I trusted those people in white; I handed over my daughter without hesitation. It isn't possible to go back in time. I must not keep looking back, yet I can't stop doing it, it's an obsession. Nothing exists but the unremitting certainty of this hospital; the rest of my life is veiled in heavy mist.

Willie, who after a few days had to return to his work in California, calls every morning and every night to offer support, to remind me that we love each other and have a happy life on the other side of the ocean. His voice comes to me from very far away, as if I had dreamed him and there was no wood house high above San Francisco Bay, no ardent lover now a distant husband. It also seems I have dreamed my son Nicolás, my daughter-in-law Celia, and little Alejandro with his giraffe eyelashes. Carmen, my agent, comes from time to time with sympathies from my editors or news about my books, but I don't know what she's talking about. Nothing exists but you, Paula, and this space without time in which we both are trapped.

In the long, silent hours, I am trampled by memories, all happening in one instant, as if my entire life were a single, unfathomable image. The child and girl I was, the woman I am, the old woman I shall be, are all water in the same rushing torrent. My memory is like a Mexican mural in which all times are simultaneous: the ships of the Conquistadors in one corner and an Inquisitor torturing Indians in another, galloping Liberators with blood-soaked flags and the Aztecs' Plumed Serpent facing a crucified Christ, all encircled by the billowing smokestacks of the industrial age. So it is with my life, a multilayered and ever-changing fresco that only I can decipher, whose secret is mine alone. The mind selects, enhances, and betrays; happenings fade from memory; people forget one another and, in the end, all that remains is the journey of the soul, those rare moments of spiritual revelation. What actually happened isn't what matters, only the resulting scars and distinguishing marks. My past has little meaning; I can see no order to it, no clarity, purpose, or path, only a blind journey guided by instinct and detours caused by events beyond my control. There was no deliberation on my part, only good intentions and the faint sense of a greater design determining my steps. Until now, I have never shared my past; it is my innermost garden, a place not even my most intimate lover has glimpsed. Take it, Paula, perhaps it will be of some use to you, because I fear that yours no longer exists, lost somewhere during your long sleep—and no one can live without memories.

My mother returned to her parents' home in Santiago. At that time, a failed marriage was considered the worst fate that could befall a woman, but as yet she did not know that, and returned with her head high. Ramón, the captivated consul, conveyed her, her children, the daunting Margara, the dog, and the trunks and boxes with the silver platters to the ship. As he bid her goodbye, he held her hands in his and repeated his promise to look after her forever, but she, distracted by the task of arranging her part in the limited space of the stateroom, rewarded him with the faintest of smiles. She was not unaccustomed to men's attentions, and she had no reason to suspect that this insecure-looking official was to play an essential role in her future. Neither had she forgotten that he had a wife and four children. As for the rest, she was besieged by more urgent matters: the newborn was gasping for breath like a fish on dry land, the other two children were sobbing with fright, and Margara had lapsed into one of her surly, reproachful silences. Only when my mother heard the sound of the engines and the hoarse blast announcing the ship's departure did she feel the first breath of the winds fast overtaking her. She could count on the refuge of her parents' home, but she could not go back to her single days; it was as if she were a widow, she would have to assume responsibility for her children. She was beginning to wonder how in the world she would cope, when the slamming of the waves brought back the memory of the prawns of her honeymoon and she smiled with relief—at least she was nowhere in the vicinity of her bizarre husband. She was just twenty-five and had no idea how she would support herself, but it was not for nothing that the adventurous blood of that remote Basque sailor flowed through her veins.

That is how I came to grow up in my grandparents' house. Well, I say "grow" in a manner of speaking; the truth is that I never did grow much. With tremendous effort, I reached five feet, where I remained until a month ago when I noticed that the bathroom mirror seemed higher on the wall. "Oh, piffle, you're not shrinking, it's just that you've lost weight and you're not wearing your heels," my mother consoled me, but I noticed she was observing me with a worried look. When I say it was hard work to grow, I am not speaking metaphorically; they tried everything possible to make me taller, except hormones. When I was young they were still experimental, and Benjamin Viel, our family physician and my mother's enduring Platonic love, was afraid I would grow a mustache—although a mustache wouldn't have been all that bad, you can always shave it off. Instead, for years I went to a gym where they suspended me from a system of cords and poles in the hope that gravity would stretch my skeleton. In my nightmares, I see myself hanging upside down by my ankles, but my mother swears that is pure fantasy, I never experienced anything that cruel. I was suspended by my neck, using an apparatus that prevented instantaneous death by hanging. The torment was for naught, however; all it did was lengthen my neck. The first school I attended was run by German nuns, but I didn't last long there. I was expelled at the age of six for perversion, having organized a contest to show off our underpants, although the true reason may have been that my mother had scandalized a prudish Santiago society by not having a husband. From the nuns, I went to a more understanding English school, where such underwear exhibitions had little consequence as long as they were performed discreetly. I am sure that my childhood would have been different had Memé lived longer. My grandmother was training me to be an Illuminata; the first words she taught me were in Esperanto, an unpronounceable mishmash she expected to be the universal language of the future, and I was still in diapers when she first sat me down at the table of the spirits. All those splendid possibilities ended with her death. Our family home, a delight when she was presiding over it with her gatherings of intellectuals, Bohemians, and lunatics, became at her death a cheerless and empty place populated only by currents of air. Smells from that time endure in my memory: paraffin stoves in the winter and burnt sugar in summer, when a huge bonfire was lighted in the patio to make blackberry jam in a gigantic copper kettle. After my grandmother died, no birds sang in the cages, no more sonatas were played on the piano, all the plants and flowers withered and died, the cats escaped to run wild on the rooftops, and one by one all the other domestic animals perished: the rabbits and hens ended up in stews, and the nanny goat got out in the street one day and was run over by the milkman's cart. The only survivor was the dog, Pelvina López-Pun, dozing beside the drapes that divided the drawing room from the dining room. I wandered among heavy Spanish furniture, marble statues, and pastoral paintings, calling my grandmother's name, seeking her among the piles of books that filled every corner and reproduced at night in an uncontrollable orgy of printed paper. A tacit boundary divided the part of the house occupied by the family from the kitchen, patios, and servants' quarters where I spent most of my life. Theirs was a badly ventilated, dark subworld of rooms furnished only with a cot, a chair, and a rickety chest of drawers, and decorated with calendars and color prints of saints. That was the sole refuge of those women who labored from sunup to sundown, the first to get up in the morning and the last to go to bed at night, after serving dinner and cleaning up the kitchen. They were free every other Sunday. I don't remember their ever having a family or taking a vacation. They grew old serving, and died in our house. Once a month a large, slightly dim-witted man came to wax the floors. He strapped steel wool on his feet and danced around in a pathetic samba, scrubbing the parquet clean; then on hands and knees he applied wax with a rag, and finished with a stout brush to bring the wax to a high shine. The laundress also came once a week, a nondescript woman, all skin and bones, with two or three little ones clinging to her skirts and a mountain of dirty clothes balanced on her head. Each piece was counted, so that nothing would be missing when it was returned clean and ironed. Every time I happened to witness the humiliating process of counting the shirts, napkins, and sheets, I ran to hide among the plush drapes of the drawing room, to be close to my grandmother. I didn't know why I was crying. I know now; I was crying of shame. Memé's spirit reigned in the drapes—I suppose that is why the old dog never moved from there. The servants, on the other hand, believed my grandmother roamed the cellar, the origin of mysterious sounds and faint lights, and so never went down there. I knew the source of those phenomena very well, but had my own reasons for not telling. I searched for my grandmother's translucent face on the theatrical curtains of the drawing room; I wrote messages on scraps of paper, folded them with care, and pinned them onto the heavy cloth where she would find them and know I had not forgotten her.

Memé left this world with great simplicity. No one took note of her preparations for her journey to the Beyond until the end, when it was too late to intervene. Aware that it requires supreme airiness to detach oneself from the earth, she lightened her load. She rid herself of earthly goods and eliminated all superfluous emotions and desires, keeping only the barest essentials. She wrote a few letters and then, as her last act, took to her bed, never to get up again. She lay dying for a week, attended by her husband, who used every medication within his power to prevent her from suffering, as her life drained away and a muted drum thudded in her chest. There was no time to inform anyone, yet her friends from the White Sisterhood received a telepathic message and came at the last instant to deliver messages for the benevolent souls that for years they had summoned to the Thursday sessions around the three-legged table. This marvelous woman left no physical trace of her presence other than a silver mirror, a prayer book with mother-of-pearl covers, and a fistful of wax orange blossoms, remnants of her bridal headdress. Neither did she leave me many memories, and those I have are surely deformed by a child's view of that time and by the passing of years. None of that matters, though, because she has always been with me. When her asthma or anxiety made it hard for her to breathe, she hugged me close so my warmth would relieve her. That is the most vivid image I have of her: rice paper skin, gentle fingers, the wheezing, her affectionate hug, the scent of cologne, and an occasional hint of the almond lotion she rubbed on her hands. I heard people talk about her, and I hoard her few remaining relics in a tin box. All the rest I have invented, because we all need a grandmother. Not only has she played that role to perfection—despite the inconvenience of her death—but she also inspired the character I love most of all those in my books: Clara . . . clearest, clairvoyant Clara, of *The House of the Spirits*.

My grandfather could not accept the loss of his wife. I believe they lived in irreconcilable worlds and at fleeting moments loved one another with a painful tenderness and secret passion. Tata had all the vitality of a practical man: he was healthy, enterprising, and loved sports. She was alien to this earth, ethereal and unreachable. Her husband had to satisfy himself with living beneath the same roof but in a different dimension, never really possessing her. Only on a few solemn occasions—such as the birth of their children, when he received them with his own hands, or when he held her in his arms as she was dying—did he have the sensation that she truly existed. He tried a thousand times to capture the airy spirit that flashed past him like a comet, leaving behind an enduring trail of astral dust, but always ended with the feeling she had escaped him. At the end of his life, after he had lived for nearly a century and all that was left of the energetic patriarch was a shadow gnawed by loneliness and the implacable corrosion of the years, he abandoned the idea of ever owning her completely, as he had hoped in his youth; only then was he able to embrace her on equal terms. It was then that the shadow of Memé took on precise outlines and she became the tangible creature who accompanied him in the meticulous reconstruction of his memories and the ailments of his old age. Newly widowed, however, he felt betrayed. He accused Memé of having abandoned him halfway along the road. His mourning was dark as a crow's wing; he painted the furniture black and, to avoid further suffering, tried to eliminate affection from his existence—never totally succeeding. He was a man defeated by his own gentility. He lived in a large room on the first floor of the house, where the hours were marked by the funereal striking of a grandfather's clock. His door was always closed and I never dared knock, but every morning I stopped by to say hello before school, and sometimes he authorized me to search for a chocolate he had hidden for me. I never once heard him complain; his fortitude was heroic, but tears often filled his eyes, and when he thought he was alone, he talked with his wife's memory. Once bowed by years and sorrow, he could no longer contain those tears; he used to brush them away with his fists, infuriated by his own weakness. "Caramba," he would growl, "I'm getting old." When he became a widower he abolished flowers, desserts, and music—any source of joy—from his life; silence spread through his house, and his soul.

*   *   *

My parents' situation was ambiguous because there is no divorce in Chile; it was not difficult, however, to convince Tomás to annul the marriage, and so my brothers and I became the children of a single mother. My father, who apparently had no desire to pay child support, forfeited the oversight of his issue and quietly disappeared, while the social circle around my mother tightened to fend off any scandal. The one thing my father asked for when he signed the annulment was the return of his family coat of arms—three starving hounds on a blue field—a wish readily granted since my mother, indeed, the whole family, burst out laughing every time they saw it. With the withdrawal of that ironic sign of nobility went any blue blood we might claim; a stroke of a pen wiped out our paternal lineage. My grandfather would not allow any mention of his former son-in-law, but neither would he tolerate complaints in his presence; after all, he had warned his daughter not to marry. My mother obtained a modest position in a bank, where the main attraction was the possibility of retiring at full salary after thirty-five years of service, and the major drawback was the lust of the director, who kept pinning her in corners. A couple of bachelor uncles also lived in our large house; their only duty seems to have been to fill my childhood with unpleasant surprises. My favorite was Uncle Pablo, a brooding, solitary young man with dark skin, passionate eyes, flashing teeth, and stiff black hair he combed straight back in the manner of Rudolf Valentino. He was never without his overcoat with huge pockets in which he hid books he stole from public libraries and the homes of friends. I begged him many times to marry my mother, but he explained that incestuous relationships always produce Siamese twins. After that, I shifted my aim and made the same plea to Dr. Benjamin Viel, for whom I felt unreserved affection. Uncle Pablo was a strong ally; he slipped money into his sister's pocketbook, helped her with us children, and defended her against gossip and other affronts. Opposed to sentimental displays, he never allowed anyone to touch him, or even get within breathing distance; he considered the telephone and the mail to be invasions of privacy, always laid an open book beside his place at the table to discourage attempts at conversation, and then tried to intimidate the person next to him with his barbaric table manners. We all knew, though, that he was a compassionate soul who secretly, hoping no one would suspect, lent a hand to a true army of needy persons. He was Tata's right arm, his best friend, and his partner in the enterprise of raising sheep and exporting wool to Scotland. The household servants adored him and, despite his unsociable silences, his peculiarities and practical jokes, he had a legion of friends. Many years later, this eccentric man hopelessly bitten by the reading bug fell in love with a delightful cousin who had been reared in the country, where life was lived in terms of hard work and religion. That branch of the family, very formal and conservative, had to call on all their restraint to endure the bizarre behavior of their daughter's suitor. One day, for instance, my uncle bought a cow's head in the market, then spent two days scraping it clean inside—to the revulsion of us children, who had never seen anything so foul or monstrous at close range. The next Sunday, when the task was complete, he showed up after mass at his sweetheart's house, dressed in a tuxedo and wearing the head like a tribal mask. The servant who opened the door never blinked an eye, she just stood aside and said, "Come in, don Pablo." My uncle's bedroom was filled with floor-to-ceiling bookshelves, and in the center was an anchorite's cot where he spent a major portion of the night reading. He was the one who convinced me that in the dark the characters escaped and roamed through the house. I used to hide my head under the sheets because I was afraid of the devils in the mirrors and that throng of characters wandering about the house reliving their adventures and desires: pirates, courtesans, bandits, witches, and fair damsels. At eight-thirty I was supposed to turn off the light and go to sleep, but Uncle Pablo gave me a flashlight so I could read under the covers; ever since, I have enjoyed the vice of secret reading.

It was impossible to be bored in a house filled with books and outrageous relatives, a forbidden cellar, litter after litter of kittens— which Margara drowned in a bucket of water—and a kitchen radio that was turned on behind my grandfather's back to blare popular songs, news of bloodcurdling crimes, and serialized dramas. My uncles invented a game they called Ruffin, for "roughing up the ruffians," a ferocious entertainment that consisted basically of teasing us children until they made us cry. They never ran out of ideas, from pasting our ten-peso allowances on the ceiling, where we could see them but not reach them, to offering us bonbons from which, using a syringe, they had removed the chocolate filling and replaced it with hot chili sauce. They used to push us from the top of the stairs in cardboard boxes, hold us upside down over the toilet and threaten to pull the chain, fill the washbasin with alcohol and light it, offering us money to put our hands in the flame, and stack up my grandfather's used tires and drop us inside, where we screamed with fear in the dark, half choked by the smell of rotted rubber. When we traded in an old gas stove for a new electric one, they stood us on the burners, turned them on low, and, as we hopped from one foot to the other, began to tell us a story to see whether the heat on the soles of our shoes was more compelling than our interest in the tale. My mother defended us like a lioness, but she was not always there to protect us. Tata, on the other hand, had the idea that Ruffin built character and was a necessary part of our education. The theory that childhood must be a period of placid innocence did not exist then, this is something North Americans invented later. It was believed that life was hard, and it was therefore good for us to temper our nerves. Didactic methods were based on endurance; the more inhuman tests a child survived, the better prepared he would be to face the hazards of adulthood. I admit that I suffered no ill effects and that if I had conformed with that tradition I would have martyred my own children and now be doing the same with my grandson—but I am too softhearted. Some summer Sundays, the whole family would go to San Cristobal, a hill in the center of Santiago that used to be a wilderness but today is a park. Sometimes Salvador and Tencha Allende came along with their three daughters and their dogs. Allende was already a well-known politician, the most aggressive deputy on the Left and the target of the Right's odium, but to us he was just another uncle. We would struggle up the faintly marked trails through weeds and tall grasses, burdened down with baskets and wool shawls. Once there, we looked for an open space with a view of the city below—just as I would do during the military coup twenty years later, but for very different reasons—and kept an eye on the picnic, defending pieces of chicken, boiled eggs, and turnovers from the dogs and the invincible advance of the ants. The adults would rest while we cousins hid in the bushes to play doctor. From time to time you could hear the distant roar of a lion from the zoo on the other side of the hill. Once a week they used to feed them live animals, so that the excitement of the hunt and charge of adrenaline would keep them healthy: the big cats devoured an ancient burro, the boas gorged on mice, and the hyenas feasted on rabbits. Everyone said that was where all the dogs and cats from the pound ended up, and that there was a long list of people waiting for an invitation to watch that bone-chilling spectacle. I dreamed of the poor creatures thrust into the cages with the great carnivores, and writhed in anguish thinking of the early Christians in the Roman coliseum; I knew in my heart that if I was asked to choose between renouncing my faith and becoming lunch for a Bengal tiger, heresy would win hands down. After we ate we would run back down the hill, pushing and shoving, and rolling down the steepest part. Salvador Allende always took the lead with his dogs, and his daughter Carmen Paz and I were always the last, reaching the bottom with scraped hands and knees after all the others had grown tired of waiting for us. Except for those Sundays, and summer vacations, life was all sacrifice and hard work. Those were very difficult years for my mother; she had to contend with poverty, gossip, and the snubs of people who had been her friends. Her salary at the bank was barely pin money, and she rounded it out by making hats. It seems I can see her now at the dining table—the same Spanish oak table I use today as a desk in California—trying out various velvets, ribbons, and silk flowers. She would ship the hats off in round boxes to Lima, where they ended up adorning the heads of the cream of Peruvian society. Even so, she could not have survived without help from Tata and Uncle Pablo. In school, I was given a scholarship that depended on my grades. I don't know how she obtained it, but it must have cost more than one humiliation. She spent hours standing in line in hospitals with my brother Juan who, thanks to Margara's wooden spoon, had learned to swallow, but who suffered horrible intestinal upsets and had become a case study for doctors until Margara discovered he was eating toothpaste and cured him with a razor strap. My mother was truly overwhelmed by her responsibilities; she suffered unendurable headaches that kept her in bed for two or three days at a time, leaving her completely sapped. She worked hard and long but had little control over her life or those of her children. Margara, who gradually grew into an absolute tyrant, tried every way she could to come between us. When my mother came home from the bank in the evening, we would already be bathed, fed, and put to bed. "Don't get the children all stirred up," she would grumble, and to us she would say, "Don't bother your Mama, she has a headache." My mother clung to her children with all the force of her loneliness, and tried to compensate for her absence and the poverty of our lives with flights of imagination. All three of us slept in the same room with her, and at night, the only time we were together, she told us stories about our ancestors and fantastic tales spiced with black humor. She made up an imaginary world where we were all happy and human vices and the merciless laws of nature were forbidden. Those conversations in low voices, all in the same room, each of us in our own bed but so close we could touch, were the best part of those years. That was where my passion for stories was born, and I call upon those memories when I sit down to write.

Pancho, the least cowed by our uncles' "Ruffin," was a blond little boy, sturdy and calm, but if he lost patience he could turn into a tiny beast with a savage bite. Margara adored him and called him her King; he was lost when she was out of the house. As an adolescent he left home to join a strange sect that lived in the desert region of northern Chile. We heard rumors that they tripped to other worlds on hallucinogenic mushrooms, indulged in unspeakable orgies, and brainwashed the young to make them slaves of the leaders. I never learned the truth, because no one who lived through that experience ever spoke of it—but they were marked by it. My brother renounced his family, cut all emotional ties, and hid behind a shell that nevertheless failed to protect him from pain and insecurity. Eventually, he *twice* married and divorced *two* wives, had children, and has lived nearly all his adult life outside Chile. I doubt that he will ever return. There is not much I can say about him because I don't know him. Like my father, he is a mystery to me.

Juan was born with the rare gift of likableness. Even now, a solemn professor in the mature years of his life, people immediately are attracted to him. When he was little, he looked like an angel, with dimpled cheeks and a helpless air capable of melting the hardest heart. Small, but prudent and astute, his many illnesses hampered his growth and condemned him to eternal poor health. We thought of him as the intellectual of the family, a true genius. At five, he could recite long poems and instantly calculate how much change we should get from a peso if we bought three caramels at eight cents apiece. He earned two master's degrees and a doctorate from North American universities, and currently is working toward a degree in theology. He was a professor of political science, an agnostic and a Marxist, but after experiencing a spiritual crisis he decided to seek the answer to humanity's problems in God. He abandoned his teaching position and began divinity studies. Because he is married, he can never become a Catholic priest, a choice he would have preferred because of family tradition, so he opted to become a Methodist—to the initial discomfort of my mother, who knew very little about that church and could picture the genius of the family reduced to singing hymns in a public square while accompanying himself on the guitar. Such sudden conversions are not rare among my mother's people; I have many mystical relatives. I cannot imagine my brother preaching from a pulpit, because no one would understand his learned sermons—especially in English—but he will be an outstanding professor of theology. When he learned that you were ill, he dropped everything, caught the first plane, and came to Madrid to give me support. "We must have hope that Paula will get well," he keeps telling me.

Will you get well, Paula? I look at you in that bed, connected to a half dozen tubes and wires, unable even to breathe without help. I scarcely recognize you; your body has changed and your mind is in shadows. What goes through your thoughts? Tell me about your loneliness and your fears, about the distorted visions, the pain in your rock-heavy bones, the menacing silhouettes leaning over your bed, the voices, the murmurs, the lights. Nothing must make any sense to you. I know you hear because you flinch at the sound of metal on metal, but I don't know whether you understand what it is. Do you want to live, Paula? You spent your life trying to be one with God. Do you want to die? Perhaps you have already begun.

What meaning do the days have for you now? Have you returned to
the place of total innocence, to the waters of my womb, like the fish
you were before you were born? I count the days, and they are too
many. Wake up, Paula, please wake up. . . .

I place one hand over my heart, close my eyes, and concentrate.
There is something dark inside. At first it is like the night air, transparent shadow, but soon it is transformed into impenetrable lead. I
try to lie calmly and accept the blackness that fills my inner being as
I am assaulted by images from the past. I see myself before a large
mirror. I take one step backward, another, and with each step
decades are erased and I grow smaller, until the glass returns the
reflection of a seven-year-old girl. Me.

It has been raining for several days; I am leaping over puddles,
my leather bag bouncing against my back. I am wearing a blue coat
that is too large for me and a felt hat pulled down to my ears; my
shoes are sodden. The huge wooden entry door, swollen by rain, is
stuck; it takes all my weight to pull it open. In the garden of my
grandfather's house is a gigantic poplar with roots growing above
the ground, a scrawny sentinel standing guard over property that
appears abandoned—shutters hanging from their hinges, paint
peeling from walls. Outdoors it is just getting dark, but inside it is
already deepest night. All the lights are off, except in the kitchen. I
walk through the garage toward the light. The walls of the cavernous
kitchen are spotted with grease, and large blackened saucepans and
spoons hang from iron hooks. One or two fly-specked lightbulbs
cast a dull light on the scene. Something is bubbling in a pot and the
kettle is whistling; the room smells of onion, and an enormous
refrigerator purrs in a corner. Margara, a large woman with strong
Indian features and a thin braid wound around her head, is listening
to a serial on the radio. My brothers are sitting at the table with
cups of hot cocoa and buttered bread. Margara does not look up.
"Go see your mother, she's in bed again," she scolds. I take off my
coat and hat. "Don't strew your things about; I'm not your slave, I
don't have to pick up after you." She turns up the volume on the
radio. I leave the kitchen and confront the darkness in the rest of
the house. I feel for the light switch and a pale glow barely fills the

hall with its several doors. A claw-foot table holds the marble bust of a pensive girl; there is a mirror with a heavy wood frame, but I don't look because the Devil might be reflected in it. I shiver as I climb the stairs; currents of air swirl through an incomprehensible hole in this strange architecture. Clinging to the handrail, I reach the second floor. The climb seems interminable. I am aware of silence and shadows. I walk to the closed door at the end of the hall and tiptoe in without knocking. A stove furnishes the only illumination; the ceilings are covered with the accumulation of years of paraffin soot. There are two beds, a bunk, a sofa, tables and chairs—it is all I can do to make my way through the furniture. My mother, with Pelvina López-Pun asleep at her feet, is lying beneath a mountain of covers, her face half-hidden on the pillow: straight nose, high cheekbones, pallid skin, finely drawn eyebrows above closed eyes. "Is it you?" A small, cold hand reaches out for mine.

"Does it hurt a lot, Mama?"

"My head is bursting."

"I'll go get you a glass of warm milk and tell my brothers not to make any noise."

"Don't leave. Stay here with me. Put your hand on my forehead, that helps."

I sit on the bed and do as she asks, trembling with sympathy, not knowing how to free her from that crushing pain. Blessed Mary, Mother of God, pray for us sinners now and at the hour of our death, Amen. If she dies, my brothers and I are lost; they will send us to my father. The mere idea terrifies me. Margara is always telling me that if I don't behave I will have to go live with him. Could it be true? I have to find out, but I don't dare ask my mother, it would make her headache worse. I mustn't add to her worries or the pain will grow until her head explodes. I can't mention it to Tata, either; no one may speak my father's name in his presence. "Papa" is a forbidden word, and anyone who says it stirs up a hornet's nest. I'm hungry, I want to go down to the kitchen and drink my cocoa, but I must not leave my mother, and besides, I don't have the courage to face Margara. My shoes are wet and my feet feel like ice. I stroke my mother's poor head and concentrate: everything depends on me now. If I don't move, and pray hard, I can make the pain go away.

I am forty-nine years old. I place one hand over my heart and say in a little girl's voice: I do not want to be like my mother, I will be like my grandfather—independent, healthy, strong. I will not allow anyone to order me about, and I will not be beholden to anyone. I want to be like my grandfather and protect my mother.

I think Tata was always sorry I wasn't a boy; had I been, he could have taught me to play jai alai, and use his tools, and hunt. I would have been his companion on the trips he made every year to Patagonia for the sheepshearing. In those days one traveled south by train, or by automobile over twisting dirt roads that could turn into quagmires, immobilizing cars until a team of oxen pulled them free. Lakes were crossed by rope-drawn ferries, and mountains on muleback. Those were demanding expeditions. My grandfather slept beneath the stars, wrapped in a heavy Castilian blanket; he bathed in raging rivers fed by snowmelt from the peaks and ate garbanzo beans and tinned sardines until he reached the Argentine side of the mountain. There a crew was waiting for him with a truck and a lamb roasting over a slow fire. Rough men, they hunkered around the fire in silence. They lived in a vast, forsaken landscape where the wind tore the words from their mouths. With gaucho knives they sliced off great hunks of meat and devoured them, their gaze fixed on the glowing coals. One of them might strum a plaintive song on his guitar while the maté passed from hand to hand, the aromatic brew of bitter green yerba they drink there like tea. I treasure indelible memories of the one trip to the south I made with my grandfather—even though I was so carsick I thought I would die, a mule threw me twice, and then as I watched them shearing the sheep I was struck dumb, unable to speak until we returned to civilization. The sheepshearers, who were paid by the animal, could zip off a fleece in less than a minute, but, however careful they were, they often sliced off strips of skin with the wool, and I saw more than one wretched lamb split open, its guts stuffed back any which way in its belly before being stitched up with an upholstery needle and returned to the flock with the hope it would survive and continue to produce wool.

My love for heights, and my relationship with trees, originated with that trip. I have returned several times to the south of Chile and I always feel the same indescribable love for the landscape. Crossing the cordillera of the Andes is engraved in my soul as one of the true epiphanies of my existence. Now, and during other critical moments when I try to remember prayers and cannot evoke the words or the rituals, the only vision I can turn to for consolation is that of those misty paths through the chill forest of gigantic ferns and tree trunks rising toward the heavens, the sheer mountain passes, and the sharp profile of snow-covered volcanoes reflected in emerald lakes. To be one with God must be very much like being in this extraordinary realm. In my memory, my grandfather, the guide, and the mules have disappeared. I am alone, walking in solemn silence through that temple of rock and vegetation. I am breathing clean air cold and wet with rain. My feet sink into a carpet of mud and rotted leaves; the scent of the earth is a sword piercing my bones. Effortlessly, I walk and walk along the narrow, misty paths, yet never leave that undiscovered world surrounded with century-old trees, fallen trunks, strips of aromatic bark, and roots bursting through the earth like mutilated, vegetal hands. On the path, my face is brushed by strong spiderwebs, lace tablecloths pearled with drops of water and phosphorescent-winged mosquitoes. Here and there I glimpse the brilliant scarlet and white of copihues and other flowers that live at these heights tangled among the trees like glittering beads. You can feel the breath of the gods, throbbing, absolute presences in this resplendent domain of precipices and high walls of black rock polished by the snow to the sensual perfection of marble. Water, and more water. Thin crystalline serpents slip through fissures of rock into the hidden depths of the mountains and join together in small brooks and sounding waterfalls. Suddenly I am startled by the scream of a bird or thud of a rock rolling from above, but the enveloping peace of this vastness descends again, and I realize I am weeping with happiness. That trip, with all its obstacles and hidden dangers, its desired solitude and breathtaking beauty, is like the journey of my own life. This memory is sacred to me; this memory is my country. When I say Chile, this is what I think of. Time and time again I have tried to recapture the emotion that forest stirs in me, a feeling more intense than the most perfect orgasm, than the longest ovation.

*   *   *

Every year when the wrestling season began, my grandfather would take me to the Teatro Caupolicán. I always wore my Sunday best, my patent leather shoes and white gloves contrasting sharply with the scruffy appearance of the crowd. Thus attired, and holding tight to the hand of the grand old man at my side, I pushed my way through the roaring spectators. We always sat in the first row, "So we can see the blood," Tata used to say with ferocious anticipation. Once, one of the gladiators landed right on us, a savage mass of sweaty flesh that flattened us like cockroaches. My grandfather had prepared many times for that eventuality, yet when it came he did not know how to react and, instead of beating the man to a pulp with his cane, as he had always said he would, he greeted him with a cordial handclasp to which the man, equally nonplussed, replied with a timid smile. That was one of the great disillusions of my childhood. Tata was demoted from a barbarous Mount Olympus where he had until then occupied the single throne and reduced to human dimensions. I believe that my rebelliousness dates from that moment.

The favorite of the crowd was The Angel, a handsome man with long blond hair, always costumed in a blue cape with silver stars, white boots, and a ridiculously tiny pair of trunks that barely covered his private parts. Every Saturday he bet his magnificent yellow locks against the challenge of the terrible Kuramoto, a Mapuche Indian who wore a kimono and wooden clogs and pretended to be Japanese. They engaged one another in spectacular combat, biting, twisting necks, kicking genitals, and sticking fingers in each other's eyes, while my grandfather, holding his beret in one hand and brandishing his cane in the other, yelled "Kill him! Kill him!"—indiscriminately, since it didn't matter to him who murdered whom. Two out of three contests, Kuramoto vanquished The Angel; with the decision, the referee would produce a pair of scintillating scissors and before the respectful silence of the crowd the phony Nipponese warrior would cut off his rival's curls. The miracle that one week later The Angel again displayed shoulder-length hair was irrefutable proof of his divinity.

The high point of the night, however, was always The Mummy,

who for years filled my nights with terror. The lights in the theater would dim and we would hear a scratchy recording of a funeral march, at which point two Egyptians, profiled against lighted torches, would appear, followed by another four carrying a gaudily painted sarcophagus on a bier. The four would lower the mummy case to the floor of the ring and take one or two steps backward, all the while chanting in some dead tongue. Frozen with dread, we watched as the lid opened and a gauze-swathed humanoid figure emerged—apparently in perfect health, to judge by all the roaring and breast-beating. The Mummy did not have the mobility of the other wrestlers, but relied on formidable kicks and battering, stiff-armed blows that slammed opponents into the ropes and decked referees. Once, one of those hammer blows split Tarzan's head, and when we got home my grandfather at last could exhibit some red stains on his shirt. "This isn't blood, or anything near; it's tomato sauce," Margara grumbled as she was soaking the shirt in chlorine. Those showmen occupied a nook in my memory, and many years later I tried to resuscitate them in a story, but the only one that had left a lasting impression was The Widower. He was a wretch of a man in the fortieth year of his miserable existence, the antithesis of a hero, who entered the ring wearing an old-fashioned bathing suit, the kind men wore at the beginning of the century: black wool jersey to his knees, with a U-neck top and suspenders. A rubber swim cap added the last touch of pathos. He was met with a storm of jeers, insults, threats, and projectiles, but by clanging the bell and blowing his whistle the referee finally restored order to the unruly mob. The Widower then raised his reed-thin voice to announce that this would be his last fight because he had serious back trouble and had been profoundly depressed since the passing of his saintly wife—might she rest in peace. When that fine woman had shuffled off this mortal coil, she had left him in sole charge of their two young children. When the boos had reached the noise level of a full-fledged battle, two little boys with sorrowful expressions climbed between the ropes and clung to The Widower's knees, begging him not to fight because he'd be killed. A sudden silence would fall over the crowd, as I whispered my favorite poem: *Hand in hand, two orphan lads / toward the graveyard slowly wend / Upon their father's tomb they kneel / and up to God sweet prayers they send.* "Quiet," Tata would say, jabbing me with his elbow. In a voice broken with sobs, The Widower would explain that he had to support his children, and so would take on the Texas Assassin. You could hear a flea jump in that enormous hall. In one instant, a savage thirst for mayhem and blood was transformed into teary compassion, and a warmhearted shower of coins and bills rained down on the ring. The orphans quickly gathered the loot and skedaddled, as the Texas Assassin strutted toward the ring, dressed—I never knew why—as a Roman galley slave and slashing the air with a whip. Naturally, The Widower always took an unholy drubbing, but as the winner left he had to be protected by armed guards from a public ready to make mincemeat of him, while the bruised Widower and his young sons were borne off by kindly hands that, as a bonus, also bestowed sweets, money, and blessings.

"Poor devil, it's a terrible thing, being widowed," my grandfather would comment, openly moved.

In the late sixties, when I was working as a journalist, I was assigned a feature on the "Grunt and Groan Game," as Tata called that unique sport. At twenty-eight, I still believed in objective reporting, and had no choice but to write about the miserable lives of the pitiful combatants, to unmask the tomato-pulp blood, the glass eyes clutched in the grappling hook hands of Kuramoto as the blinded loser staggered away howling and covering his face with blood-smeared hands, or to report on the moth-eaten wig of The Angel, now so old he must surely have been the model for Gabriel García Márquez's best short story, "A Very Old Man with Enormous Wings." My grandfather read my article with clenched teeth, and it was a week before he would speak to me again.

My childhood summers were spent at the beach, where our family owned a huge, rundown old house by the sea. We left in December, before Christmas, and returned at the end of February, black from the sun and stuffed with fruit and fish. The trip, today an easy hour on the thruway, was then an odyssey that took the entire day. Preparations began a week in advance, as boxes were filled with food, sheets, and towels, bags and baskets with clothes, and the parrot—a nasty bird that would as soon as not nip off a finger if you got too close—forced into its cage. It goes without saying that Pelvina López-Pun also made the trip. The only ones to stay in town were the cook and the cats, wild creatures by now that fed on mice and pigeons. My grandfather owned a black English touring car that was as heavy as a tank, with a rack on the roof for strapping on the mountain of bundles. Pelvina rode in the open trunk with the lunch, which she never disturbed because as soon as she saw the suitcases she fell into a profound canine melancholy. Margara always brought basins, wet cloths, ammonia, and a bottle of *tisana,* a sweet, home-brewed chamomile tea to which she attributed the nebulous virtue of contracting the stomach. None of those precautions, however, could prevent carsickness. My mother, we three children, and Pelvina began to languish long before we left Santiago; as we turned onto the highway, we began to moan with agony, and by the time we reached the curving road through the hills, we entered a twilight zone. Tata, who had to stop every so often so we could get down, half swooning, to breathe and stretch our legs, fought the wheel of that old motorcar, cursing the fortune that led us to summer at the beach. We always stopped at farms along the way to buy goat cheese, melons, and jars of honey. Once he bought a live turkey to fatten; the countrywoman from whom he acquired it was large— clearly an understatement—with child, and my grandfather, with his customary chivalry, offered to catch the bird for her. Even half-sick, we were wildly entertained by the memorable spectacle of that lame old man in hot pursuit of the turkey. Finally he hooked his cane around the bird's neck and tackled it amid a whirlwind of dust and feathers. We watched him as he limped back to the car, covered with droppings but with the trophy safely beneath his arm, its feet tightly bound. How could anyone have foreseen that Pelvina would shake off her lassitude long enough to bite off the bird's head before we reached our destination? Nothing would take out the blood-stains, which remained for the life of the car as an eternal reminder of those calamitous journeys.

That summer watering place was a world of women and chil-dren. La Playa Grande was a paradise that lasted until a petroleum refinery was set up nearby that forever fouled the clear ocean water and frightened away the sirens, who were never again heard along those shores. At ten in the morning, uniformed nannies would begin to arrive with children in tow. They settled down to knit, watching their charges out of the corner of their eyes, always from the same identical spot on the beach. The oldest families, who owned the grand houses, positioned themselves beneath tents and umbrellas in the precise center; to the left were the newly rich, the tourists, and the middle class who rented the houses on the hills; and at the extreme right were the day-trip hoi polloi who came down from Santiago in rattletrap buses. In a bathing suit, everyone looks more or less equal; every person, nevertheless, immediately recognized his God-given place. In Chile, the upper class tends to have a European appearance; as you descend the social and economic scale, indigenous features become more pronounced. Class consciousness is so strong that I never saw one person violate the defining boundaries. At noon the mothers would arrive, carrying large straw hats and bottles of the carrot juice they used for rapid tanning. About two, when the sun was at its zenith, everyone retired for lunch and a siesta. Soon after, the teenagers appeared, essaying an air of boredom; ripening girls and world-weary young males who lay in the sand to smoke and rub against each other until excitement obliged them to seek relief in the sea. Every Friday night, the husbands arrived from Santiago, and Saturday and Sunday the character of the beach changed. Mothers sent their children on walks with nannies and gathered in groups in their best swimsuits and straw hats, competing for the attention of each other's spouses, a pointless endeavor, really, since the men scarcely glanced at them; they were much more interested in talking politics—the only topic in Chile—and counting the minutes before they could go back to the house to eat and drink like Cossacks. My mother, seated like an empress at the center of the center of the beach, took the sun in the mornings and in the late afternoons went to the casino, where she had discovered a system that allowed her to win enough daily to pay her expenses. To prevent our being dragged out to sea and drowning, Margara tied us to her with ropes she kept wound around her waist while she continued to knit endless sweaters for the winter. When she felt a tug, she would look up briefly to see who was in difficulty and then haul the victim back to safety. We suffered that humiliation every single day, but we forgot the other children's teasing as soon as we jumped into the water. We played until we were blue with cold; we collected conchs and other seashells; we ate sand-sprinkled cakes and half-melted lemon ices sold by a deaf-mute from a little cart filled with salted ice. Every evening, my mother took my hand and walked with me to the rocks to watch the sunset. We waited to make a wish on the last ray, which sparks green fire at the precise instant the sun sinks below the horizon. I always wished for my mother not to find a husband, and I suppose that she wished exactly the opposite. She would tell me about Ramón, whom, influenced by her description, I imagined as an enchanted prince whose principal virtue consisted of distance. Tata left us at the beach at the beginning of summer and returned almost immediately to Santiago. It was the one time he could enjoy a little peace; he liked the empty house, and playing golf and cards at the Union Club. If he appeared some weekend, it was not to indulge in relaxation but to test his strength, swimming for hours in the strong, ice-cold waves, fishing, or making badly needed repairs on a house eternally deteriorating from dampness. He sometimes took us to a place that had milk fresh from the cow, a dark, stinking shed, where a peasant with filthy fingernails squirted milk directly into tin cups. We drank the warm, creamy liquid, along with occasional flies floating in the foam. My grandfather, who did not believe in hygiene and was a proponent of immunizing children through direct contact with the source of infection, would shake with laughter when we swallowed a live fly.

The local inhabitants greeted the invasion of the summer people with a mixture of animosity and enthusiasm. They were modest folk, nearly all fishermen, or tradesmen and owners of small plots along the river where they cultivated tomatoes and lettuce. They took great pride in the fact that nothing ever happened in their peaceful little town. One winter, however, a well-known artist was found crucified on the mast of a sailboat. I heard only snatches of talk, as the subject was not considered appropriate for children, but years later I learned some of the particulars. The entire town had conspired to muddy the waters by confusing evidence and covering up proof, and the police did not make too great an effort to clear up the dark crime because everyone knew exactly who had nailed the body to the mast. This artist lived year-round in his house on the coast, devoted to his painting, his collection of classical records, and taking long walks with his dog, a purebred Afghan hound so lean people thought it must be a cross between a dog and an eagle. The handsomest among the young fishermen posed as models for the artist's paintings, and soon became his drinking companions. At night, music filled every corner of the house, and more than once the men did not return home or go to work for days at a time. Mothers and sweethearts tried in vain to reclaim their men, until, their patience exhausted, they quietly began to plot an end to the problem. I can picture them, whispering while they repaired the nets, exchanging winks from their stalls in the market, and passing along countersigns for the witches' Sabbath to come. On the night in question, they slipped like shadows along the beach, approached the large house, entered silently, without disturbing the drunken slumbers of their men, and carried out what they had to do—hammers firm in their hands. They say that the svelte Afghan suffered the same fate as its master.

I have had reason from time to time to visit the fishermen's miserable huts, with their clinging odors of charcoal and fishing gear, and I felt the same discomfort I did in the rooms of our servants. In my grandfather's house, which was as long as a railroad, the walls were so thin that our dreams intermingled at night. In the salt air, water pipes, anything metal, promptly surrendered to the pernicious leprosy of rust. Once a year the whole house had to be repainted and the mattresses ripped open to wash and sun-dry the mildewed wool. The house was built beside a hill, which Tata had had sliced off like a cake, with no thought for erosion; the happy result, however, was a gully with a continuous flow of water that fed gigantic clumps of pink and blue hydrangeas that bloomed all year round. On the top of the hill, reached by endless stairs, lived a fisherman's family. One of their children, a young man with hands calloused from the onerous task of tearing shellfish from rocks, once took me into the woods. I was eight. It was Christmas Day.

* * *

This is the moment, however, to focus on the only one of my mother's lovers to interest us; she paid very little attention to any of the others, and they simply fade from this story. Ramón had separated from his wife, who had returned to Santiago with their children, and was working in the embassy in Bolivia, saving every cent to finance an annulment, the traditional procedure in Chile where because of the absence of divorce laws one must resort to tricks, lies, and perjury. Years of deferred love had served to change his personality; he had freed himself of the guilt instilled by a despotic father, and distanced himself from the constraining straitjacket of the Church. Through passionate letters and a smattering of telephone calls, he had succeeded in routing several rivals as powerful as a dentist who was a magician in his free time and could pull a live rabbit from a pail of boiling oil; the king of pressure cookers who introduced those devices into Chile, altering forever the slow rituals of the national kitchen; and various other gallants who might have become our stepfather—including my own favorite, Dr. Benjamin Viel, tall and straight as a lance, whose contagious laughter rang through my grandfather's house. My mother assures me that the one love of her life was Ramón, and as they are both still living, I will not contradict her. Two years after we left Peru, they plotted a rendezvous in the north of Chile. For my mother, the risks of that clandestine meeting were enormous; it was a definitive step toward the forbidden, a rejection of her prudent life as a bank employee and the advantages of self-sacrificing widowhood in her father's home, but youth and the force of frustrated desire won out over scruples. She spent months planning this adventure, her only accomplice my Uncle Pablo, who did not want to know the lover's identity, or any of the details, but bought his sister the most elegant traveling outfit money could buy and filled her pocketbook with cash—in case she repented along the way and decided to come home, he said—and then, still silent as the Sphinx, drove her to the airport. She left defiantly, without any explanation to my grandfather, because she assumed he would not understand the overpowering call of love. She returned a week later, transformed by the experience of sated passion and, upon descending from the plane, found Tata, all in black and deadly serious, waiting with open arms; he clasped her to his bosom, silently forgiving her. I must suppose that during those fleeting days Ramón had fulfilled with interest the burning promises of his letters; that would explain my mother's decision that she would wait for him for years, hoping that one day he would slip free of his matrimonial bonds. Their tryst, and its consequences, seemed to dim with the passing weeks. My grandfather, who mistrusted long-distance love affairs, never broached the subject and, as my mother was similarly silent, he came to believe that the inevitable pulverization of time was grinding down their passion. He was, therefore, more than a little surprised when he learned of the lover's abrupt appearance in Santiago. As for me— nearly convinced that the enchanted prince lived in a fairy tale and was not a real person at all—I panicked; the idea that my mother might become so enamored of him that she would abandon us tied my stomach in knots. Ramón, it seems, had learned that a mysterious suitor with better prospects than his own had appeared on the horizon—I like to think it was Benjamin Viel, but have no proof— and, without a backward look, he left his post in La Paz and bought a seat on the first plane for Chile. As long as he had been out of the country, his separation from his wife had not been too noticeable, but when he returned to Santiago, and not to the conjugal abode, the situation exploded: relatives, friends, and acquaintances mobilized in a tenacious campaign to return him to his legitimate hearth. I will never forget the day that my brothers and I were walking down the street with Margara and as we passed an obviously wealthy woman she screamed, "Your mother's a slut!" In view of the stubbornness of the recalcitrant husband, his uncle the bishop came to call on my grandfather to demand his intervention. Exalted with Christian fury and enveloped in the odor of sanctity—he hadn't bathed in fifteen years—he updated the list of my mother's sins, a Bathsheba sent by the Evil One to beguile mortal men. My grandfather was not one to accept such rhetoric when it was directed toward a member of his family, nor to let himself be run over by a priest, however saintly his fame, but he realized that the scandal must be met head on, before it was too late. He arranged a meeting with Ramón in his office, to deal with the problem at its root, but found himself confronting a will as stony as his own.

"We are in love," Ramón reported respectfully, but with a firm voice and using the plural, even though recent letters had sowed some doubts about the reciprocity of that love. "Allow me to prove to you that I am a man of honor, and that I can make your daughter happy." My grandfather's eyes bore into Ramón, trying to perceive his most secret intentions, but he must have liked what he saw.

"All right," he decided finally. "If that's how it is, you are coming to live in my house, because I don't want my daughter off by herself God knows where. And in passing, I warn you to take good care of her. The first whiff of any monkey business and you will have me to contend with. Is that clear?"

"Perfectly," the provisional fiancé replied, trembling slightly, but not lowering his eyes.

That was the beginning of a thirty-year unqualified friendship between an improbable father-in-law and an illicit son-in-law. Soon afterward, a truck arrived at our house and disgorged into our patio an enormous crate which in turn vomited out an infinitude of household goods. The first time I saw my Tío Ramón, I thought my mother was playing a joke. *That* was the prince she had been sighing over? I had never seen such an ugly man. Until then, my brothers and I had slept beside our mother; that night my bed was transferred to the ironing room, surrounded by wardrobes with diabolical mirrors, and Pancho and Juan were moved into Margara's room. I still did not realize that something basic had changed in the family order, even though when our Aunt Carmelita came to visit, Ramón made a hasty exit through a window. The truth was revealed to me later, one day when I came home from school at an inopportune hour, went into my mother's bedroom without knocking, as I always had, and found her sleeping her siesta with that stranger we were to call Tío Ramón. I was stabbed by a fit of jealousy I did not recover from until ten years later, when I was at last able to accept him. He took charge of us children, just as he had promised that memorable day in Lima. He raised us with a firm hand and unfailing good humor; he set limits and sent clear messages, without sentimental demonstrations, and without compromise. I recognize now that he put up with my contrariness without trying to buy my esteem or ceding an inch of his authority, until he won me over totally. He is the only father I have known, and now I think he is really handsome!

MY MOTHER'S LIFE IS A NOVEL SHE HAS FORBIDDEN ME TO WRITE; I cannot reveal her secrets and mysteries until fifty years after her death, but by then, if my descendants honor my instructions and scatter my ashes at sea, I shall be food for the fish. Even though we rarely agree on anything, I have loved her longer than anyone in my lifetime. Our relationship began the day of my conception and has already lasted a half-century; it is, furthermore, the only truly unconditional love—neither one's children nor one's most fervent lovers love in that way. She is with me now in Madrid. She has the silver hair and the wrinkles of her seventy years but her dark green eyes still blaze with the old passion, even after the grief of these last months, which tends to make everything opaque. We share a couple of hotel rooms a few blocks from the hospital, where we have a small oven and refrigerator. We live primarily on the thick chocolate and crullers we buy in a little shop, although sometimes in our small kitchen we prepare a robust lentil and sausage soup that would raise Lazarus from the dead. We wake very early, while it is still dark; Mother lies in bed awhile as I hurriedly dress and brew coffee. I leave first, picking my way through the dirty snow and ice, and an hour or two later she joins me in the hospital. We spend the day in the corridor of lost steps, next to the door to the intensive care unit, just the two of us, until evening, when Ernesto comes from work and your friends and the nuns from your school drop by to visit. In keeping with the regulations, we can cross that ominous threshold only twice a day; we dress in green surgical gowns, slip plastic bags over our shoes, and walk the twenty-one long steps to your room, Paula, our hearts in our throats. Your bed is the first on the left; there are twelve beds in the room, some empty, some occupied. Cardiac and postoperative patients, victims of accidents, drugs, and failed suicides stay for a few days and then disappear; some return to life, others are wheeled out under a sheet. Beside you is don Manuel, slowly dying. Sometimes he raises himself a little to look at you with pain-clouded eyes. "How beautiful your daughter is!" he tells me. Almost always, he asks what happened to you, but he is so deep in the misery of his own illness that as soon as I tell him, he forgets. Yesterday I told him a story, and for the first time he listened with all his attention. Once there was a princess who on the day she was baptized received many gifts from her fairy godmothers, but, before her mother could stop him, one wicked sorcerer placed a time bomb in her body. When the young girl had lived twenty-eight happy years, everyone had forgotten the curse, but the clock was ticking on, inexorably counting down the minutes. Then one terrible day the bomb noiselessly exploded. Enzymes lost their way in the labyrinth of her veins, and the girl sank into a sleep deep as death. "May God watch over your princess," don Manuel sighed.

To you I tell different stories, Paula.

My childhood was a time of unvoiced fears: terror of Margara, who detested me; fear that my father would come back to claim us, or that my mother would die or get married; fear of the devil, of my uncles' games of Ruffin, or of the things bad men can do to little girls. Don't ever get into an automobile with someone you don't know, Don't speak to anyone in the street, Don't let anyone touch your body, Never go anywhere near the gypsies. I always believed I was different; as long as I can remember I have felt like an outcast, as if I didn't really belong to my family, or to my surroundings, or to any group. I suppose that it is from that feeling of loneliness the questions arise that lead one to write, and that books are conceived in the search for answers. My consolation in moments of panic was the ever-present spirit of Memé, who would emerge from the folds of the drapes to keep me company. The cellar was the dark belly of the house, a locked and forbidden place I entered by slipping through a cellar window. I felt at home in that damp-smelling cave where I used to play, defeating the darkness with lighted candles, or with the same flashlight I used when I read under the covers at night. I spent hours in the silent games, secretive reading, and complicated ceremonies lonely children invent. I had stored away a good supply of candles stolen from the kitchen, and I had a box where I kept bread and cracker crumbs to feed the mice. No one suspected my excursions into the depths of the earth; the servants attributed the noises and lights to my grandmother's ghost, and never came anywhere near. My subterranean kingdom consisted of two large, low-ceilinged rooms with a hard dirt floor; all the bones of the house were exposed there, the guts of the plumbing, the fright wig of the electric wires. There were piles of broken furniture, ripped mattresses, heavy, ancient suitcases for sea voyages no one remembered now. In one metal trunk bearing my father's initials, I found a collection of books, a fabulous inheritance that illuminated those childhood years, *A Child's Treasury of Literature*: Salgari, Shaw, Verne, Twain, Wilde, London, and others. In my mind, they were forbidden books, since they had belonged to that T.A. whose name could not be spoken aloud. I never dared take them into the daylight but, with the help of my candle, I gobbled them down with the voraciousness inspired by secrecy—as years later I hid to devour *A Thousand and One Nights*. In fact there were no censored books in that house; no one had time to keep an eye on the children, much less their taste in books. When I was nine I dove into the complete works of Shakespeare, my first gift from Tío Ramón, a beautiful edition that I read through several times, never thinking of literary quality, only intrigue and tragedy—that is, for the same reasons that earlier I had listened to serials on the radio and that now I write fiction. I lived every story as if it were my own life; I was each of those characters, especially the villains, who were much more attractive to me than the virtuous heroes. My imagination inevitably tilted toward the lurid. If I read about redskins scalping their enemies, I presumed that the victims lived on, and continued their battle wearing tight-fitting bison skin caps to contain the brains spilling through cracks in their hairless craniums—and from there it was only a step to imagining that their ideas leaked out as well. I drew characters on bristol board, cut them out, and propped them up with toothpicks; those were my first ventures in theater. I told stories to my stupefied brothers, terrible tales of suspense that filled their days with terror and their sleep with nightmares, as years later

I entertained my children—and also a few men in the intimacy of our bed, where a well-told fable tends to be the most powerful aphrodisiac.

Tío Ramón had a substantial influence on many aspects of my character, although in some instances it has taken me forty years to relate his teaching with my actions. He was half-owner, with a friend, of a Ford that had seen much better days. Tío Ramón drove it Mondays, Wednesdays, Fridays, and every other Sunday, yielding it to his friend the rest of the week. One of the Sundays he had the car, he took my brothers, my mother, and me to The Open Door, a farm on the outskirts of Santiago where they housed nonviolent mental patients. He knew the place well, because he had spent childhood vacations there as the guest of relatives who administered the agricultural operations. We entered the grounds by joggling along a dirt road lined with large plane trees arching greenly overhead. On one side were pastures, and on the other the buildings, encircled by an orchard of fruit trees where a few peaceful inmates in faded smocks were aimlessly roaming. They rushed to meet us, running alongside the car, poking their hands and faces through the windows, and yelling, "Hello! Hello!" We shrank back in our seats, terrified, as Tío Ramón greeted them by name; some had been there for years, and he had played with them as a boy. For a reasonable price, he negotiated with the supervisor to let us go into the orchard.

"Get out, children, these are nice people," Tío Ramón ordered. "You can climb the trees, eat all you want, and also fill this sack. *We are filthy rich.*"

I don't know how he arranged it, but the patients helped us. We soon lost our fear of them, and all of us ended up in the branches, streaming with juice, wolfing down apricots and pulling them from the branches by handfuls to drop into our sack. If we bit into one that wasn't sweet enough, we threw it away and picked another. We bombed each other with ripe apricots: a true orgy of bursting fruit and laughter. We ate till we could eat no more, then kissed our new friends goodbye and piled into the old Ford for the return trip, continuing to stuff ourselves from the overflowing bag of fruit until stopped by stomach cramps. That day, for the first time ever, I realized that life can be generous. I had never experienced anything similar with my grandfather, or any other member of my family, all of whom believed that paucity is a blessing and avarice a virtue. From time to time, Tata would appear with a tray of little cakes, always counted out, one for each: never too many and never too few. Money was sacred and we children were taught early on how difficult it was to earn it. My grandfather had a fortune, but I never suspected that until much later. Tío Ramón was poor as a churchmouse, but I didn't know that either, because he always showed us how to enjoy the little we had. At the most difficult moments of my life, when it has seemed that every door was closed to me, the taste of those apricots comes back to comfort me with the notion that abundance is always within reach, if only one knows how to find it.

My memories of childhood are dramatic, like everyone else's, I suppose, because the banalities are lost; with me, it may also be my sense of the tragic. They say that geography can determine character. I come from a very beautiful land, but one battered by calamities: summer droughts; winter floods when irrigation ditches overflow and the poor die of pneumonia; rising rivers from melting snow in the mountains and seaquakes that with a single wave wash ships onto dry land, stranding them in the middle of a plaza; wild fires and erupting volcanoes; plagues of flies, snails, and ants; apocalyptic earthquakes and an uninterrupted string of minor temblors that no one even notices; and if to the poverty of half the population we add isolation, there is more than enough material from which to construct melodrama.

Pelvina López-Pun, the dog that was placed in my cradle from the day I was born, with the idea of immunizing me against epidemics and allergies, was a lascivious bitch that every six months was inseminated by some street cur despite the ingenious subterfuges improvised by my mother—such as outfitting her in rubber pants. When Pelvina was in heat, she would push her rear against the iron fence in the garden as an impatient pack of mutts waited to offer their love through the bars. Often when I came home from school I would find a dog stuck on one side, Pelvina howling on the other, and my uncles, weak with laughter, trying to separate them with blasts of cold water from the garden hose. Afterward, Margara would drown the litter of newborn pups, just like the kittens. One summer we were all ready to leave for vacation but had to postpone the trip because Pelvina was in heat and could not be taken anywhere in that condition; we had no pen at the beach, and it had been demonstrated that the rubber pants were little protection against the onslaught of true passion. Tata threw such a fit that my mother decided to put an ad in the newspaper: "Purebred bulldog bitch, European papers, sweet tempered, seeking loving owners who can appreciate her." She explained her reasons to us but we thought the whole idea was unspeakable, and deduced that if she was capable of getting rid of Pelvina she could do the same to any of us. We begged in vain. On Saturday a couple came to the house who were interested in adopting her. Hidden beneath the stairway, we could see Margara's hopeful smile as she led them to the drawing room—that woman hated the dog as much as she did me. Soon Mother came out to look for Pelvina, to show her off to the potential buyers. She searched the house from top to bottom before she found all of us in the bathroom; my brothers and I had locked ourselves in with the dog, after shaving patches on her back and painting them with Mercurochrome. Pushing and threatening, Mother managed to open the door; Pelvina shot down the stairs and leaped onto the sofa with the couple, who at the sight of the apparent sores screamed and fell over one another to get to the door before they were infected. Three months later, Margara had to do away with a half-dozen bastard pups, as we burned in flames of guilt. Soon thereafter, Pelvina mysteriously died; there is little doubt that Margara had something to do with the death.

That same year, I was informed at school that babies are not brought by the stork but grow like melons in their mother's belly, and also that there was no such thing as good old Santa Claus, it was your parents who bought your Christmas presents. The first part of that revelation had little effect on me because I did not intend to have children just yet, but the second part was devastating. I planned to stay awake all Christmas Eve to discover the truth, but my best efforts failed, and I fell asleep. Tormented by doubts, I had written a letter, a kind of trap, asking for the impossible: another dog, a host of friends, and a list of toys. When I woke on Christmas morning, I found a box containing bottles of tempera paint, brushes, and a clever note from that wretched Santa—whose writing looked suspiciously like my mother's—explaining that in order to teach me to be less greedy, he had not brought what I asked; instead, he was offering the walls of my room, where I could paint the dog, the friends, and the toys I had requested. I looked around and saw that several stern old portraits had been removed, along with a lamentable Sacred Heart of Jesus, and on the bare wall facing my bed was a color reproduction cut from an art book. My disenchantment immobilized me for a few minutes, but finally I pulled myself together sufficiently to examine the picture, which turned out to be a work by Marc Chagall. At first, all I could see were anarchical smudges, but soon I discovered on that small piece of paper an astounding universe of blue brides tumbling head over heels through the air and a pale musician floating amid a seven-armed candelabrum, a red nanny goat, and other mutable characters. There were so many different colors and objects that I was a long time taking in the marvelous disorder of the composition. That painting had music: a ticking clock, moaning violins, bleating goats, fluttering wings, and endless streams of words. It also had scents: lighted candles, wildflowers, an animal in heat, women's lotions and creams. The whole scene seemed bathed in the nebula of a happy dream; on one side the atmosphere was as warm as an afternoon siesta, and on the other you could feel the cool of a country night. I was too young to be able to analyze the artistry, but I remember my surprise and curiosity: that Chagall was an invitation to a game. I asked myself, fascinated, how it was possible to paint like that, without an ounce of respect for the norms of composition and perspective my art teacher was trying to instill. If this artist can do whatever he pleases, so can I, I concluded, opening the first bottle of tempera. For years I painted—freely, with unbounded pleasure—a complex mural in which were registered my desires, fears, rages, childhood doubts, and growing pains. In a place of honor, surrounded by delirious flora and impossible fauna, I drew the silhouette of a boy with his back turned as if looking at the mural. It was the portrait of Marc Chagall, with whom I had fallen in love as only children can. At the time I was furiously decorating the walls in my house in Santiago, Chile, the object of my love was sixty years older than I; he was famous throughout the world, he had just ended a long period of widowhood with a second marriage, and he lived in the heart of Paris . . . but distance and time are fragile conventions. I thought Chagall was a boy my own age and years later, in April 1985, when he died in the ninety-seventh year of his eternal youth, I found that in fact he had always been the boy I imagined. When we left that house and I had to bid my mural goodbye, my mother gave me a notebook in which to note down things I previously had painted: a notebook to record my life. "Here, write what's in your heart," she said. That is what I did then, and that is what I am doing now in these pages. What else can I do? I have time left over. I have the whole future ahead of me. I want to give it to you, Paula, because you have lost yours.

Here everyone calls you *la niña,* " the little girl"; it must be because of your schoolgirl face and the long hair the nurses braid for you. They have asked Ernesto's permission to cut it—it is an ongoing struggle to keep it clean and free of tangles—but they haven't done it as yet; the idea makes them sad. They have never seen you with your eyes open, so they think your hair is your most beautiful feature. I believe they are a little in love with your husband because they are so touched by his devotion. They see him leaning over your bed, whispering to you as if you could hear, and wish they could be loved like that. Ernesto takes off his jacket and presses it against your lifeless hands. "Feel it, Paula, it's me; this is your favorite jacket, do you remember it?" He has recorded secret messages he leaves on your earphones so you can hear his voice when he's not there; he brings cotton scented with his cologne and places it beneath your pillow so his aroma will stay with you. Love roars down on the women of our family like a gale-force wind; that is what happened to my mother with Tío Ramón, to you with Ernesto, to me with Willie, and I suppose the same thing will happen to generations of our girls to come. One New Year's Day, after I was living with Willie in California, I called you to give you a long-distance hug and to talk over the old year and ask what your wish was for the 1988 just beginning. "I want a man, a love like yours," was your immediate response. Scarcely forty-eight hours later, you called me back, euphoric.

"I have it, Mama! Last night at a party I met the man I'm going to marry," and the words poured out; you told me that from the first instant it was like wildfire; you looked at each other with instant recognition, you knew this was meant to be.

"You sound like a corny romance novel, Paula. How can you be so sure?"

"Because it made me so queasy I had to leave. Thank goodness, he came right behind me. . . ."

A normal mother would have warned you against a passion like that, but I have no moral authority to impose temperance, so what followed was one of our typical conversations.

"Fantastic, Paula. Are you going to live with him?"

"I have to finish my studies first."

"You're going to go on with them?"

"You don't think I'd throw it all over?"

"Well, if he's the man of a lifetime . . . "

"Slow down, Mama, I've only just met him."

"Well, I just met Willie, too, and you see where I am. Life is short, Paula."

"Shorter at your age than mine. All right, I won't go for the doctorate, but at least I want to finish the M.A."

And that's what you did. You completed the degree with honors, and then left to go live with Ernesto in Madrid. You both found work, he as an electronics engineer and you as a volunteer school psychologist, and shortly afterward you were married. On the first anniversary of your wedding you were in a coma, and as a gift your husband brought you a love story he whispered in your ear, kneeling beside you, while the nurses watched, moved, and don Manuel wept in the bed beside you.

Ah, carnal love! My first galloping attack struck when I was eleven. Tío Ramón had been reassigned to Bolivia, but this time he took my mother and the three of us children. They were not free to marry, and the government would pay expenses only for a legal family. Mother and Tío Ramón, however, ignored the malicious gossip and despite formidable obstacles set about nurturing their problem-plagued relationship. They succeeded admirably, and today, more than forty years later, they are a legendary couple. La Paz is an extraordinary city, so near heaven, and with such thin air, that you can see the angels at dawn. Your heart is always about to burst, and your gaze is lost in the consuming purity of endless vistas. Mountain chains, purple hills, rocks and splashes of earth in saffron, violet, and vermilion tones encircle the long, narrow valley from which this city of contrasts spills. I remember narrow streets rising and falling like party streamers, little hole-in-the-wall shops, broken-down buses, Indians dressed in bright wool, the ever-present wad of coca leaves staining their teeth green. The bell towers of hundreds of churches, and the courtyards where Indian women sat to sell dried yucca and purple maize and little mounds of dried llama fetuses for curative poultices, all the while fanning away flies and nursing their babies. The smells and colors of La Paz are inscribed in my memory as an inseparable part of the slow and painful awakening of adolescence. The ambiguity of my childhood ended at the precise moment we moved from my grandfather's house. The night before we left, I crept out of bed, went downstairs, carefully avoiding the treads that creaked, and felt my way through the dark ground floor to the drawing room drapes where Memé was waiting to tell me that I must not be sad because she had nothing more to do in that house and was ready to go with me; she said that I should get her silver mirror from Tata's desk, and take it with me. I will be there from now on, she added, always with you. For the first time in my life, I dared to open the door of my grandfather's room. Light from the street filtered through the slats of the shutters, and my eyes were by now accustomed to the darkness. The grandfather clock struck three. I could see Tata's motionless body and austere profile; he was lying on his back, rigid as a corpse in that room filled with funereal furniture. I would see him exactly like that thirty years later, when he came to me in a dream to reveal the ending for my first novel. Ever so quietly, I glided toward his desk—passing so close to his bed that I could sense his widower's loneliness—and opened his drawers one by one, terrified that he would wake and catch me in the act of stealing. I found the baroque-handled mirror next to a tin box I did not dare touch. I took it in both hands and tiptoed out of the room. Safely back in bed, I peered into the shining glass where I had so often been told demons appear at night; I suppose I saw my ten-year-old face, round and pale, but in my imagination I saw Memé's sweet image, telling me good night. Early the next morning I added the last touch to my mural, a hand writing the word "Adios." That day was filled with confusion, contradictory orders, hasty farewells, and superhuman efforts to fit the suitcases on top of the automobiles that were to drive us to the port to take the ship north. The rest of the journey would be undertaken on a narrow-gauge train that climbed toward the heights of Bolivia at the pace of a millenarian snail. The sight of my grandfather—in his mourning, and with his cane and his Basque beret—standing at the door of the house where I grew up marked the end of my childhood.

Evenings in La Paz are a conflagration of stars, and on moonless nights you can see them individually, even those that died millions of years ago and those that will be born tomorrow. Sometimes I used to lie on my back in the garden to gaze at those awe-inspiring skies and feel the vertigo of death, falling and falling toward the depths of an infinite abyss. We lived in a compound of three houses that shared a common garden; in front of us was a celebrated oculist, and behind, an Uruguayan diplomat who was rumored to be homosexual. We children thought that he suffered from an incurable disease. We always said hello with great sympathy, and once were so bold as to ask him whether "homosexuality" hurt very much. After school, I sought solitude and silence in the paths of that large garden; I found hiding places for the notebook with the record of my life and secret places to read, far away from the noise of the city. We attended a coeducational school; until then my only contact with boys had been my brothers, but they didn't count. Even today I think of Pancho and Juan as asexual, like bacteria. For her first history lesson, the teacher lectured on Chile's nineteenth-century wars against Peru and Bolivia. In my country, I had been taught that the Chileans won battles because of their fearless valor and the patriotism of their leaders, but in that class I learned about the atrocities committed by my compatriots against civilian populations. Chilean soldiers, drugged on a mixture of liquor and gunpowder, swept into occupied cities like barbarian hordes. With fixed bayonets and slaughtering knives, they speared babies, gutted women, and mutilated men's genitals. I raised my hand to defend the honor of our armed forces—not yet suspecting what they are capable of—and was greeted by a hail of spitballs. I was sent from the room, amid hisses and catcalls, and told to stand in the corridor with my face to the wall. Holding back my tears, so no one would see my humiliation, I fumed for forty-five minutes. During that traumatic time, my hormones—until then totally unknown to me—erupted with the force of a volcano. "Erupt" is not an exaggeration: that day I had my first menstrual period. In the opposite corner, also facing the wall, stood a fellow culprit, a tall boy, skinny as a broom, with a long neck, black hair, and enormous, protruding ears that from the rear gave him the air of a Greek amphora. I have never seen more sensual ears. It was love at first sight; I fell in love with those ears before I ever saw his face, with such vehemence that in the next months I lost my appetite and then, from eating so little and sighing so much, became anemic. My romantic rapture was devoid of sexuality; I did not connect what had happened in my childhood—the pine forest beside the sea, and the warm hands of a young fisherman—with the pristine sentiments inspired by those extraordinary appendages. I was a victim of that chaste, and therefore much more devastating, love for two years. I remember that time in La Paz as a succession of fantasies in our shady garden, ardent pages in my notebooks, and storybook daydreams in which a pitcher-eared knight rescued me from the maws of a dragon. To top everything off, the entire school knew of my enslavement, and because of my infatuation and my unarguable nationality, I became the prime victim of the most offensive schoolyard pranks. My love was destined for failure; the object of my passion treated me with such indifference that I came to believe I was invisible in his presence. Not long before our final departure from Bolivia, a fight broke out on the playground in which—I shall never know how—I ended up with my arms around my idol, rolling in a dustdevil of fists, hair-pulling, and kicking. He was much larger than I and, although I put into practice every trick I had learned at the Teatro Caupolicán wrestling matches with my grandfather, I was bruised and bloody-nosed at the end. In a moment of blind fury, however, one of those ears came within range of my teeth and I had the satisfaction of stealing an impassioned nip. For weeks I walked on air. That was the most erotic encounter of a long lifetime, a combination of intense pleasure from the embrace and no-less-sharp pain from the pummeling. Given that masochistic awakening of lust, another, less fortunate woman might today be the complaisant victim of a sadist's whip, but as it worked out, I never again had occasion to practice that particular hold.

Shortly after, we left Bolivia forever, and I never saw the ears again. Tío Ramón flew directly to Paris, and from there to Lebanon, while my brothers and mother and I made the long descent by train to a port in the north of Chile; from there we took an Italian steamer to Genoa, then a bus to Rome, and from there we flew to Beirut. It was a journey of two months, and I believe it was a miracle my mother survived. We traveled in the last car of the train, in the company of an enigmatic Indian who never spoke a single word and spent the entire trip kneeling on the floor beside a small stove, chewing his coca, scratching his lice, and gripping an archaic rifle. Day and night his small, oblique eyes watched us, his expression impenetrable. We never saw him sleep. My mother was sure that at some unguarded moment he would murder us, even though she had been assured he had been hired to protect us. As the train moved slowly across the desert, inching past dunes and salt mines, my brothers often jumped down and ran alongside. To upset my mother, they would fall behind, feigning exhaustion, and then yell for help because the train was leaving them behind. On the ship, Pancho caught his fingers so often in the heavy metal hatches that finally no one would respond to his howls, and Juan caused an uproar one day by disappearing for several hours. While playing hide-and-seek, he had fallen asleep in an unoccupied stateroom; he wasn't found until a blast from the ship's whistle waked him, just as the captain was prepared to back down the engines and lower lifeboats to search for him; in the meantime, two brawny petty officers were forcibly restraining my mother to prevent her from diving into the Atlantic. I fell in love with all the sailors with a passion nearly as violent as that inspired by my young Bolivian, but I suspect they had eyes only for my mother. Although those slender young Italians stirred my imagination, even they could not cure me of my shameful vice of playing with dolls. Locked tight in my stateroom, I rocked them, bathed them, gave them their bottles, and sang in a low voice—in order to hear anyone coming—while my fiendish brothers threatened to take my dolls up on the deck and expose them to the crew. However, when we disembarked in Genoa, both Pancho and Juan, loyal under fire, were carrying a suspicious, towel-wrapped bundle under one arm while I hung behind, sighing, to bid the sailors of my dreams goodbye.

We lived in Lebanon for three surreal years, which allowed me to learn some French and to travel to most of the surrounding countries—including the Holy Land and Israel, which in the decade of the fifties, as now, existed in a permanent state of war with the Arabs. Crossing the border by car, as we did more than once, was a sobering experience. We lived in a large, ugly, modern apartment. From the terrace, we could look down on a market and the Guard Headquarters that played important roles later when the violence began. Tío Ramón set aside one room for the consulate, and hung the shield and flag of Chile on the front of the building. None of my new friends had ever heard of that country; they thought I came from China. In general, in that time and in that part of the world, girls were confined to house and school until the day of their marriage—if they had the misfortune to marry—the moment at which they exchanged a paternal prison for a conjugal one. I was shy, and kept very much to myself. Elvis Presley was already fat before I ever saw him in a film. Our family life was not smooth; my mother did not adapt well to the Arab culture, the hot climate, or Tío Ramón's authoritarianism; she suffered headaches, allergies, and sudden hallucinations. Once we packed our suitcases to return to my grandfather's house in Santiago because she swore that an Orthodox priest in full liturgical vestments was spying on her bath through a transom. My stepfather missed his own children but had little contact with them; communications with Chile could be delayed for months, contributing to the feeling that we lived at the end of the world. Finances were extremely tight; money was laboriously stretched out in weekly accountings, and then, if anything was left over, we went to the movies or to an indoor ice-skating rink, the only luxuries we could allow ourselves. We lived decently, but on a level different from that of other members of the diplomatic corps or the social circle we frequented, for whom private clubs, winter sports, the theater, and vacations in Switzerland were the norm. My mother made herself a long silk dress for gala receptions; she transformed it in miraculous ways with a brocade train, lace sleeves, or velvet bow at the waist. I suspect that people focused on her face, however, not her clothes. She became expert in the supreme art of keeping up appearances; she prepared inexpensive dishes, disguised them with sophisticated sauces of her own invention, and served them on her famous silver trays; she made the living room and dining room elegant with paintings from my grandfather's house and tapestries bought on credit on the docks of Beirut, but everything else was at best modest. Tío Ramón's unbending optimism never flagged. With all the problems my mother had, I have often wondered what kept them together during that time, and the only answer that comes to me is, the tenacity of a passion born of distance, nourished with love letters, and fortified by a veritable Everest of obstacles. They are very different, and it is not unusual for them to argue to the point of exhaustion. Some of their battles were of such magnitude that they were dubbed with a name of their own and given a place in the family archive of anecdotes. I admit that I did nothing to facilitate their living together; when I realized that my stepfather had arrived in our lives to stay, I declared all-out war. Today it shames me to recall all the times I plotted horrible ways to kill him. His role was not easy; I cannot imagine how he was able to rear the three Allende children who fell into his lap. We never called him Papa, because that word brought back bad memories, but he earned his avuncular title, Tío Ramón, as a symbol of admiration and confidence. Today, at seventy-five, hundreds of persons scattered across five continents—including no few government officials and members of Chile's diplomatic corps—call him Tío Ramón for the same reason.

In at attempt to provide continuity to my education, I was sent to an English school for girls whose objective was to build character through trials of rigor and discipline—none of which much impressed me because it was not for nothing I had emerged unscathed from my uncles' famous Ruffin games. The goal of that teaching was for all students to memorize the Bible. "Deuteronomy, chapter five, verse three," Miss St. John would intone, and we had to recite it without stopping to think. In this way, I learned a little English, and also perfected to absurdity the stoic sense of life already implanted by my grandfather in the big old house with swirling currents of air. Both the English language and stoicism in the face of adversity have been beneficial; most of what other skills I possess Tío Ramón taught me by example and a methodology that modern psychology would consider brutal. He acted as consul general for several Arab countries, using Beirut as his base, a magnificent city that was considered the Paris of the Middle East: traffic was tied up by camels and sheikhs' Cadillacs with gold bumpers, and Muslim women, draped in black with only a peephole for their eyes, shopped in the souks elbow to elbow with scantily clad foreigners. On Saturdays, some of the housewives in the North American colony liked to wash their cars wearing shorts and bare midriff tops. Those Arab men who rarely saw women without veils came from remote villages, harrowing journeys by burro, to attend the spectacle of the half-naked foreign women. The locals rented chairs and sold coffee and syrupy sweets to the spectators lined up in rows on the opposite side of the street.

Summers were as hot and humid as a Turkish bath, but my school was ruled by norms imposed by Queen Victoria in a foggy, late-nineteenth-century England. Our uniform was a medieval cassocklike affair of coarsely woven cloth that closed with ties because buttons were considered frivolous; we wore orthopedic-looking shoes and a pith helmet–style hat pulled down to our eyebrows, an outfit that would take the wind out of anyone's sails. Food was fodder for shaping character; every day we were served unsalted rice, and twice a week it was burned; on Monday, Wednesday, and Friday, it was accompanied by vegetables, Tuesday, by yogurt, and Thursday, by boiled liver. It was months before I could refrain from gagging when I saw those pieces of gray organs floating in tepid water, but in the end I found them delicious, and eagerly awaited Thursday lunch. Since then, I have never met a meal I cannot eat, including English food. The girls came from many regions, and almost all were boarding students. Shirley was the prettiest girl in the school; she looked good even in our uniform hat. She came from India, had blue-black hair, made up her eyes with a pearly powder, and walked with the gravity-defying step of a gazelle. Behind closed bathroom doors, she taught me to belly dance, an accomplishment that has not done me much good since I have never had enough nerve to seduce a man by shaking and grinding. One day, soon after her fifteenth birthday, Shirley was removed from the school and taken back to her country to be wed to a fifty-year-old merchant her parents had chosen for her, a man she had never seen but knew only from a hand-tinted studio portrait. Eliza, my best friend, was straight out of a novel: an orphan, she was raised like a servant by sisters who had stolen her share of their inheritance; she sang like an angel and had plans to run away to America. Thirty-five years later, we met in Canada. She had fulfilled her dreams of independence; she owned her own business, had a fine mansion, a car with a telephone, four fur coats, and two spoiled dogs, but she still weeps when she remembers her childhood in Beirut. While Eliza was saving her pennies to flee to the New World, and the beautiful Shirley was fulfilling her destiny in an arranged marriage, the rest of us were studying the Bible and whispering about a certain Elvis Presley, whom none of us had seen or heard but who was said to create havoc with his electric guitar and rotating pelvis. I rode the school bus every day, the first to be picked up in the morning and the last to be left off in the afternoon. I spent hours circling around the city, an arrangement I liked because I didn't much want to go home. When I was eventually delivered, I often found Tío Ramón sitting in his undershirt beneath the ceiling fan, trying to move more air with a folded newspaper and listening to boleros.

"What did the nuns teach you today?" he would ask.

I particularly remember one day replying, sweating, but phlegmatic and dignified in my dreadful uniform, "They're not nuns, they're Protestant ladies. And we talked about Job."

"Job? That idiot God tested by sending every calamity known to mankind?"

"He wasn't an idiot, Tío Ramón, he was a saintly man who never denied the Lord, no matter how much he suffered."

"Does that seem right? God makes a bet with Satan, punishes poor Job unmercifully, and wants to be loved by him besides. That is a cruel, unjust, and frivolous God. A master who treated his servants that way would deserve neither loyalty nor respect, much less adoration."

Tío Ramón, who had been educated by Jesuits, was intimidatingly emphatic and implacably logical—the same skills he used in squabbles with my mother—as he set out to prove the stupidity of the biblical hero whose attitude, far from setting a praiseworthy example, demonstrated a personality disorder. In less than ten minutes of oratory, he had demolished all Miss St. John's virtuous teachings.

"Are you convinced that Job was a numskull?"

"Yes, Tío Ramón."

"Will you swear to that in writing?"

"Yes."

The consul of Chile crossed the couple of yards that separated us from his office and composed on letterhead paper a document with three carbons saying that I, Isabel Allende Llona, fourteen years old, a Chilean citizen, attested that Job, he of the Old Testament, was a dolt. He made me sign it, after reading it carefully—"because you must never sign anything blindly"—then folded it and put it in the consulate safe. He went back to his chair beneath the ceiling fan and, heaving a weary sigh, said:

"All right, child, now I shall prove that you were correct in the first place, and that Job was a holy man of God. I shall give you the arguments you should have used had you known how to think. Please understand that I am doing this only to teach you how to debate, something that will be very helpful in life." And he proceeded to dismantle his previous arguments and convince me of what I had firmly believed in the first place. In a very few minutes, I was again defeated, and this time on the verge of tears.

"Do you accept that Job was right to remain faithful to his God despite his misfortunes?"

"Yes, Tío Ramón."

"Are you absolutely sure?"

"Yes."

"Would you sign a document?"

And he composed a second statement that said that I, Isabel Allende Llona, fourteen years old, a Chilean citizen, was retracting my earlier opinion and instead agreeing that Job acted correctly. He handed me his pen, but just as I was about to sign my name at the bottom of the page he stopped me with a yell.

"*No!* How many times have I told you not to let anyone twist your arm? The most important thing in winning an argument is not to vacillate even if you have doubts, let alone if you are wrong!"

That is how I learned to defend myself, and years later in Chile I participated in an intermural debate between our girls' school and San Ignacio, which was represented by five boys with the mien of criminal lawyers, and two Jesuit priests whispering instructions to them. The boys' team arrived with a load of books they consulted to support their arguments and intimidate their opponents. My only resource was the memory of those afternoons with Job and my Tío Ramón in Lebanon. I lost, of course, but at the end my team paraded me around on their shoulders as our macho rivals retreated haughtily with their cartload of arguments. I do not know how many statements with three carbons I signed in my adolescence on topics as wildly diverse as biting my fingernails and the threatened extinction of whales. I believe that for a few years Tío Ramón kept some of them—for example, the one in which I swear that it is his fault that I will never meet any men and will end up an old maid. That was in Bolivia, when at age eleven I threw a tantrum because he did not let me go to a party where I thought I would see my beloved Big Ears. Three years later I was invited to a different party, this one in Beirut at the home of the U.S. ambassador and his wife. That time I had the good sense not to want to go because the girls had to play the part of passive sheep; I was sure that no boy in his

right mind would ask me to dance, and I could not think of a worse
humiliation than being a wallflower. That time my stepfather forced
me to attend because, he said, if I did not overcome my complexes
I would never have any success in life. The day before the party, he
closed the consulate and dedicated the afternoon to teaching me to
dance. With single-minded tenacity, he made me sway to the
rhythm of the music, first holding the back of a chair, then a broom,
and finally him. In several hours I learned everything from the
Charleston to the samba. Then he dried my tears and drove me to
buy a new dress. As he left me at the party, he offered a piece of
unforgettable advice, one I have followed at crucial moments of my
life: *Remember that all the others are more afraid than you*. He added that
I should not sit down for a second, but should take up a position
near the record player . . . oh, and not eat anything, because it takes
tremendous courage for a boy to cross a room and go up to a girl
anchored like a frigate in her chair and with a plate of cake in her
hand. Besides, the few boys who know how to dance are the same
ones who change the records, so you want to be near the player. At
the entrance to the embassy, a cement fortress in the worst fifties
style, there was a cage of huge black birds that spoke English with a
Jamaican accent. I was greeted by the ambassador's wife—in some
sort of admiral get-up and with a whistle around her neck for giving
instructions to the guests—and led to an enormous room swarming
with tall, ugly adolescents with pimply faces, all chewing gum, eating
french fries, and drinking Coca-Cola. The boys were wearing plaid
jackets and bow ties, and the girls had on circle skirts and angora
sweaters that left a flurry of hair in the air but revealed enviable
protuberances on their chest. I, on the other hand, had nothing to
put in a brassiere. They were all wearing bobby socks. I felt totally
alien; my dress was a disaster of taffeta and velvet, and I didn't know
a soul there. Panic-stricken, I stood and fed cake crumbs to the
black birds until I remembered Tío Ramón's instructions. Trembling, I removed my shoes and headed toward the record player.
Soon I saw a male hand stretched in my direction and, unable to
believe my luck, was borne off to dance a sugary tune with a boy
who had flat feet and braces on his teeth and was not half as grace-
ful as my stepfather. It was the time when everyone danced cheek-

to-cheek, a feat usually denied me even today, since my face comes about to a normal man's breastbone; at this party, barely fourteen and not wearing my shoes, my head was at the level of my partner's belly button. After that first ballad, they played a whole record of rock 'n' roll. Tío Ramón had never even heard of that, but all I had to do was watch the others for a few minutes and apply what I had learned the afternoon before. For once, my size and my limber joints were a plus: it was a breeze for my partners to toss me toward the ceiling, twirl me through the air like an acrobat, and catch me just before I broke my neck on the floor. I found myself performing arabesques, lifted, dragged, whipped around, and bounced by a variety of youths who by this point had shed their plaid jackets and bow ties. I had no complaint. I was not a wallflower that night, as I had dreaded, but danced until I raised blisters on my feet, in the process acquiring the assurance that it is not so difficult to meet men after all, and that certainly I would not be an old maid. I did not, however, sign a document to that effect. I had learned not to let anyone twist my arm.

Tío Ramón had a three-sectioned wardrobe that could be taken apart when we moved, in which he locked his clothes and treasures: a collection of erotic magazines, cartons of cigarettes, boxes of chocolates, and liquor. My brother Juan discovered a way to open it with a bent wire, and we became expert sneak thieves. If we had taken only a few chocolates or cigarettes, he would have noticed, but we would sneak an entire layer of chocolates and reseal the box so perfectly it looked unopened, and we filched entire cartons of cigarettes, never a few, or a pack. Tío Ramón first became suspicious in La Paz. He called us in, one by one, and tried to get us either to confess or to inform on the guilty party. Neither gentle words nor threats were any good: we thought that to admit to the crime would be stupid and, in our moral code, betrayal among siblings was unpardonable. One Friday afternoon when we got back from school, we found Tío Ramón and a man we didn't know waiting for us in the living room.

"I have no patience with your disregard for the truth; the least I can expect is not to be robbed in my own home. This gentleman is a police detective. He will take your fingerprints, compare them with the evidence on my wardrobe, and we will know who the thief is. This is your last chance to confess the truth."

Pale with terror, my bothers and I stared at the floor and clamped our jaws shut.

"Do you know what happens to criminals? They rot in jail," Tío Ramón added.

The detective pulled a tin box from his pocket. When he opened it, we could see the black inkpad inside. Slowly, with great ceremony, he pressed each of our fingers to the pad, then rolled them onto a prepared cardboard.

"Have no worry, Señor Consul. Monday you will have the results of my investigation," the man assured Tío Ramón as he left.

Saturday and Sunday were days of moral torture; hidden in the bathroom and the most private corners of the garden, we whispered about our black future. None of us was free of guilt; we would all end up in a dungeon on foul water and dry bread crusts, like the Count of Monte Cristo. The following Monday, the ineffable Tío Ramón called us into his office.

"I know exactly who the thief is," he announced, wiggling thick, satanic eyebrows. "Nevertheless, out of consideration for your mother, who has interceded in your behalf, I shall not incarcerate anyone this time. The culprit knows I know who he or she is. It will remain between the two of us. I warn all of you that on the next occasion I shall not be so softhearted. Do I make myself clear?"

We stumbled from the room, grateful, unable to believe such magnanimity. We did not steal anything for a long time, but a few years later in Beirut I thought about it again, and was struck by the suspicion that the purported detective was actually an embassy chauffeur—Tío Ramón was quite capable of playing such a trick. Bending a wire of my own, I again opened the wardrobe. This time, in addition to the predictable treasures, I found four red leather-bound volumes of *A Thousand and One Nights*. I deduced that there must be some powerful reason these books were under lock and key, and that made them much more interesting than the bonbons, cigarettes, or erotic magazines with women in garter belts. For the next three years, every time Tío Ramón and my mother were at some cocktail party or dinner, I read snatches of the tales, curled up inside the cabinet with my faithful flashlight. Even though diplomats necessarily suffer an intense social life, there was never enough time to finish those fabulous stories. When I heard my parents coming, I had to close the wardrobe in a wink and fly to my bed and pretend to be asleep. It was impossible to leave a bookmark between the pages and I always forgot my place; worse yet, entire sections fell out as I searched for the dirty parts, with the results that innumerable new versions of the stories were created in an orgy of exotic words, eroticism, and fantasy. The contrast between the puritanism of my school, where work was exalted and neither bodily imperatives nor lightning flash of imagination allowed, and the creative idleness and enveloping sensuality of those books branded my soul. For decades I wavered between those two tendencies, torn apart inside and awash in a sea of intermingled desires and sins, until finally in the heat of Venezuela, when I was nearly forty years old, I at last freed myself from Miss St. John's rigid precepts. Just as in my childhood I hid in the basement of Tata's house to read my favorite books, so in full adolescence, just as my body and mind were awakening to the mysteries of sex, I furtively read *A Thousand and One Nights*. Deep in that dark wardrobe, I lost myself in magical tales of princes on flying carpets, genies in oil lamps, and appealing thieves who slipped into the sultan's harem disguised as old ladies to indulge in marathon love fests with forbidden women with hair black as night, pillowy hips and breasts like apples, soft women smelling of musk and eager for pleasure. On those pages, love, life, and death seemed like a gambol; the descriptions of food, landscapes, palaces, markets, smells, tastes, and textures were so rich that after them the world has never been the same to me.

I dreamed you were twelve years old, Paula. You were wearing a plaid coat; your hair was pulled back from your face with a white ribbon and the rest fell loose over your shoulders. You were standing in the center of a hollow tower, something like a grain silo filled with hundreds of fluttering doves. Memé's voice was saying, *Paula is dead.* You began to rise off the ground. I ran to catch you by the belt of your coat but you pulled me with you, and we floated like feathers, circling upward. I am going with you, take me, too, Paula, I begged. Again my grandmother's voice echoed in the tower: *No one can go with her, she has drunk the potion of death.* We kept rising and rising; I was determined to hold you back, nothing would take you from me. Overhead was a small opening through which I could see a blue sky with one perfect white cloud, like a Magritte painting, and then I understood, horrified, that you would be able to pass through but that the aperture was too narrow for me. I tried to hold you back by your clothing; I called to you, but no sound came. For a few precious instants, I could see as you drifted higher and higher, and then I began to float back down through the turbulence of the doves.

I awoke crying your name, and it was minutes before I realized I was in Madrid, and recognized the hotel room. I threw on my clothes before my mother had time to stop me, and ran toward the hospital. Along the way I found a taxi, and soon I was frantically beating on the door to intensive care. A nurse assured me that nothing had happened to you, that everything was the same, but I begged so hard, and was so visibly shaken, that she allowed me to come see you for a minute. I made sure that the machine was pumping air into your lungs, and that you weren't cold; I kissed your forehead, and went out in the corridor to wait for morning. They say that dreams don't lie. With the first light of day, my mother arrived. She brought a thermos of freshly brewed coffee and *rosquillas* still warm from the bakery.

"Don't worry, it wasn't a bad omen, it didn't have anything to do with Paula. All of the characters are you," she explained. "You are the twelve-year-old girl, still flying free. But your innocence also ended then. The girl you were died; the potion of death was what all of us women swallow sooner or later. Have you noticed how at puberty the Amazon-like energy we are born with fades and we turn into doubt-filled creatures with clipped wings? The woman left trapped in the silo is also you, a prisoner of the restrictions of adult life. The female condition is a disgrace, Isabel, it's like having rocks tied to your ankles so you can't fly."

"And what do the doves mean, Mama?"

"An agitated spirit, I suppose. . . ."

Every night dreams wait for me crouched beneath the bed with their bag of horrific visions—bell towers, blood, doleful wailing— but also with an ever-renewed harvest of fleeting, happy images. I have two lives, one waking, the other sleeping. In the world of my dreams, there are landscapes and people I already know; there I explore infernos and Edens; I fly through the black night of the cosmos and descend to the bottom of the sea where a green silence reigns; I meet dozens of children of all kinds, impossible animals, and the delicate ghosts of my most loved dead. Through the years I have discovered the keys to understanding these stories of the night, and I have learned to decipher their codes; now the messages are clearer and they help me illuminate the mysterious areas of everyday life and of my writing.

But back to Job. I have been thinking a lot about him these days. It occurs to me that your illness is a trial like those visited upon that poor man. It is a terrible arrogance on my part to imagine that you are lying in this bed so that we—we who wait in the corridor of lost steps—can be taught something, but the truth is that there are moments when I believe that. What do you want to teach us, Paula? I have changed a lot during these interminable weeks, all of those who have lived through this experience have changed—especially Ernesto, who seems to have aged a hundred years. How can I console him when I myself am without hope? I wonder whether I will ever laugh with pleasure again, embrace a cause, eat with gusto, write a novel. "Of course you will. Soon you will be celebrating with your daughter and this nightmare will be forgotten," my mother promises. She is seconded by the porphyria specialist, who assures us that once the crisis is past, patients recover completely. I have a premonition, though, Paula, I can't deny it. This has gone on too long, and you are no better; in fact, it seems to me you are worse. Your grandmother does not give an inch; she keeps a normal routine, and has the energy to read the newspaper, even to go shopping. "I have only one regret in this life, and that is for the things I didn't buy," that sinful woman tells me. We have been here a long time, and I want to go home. Madrid holds bad memories for me; I suffered through a bad love affair here, one I would prefer to forget. During this dreadful time, however, I have made my peace with this city and its inhabitants. I have learned to find my way through its broad majestic avenues and the twisted streets of its centuries-old barrios; I have come to terms with Spanish customs: their smoking, their two-fisted consumption of coffee and liquor, their staying up till dawn, the mind-numbing amount of fat they eat, and their never exercising. Even so, people here live as long as Californians—and much more happily. Once in a while we have dinner at a neighborhood restaurant, always the same one because my mother has fallen in love with the waiter. She likes ugly men, and this one could win a contest. He is burly from the waist up, with the massive hunched shoulders and long arms of an orangutan, but from the waist down he is a dwarf, with spindly little legs. My mother follows him with her seductive gaze, her mouth sometimes agape as she watches him, her spoon frozen in air. For seventy years, she has cultivated the reputation of being spoiled; all of us have protected her from stressful emotions, thinking she could not bear up, but during this crisis her true character has come to light: she is a fighting bull.

In terms of the cosmos and the long course of history, we are insignificant; after we die nothing will change, as if we had never existed. Nevertheless, by the measures of our precarious humanity, you, Paula, are more important to me than my own life, or the sum of almost all other lives. Every day several million persons die and even more are born, but, for me, you alone were born, only you can die. Your grandmother prays for you to her Christian God, and I sometimes pray to a smiling, pagan Goddess overflowing with gifts, a divinity who knows nothing of punishment, only pardon, and I speak to Her with the hope that She will hear me from the depths of time, and help you. Neither your grandmother nor I have had any response, we are encased in this abysmal silence. I think of my great-grandmother, of my clairvoyant grandmother, of my own mother, of you, and of my granddaughter who will be born in May, a strong female chain going back to the first woman, the universal mother. I must harness these nurturing forces for your salvation. I do not know how to reach you; I call but you don't hear me. That is why I am writing to you. The idea of filling these pages was not mine; it has been weeks since I took any initiative. As soon as she heard of your illness, my agent came to give me support. As a first measure, she dragged my mother and me to an inn where she tempted us with suckling pig and a bottle of Rioja wine, which settled like a stone in our stomach but also had the virtue of making us laugh again. Then she surprised us in the hotel with dozens of red roses, nougats from Alicante, and an obscene-looking sausage—the one we are still using to make lentil soup—and in my lap she deposited a ream of lined yellow paper.

"My poor Isabel. Here, take this and write. Unburden your heart; if you don't you are going to die of anguish."

"I can't, Carmen. Something has broken inside. I may never write again."

"Then write a letter to Paula. It will help her know what happened while she was asleep."

And this is how I entertain myself in the empty moments of this nightmare.

WILL YOU KNOW I AM YOUR MOTHER WHEN YOU WAKE, PAULA? OUR family and friends never falter; so many visitors come during the evening that we resemble a tribe of Indians. Some come from very far, spend a few days, and return to their normal lives, among them your father, who has a half-finished construction project in Chile, and must go back. During these weeks of shared sorrow in the corridor of lost steps, I have been remembering the good times of our early years together; unimportant grudges have been receding, and I have learned to prize Michael as an old and loyal friend. I feel a quiet consideration for him. It is difficult for me to imagine that once we made love, or that by the end of our relationship I had come to detest him. Two women friends and my brother Juan came from the United States, Tío Ramón from Chile, and Ernesto's father directly from the Amazon jungle. Nicolás cannot make the trip because his student visa would not allow him to reenter the United States, and also because he should not leave Celia and their son alone. It's better that way, I would rather your brother not see you as you are. And Willie comes, too, crossing the world every two or three weeks to spend a Sunday with me, and make love as if it were the last time. I wait at the airport in order not to lose even a minute with him. I watch as he deplanes, pulling the little cart with his suitcases, a head taller than anyone else, his blue eyes anxiously looking for me in the crowd, his smile radiant when he spots me from below. We run to meet each other and his embrace lifts me off my feet. I smell his leather jacket, feel the roughness of his twenty-hour beard, his lips pressed hard against mine, and then we are in the taxi; I huddle against him as his long fingers renew their knowledge of me and he whispers, "My God, how I've missed you! You've lost weight, you're nothing but bones." But suddenly he remembers why we've been apart, and in a different voice he asks about you, Paula. We have been together for more than four years, and I still feel the indefinable alchemy of our first meeting, a powerful attraction that time has colored with other sentiments but is still the essence of our union. I don't really know what it consists of, or how to define it, because it is more than sexual attraction, though at first I thought that's what it was. Willie says that we are two fighters fired by the same kind of energy, that together we have the strength of a racing train; we can achieve any goal together, he says, and united we are invincible. We both trust the other to guard our back, to be loyal, not to lie, to offer support in moments of weakness, to steady the helm when the other goes off course. I think there is also a spiritual component; if I believed in reincarnation, I would think that it was our karma to meet and love each other in every life, but I won't speak of that yet, Paula, I will just confuse you. In our urgent coming together, desire and sorrow blend into one. I cling to Willie, seeking pleasure and consolation——two things this man who has suffered knows how to give——but your image, Paula, submerged in your mortal sleep, comes between us, and our kisses turn to ice.

"Paula cannot make love with her husband for a long time, maybe never again. Ernesto isn't even thirty yet, and his wife could be an invalid for the rest of her days. How can there be such injustice? Why did it happen to her and not me—I've already lived and loved so well."

"Don't think about that, there are many ways to love," Willie tells me.

It's true, love has unexpected resources. In the brief minutes you can be together, Ernesto hugs and kisses you, in spite of the array of tubes. "Wake up, Paula, I'm waiting for you; I miss you, I need to hear your voice; I am so filled with love for you I am going to burst. Please come back," he begs you. I picture him at night when he goes back to his empty house and lies next to the hollow left by your shoulders and hips. He must imagine you beside him, with your fresh smile, recall how your skin felt as he caressed you, the harmony of your silences, the lovers' secrets whispered in the night. He remembers the times you danced till you were drunk with the music, so attuned to each other's steps that you seemed a single being. He sees you moving like a reed, your long hair wrapping you both in the rhythm of the music, your slim arms around his neck, your lips on his ear. Oh, your grace, Paula! Your sweetness, your unpredictable intensity, your fierce intellectual discipline, your generosity, your insane tenderness. He misses your jokes, your laughter, your ridiculous tears at the movies and your serious tears when you empathized with someone's suffering. He remembers the time in Amsterdam you hid from him in the cheese market and he was beside himself, yelling for you everywhere, to the astonishment of the Dutch merchants. He wakes, soaked with sweat. He sits on the side of the bed in the darkness and tries to pray, to concentrate on his breathing and the sensations of his body, seeking peace, as he has learned in aikido. Perhaps he goes out on the balcony to gaze at the stars in the Madrid sky, and repeats to himself that he cannot lose hope, he must be patient, everything will be all right, soon you will be with him again. He feels the blood beating at his temples, his veins throbbing, the fire in his chest, he is choking, and he pulls on his sweatpants and goes for a run through the empty streets, but nothing helps to calm the agitation of frustrated desire. Your love is newly born, the first page in a blank notebook. "Ernesto is an old soul, Mama," you told me once, "but he hasn't lost his innocence; he has the gift of play, of amazement, of loving and accepting me unconditionally, without making judgments—the way children love. Since we have been together, something has opened up inside me; I have changed. I see the world differently, and I like myself more because I see myself through Ernesto's eyes." And he, Paula, has confessed to me in the moments of his greatest terror that he cannot live without you, that he never imagined he would find the visceral rapture he feels when he takes you in his arms; he says you are his perfect complement, and that he loves you and wants you to a point beyond pain, that he regrets every hour you were apart. "How could I know our happiness would be so short-lived? I dream of her, Isabel," he has told me, trembling. "I dream constantly of being with her again, and making love till we are senseless. I can't explain these images that assail me and that only she and I know; her absence is like a hot coal in my heart. I cannot stop thinking of her for an instant, Paula is the only woman for me, the companion I dreamed of, and found." How strange life is, Paula! Only a short while ago I was a distant, rather formal mother-in-law for Ernesto. Now we are confidantes, the most intimate friends.

The hospital is a gigantic building intersected by corridors where it is never night and the temperature never changes; day is captive in the electric lights and summer in the heating. Routines are repeated with irritating precision. This is the realm of pain; you come here to suffer, and all of us understand that. The misery of illness makes everyone equal. There are no rich or poor; when you cross this threshold, privilege blows away like smoke, and we are all humbled. My friend Ildemaro came from Caracas on the first flight he could wangle during an interminable strike of airline pilots, and stayed with me for a week. For more than ten years, this cultivated and gentle man has been like another brother to me, an intellectual mentor and companion during times I felt cut off from my country. As he hugged me, I felt an absurd certainty: you would react to his presence, and when you heard his voice you would wake up. He took advantage of being a physician to question the specialists and read the charts, tests, and X rays; he checked you over from head to foot, with the care that distinguishes all his actions and with the special affection he feels for you. When he came out of your room, he took my hand and we went outside and walked through the streets around the hospital. It was very cold.

"How do you find Paula?"

"She's very ill. . . ."

"That's how porphyria is. They assure me she will recover completely."

"I love you too much to lie to you, Isabel."

"Tell me the truth, then. Do you think she might die?"

"I do," he replied after a long pause.

"Might she stay in the coma for a long time?"

"I hope not, but it is a possibility."

"And if she never wakes again, Ildemaro?"

We stood silently beneath the rain.

I will try not to be sentimental, I know how much you hate that, Paula, but you will have to forgive me if sometimes I break down. My nerves are shattered. Am I going crazy? I don't know what day it is, I've lost interest in news of the world, the hours drag by painfully in an eternal waiting. I'm allowed to see you for such a short time, and I fritter the day away waiting for those moments. Twice a day, the door to intensive care opens and the nurse on duty calls the name of a patient. When she says "Paula," I go in, shivering. I can't help it, I can never get used to the humming of the respirator, to the monitors and needles, to seeing you always asleep, your feet bandaged and your arms bruised purple. As I hurry toward your bed along the white corridor that stretches endlessly before me, I call on Memé, Granny, Tata, and all my beloved spirits; I beg them to let me find you better, without any fever, your heart regular, your breathing tranquil, and your blood pressure normal. I say hello to the nurses and to don Manuel, who is growing worse every day; he can barely speak now. I bend down to you, and sometimes I dislodge some cable and an alarm sounds. I examine you inch by inch, observe the numbers and lines on the screens, the entries in the open book on a table at the foot of your bed—futile tasks, because I understand none of it, but with these meaningless ceremonies you belong to me again, as you did when you were a baby and entirely dependent on me. I place my hands on your head and your breast and try to transmit health and energy. I visualize you inside a glass pyramid, isolated from harm in a magic space where you can get

well. I call you all the pet names I have ever given you and tell you a
thousand times, I love you, Paula, I love you, and repeat it over and
over until someone touches my shoulder and tells me the visit is
over, I must leave. I give you one last kiss and walk, now slowly, to
the door. My mother is waiting outside. I give her an optimistic
thumbs up, and we try to smile. Sometimes we don't succeed.

Silence, I crave silence. The noise of the hospital and the city
have seeped into my bones. I long for the quiet of nature, the peace
of my house in California. In the hospital the only place free of
noise is the chapel. I go there to look for refuge in which to think
and read and write. I accompany my mother to mass, where usually
we are the only ones present and the priest officiates for us alone.
Above the altar, upon a wall of black marble, bleeds a Christ
crowned with thorns; I cannot look at that poor tormented body. I
do not know the liturgy, but from hearing the ritual words so often I
begin to feel the strength of the myth: bread and wine, fruit of the
earth and labor of man, converted into the body and blood of
Christ. The chapel is behind the intensive care room, but to get
there we have to make a complete circle around the building. I have
calculated that your bed is precisely on the other side of the chapel
wall and that I can send thoughts straight to you. Mother insists that
you won't die, Paula. She is negotiating the matter directly with
heaven; she tells God that you have lived to serve others, that you
have much good yet to do in this world, and that your death would
be a senseless loss. Faith is a gift; God looks into your eyes and
speaks your name. That is how He chose you, but He pointed his
finger at me only to fill me with doubt. My uncertainty began when
I was seven, the day of my First Communion, as I walked down the
nave of the church, dressed in white and wearing a veil, a rosary in
one hand and a ribbon-tied candle in the other. Fifty little girls in
two rows marching to the chords of the organ and the novices'
choir. We had rehearsed so many times that I had memorized every
gesture, but the point of the sacrament had escaped me. I knew that
if I chewed the consecrated Host I would burn in eternal hellfire,
but I did not remember it was Jesus I was receiving. As I neared the
altar, my candle broke in two. It just broke, without provocation,
the upper half hanging by the wick like the neck of a dead swan, and

I felt that someone from on high had pointed to me, amid all my companions, to be punished, perhaps for some sin I might have forgotten to confess the day before. In fact, I had elaborated a long list of major sins to impress the priest. I did not want to bore him with bagatelles, and I had also reasoned that if I did penance for mortal sins, even though I hadn't committed them, the venial sins would be pardoned in the lot. I confessed everything imaginable, even things I didn't know the meaning of: homicide, fornication, lies, adultery, sins against my parents, impure thoughts, heresy, envy. . . . The priest listened in stunned silence, then, aggrieved, rose to his feet and signaled to a nun. They muttered a few minutes and she seized me by the arm and led me to the sacristy, where with a deep sigh she washed out my mouth with soap and made me pray three Ave Marias. In the evening, the hospital chapel is dimly lighted by votive candles. Yesterday I surprised Ernesto and his father there—heads in hands, broad shoulders sagging—and did not dare go to them. They look very much alike. Both are large, dark, and sturdy, with Moorish features and a way of moving that is a rare mixture of virility and gentleness. Ernesto's father's deeply tanned skin, his short gray hair and wrinkles like knife scars speak of his adventures in the jungle and forty years of living with nature. He seems indestructible, and that is why I was so moved to see him on his knees. He has become his son's shadow; he never leaves him by himself, in the same way my mother is always at my side. He accompanies Ernesto to his aikido classes, and they walk for hours in the country, until both are exhausted. "You need to burn off that energy or you'll explode," he tells Ernesto. He takes me to the park on nice days, sits me down facing the sun, and tells me to close my eyes and feel the warmth on my skin, to listen to the sound of the birds and the water and the distant traffic and see if that will help calm my nerves. When he heard about his daughter-in-law's collapse, he immediately flew from the depths of the Amazon to be with his son. He does not like cities or populous areas, the hospital gives him claustrophobia, people bother him, he paces the corridor of lost steps with the sad impatience of a caged beast. You have more courage than the most macho of men, Isabel, he says, with great seriousness, and I know that is the most flattering thing a man accustomed to killing snakes with a machete can think of me.

Physicians come from other hospitals to observe you; they have never seen such a complex case of porphyria. You have become an example, and I am afraid you will earn a certain fame in medical textbooks. The illness struck like a thunderbolt, sparing nothing. Your husband is the only one who is at peace; the rest of us are terrified, but even he talks about your death and other, even worse, possibilities.

"Nothing has any meaning without Paula, nothing is worth the effort. Since she closed her eyes, the light has gone from the world," he says. "God *can't* take her from me, else why did He bring us together? We have so much life ahead of us. This is a cruel test, but we will come out of it. I will never leave her, I will never love anyone else; I will protect her and care for her always. Whatever happens, even if illness or death separates us physically, we are destined to meet again and be together through eternity. I can wait."

"I'm sure she will recover, Ernesto, but it will be a long convalescence. Be prepared for that. You will take her home, I'm sure. Can't you just imagine that day?"

"I think of it every minute. I will carry her up the three flights of stairs. I will fill the apartment with flowers. . . ."

Nothing frightens him; he thinks of you as his spiritual companion, safe from the vicissitudes of life or death; he is not alarmed by your motionless body or your absent mind; he tells us he is in contact with your soul, that you can hear him, that you have feelings and emotions, that you are not a vegetable as the machines you are connected to attest. Skeptical, the physicians shrug their shoulders, but the nurses are swayed by this obstinate love and sometimes they allow him to visit you out of hours because they know that when he takes your hand the readings on the screens change. Perhaps the intensity of feelings can be measured by the same apparatus that monitors heartbeats.

One day more of waiting, one day less of hope. One day more of silence, one day less of life. Death wanders freely through the hallways, and my task is to distract it, so it cannot find your door.

"How long and puzzling life is, Mama!"

"At least you can write about it to try to understand," she replied.

Lebanon in the fifties was a flourishing country, the bridge between Europe and the extremely wealthy Arab emirates, a natural cross-roads for several cultures, a tower of Babel where dozens of tongues were spoken. All the commerce and banking in the region passed through Beirut; by land came swaying caravans of merchandise, by air, the newest fads from Europe, and by sea, so many ships they had to wait their turn to anchor in the port. Veiled, black-robed women carrying bundles and packages and pulling their children by the hand scurried through the streets, eyes always lowered, while idle men congregated in the cafés. Burros, camels, crowded buses, motorcycles, and cars stopped as one at the traffic lights as shepherds dressed in the same fashion as their biblical ancestors crossed the avenues herding flocks of sheep toward the slaughterhouse. Several times a day the high keening of the muezzin called the faithful to prayer from the minarets of the mosques, chiming with bells from Christian churches. The smart shops of that capital offered the best of the world's goods, but we were more often drawn to the souks, the labyrinths of narrow alleyways lined with countless shops where it was possible to buy anything from fresh eggs to relics of the pharaohs. I can still smell those markets! All the aromas of the planet wafted through those twisting streets, a mélange of exotic vapors, food fried in sheep lard, baklava, garbage and excrement floating in open drains, animal sweat, leather dyes, cloying perfumes of incense and patchouli, coffee freshly boiled with cardamom seeds, spices of the Orient—cinnamon, cumin, pepper, saffron. . . . From the outside, the bazaars seemed insignificant, but each of them stretched inward through a series of roomlike areas with glittering lamps, trays, and amphoras inscribed with intricate calligraphic designs, rugs covering the floor, draped from the walls, and lying in rolls in the corners, furniture of carved wood with ivory, bronze, and mother-of-pearl inlay swamped beneath piles of tablecloths and embroidered *babouches*. Merchants came out to meet their customers and nearly dragged them inside those Ali Baba caves glutted with treasures. They would offer basins filled with rosewater for washing your hands and then serve a black, sugary coffee—the best in the world. Bargaining was an essential component of the transaction; my mother understood that from the first day. Upon hearing the opening price, she would reply with a horrified exclamation, throw up her hands, and start toward the door with a determined step. The seller would seize her arm and haul her back, swearing that this was the first sale of the day, that she was his sister, that she would bring him luck, and that he was therefore prepared to listen to her proposition, even though the object in question was unique and the price more than fair. Impassive, my mother would offer half, while the rest of us rushed for the door, red with embarrassment. The store owner would pound his forehead with his fist, calling on Allah as witness. "Do you want to ruin me, my sister? I have children, I am an honest man. . . ." After three cups of coffee and nearly an hour of haggling, the object would change ownership. The merchant would be smiling with satisfaction and my mother would rejoin us in the street, certain she had acquired a bargain. At times, a couple of shops farther along she would find the same piece for much less than she had paid; that ruined the day but not the temptation to buy again. This was the process she followed during a trip to Damascus when she negotiated the cloth for my wedding dress. I was fourteen and had no relation of any kind with any male except my brothers, my stepfather, and the son of an affluent Lebanese merchant who visited from time to time under the vigilant eye of his parents and mine. He was so rich that he had a chauffeured motor scooter. On the wave of the vogue for Italian Vespas, he pestered his parents until they bought him one; his father did not, however, want to run the risk of losing his firstborn in a crash of some vehicle for suicides, so he hired a chauffeur to drive the boy regally mounted behind. In any case, I was considering the idea of becoming a nun, in order to conceal that I could not snare a husband, and that is what I tried to convey to my mother in the market in Damascus, but she insisted. "Don't be foolish," she said, "this is the chance of a lifetime." We left the bazaar with meters and meters of white, silk-embroidered organza, besides several tablecloths for my hope chest and a carved wooden screen that has survived three decades, countless moves, and exile.

Even the incentive of bargains was not enough to make my mother feel comfortable in Lebanon; she had the sensation she was a prisoner in her own skin. Women were not supposed to go out alone because in close quarters a disrespectful hand might dart out and offend them, and if they tried to defend themselves they were met with a chorus of hostile jeers. Only ten minutes from our house was an endless white sand beach and a warm ocean inviting us to cool off during the dog days of August. We had to go as a family, always in a tightly knit group to protect ourselves against other swimmers' busy hands; it was impossible to lie on the sand, that was an open invitation to trouble, and as soon as our heads broke the surface of the water we ran to the refuge of a cabana rented for that purpose. The climate, the cultural differences, the strain of speaking French and mumbling a little Arabic, the juggling act of making ends meet, the absence of friends and family, all overwhelmed my mother.

Lebanon had found a way to live in peace and prosperity despite the religious wars that had torn the region for centuries. During the Suez Canal crisis, however, growing Arab nationalism profoundly divided politicians, and rivalries became irreconcilable. Violent uprisings culminated in July 1958, with the landing of the United States Sixth Fleet. Installed on the third floor of a building located at the confluence of Christian, Muslim, and Druze barrios, we were in a privileged position for observing the skirmishes. Tío Ramón made us place mattresses in front of the windows to stop any stray bullets, and forbade us to watch from the balcony; meanwhile, my mother managed somehow to keep the bathtub filled with water and to obtain fresh supplies of food. During the worst weeks of the crisis, a sunset curfew was imposed; only military personnel were authorized to move through the streets, but in fact that was the hour of a tacit truce when housewives bargained in the black market and men did business. From our forbidden terrace we witnessed ferocious gun battles between opposing groups that lasted most of the day, but at dusk everything stopped as if by enchantment and, under cover of night, furtive figures slipped out to trade with the enemy and mysterious packages passed from hand to hand. We saw prisoners, naked from the waist up and handcuffed to wood poles, flogged in the courtyard of the guard station, and just within our field of vision was the fly-covered corpse of a man with a slit throat who was left in the street for two days to frighten the Druze. We also witnessed the revenge, when two veiled women left a burro with a load of olives and cheeses standing in the street. As expected, the soldiers confiscated the burro and shortly after we heard the explosion that pulverized neighborhood windows and left the barracks courtyard a pool of blood and torn flesh. Even with that violence, I have the impression that the Arabs never truly took the U.S. landing seriously. When their ships sailed into the bay with cannons at the ready, Tío Ramón obtained a pass and took us to see them. There was a huge crowd of curiosity seekers on the docks, waiting to do business with the invaders and get permission to board the aircraft carriers. LSTs like monsters of steel opened their jaws and vomited out landing craft filled with armed-to-the-teeth marines who were greeted with a salvo of applause from the beach, and the minute these bold warriors touched dry land they were surrounded by a raucous mob trying to sell them everything from parasols to hashish and Japanese condoms shaped like brightly colored fish. I can imagine that it wasn't easy for officers to maintain the morale of their troops or to prevent them from fraternizing with the enemy. The next day at the indoor skating rink I had my first contact with the most powerful armed force in the world. I had skated all afternoon among hundreds of uniformed youths with shaved hair and tattooed arms, who were drinking beer and talking in a guttural lingo very different from what Miss St. John had attempted to teach at the British school. I could barely communicate with them, but even if we had spoken the same language, we wouldn't have had much to say to each other. That memorable day, though, I received my first kiss on the lips; it was like biting a frog that smelled of chewing gum, beer, and tobacco. I have no idea which one kissed me, because I couldn't tell him from the others—they all looked alike—but I do remember that from that very moment I decided to explore the matter of kisses. Unfortunately, I had to wait quite a while to pursue my research, because as soon as Tío Ramón discovered that the city was crawling with marines hungry for girls, he redoubled his vigilance and I was confined to the house like a flower of the harem.

It was my good fortune that my school was the only one not to close its doors when the crisis began. My brothers, on the other hand, could not go to class and had to spend months of lethal boredom penned up in the apartment. Miss St. John considered that the war was a vulgar occurrence that had nothing to do with the English, and therefore preferred to ignore it. The street in front of the school was cut into two zones separated by piled-up sandbags protecting the two sets of combatants. In newspaper photos, the men and their weaponry were terrifying, but seen behind their barricades from high atop the building they looked like vacationers on a picnic. Among their sandbags, they listened to the radio, cooked, received visits from wives and children, and whiled away the hours napping or playing cards and checkers. Sometimes they arranged a brief ceasefire in order to go for water or cigarettes. The unflappable Miss St. John jammed the green hat reserved for grand occasions firmly on her head and marched out to confer in her atrocious Arabic with the inconsiderate individuals who were obstructing passage in the street and to ask them to allow the school bus through, while the frightened teachers and few girls still in attendance observed from the roof. I have no idea what arguments she wielded, but the fact is that the vehicle continued to operate, and on time, right to the very end when I was the last student riding. I was careful not to tell at home that other parents had withdrawn their children from the school, and I certainly never mentioned the daily negotiations between the driver and the men on the barricades who allowed us to pass. I attended classes until the establishment was deserted and Miss St. John courteously asked me not to return for a few days—"until this disagreeable incident has been resolved and people return to their senses." By then the situation had become very violent, and a spokesman for the Lebanese government had advised diplomats to send their families home because their safety could not be guaranteed. After several secret councils, Tío Ramón put my brothers and me on one of the last commercial flights to leave Beirut. The airport was swarming with men scrambling to get out; some tried to take their wives and daughters as a kind of cargo—as they did not consider them whole human beings, they could not understand the need to buy tickets for them. Then, to the alarm of the French stewardess, as soon as we were airborne a woman wrapped head to foot in some dark cloth set up a small kerosene burner in the aisle of the plane to prepare food.

My mother stayed behind in Beirut with Tío Ramón for a few months, until they were transferred to Turkey. In the meantime, the U.S. marines had returned to their carriers and sailed away without a trace, taking with them the corroboration of my first kiss. These were the circumstances of our return to the opposite side of the world and my grandfather's house in Chile. I was fifteen, and it was the second time I had ever been away from my mother—the first was the time she joined Tío Ramón for their romantic tête-à-tête in the north of Chile, the one that consecrated their love affair. I did not know at the time that we were going to be separated for most of the remainder of our lives. I began writing her my first letter on the plane; I have continued to write almost every day over the years, and she has done the same. We stack this correspondence in a basket and at the end of the year tie it with a red ribbon and put it away on a closet shelf; we have collected mountains of pages this way. We have never reread them, but we know that the record of our lives is safeguarded against poor memory.

Up till then, my education had been chaotic. I had learned a little English and French, memorized a good part of the Bible, and absorbed Tío Ramón's lessons in self-defense, but I lacked the most elemental knowledge for functioning in this world. When I reached Chile, my grandfather decided that with some help I could finish my schooling in a year, and prepared to teach me history and geography himself. Later he found out that I also did not know how to add, and so he enrolled me in private math classes. The teacher was a tiny old lady with jet-dyed hair and several missing teeth, who lived far away from us in a modest house cluttered with gifts from fifty years' worth of students and permeated with the abiding odor of cooked cauliflower. I had to take two buses to get there, but it was worth the effort because that woman succeeded in cramming enough numbers in my head to allow me to pass the examination, after which they were permanently erased. Boarding a bus in Santiago could be fraught with danger, it required a resolute temperament and an acrobat's agility. The bus never ran on time; you had to wait for hours, and then when it came it was jammed, with so many passengers hanging from the doors that it tilted to one side. My stoic formation and double joints helped me survive in this daily warfare. I shared the class with five other students, one of whom always sat beside me, lent me his notes, and walked me to the bus stop. While we stood patiently waiting in sunshine or rain, he listened, never commenting, to my exaggerated tales about trips to places I could not locate on the map but had read about in my grandfather's *Encyclopædia Britannica*. When the bus came, this friend helped me clamber over the cluster of humanity bulging from the entrance, pushing me from the rear with both hands. One day he invited me to go to the movies. I told Tata I had to stay and study with the teacher, and set off with my beau to a neighborhood theater where they happened to be showing a horror film. When the antediluvian lizard head of the Monster from the Green Lagoon appeared only a few centimeters from the inattentive maiden swimming there, I let out a yell, and he used the excuse to grab my hand. The boy, I mean, not the monster. The rest of the movie went by in a haze. I cared nothing about the fangs of the giant reptile or the fate of the stupid blonde paddling in the lagoon; my attention was focused on the warmth and moistness of that hand caressing mine—an experience nearly as sensual as biting the ear of my beloved in La Paz and a thousand times greater than the North American soldier's kiss stolen in the Beirut ice-skating rink. I was walking on air when I reached my grandfather's house, convinced that I had met the love of my life and that our intertwined hands signified a formal engagement. I had heard my friend Eliza in Lebanon say that a girl could get pregnant by splashing in the same swimming pool with a boy, and I suspected, logically, that an entire hour of intermingling the sweat of our hands could have the same effect. I lay awake all night, imagining my future married life and anxiously awaiting the next math class. The next day, however, my friend did not show up; all during class I sat in torment, watching the door, but he did not come that day, or the rest of the week, or ever again; he simply vanished. Eventually, I recovered from that humiliating abandonment, and for years completely forgot about him. Twelve years later, however, I felt as if I had seen him again; that was the day I was called to the morgue to identify my father's corpse. I have asked myself many times why that boy disappeared so suddenly, and, from turning it over and over in my mind, finally reached a dark conclusion, but I think I would rather let the matter drop, because only in soap operas do lovers discover one day that they are brother and sister.

One of the reasons I forgot my short-lived love was that I met another boy—and here, Paula, is where your father enters the story. Michael had English roots. He was from one of those families that have lived and died in Chile for generations but still call England "home." They read weeks-old English newspapers and maintain a nineteenth-century lifestyle and social code appropriate to the arrogant subjects of a great Empire, a way of life not found today even in the heart of London. Your paternal grandfather worked for a North American copper company in the north of Chile, in a town so insignificant it rarely appears on maps. The gringo colony consisted of twenty or so houses surrounded by a barbed-wire fence, a sphere in which—with air-conditioning, bottled water, and a profusion of catalogs from which they could order from the United States anything from condensed milk to terrace furniture—the inhabitants attempted to reproduce as faithfully as possible the mode of life of their home cities. Each family dutifully cultivated a garden, despite harsh sun and drought. The men played golf among the sandpits and the ladies competed in contests for best roses and pies. On the other side of the fence were the Chilean laborers who lived in rows of shacks with common bathrooms, their only diversions a soccer field drawn with a stick on the hard dirt of the desert and a bar on the outskirts of the camp where they got drunk every weekend. It was said that there was also a brothel, although I never found it when I went looking, perhaps because I was expecting at least a red light and the house must have been in a hovel indistinguishable from all the others. Michael was born and lived the first years of his life in that place, in Edenic innocence, protected from all harm, until he was sent to a British boarding school in the center of Chile. I think he did not have the slightest idea he was in Chile until he was old enough for long pants. His mother, whom everyone remembers as Granny, had large blue eyes and a heart that never knew an unkind thought. Her life was lived between kitchen and garden; she smelled of fresh baked bread, butter, and plum preserves. Years later, when she had given up her dreams, she smelled of alcohol, but not many knew that because she kept a prudent distance and covered her mouth with her handkerchief when she talked, and also because you, Paula, who were eight or nine, hid the empty bottles so no one would discover her secret. Michael's father was a good-looking man, dark as an Andalusian but very proud of the German blood that coursed through his veins. He cultivated virtues he considered Teutonic, and grew to be the model of an honest, responsible, and punctual man, although he was also inflexible, authoritarian, and cold. He never touched his wife in public, but he always called her "my young lady," and his eyes shone when he looked at her. He spent thirty years in that North American camp earning sound U.S. dollars, retired when he was fifty-eight, and moved to Santiago, where he built a house on the edge of a private golf club. Michael grew up in a boys' school dedicated to study and manly sports, separated from his mother, the only person who could have taught him to express his feelings. During his vacations, he and his father shared polite conversation and chess games. I met Michael soon after his twentieth birthday, when he was in his first semester of civil engineering. He rode a motorcycle and lived in an apartment with a housekeeper who treated him like a young lord; he never washed a pair of socks or boiled an egg. He was tall, young, handsome, and very slender, with large caramel-colored eyes, and he blushed when he was nervous. A mutual girlfriend introduced us. He came to see me one day under the pretext of helping me with my chemistry, and soon asked formal permission from my grandfather to take me to the opera. We went to see *Madama Butterfly*, and I—totally ignorant about anything musical—thought it was a comedy, and laughed aloud when I saw a rain of pink plastic flowers falling from the ceiling over a fat woman singing at the top of her lungs as she knifed herself in the belly before her son, a pitiful child, blindfolded and waving a flag in each hand. That was the beginning of a long, sweet courtship destined to last many years before being consummated, since Michael had six years of university course work

ahead of him and I was still in school. It was several months before
we held hands at the Wednesday concert, and almost a year before
our first kiss.

"I like this young man, he is going to improve the race," my
grandfather chuckled when finally I admitted that we were in love.

DEATH LAID ITS HANDS ON YOU MONDAY, PAULA. IT CAME AND POINTED
to you, but found itself face to face with your mother and grandmother and, for now, has backed off. It is not defeated, and is still
circling round, grumbling, in its swirl of dark rags and clicking
bones. You were on the other side for a few minutes, and in fact no
one can explain how or why you are back. We had never seen you so
ill; you were burning with fever, and we could hear a terrifying
rumble from your chest and see the whites of your eyes through a
slit between your eyelids. Suddenly your blood pressure plummeted
almost to zero and the alarms on the monitors sounded and the
room filled with people, all working so hard around you that they
forgot about us, and that was how we came to be present when your
soul escaped your body, as they injected drugs and administered
more oxygen and tried to make your exhausted heart start beating
again. They rolled in a machine to give you electric shocks, terrible
charges that lifted you from the bed. We heard orders, tense voices,
running; other doctors came with new machines and new syringes.
Who knows how many minutes went by, it seemed hours, an eternity. We couldn't see you; the bodies of the people attending you
blocked our view, but your anguish and the triumphant breath of
Death were all too clear. There came a moment when all the feverish agitation suddenly congealed, as in a photograph, and then I
heard my mother's muted murmur begging you to fight, Paula,
commanding your heart to keep on beating in the name of Ernesto
and the precious years you had still to live and for the good you had
yet to give. Time stopped on the clocks; the green curves and peaks
on the screens flattened into straight lines and a buzz of distress
replaced the shriek of the alarms. Someone said, "There's nothing

more we can do. . . ," and another voice added, "She's gone." People moved away; some left the room, and we could see you, lying motionless and pale, like the marble statue of a girl. Then I felt my mother's hand in mine, pulling me forward, and we walked to your bedside and without a single tear we offered you the entire reservoir of our energy, all the health and strength of our most recondite genes from Basque sailors and indomitable American Indians, and in silence we invoked all the gods known and yet to be known, and the beneficent spirits of our ancestors, and the most formidable forces of life, to race to your rescue. Our unvoiced wail was so intense that from fifty kilometers away Ernesto heard it, clear as a bell; he knew that you were on the edge of the abyss and started immediately for the hospital. In the meantime, the air around your bed was frozen and time was suspended, but when the clock again began to mark the seconds, Death had lost. The vanquished doctors had left and the nurses were preparing to disconnect the tubes and cover you with a sheet, when one of the magic screens gave a sigh and the capricious green line began to undulate, signaling your return to life. Paula! my mother and I cried in a single voice, and the nurses repeated, Paula! and the room was filled with your name.

Ernesto arrived an hour later; he had burned up the highway and streaked through the city like lightning. He had never, ever, doubted you would get well, but on this occasion, defeated, kneeling in the chapel, he prayed only that your martyrdom would end and you would find rest. Even so, when he put his arms around you the next morning, the vehemence of his love and his desire to keep you with him were more powerful than resignation. He feels your body in his own; he knows your state before the clinical diagnoses; he perceives signs invisible to other eyes and is the only one who seems to communicate with you. "Live, live for me, for us, Paula, we're a team," he begged. "You'll see, everything will be fine. Don't leave me, I will be your support, your refuge, your friend; I will heal you with my love. Remember that blessed third of January when we met and everything changed forever. You can't leave me now, we've just begun, we have a half a century ahead of us." I don't know what other pleas and secrets and promises he whispered in your ear on that dark Monday, or how he instilled the wish to live in every kiss he gave you, but I am sure that you are breathing today because of his tender tenacity. Your life is a mysterious victory of love. You have lived through the worst of the crisis; they are giving you the exact dose of antibiotics, they have controlled your blood pressure, and little by little your fever is going down. You are back where you were. I don't know what this kind of resurrection means. You have been in a coma for more than two months, and I am not fooling myself, Paula, I know how ill you are, but you can recover completely. The porphyria specialist swears that you have no brain damage, that the illness has attacked only the peripheral nerves. What blessed words. I repeat them over and over as a kind of magic spell to save you. Today they turned you on your side in the bed and in spite of the tortured look of your poor body your face was the same, you looked as beautiful as a sleeping bride, with blue shadows under your long eyelashes. The nurses have sprayed you with cologne and combed your hair into a long braid that hangs from the bed like a sailor's rope. There are no signs of your conscious intelligence, but you are alive, and your spirit is still within you. Breathe, Paula, you must breathe. . . .

My mother keeps bargaining with God. Now she is offering him her life for yours. She says that, after all, seventy years is a long time, a lot of weariness and pain. I would gladly take your place, too, Paula, but there are no illusionist's tricks that can let me do that; each of us, grandmother, mother, daughter, must live out her own destiny. At least we are not alone, we are three. Your grandmother is tired; she tries to hide it but her years weigh on her, and during these months of suffering in Madrid the winter has crept into her bones. There is no way to keep her warm; she sleeps beneath a mountain of blankets and in the daytime she goes around in sweaters and wool scarves but can't stop shivering. I had a long talk with Tío Ramón by telephone, asking him to convince her that it's time for her to go back to Chile. I hadn't been able to write for several days. Only now that you are beginning to emerge from death's grip do I return to these pages.

My discreet relationship with Michael flowered circumspectly, in the old-fashioned way, in the living room of Tata's house, between cups of tea in the winter and ice cream in the summer. The discovery of love and the happiness of feeling accepted transformed me; my shyness was replaced by a more explosive temperament, and the long periods of angry silence of my childhood and adolescence ended. Once a week, we went on Michael's motorcycle to hear a concert. Every other Saturday I was allowed to go to the movies, as long as I got home early, and some Sundays my grandfather invited Michael to the family dinner, a true tourney of endurance. The feast alone was a bone-crushing ordeal: seafood appetizers, spicy meat pies, *cazuela,* a hearty chicken and corn and vegetable dish, or *pastel de choclo,* a corn soufflé over a meat base, a blancmange-filled cake— *torta de manjar blanco*—wine and fruit, and a gigantic jug of *pisco* sours, the most lethal of Chilean drinks. In that agape, everyone at the table tried to outdo the other in how much they could down, and sometimes, just for the thrill of the challenge, they asked for fried bacon and eggs before the dessert. The survivors won the privilege of demonstrating their particular madness. By the time coffee was served, everyone was arguing at the top of his lungs and, before the dessert liqueurs were passed, they had sworn this would be the last Sunday for the family bash. The following week, nevertheless, and with only minor variations, they suffered through the same mortification, because not to attend would have been an inconceivable snub my grandfather would never have forgiven. I dreaded those gatherings almost as much as the luncheons at the home of Salvador Allende, where his daughters, my cousins, always stared at me with veiled scorn because I didn't know what the devil they were talking about. They lived in a small, cozy house crowded with works of art, good books, and photographs that if they still exist are valuable historical documents. Politics was the one topic in this intelligent and well-informed family. The conversation was on a high plane, primarily about world events but occasionally coming down to earth to include the latest inside gossip about Chile, but in either case, I was in outer space. The only books I was reading then were science fiction, and while with socialist fervor the Allendes plotted the transformation of the nation, I was wandering from asteroid to asteroid in the company of extraterrestrials as elusive as my grandmother's ectoplasms.

The first time that Michael's parents came to Santiago, he took me to meet them. My future in-laws were waiting to take five o'clock tea: starched tablecloth, hand-painted English porcelain, homemade cakes. They welcomed me graciously; I felt they had accepted me even before they met me, grateful for the love I showered on their son. Michael's father washed his hands a dozen times during my brief visit and when he sat down at the table, pushed back the chair with his elbows in order not to soil his hands before eating. Toward the end of my visit, he asked me whether I was related to Salvador Allende, and when I said yes, his expression changed but his natural courtesy prevented him from stating his views on that subject at our first meeting, there would be other times. Michael's mother charmed me from the moment I met her; she was an innocent, incapable of a mean thought; her goodness glowed in her liquid aquamarine eyes. She accepted me without reservation, as if we had known each other for years, and that afternoon we sealed a secret pact of mutual aid that would be very comforting through the painful trials to come. Both of Michael's parents must have wished for their son a calm, discreet girl from the English colony; it could not have been difficult for them to perceive my character flaws from the beginning. It is, therefore, all the more admirable that they opened their arms to me so promptly. I began working when I was seventeen, and haven't stopped since. I had no idea what I was going to do after graduation, I should have considered attending the university, but I was confused. I wanted to be on my own, and besides, I intended to be married soon and have children, because that was what girls did in those days. My mother, who knew me better than anyone, suggested I study theater, but I thought that idea was preposterous. Since I wasn't trained for anything else, I started looking for a job as a secretary the day after graduation. I had heard that they paid well at the United Nations, and decided to capitalize on my knowledge of English and French. In the telephone directory, prominently displayed, I found the strange designation FAO and, without the least idea of what it stood for, showed up at their doorstep, where I was greeted by a young man with a colorless face.

"Who is the owner here?" I asked pointblank.

"I don't know. . . . I don't think there there is an *owner*," he murmured, slightly perturbed.

"Then who is in charge?"

"Don Hernán Santa Cruz." This time there was no hesitation.

"I want to speak with him."

"He is presently in Europe."

"So who is in charge of hiring when he isn't here?"

The young man referred me to an Italian count. I requested an interview, and as soon as I stood before the impressive desk of the handsome Roman I rattled off that Señor Santa Cruz had sent me to see him about a job. This aristocratic official had no reason to suspect that I wouldn't know his superior if I saw him, and so he agreed to try me for a month, even after I had presented the lowest score on the typing exam of anyone in the history of the Food and Agricultural Organization of the UN. They had sat me down before a heavy old Underwood and told me to write a letter with three carbons—failing to mention that it should be a business letter. Instead, I composed a letter of love and despair—as well as one punctuated with errors, the keys seemed to have a life of their own. I also put the carbons in upside down and the copies came out on the back of the page. Hoping to place me where I could do the least damage, they temporarily assigned me as secretary to a forestry expert from Argentina whose mission was to conduct a world census of trees. I was aware that my luck could not hold out forever, and gave myself four weeks to learn to type, answer the telephone, and serve coffee like a professional, secretly praying that the redoutable Santa Cruz would suffer a fatal accident and never return. My prayers, however, went unheard and precisely at the end of one month the director of the FAO showed up, an enormous man with the look of an Arab sheikh and a voice like thunder before whom employees in general and my Italian nobleman in particular bowed with respect, not to say terror. Before he could learn of my existence through other channels, I went to his office and told him I had taken his sainted name in vain and was prepared to do the necessary penance. My confession was met with paroxysms of laughter.

"Allende? Which Allendes do you come from?" he roared finally, after wiping away his tears.

"I think my father is named Tomás."

"What do you mean, *think*? How can you not know your father's name?"

"We can never be sure who our father is," I replied haughtily, "only our mother."

"Tomás Allende, eh? I know who he is! A very intelligent fellow . . . ," and Santa Cruz sat staring into space, like someone dying to tell something he can't.

Chile is the size of a pocket handkerchief, and it turns out that this gentleman with the air of a sultan was one of Salvador Allende's closest childhood friends; he also knew my mother and stepfather well. For those reasons, he did not kick me out, as the Roman count had expected, but had me transferred to the Department of Information, where someone with my imaginative gifts, he explained, might be better utilized than in copying forestry statistics. They put up with me in the FAO for several years. I made friends there, learned the rudiments of journalism, and had my first opportunity to work in television. In my free time I translated popular novellas from English to Spanish. These romantic—actually, overtly erotic—tales were all cut from the same cloth: beautiful, innocent, and penniless young girl meets mature, strong, powerful, virile, and lonely man disappointed in love in some exotic setting, for example, a Polynesian island where she works as a governess and he owns a plantation. She is always a virgin, even if a widow, with satiny breasts, velvety lips, and eyes like watered silk, while he has silver temples, golden skin, and steely muscles. The landowner is superior to the virgin in every way, although she is good, and pretty. After sixty pages of burning passion, jealousy, and incomprehensible intrigues, they marry, of course, and the material maiden is deflowered by the metallic male in a racy final scene. It took enormous character to remain faithful to the original versions, and even with all Miss St. John's stalwart efforts behind me, mine was not sufficiently strong. Almost without realizing, I began to slip in small modifications to better the heroine's image; it began with subtle changes in the dialogue, so she would not seem completely moronic, then gradually I followed the flow of my inspiration and changed the denouement so that sometimes the virgin might end her days selling arms in the Congo and the plantation owner set off for Calcutta to care for lepers. I did not last very long in this work; in fact, after only a few months, I was let go. By then my parents had returned from Turkey and I was living with them in a large Spanish-style adobe and red tile–roof house in the foothills, where it was difficult to catch a bus and nearly impossible to obtain a telephone. The house had a tower, five acres of orchards, a melancholy cow that never gave milk, a pig we had to chase out of the bedrooms with a broom, hens, rabbits, and a huge squash vine growing in the roof tiles. The large, ripened fruit tended to roll off, endangering anyone who had the bad luck to be standing below. Catching the bus to get back and forth from the office became an obsession. To get there on time, I got up every morning at dawn, but by the time I got off work the buses were always full, so I started going to my grandfather's house to visit and wait to squeeze onto a later one with fewer passengers. That was the origin of my custom of seeing him every day, and it became so important to both of us that I missed only when he lived at the beach, when my children were born, a few days at the beginning of the military coup, and once when I wanted to dye my hair yellow and the beautician bungled the job and it turned green. I didn't dare show up at Tata's until I had bought a wig in my own color. In the winter our house was a clammy dungeon with holes in the roof, but in the spring and summer it was enchanting, with big clay pots spilling over with petunias, buzzing bees, songbirds, the perfume of flowers and fruit, the pig bumbling between visitors' legs, and pure mountain air. Sunday dinners were moved from Tata's house to my parents', where the tribe continued to meet faithfully every week, following some urge to destroy itself. Michael, who had come from a placid home ruled by extreme courtesy, and who had been conditioned to hide his emotions at all times—except on the sports fields where one was free to behave like Genghis Khan—was a mute witness to the outlandish passions of my family.

That year my Uncle Pablo died in a bizarre accident. He was flying over the Atacama Desert in a small plane when it blew up in midair. Witnesses saw the explosion and an incandescent ball of fire flashing through the skies, but there were no traces of the crash and after meticulously combing the area the rescue teams returned empty-handed. There was nothing to bury; the funeral was held with a symbolic coffin. The disappearance of this man I had loved dearly was so abrupt and total that I cultivated the fantasy that he had not really been reduced to ash and scattered across the dunes; perhaps he had miraculously been saved but had suffered irreparable trauma, and today, somewhere, a serene septuagenarian with no memory is wandering about unmindful of the young wife and four children he left behind him years ago. He was married to one of those rare individuals with a diaphanous soul destined to become even more pure with hard times and suffering. My grandfather received the bitter news without a flicker of emotion; his lips tightened, he stood up, leaned on his cane, and hobbled outside so that no one could see the expression in his eyes. He never again spoke of his favorite son, just as he never mentioned Memé. For that valiant old man, the deeper the wound, the more private the grief.

I was three years into a relatively chaste love affair when I first heard the women in the office talking about a marvelous pill that would prevent pregnancy; it had revolutionized the cultures of Europe and the United States, they said, and was now available in a few local pharmacies. I investigated further and learned that one had to have a prescription to buy it. I did not dare go to the ineffable Dr. Benjamin Viel, who by then was the guru of family planning in Chile, but neither could I work up the nerve to talk with my mother. She had enough problems with two adolescent sons, and didn't need to add magic pills for an unmarried daughter to her list. My brother Pancho had vanished, following the footsteps of a weird prophet who attracted disciples by proclaiming himself the new Messiah. The fact was that he owned a grocery store, and his whole program was nothing more than an elaborate theological scam, but the truth came out only much later, after my brother, and many other young people, had wasted years pursuing a myth. My mother did everything she could to retrieve her son from that mysterious sect, and more than once went to bring him home when he had scraped bottom and wanted help from the family. She would find him in some dark hovel, hungry, ill, and let down, but as soon as he gained enough strength he would disappear again and it would be months before we knew where he was. Once we heard that he was in Brazil, learning voodoo, and another time in Cuba training to be a revolutionary; none of those rumors was reliable and the truth was we never really knew anything. During this same period, my brother Juan was spending a couple of miserable years enrolled in the National Air Academy. Almost immediately, he realized that he lacked the aptitude or the endurance for that career, that he detested the absurd principles and military ceremonies, that he really didn't give a damn about the nation itself, and that if he didn't get out of there soon he would either perish at the hands of the older cadets or commit suicide. He did run away one day but his desperation did not carry him very far; he arrived home with his uniform in tatters, terrified, and stammering that he had deserted and when they caught him he would be subjected to a military trial, and even if he escaped the firing squad for having betrayed his country he would spend the rest of his young life in the black hole. My mother acted expeditiously; she hid him in the pantry, made a vow to the Virgen del Carmen, patron saint of Chile's armed forces, in exchange for her aid, made a quick trip to the beauty salon, and then put on her best outfit and requested an audience with the director of the Academy. Once there, she did not give him an opportunity to open his mouth; she threw herself on him, got a firm grip on his jacket, and shouted that he alone was responsible for her son's situation, and why was he not aware of the humiliation and torture the cadets suffered, and that if anything happened to Juan she would drag the good name of the Academy through the mud, and then continued to bombard him with arguments and shake him until the general, conquered by those panther eyes and the vehemence of unleashed maternal instinct, allowed my brother to return to the ranks.

To get back to the pill, however. Michael and I never talked about the gross details of sexual relationships, our puritanical upbringing was too inhibiting. Our petting in some dark corner of the garden left us both exhausted, and me furious. I was slow to understand the mechanics of sex because I had never seen a man naked—except for marble statues with little baby peters—and I was not very clear about what an erection consisted of: when I felt something hard in Michael's pants pocket, I thought it was motor-cycle keys. My secret reading of *A Thousand and One Nights* in Lebanon had left my head filled with metaphors and poetic flour-ishes; what I needed was a simple manual. Later, when the differ-ences between men and women became clear, and I was apprised of the function of something as uncomplicated as a penis, I felt cheated. I didn't see then, and I don't see now, the moral difference between those steamy sessions of unsatisfactory pawing and renting a hotel room and doing whatever your fancy dictates, but neither Michael nor I dared suggest that. I suspect that many girls my age did not hold back, but in those days of collective hypocrisy the sub-ject was taboo. Everyone improvised as best he or she could, suffer-ing inflamed hormones, a guilty conscience, and the fear that after "going all the way" the boy not only might evaporate from the scene but, even worse, divulge his conquest. The role of the male was to attack and ours to defend, pretending that sex did not interest us because it was not good form to appear to be collaborating in your own seduction. How different things were for you, Paula! You were sixteen when you came one morning to ask me to take you to a gynecologist because you wanted to learn about contraceptives. Mute with shock—because I realized your childhood had ended and you were beginning to escape my influence—I went with you. "Let's not say anything about this, please; I don't think anyone would understand that you helped me," you advised me. When I was your age, I was in a muddle, cowed by apocalyptic warnings: Be careful about accepting a drink, it might be drugged with those powders they give cows to bring on their breeding season, or, Don't get into his car because he will take you somewhere in the country and you know what can happen then. From the beginning, I rebelled against the double standard that allowed my brothers to go out all night and come back at dawn smelling of liquor, with never a word of rebuke. Tío Ramón used to call them in and close the door for a private "man's talk," things my mother and I had no right to comment on. It was considered normal that they would slip into the maid's room at night, and they made jokes about it that made it doubly offensive to me, because added to macho arrogance was abuse of class. Imagine the scandal if I had invited the gardener to my bed! In spite of my rebelliousness, though, I was paralyzed by fear of the consequences of sex; nothing cools one off like the threat of an unwanted pregnancy. I had never seen a condom—except those fish rubbers the Lebanese merchants sold to marines in Beirut, the ones I thought were birthday party balloons. The first condom I ever held in my hand you showed me in Caracas, Paula, when you were going around everywhere with that kit for your human sexuality course. "That takes the cake! To think that at your age you don't know how to use one of these," you said that day. I was over forty, had published my first novel, and was writing the second. Now I am astonished by such ignorance from someone who had read as much as I. There was also that incident in my childhood that should have given me some inkling about sex, or at least provoked my curiosity about learning more, but I had locked that in the deepest corner of my memory.

That Christmas Day in 1950, I was walking along the beach promenade, a raised terrace edged with geraniums. I was eight years old. I was sunburned—my nose was raw and my face covered with freckles. I was wearing a white piqué sundress and a necklace of small shells strung on a thread. I had painted my fingernails with red water colors, so my fingers looked as if they had been smashed, and I was pushing a little wicker buggy holding my newest doll, a sinister rubber baby with one orifice in her mouth and another between her legs, so water that went in above came out below. The beach was deserted; the night before, the village inhabitants had eaten late, attended midnight mass, and celebrated till early morning, and no one was up yet. At the end of the walkway was an area of huge rocks where the ocean erupted in roaring bursts of foam and seaweed; the light was so intense that colors paled in the incandescent whiteness of the morning. I seldom wandered so far from home, but that day I was looking for the perfect place to give my doll her bottle and change her diaper. Down below, among the rocks, a man came out of the sea; he was wearing goggles and had a tube in his mouth that he jerked out roughly, gasping for air. Around the waist of his threadbare black bathing trunks was a rope where he had tied the curved knives that were his tools for gathering shellfish. In his hand he had three sea urchins, which he dropped into a sack and then lay down on a large rock to rest. His smooth, hairless skin was like tanned leather, and his hair was black and curly. He reached for a bottle and gulped long drafts of water, gathering strength to dive again. With the back of his hand he brushed the hair from his face and rubbed his eyes; that was when he looked up and saw me. At first he may not have realized how old I was; all he saw was a figure rocking a small bundle in her arms, and in the reverberating late-morning light he could have mistaken me for a mother with her baby. He whistled to me and lifted his hand to wave. I stood up, slightly distrustful, but curious. By then his eyes had adjusted to the sun and he recognized me; he waved again and shouted to me not to be afraid, and not to run away because he had something for me. He took two sea urchins and half a lemon from his sack and began to climb the rocks. "You've really changed," he said. "Last year you were just a little runny-nosed kid like your brothers." I took a couple of steps backward, but then I recognized him, too, and returned his smile, putting my hand over my mouth because my new teeth weren't all in yet. I knew him because he often came by our house at the end of the day to see if we wanted anything: Tata always insisted on personally selecting the fish and shellfish. "Come over here and sit by me and let me see your dolly. If she's rubber, I bet she can swim; let's go put her in the water. I'll look after her for you, nothing will happen. Look, I have a whole bag of sea urchins down there, and this afternoon I'll bring some by your grandfather's. You want to taste one?" He took one in his large calloused hand, indifferent to the sharp spines, placed the hooked tip of his knife under the crown, just where the shell is circled with a little string of pearls, and pried it open. An orangish cavity appeared, filled with viscera awash in a dark liquid. He held the cup of the shell to my nose and told me that that was the smell of the bottom of the ocean and of women when they are hot. I sniffed, timidly at first, and then with pleasure at the strong aroma of iodine and salt. He explained that a sea urchin should be eaten only when it's alive, that otherwise it's deadly poisonous. He squeezed a few drops of lemon juice into the shell and showed me how the little tongues moved, stung by the acid. He broke one off, tipped his head back, and slipped it into his mouth as a thread of dark juice trickled from his thick lips. I agreed to try it—I had seen my grandfather and my uncles empty several shells into a bowl and wolf down the contents with chopped onion and cilantro—and he pulled off another piece and put it in my mouth. It was soft and flabby but with a rough texture, a little like a wet towel. The taste and smell are not like anything else; at first the iodine was repellent, but then the succulent, palpitating meat filled my mouth with distinct and inseparable savors. One by one, he stripped the pieces of rosy flesh from the shell, giving me some and eating some himself. Then he opened the second sea urchin and we ate it, too, laughing and spattering juice and sucking each other's fingers. Last, he poked at the bloody bottom of the shells and picked out the tiny sea spider that is nourished by the urchin and is pure, concentrated flavor. He put one on the tip of his tongue and waited, mouth open, for it to sidle farther back, then crushed it against his palate and showed me the squashed creature before he swallowed it. I closed my eyes. I felt his thick fingers tracing the outlines of my lips, tickling the tip of my nose, and my chin. I opened my mouth and something was on my tongue, but when I felt the tiny moving feet I gagged and spit out the spidery crustacean. "Silly," he said, as he picked it out of the rocks and ate it. "You know, I don't believe your dolly can pee pee, let me see, show me the little hole. Is it a boy or a girl doll? You don't know? Well, does it have have a pecker or not?" And then he looked at me with an indecipherable expression and suddenly took my hand and placed it on his sex. I felt something under the damp cloth of his bathing suit, something that moved, something like a piece of garden hose. I tried to pull my hand away but he held it there firmly while in an altered voice he whispered not to be afraid, that he wouldn't do anything bad, just things that felt good. The sun grew warmer, the light whiter, and the roar of the ocean louder, while beneath my hand that tool of eternal damnation began to come to life. At that instant, Margara's voice called from the distance, breaking the spell. Startled, the man stood and pushed me away from him; he picked up his knife, and leaped down the rocks toward the sea. Halfway down, he paused, turned, and pointed to his groin. "You want to see what I have here? You want to know how your Papa and Mama do it? They do it like dogs but, oh, much nicer; wait for me here this afternoon during siesta time, about four, and we'll go to the woods where no one can see us." An instant later he disappeared among the waves. I put my doll in the buggy and walked back toward the house. I was trembling.

We always had Sunday dinner under the grape arbor in the patio with the hydrangeas, gathered around a large table with white tablecloths. That day the entire family was celebrating Christmas; there were hanging garlands, as well as pine branches and plates of nuts and crystallized fruit on the table. We had turkey left from the night before, tomato and lettuce salad, sweet corn, and an enormous conger eel baked in butter and onion. It was served whole: tail, huge head with entreating eyes, and unmarred skin like a glove of tarnished silver, which my mother peeled off with a single flourish, exposing the gleaming flesh. Jugs of white wine with peaches passed from hand to hand, along with trays of rolls warm from the oven. As always, everyone was talking at high volume. My grandfather, in shirtsleeves and a straw hat, was the only one aloof from the uproar; he was absorbed in the task of removing the seeds from a chili pepper before filling it with salt; soon he had a salty, spicy liquid that would bore through cement, which he drank with obvious relish. We children all sat at one end of the table, five boisterous cousins fighting over the most golden rolls. I still had the taste of the sea urchins in my mouth, and all I could think of was that I had to be there at four. The maids had prepared the airy, cool bedrooms, and after lunch the family retired to rest. We cousins had cots in the same room, and it wasn't easy to slip out during siesta because of Margara's all-seeing eye. After a while, though, she went to her own room—even she got tired. I waited for my cousins to surrender to sleep and for the house to grow calm, then got out of bed, very quietly, put on my sundress and sandals, hid my doll under my bed, and went out. The wood floor creaked with every step, but in that house something was always making noise: the floorboards, the pipes, the motor of the refrigerator or the water pump, mice, and Tata's parrot that spent the summer insulting us from its perch.

The young fisherman was waiting at the end of the beach walk, dressed in dark pants, a white shirt, and rubber-soled shoes. As I came near, he starting walking, and I followed without a word, like a somnambulist. We crossed the street, turned into an alley, and began to climb the hill toward the woods. There were no houses there, only pines, eucalyptus, and scrub; the air was cool, almost cold, because the sun rarely penetrated the heavy shade of that green canopy. The sharp combined fragrance of the trees and the clumps of wild thyme and mint blended with exhalations from the sea. Green lizards scuttled across dried leaves and pine needles; those whispery steps, the occasional cry of a bird, and the sound of branches in the breeze were the only perceptible sounds. He took my hand and led me deep into the woods; I couldn't see anything but vegetation, I had lost my sense of direction, I couldn't hear the ocean anymore . . . I was absolutely lost. No one could see us now. I was so afraid I couldn't speak, but I didn't dare let go of that calloused hand and run, I knew he was much stronger and faster than I. Don't talk to strangers, Don't let anyone touch you, If someone touches you between your legs it's not just a mortal sin, you'll be pregnant besides, your belly will swell up like a balloon, bigger and bigger until it explodes and you die. All Margara's horrible admonitions were pounding in my ears. I knew I was doing something forbidden, but I couldn't go back or escape. I was trapped in my own curiosity, a fascination more powerful than terror. At other times in my life, I have experienced that same mortal vertigo when facing danger, and have yielded to it because I couldn't resist the urgent call to adventure. At times that temptation has been detrimental—for example, during the military dictatorship—and at others it has been enriching—as when I met Willie, and the thrill of the gamble impelled me to follow him. Finally, the fisherman stopped. "We're fine here," he said, arranging branches to form a bed. "Lie down here and put your head on my arm so the needles don't get in your hair. That's it, now, lie still, we're going to play Mama and Papa." He was panting slightly, gasping; his chapped hand stroked my face and neck, then slipped beneath the bib of my dress, feeling for my childish nipples, which contracted when he touched them, caressing me as no one had ever done before—we never even touched in my family. I felt a warm lassitude dissolving my bones and my will; a visceral panic swept over me and I began to cry. "What's the matter, silly girl? I'm not going to do anything bad," and he moved his hand from the neck of my sundress to my legs, his fingertips first feeling between them, then pushing them apart, firmly but not violently, moving up, up to my very center. "Don't cry now, let me do it, I'm just going to touch you softly with my finger, there's nothing bad about that, open your legs, relax, don't be afraid, I'm not going to put it in you, I'm not a fool, if I do anything to you your grandfather will kill me, I'm not going to fuck you, we're just going to play a little." He unbuttoned my dress and took it off, but left on my panties. I suppose he felt Tata's hot breath on his neck. His voice was hoarse now, and he was mumbling an uninterrupted stream of obscenities and endearments and kissing my face. His shirt was wet through, and he was gulping for breath, pressing hard against me. I thought I might die, my face was slick from his kisses, I was crushed by the weight of his body, choked by the reek of sweat and sea, by his wine and garlic breath, as his strong, warm fingers crawled like lobsters between my legs, pressing, rubbing, his hand covering that secret part that no one was supposed to touch. I couldn't protest, I felt something deep inside me opening, shattering, exploding in a thousand fragments, while he rubbed against me, faster and faster, in an incomprehensible paroxysm of moans and rasping breath, then slumped beside me with a choked cry that came not from him but the very depths of the earth. I had no idea what had happened, or how long I lay beside that man, naked except for my pristine blue cotton underpants. I looked for my sundress and with shaking hands clumsily put it on. He buttoned the buttons down the back and stroked my hair. "Don't cry, nothing happened to you," he said, and suddenly he jumped up, took my hand, and pulled me back down the hill toward the light. "I'll wait for you tomorrow at the same time. You *be* here, and don't say a single world to anyone about this. If your grandfather finds out, he'll kill me," he warned as we set off in different directions. But the next day, he wasn't there.

This experience must have left a scar somewhere, because in all my books, seductive or seduced children play a role, almost always without related evil, except in the case of the small black girl in *The Infinite Plan* whom two men capture and intend to harm. Resurrecting the memory of that young fisherman, I feel no repugnance or terror; quite the opposite, actually, I feel a vague tenderness for the little girl I was and for the man who did not rape me. For years I kept the secret so deeply hidden in a separate compartment of my mind that when I fell in love with Michael I did not relate it to the awakening of sexuality.

THE NEUROLOGIST AND I AGREED TO CUT OFF YOUR RESPIRATOR FOR one minute, Paula, but we did not tell the rest of the family because they still haven't recovered from that fateful Monday when you were so close to leaving us. My mother cannot talk about it without bursting into tears; she wakes at night with a vision of Death leaning over your bed. I believe that, like Ernesto, she no longer prays for you to get well but for you not to suffer any longer; as yet, however, I have not lost my will to fight to keep you. The doctor is a kind man, whose eyeglasses perched at the end of his nose and wrinkled white lab coat give him a look of vulnerability, as if he had just waked from a nap. He is the only physician here who seems sensitive to the anguish of those of us who spend our days in the corridor of lost steps. The porphyria specialist is more interested in the laboratory test tubes where he analyzes your blood every day; he seldom comes by to see you. This morning we disconnected you for the first time. The neurologist checked your vital signs and read the charts from last night, while I called on my grandmother and yours—the wonderful Granny who has been gone fourteen years now—for their help. "Ready?" he asked, peering at me over his glasses, and I responded with a nod, because I couldn't speak. He flicked a switch and the liquid hiss of the oxygen in the transparent tube in your neck suddenly was stilled. I stopped breathing, too; watch in hand, I counted the seconds, begging, commanding, you to breathe, Paula . . . please. Every instant was the lash of a whip . . . thirty, forty seconds . . . nothing; five seconds more and it seemed your chest moved a fraction, but so slightly it could have been an illusion . . . fifty seconds . . . and we couldn't wait any longer, the blood had drained from your face and I myself was nearly asphyxiated. The machine began to function, and a touch of color returned to your skin. I put away the watch, trembling; I was burning hot and soaked with perspiration. The doctor handed me a square of gauze.

"Here, you have blood on your lips," he said.

"This afternoon we'll try again, and then tomorrow, and so on, a little more each day, until she can breathe on her own," I resolved, when I could speak.

"Paula may not be *able* to breathe on her own. . . ."

"She will, Doctor. I'm going to take her out of this place and it will be easier if she helps me."

"I suppose mothers know better than anyone else. We will gradually lower the pressure of the respirator to force her to use those muscles. Don't worry, we'll see she gets plenty of oxygen"; he smiled, giving me an affectionate pat on the shoulder.

My eyes were blurred with tears as I left the room and rejoined my mother. I guess Memé and Granny stayed behind with you.

Willie came the moment he heard about the most recent crisis, and this time he was able to be away from his office five days—five whole days together! I needed that time badly. Long separations are dangerous; love can go astray in the shifting sands. "I'm afraid I'll lose you," Willie says. "I feel you're farther and farther away and I don't know how to hold you. Remember you are my woman, my soul." I haven't forgotten, but it is true that I am more distant; sorrow is a solitary road. When Willie comes he brings a blast of fresh air. Adversity has strengthened his character; nothing defeats him, he has inexhaustible stamina in the face of day-to-day struggles. He is restless and impulsive, but he is suffused with Buddhistic calm when he must endure misfortune, which makes him a stalwart companion in difficult times. He occupies every inch of our small apartment in the hotel, altering the delicate routines my mother and I have established, moving us about like two ballerinas in a rigorous choreography. Someone with the size and characteristics of Willie does not pass unnoticed; when he comes there is disorder and noise and the tiny kitchen is always busy—the entire building smells of

his delicious cooking. We rent an additional room, and we take
turns with my mother going to the hospital; that way I can have a
few hours alone with my husband. In the mornings, Willie prepares
breakfast and then calls my mother, who appears in her nightgown
and wool socks and layers of shawls, with the mark of the pillow still
creasing her cheek: a sweet little old grandmother from a bedtime
story. She crawls into our bed and we begin the day with toast and
cups of the aromatic coffee Willie has brought from San Francisco.
This man never knew what a family was until he was fifty, but he
quickly became accustomed to sharing his space with mine, and
doesn't find it strange to start the day three to a bed. Last night we
went out to eat dinner at a restaurant on the Plaza Mayor, where we
let ourselves be tempted by rowdy waiters dressed up as comic
opera smugglers, who danced attendance on us in a stone room
with vaulted ceilings; everyone was smoking and there was no venti-
lation of any kind—light years behind the North American obsession with health. We poisoned ourself with lethal dishes: fried octopus and mushrooms with garlic, pork roasted in a clay cooker—
golden, crackling, streaming fat, perfumed with herbs—and a jug of
sangria, that heavenly wine and fruit that goes down like water but
when you try to stand up hits you like a poleax at the back of the
neck. I hadn't eaten like that in weeks; my mother and I often slip
through the day with nothing but hot chocolate. I spent a terrible
night with hair-raising visions of scalded and scraped hogs screaming over their fate and live octopuses climbing my legs, and this
morning I swore to become a vegetarian like my brother Juan. No
more sins of gluttony for me. These days with Willie have renewed
me, I can feel life in my body again, forgotten for weeks; I touch my
breasts, my ribs—which I can count under my skin—my waist, my
thighs, getting to know myself again. This is me, I'm a woman, I
have a name, I'm called Isabel, I'm not turning to smoke, I have not
disappeared. I examine myself in my grandmother's silver mirror:
this person with the disconsolate eyes is me. I have lived nearly half
a century, my daughter is dying, and still I want to make love. I
think of Willie's reassuring presence and feel goosebumps rise on
my skin, and can only smile at the amazing power of desire that
makes me shiver despite my sorrow, even push death from my

mind. For a moment, I close my eyes and see clearly the first time we slept together, our first kiss, our first embrace, the astonishing discovery of a love that materialized when we least sought it, of the tenderness that took us by storm when we thought we were safely indulging in a one-night affair, of the profound intimacy we felt from the beginning, as if our entire lives had been a preparation for that meeting, of the ease, calm, and confidence with which we made love, like an old couple that has shared a thousand and one nights. And always, afterward, passions sated and love renewed, our bodies meld in sleep, not caring where one begins or the other ends, or whose hand or foot is whose, in such perfect complicity that we meet in our dreams and the next morning do not know who dreamed whom, and when one moves the other adjusts to the new angles and curves, and when one sighs the other sighs, and when one wakes the other wakes, too. "Come," Willie calls me, and I go to the man waiting in the bed and, shivering from the cold of the hospital and the outdoors and from the unshed tears that turn to frost in my veins, I take off my nightgown and huddle against the bulk of his body, wrapped in his arms until I am warm. Little by little we become aware of the other's quickening breathing, and our caresses become slower and more intense as we surrender to pleasure. He kisses me, and once again I am surprised, as I have been for four years, at how soft and cool his lips are; I cling to his strong shoulders and neck, run my hands down his back, kiss the hollow of his ears, the horrible skull tattooed on his right arm, the line of hair down his belly, and breathe in his odor of health, that odor that always excites me, lost in love, and grateful, while a river of inevitable tears pours from my cheeks onto his chest. I cry out of sorrow for you, Paula, but I suppose I am also crying for the happiness of this late love that has come to change my life.

What was my life like before Willie? It was a good life, filled with intense emotions. I have lived the extremes; few things have been easy or smooth for me, and that may be why my first marriage lasted so long: it was a tranquil oasis, a noncombat zone in between battles. Everything else was hard work, storming the bastion with sword in hand, without an instant's truce—or boredom: great successes and smashing failures; passions and loves, but also loneliness, work, losses, desertions. Until the day of the military coup I thought that my youth would last forever; the world seemed a splendid place and people essentially good. I believed evil to be a kind of mistake, an aberration of nature. All that ended abruptly on September 11, 1973, when I awakened to the brutality of existence . . . . But I haven't reached that point in these pages yet, Paula, why confuse you by leaping around in these memories? I did not end up an old maid, as I had predicted in those dramatic statements lying in Tío Ramón's strongbox; just the opposite, I married too soon. Despite Michael's promise to his father, we decided to marry before he finished engineering school because the alternative was for me to go to Switzerland with my parents, where they had been named Chile's representatives at the United Nations. If I cut corners, my salary would be enough to rent a room and keep body and soul together, but at that time in Santiago, the idea of a girl's being independent at nineteen, with a sweetheart and no oversight, was out of the question. I debated for several weeks, until my mother seized the initiative and spoke to Michael, placing him between the sword and marriage—just as I would do twenty-six years later to my second husband. Michael and I sat down with paper and pencil and came to the conclusion that two people could subsist, barely, on my salary, and that it would be worth taking a chance. My mother immediately launched into enthusiastic activity. Her first move was to sell the large Persian rug in the dining room and then announce that a wedding was an excuse to spend money like a drunken sailor, and that mine would be splendid. Quietly, she began to store provisions in a secret room in the house, so at least we wouldn't starve. She filled trunks with linens, towels, and kitchen utensils, and found out how we could get a loan to build a house. When she set the papers before us and we saw the amount of the debt, Michael felt faint. He had no job and his father, annoyed by our precipitous decision, was not inclined to help him, but my mother's powers of persuasion are staggering, and in the end we signed. The civil service took place one fine spring day in my parents' beautiful colonial house, an intimate gathering attended only by our two families—that is, nearly a hundred people. Tío

Ramón had suggested that we invite my father, who, he thought, should not be absent at such an important moment of my life, but I refused, and it was Salvador Allende who represented my father's family and signed the civil register as my witness to the wedding. Just before the judge appeared, my grandfather took me by the arm, led me aside, and repeated the words he had spoken to my mother twenty years before. "There is still time to change your mind. Don't marry him, please, think it over. Give me the sign and I will get rid of this mob. How about it?" He thought marriage was a miserable bargain for women; on the other hand, he recommended it without reservation to all his male descendants. One week later, we were married in a religious ceremony, even though Michael was Anglican and I was no longer a practicing Catholic, because the weight of the Church in the world I was born into is like a millstone around one's neck. Proudly, I walked down the aisle on the arm of Tío Ramón, who made no further suggestion regarding my father until years later, when we were called on to bury him. In photographs taken that day, the new bride and groom look like children playing dress-up: he in a tailored swallowtail coat and I swathed in clouds of the cloth acquired in the Damascus souk. In keeping with English tradition, my mother-in-law gave me a blue garter to wear for luck. The bust of my dress was stuffed with plastic foam, but with the first hug of congratulations, even before leaving the altar, my breasts were crushed concave. I lost the garter in the nave of the church, a frivolous testimony to the ceremony, and we had a flat tire on the car taking us to the reception and Michael had to take off his tail-coat and help the chauffeur change the tire, but I do not believe those were omens of bad luck.

My parents left for Geneva and Michael and I began our married life in their enormous house, with six months' rent paid by Tío Ramón and the pantry my mother had stocked like a generous magpie: there were enough sacks of grains, jars of preserves, and even bottles of wine to survive Armageddon. Even so, the house was not practical; we did not have enough furniture to fill so many rooms, or money to heat them or to hire indoor and outdoor domestic help. Perhaps worse, no one was on the property after we left every morning for the office and the university. The cow, the pig, the chickens—the very fruit from the trees—were all stolen; then thieves broke the windows and stripped us of wedding gifts and clothes. Finally, they discovered the entrance to the secret cave of the pantry and carried all that away, leaving a thank-you note on the door as the ultimate irony. That was the beginning of a string of robberies that added unwanted spice to our lives. I calculate that more than twenty times thieves have broken into houses we lived in, taking nearly everything, including three automobiles. By a miracle, my grandmother's silver mirror was never touched. Between robbery, exile, divorce, and travel, I have lost so many things that now I begin to say goodbye to something almost as soon as I buy it, because I know what a short time it will be in my hands. When the soap vanished from the bathroom and the bread from the kitchen, we decided to leave that empty, rundown, old house where spiders wove their lace on the ceilings and mice sashayed impudently through the rooms. In the meantime, my grandfather had retired, bidding farewell forever to his sheep, and had moved to the ramshackle old beach house to spend his remaining years far from the din of the capital and await death with his memories, in peace, never suspecting that he had twenty more years in this world. He turned his house in Santiago over to us, and we settled in amid solemn furniture, nineteenth-century paintings, the marble statue of the pensive girl, and the oval table in the dining room that was the stage for Memé's enchanted sugar bowl. We were not there for long, only long enough to build—on audacity and credit—the small house where my children were raised.

One month after I was married, I developed pains in my lower abdomen and from pure ignorance and confusion attributed them to a venereal disease. I did not know exactly what that was, but I supposed that it was related to sex and therefore to matrimony. I did not dare discuss it with Michael because I had learned in my family, and he in his English school, that such intimate topics are in bad taste. I certainly did not dare approach my mother-in-law for counsel, and my own mother was too far away, so I bit my lip and bore it until I was scarcely able to walk. One day as I painfully pushed a shopping cart through the market, I met the mother of my brother's former girlfriend, a suave and discreet woman I knew only slightly. Pancho was still tagging after the new Messiah and his amorous ties with the girl had been temporarily interrupted; years later, he would marry her, divorce her, then marry and divorce her a second time. This extremely pleasant woman asked me politely how I was, and before the words were out of her mouth I had clamped my arms around her neck and babbled that I was dying of syphilis. With admirable composure, she took me to a nearby tea shop, where she ordered coffee and tea cake and then questioned me on the details of my volcanic confession. The minute we finished the last forkful of cake, she escorted me to the office of a physician friend who diagnosed a urinary tract infection, possibly provoked by the icy drafts in my parents' colonial house. He prescribed bed rest and antibiotics and sent me on my way with a waggish smile. "The next time you have an attack of syphilis, don't wait so long, come see me right away," he said. This rescue was the beginning of an unbroken friendship. We adopted each other because I needed another mother and she had room to spare in her heart; she came to call herself Mama Hilda, and has beautifully fulfilled that role.

My children have determined my life; since the day they were born I have never thought of myself as an individual but as part of an inseparable trio. Once, years ago, I tried to give priority to a lover, but it did not work out and in the end I left him to return to my family. This is something we must talk about later, Paula, but for now I will pass over it. It never occurred to me that motherhood was optional, I thought it was as inevitable as the seasons. I knew I was pregnant before it was confirmed medically; you appeared to me in a dream, just as your brother, Nicolás, did later. I have not lost that gift, and now can predict my daughter-in-law's children. I dreamed my grandson Alejandro before his parents suspected he had been conceived, and I know that the child who will be born in the spring will be a girl, and will be named Andrea, though Nicolás and Celia still don't believe me and are planning to have a sonogram and are making lists of names. In the first dream I ever had of you, you were two years old and your name was Paula. You were a slender child, with dark hair, large black eyes, and a limpid gaze like that of martyrs in the stained-glass windows of some medieval churches. You were wearing a checked coat and hat, something like the classic costume of Sherlock Holmes. In the next months I gained so much weight that one morning when I stooped down to put on my shoes, the watermelon in my belly rolled up to my throat, toppling me head over heels and so definitively displacing my center of gravity that it was never restored: I still stumble my way through the world. Those months you were inside me were a time of perfect happiness; I have never since felt so closely accompanied. We learnèd to communicate in code. I knew how you would be at different periods in your life: I saw you at seven, fifteen, and twenty, I saw you with your long hair and happy laugh, in your blue jeans and your wedding dress, but I never dreamed you as you are now, breathing through a tube in your throat . . . inert . . . unconscious. More than nine months passed, and as you showed no intention of abandoning the tranquil grotto in which you floated, the doctor decided to take drastic measures and, on October 22, 1963, he opened my abdomen to bring you into the world. Mama Hilda was the only one at my side during that crisis, because Michael was in bed with a case of nerves, my mother was in Switzerland, and I did not want to notify my in-laws until everything was over. You were born with fine hair over all your body, giving you a slight resemblance to a little pink fairy armadillo, but I would not have traded you for the world, and besides, you soon shed that fuzz, leaving a delicate and beautiful baby girl with two glowing pearls in her ears that my mother insisted on giving you to continue a long-standing family tradition. I went back to work right away, but nothing was the same as before; half my time, my attention, and my energy were given to you, and I developed antennas to divine your needs even from a distance. I went to my office with dragging feet and looked for any excuse to escape; I got there late, left early, and pretended to be sick in order to stay home. Watching you grow and discover the world seemed a thousand times more interesting than the United Nations and their ambitious plans to improve the fate of the planet. I couldn't wait for Michael to get his engineering degree and support the family, so I could be with you. In the meantime, Michael's mother and father had moved to a large house a block away from where we were building ours, and were preparing to devote the rest of their lives to spoiling you. They had a naive view of life, because they had never stepped outside the small circle that protected them from ill winds; for them, the future looked rosy, just as it did to us. Nothing bad could happen if we did nothing bad. I wanted to be a model wife and mother, even if I didn't know exactly how. Michael planned to find a good job in his profession, live comfortably, travel a little, and much later inherit his parents' large house, where he would spend his old age surrounded by grandchildren and playing bridge and golf with his lifelong friends.

Tata could not put up with the boredom and solitude of the beach for very long. He had to give up his swims in the ocean because the glacial temperature of the Humboldt current fossilized his bones and his fishing expeditions because the oil refinery had wiped out both fresh and saltwater fish. He was increasingly lame and ailing, but remained faithful to his theory that illness is a natural punishment of humankind and pain is felt less if one ignores it. He kept himself going on the gin and aspirins that replaced his homeopathic pills when they ceased to have any effect. It was not too surprising they would, because when my brothers and I were children and could not resist the temptation of that ancient wood medicine cabinet filled with mysterious vials, we not only ate the homeopathic nostrums by the handful but also switched them around in the bottles. So my grandfather spent months of silence reviewing his memories and concluded that life is a crock and there is not much reason to be afraid of leaving it. "We forget," he often said, "that no matter what we do, we are on the road to death." Memé's ghost was lost in the gelid crannies of that house built for summer pleasure, not winter wind and rain. As the last straw, the parrot fell ill of a catarrh and neither the homeopathic pills nor the aspirins dissolved in gin its owner forced into its beak with a dropper did any good. One Monday morning Tata found it stone cold dead at the foot of the perch where it had sat so many years screaming insults. He had it packed in ice and sent to a taxidermist in Santiago, who shortly returned it, stuffed, with new feathers and an intelligent expression it had never worn in life. When my grandfather had made the last repairs on the house, and tired of fighting the ineluctable erosion on the hill and the plagues of ants, roaches, and mice, a year had gone by and solitude had embittered him. As a last desperate measure against boredom, he began to watch soap operas and without realizing it became ensnared in that vice; before long the fates of those cardboard characters became more important to him than those of his own family. He used to follow several at one time, and gradually the story lines blended together and he ended up lost in a labyrinth of vicarious passions. That was when he realized that the moment had come to return to civilization, before old age delivered its last blow and left him half loony. He returned to Santiago just as we were ready to move into our new house, a prefabricated cottage slapped together by a half dozen workmen and crowned by a straw thatch that gave it a touch of Africa. I renewed my old custom of visiting my grandfather in the afternoons after work. I had learned to drive and Michael and I shared a very primitive plastic vehicle with a single door in the front that took steering wheel and controls with it as it opened. I am not a good driver, and dodging through traffic in that mechanical egg was little short of suicidal. My daily visits with Tata provided me with enough material for all the books I have written, possibly for all I will ever write. He was a virtuoso storyteller, gifted with perfidious humor, able to recount the most hair-raising stories while bellowing with laughter. He held back none of the anecdotes accumulated through his many years of living: the principal historical events of the century, the excesses of our family, and the infinite knowledge acquired in his reading. The only forbidden subjects were religion and illness; he considered that God is not a topic for discussion and that anything relating to the body and its functions is private—to him, even looking in the mirror was a ridiculous vanity, and he shaved by memory. He was authoritarian by nature, but not inflexible. When I began to work as a journalist and had finally articulated a language for expressing my frustrations as a woman in that macho culture, my grandfather did not at first want to hear my arguments, which to his ears were pure poppycock, an attack upon the foundations of family and society, but when he became aware of the silence that had settled over our afternoon tea and rolls, he began to question me in an offhand way. One day I surprised him leafing through a book I thought I recognized, and with time he came to accept female liberation as a point of elemental justice; his tolerance, however, did not extend to social changes: politically, just as in religion, he was a conservative, and espoused individualism. One day, he asked me to promise to help him die, because death can be so obscenely clumsy and slow.

"How shall we do it?" I asked, amused, thinking he was joking.

"We will know when the time comes. For now all I want is your promise."

"But it's against the law, Tata."

"Don't worry about that, I shall assume all responsibility."

"Sure, you'll be in your coffin and I'll be marched off to the gallows. Besides, it must be a sin. Are you a Christian or not?"

"How dare you ask me something so personal!"

"It's a lot more personal to ask me to kill you, don't you think?"

"If you don't do it, you who are my eldest grandchild and the only one who can help me, who will? A man has a right to die with dignity!"

I realized he meant what he was saying, and finally I agreed, because he looked so healthy and strong, in spite of his eighty years, that I took it for granted I would never have to live up to my word. Two months later, he developed a cough, the dry cough of a sick dog. Furious, he buckled a saddle cinch around his waist and when he had a coughing fit gave himself a brutal tug to "subdue his lungs," as he explained it to me. He refused to go to bed, convinced that would be the beginning of the end—"From the bed to the tomb," he said—and was adamant that he would not see a doctor because Benjamin Viel was in the United States all caught up in contraceptive concerns and any doctor his own age was already dead or too sick to practice; added to that, the young doctors were a bunch of charlatans puffed up with modern theories. He put all his faith in the blind old man who "adjusted" his bones and his boxes of unpredictable homeopathic pills prescribed with more hope than knowledge. Soon my grandfather had a raging fever, and tried to cure it with ice cold showers and large glasses of gin; instead, two nights later, his head was split by a lightning bolt and a roaring earthquake filled his ears. When he could breathe again, he couldn't move: half his body had turned to granite. No one dared call an ambulance because with the half of his mouth still function- ing he growled that the first person who moved him out of his house would be disinherited—he was not, however, saved from doctors. Someone called an emergency service and, to the amaze- ment of all, who appeared but a woman wearing a silk dress and a triple strand of pearls about her neck. "I'm sorry," she apologized, "I was on my way to a party," and she began removing her kid gloves to examine the patient. My grandfather felt that in addition to being paralyzed he was hallucinating, and fought to stop this woman who with inexplicable familiarity was trying to unbutton his clothing and touch him where no one in her right mind would ven- ture. He defended himself with his last vestiges of strength, moan- ing desperately, but after a few minutes of tug-of-war, and with a smile of her painted lips, the doctor conquered. Her examination revealed that, besides the stroke, that hardheaded old goat was suf- fering from pneumonia and had also broken several ribs with his cinch-tugging act. "The prognosis is not good," she murmured to the family gathered at the foot of the bed, not counting on the patient's overhearing her. "We'll see about that!" Tata replied in a quavering voice, resolved to show this woman what a real man was made of. I was therewith relieved of fulfilling a promise lightly made. I spent the critical days of his illness at his bedside. Lying flat on his back between the white sheets, pale, motionless, with his chiseled bones and ascetic profile, he resembled the sculpted figure of a Celtic king on a marble sarcophagus. Attentive to his every movement, I silently prayed for him to keep fighting and forget his idea of dying. During those long vigils, I often wondered how I would do it in case he asked, and concluded that I would never be capable of hastening his death. In those weeks I came to realize how resistant the body is and how it clings to life, even when crushed by illness and age.

In a relatively brief time, my grandfather could speak fairly clearly, dress himself, and laboriously drag himself to the big arm- chair in the living room, where he sat rereading the encyclopedia propped before him on a music stand, squeezing a rubber ball to exercise the muscles of his hands, and slowly sipping tall glasses of water. Later I discovered that the drink wasn't water but gin, which was emphatically forbidden by the lady in pearls; as he seemed to be getting well, however, I became the one who brought it to him. He bought the gin at a corner liquor store whose proprietress often disturbed the sleep of that concupiscent old patriarch. She was a ripe widow with the energetic bosom of a soprano and heroic hindquarters, who waited on him like the favored client he was, and poured his gin into mineral water bottles to avoid problems with the rest of the family. One afternoon, my grandfather started talking about my grandmother's death, a subject he had never mentioned before. "She lives on," he said, "because I have never forgotten her, not for a single minute. She visits me, you know."

"You mean she appears to you, like a ghost?"

"She talks to me. I feel her breath on the back of my neck, her presence in my room. When I was sick, she held my hand."

"That was me, Tata."

"I'm not daft, I know that sometimes it was you. But other times, it was her."

"You won't ever die, either, Tata, because I will always remember you. I've never forgotten a single word you've told me."

"I can't trust you, though, because you change everything around. When I die there won't be anyone to rein you in, and sure as you're born, you'll go around telling lies about me," and he laughed, covering his mouth with his handkerchief because he still did not have total control of his facial muscles.

For the next few months he exercised doggedly, until he was mobile; he recovered completely and lived almost twenty years longer, time enough to know you, Paula. You are the only one who caught his eye among the throng of his grandchildren and great-grandchildren. He was not one to display his emotions, but his eyes shone when he looked at you, and he used to say, "This little girl has a special destiny." What would he do if he saw you as you are now? I think he would drive away the doctors and nurses with his cane and with his own hands tear out the tubes and probes to help you die. And if I didn't think you would get well, perhaps I would do that myself.

*   *   *

Don Manuel died today. They wheeled his body out the back door
and his family took him away to be buried in his village. Here in the
corridor of lost steps, his wife and son have shared the most painful
time of their lives with us, the anguish of every visit to intensive
care, the endless patient hours, days, weeks, of dying. In a way, we
have become a family. She brings cheeses and bread from the country to share with my mother and me; sometimes she falls asleep
from exhaustion with her head on my knees, stretched out on the
row of chairs in the waiting room, while I quietly stroke her forehead. She is a small, dark, compact woman, always in black but with
a face lined with festive wrinkles. The minute she enters the hospital, she takes off her shoes and puts on her bedroom slippers. In his
sixtieth year of life, don Manuel was strong as a horse, but after
three operations on his stomach he grew weary of humiliations and
stopped fighting. We watched him slowly decline. In the last days,
he turned his face to the wall, refusing the consolation of the chap-
lain, who often passes through this room. He died holding the hand
of his loved ones, and I, too, managed to say goodbye. Before he
escaped his body, I reminded him quietly, "Remember to speak for
Paula on the other side." His widow told me, "When your daughter
gets better, you must come visit us in the country; we have a pretty
piece of land, clean air, and the hearty food will do Paula good."
They left in a taxi, following the hearse. She seemed smaller. She
left without tears, slippers in hand.

For several days now, we have been disconnecting your respirator, always a little longer, and now you can last ten minutes on the
air you breathe yourself. You take slow, shallow breaths; the muscles
of your chest struggle against the paralysis and then lift ever so
slightly. In a week, perhaps, we can take you from this intensive care
unit and move you to a normal ward. There are no private rooms,
except for Room 0, where the dying go. I would like to take you to
a quiet, sunny place with a window that looks out on birds and
flowers; you would like that, but I'm afraid that all we can provide is
a bed in a ward. I hope my mother can last until then, I think she is
about at the breaking point.

THE WORST FOREBODINGS ASSAULT ME AT NIGHT WHEN I SENSE THE hours passing, one by one, until I hear the first faint sounds of dawn, long before light streaks the sky, and only then do I sleep— the sleep of the dead—wrapped in Willie's gray cashmere sweater. He brought it to me the first time he came, as if he knew we would be separated for a long time. This sweater has wonderful memories; to me it symbolizes the magic of our first meeting. The first weeks I was here, in order to sleep, I was taking some blue pills that are another of the many mysterious remedies my mother prescribes and generously extracts from the large satchel where from time immemorial she has accumulated medications. Once she injected me with a double dose of a tonic to be used in cases of extreme weakness—something she had acquired nineteen years before in Turkey—and nearly killed me. The aftermath of the blue pills was a drugged stupor; I awoke with my eyes crossed, and it took half the morning to reach a state of semilucidity. Then in a little street close to the hotel, I found an armoire-sized pharmacy run by a large, curt woman always in black buttoned up to her chin, to whom I told my woes. She sold me some valerian in a dark glass vial, and now, with few variations, I dream the same dream every night. I am you, Paula, I have your long hair and large eyes, your long slender fingers with your wedding band, which in fact I have worn since they handed it to me in the hospital the day you fell ill. I put it on to keep from losing it during those frantic moments, and since then have not wanted to take it off. When you regain consciousness, I will give it to Ernesto so he can slip it on your finger as he did a lit- tle more than a year ago on your wedding day. "Don't you think it's a nuisance to get married by the Church?" I inquired at the time. You shot me a stern look and, in that admonitory tone you never use with your students but sometimes favor me with, you replied that Ernesto and you were both believers, and that you wanted to consecrate your union in public because in private you had been married before God the first time you slept together. At the cere- mony, you looked like a sylvan sprite. The family came to the celebration in Caracas from all points of the globe, I from California, carrying your wedding gown, half smothered beneath a mountain of white. You got dressed in the home of my friend Ildemaro, who was as proud as if he were your father, and you asked him to drive you to the church in his old car, washed and polished for the occasion. "When I think of Paula," Ildemaro told me emotionally during a visit to Madrid during the early days of your illness, "I always see her dressed as a bride and wearing a crown of flowers."

For five days there has been a janitors' strike in the hospital. The building looks like a medieval market square; soon roaches and rats will be spreading pestilence from human to human. The strikers, surrounded by security guards, congregate at the entrance to the building and smile for the television cameras. Doctors, nurses, patients in pajamas and slippers, and others in wheelchairs, avail themselves of the opportunity to amuse themselves, chatting, smoking, and drinking coffee from the dispensing machines; although garbage mounts like sea foam, no one seems in any hurry to resolve the problem. The floor is strewn with used rubber gloves, paper cups, heaps of cigarette butts, and nauseating blobs and splotches. The families of the patients clean the rooms as well as they can, but the dirt ends up in the corridors where feet carry it right back into the same rooms. Garbage cans are overflowing, plastic bags filled to bursting are piled in every corner, the bathrooms are revolting and can't be used anymore—in fact, most have been locked: the whole building stinks like a stable. I have tried to find out if it's possible to take you to a private clinic, but they tell me that the risk of moving you is too great. It is my feeling that the risk of an infection is worse.

"Be calm," the neurologist advises me, imperturbable. "Paula is in the one clean area in the building."

"But people are carrying the contamination on their shoes! They come in and out through those filthy corridors!"

My mother leads me to a quiet spot and reminds me of the virtue of patience: "This is a public hospital, the State has no funds to settle the strike, we have nothing to gain by getting nervous, besides, Paula was raised on the water in Chile and can certainly resist a few puny Spanish germs." At that point, the nurse opened the door to authorize visits and for once called your name first. Twenty-one steps, cloth smocks, plastic bags on our shoes; the staff doesn't wear them, they just slop through all the trash, but I have to admit that in the unit everything looked as if it had recently been scrubbed. I become more nervous with every step, my heart galloping, as it always does as I approach your bedside, still furious about the strike. The nurse on the morning shift comes to meet me, the one who cries when Ernesto talks to you of love.

"Good news!" she greets me. "Paula is breathing on her own. Her fever is gone, and she seems more responsive. Talk to her, I think she hears. . . ."

I took you in my arms, then held your face in my hands and kissed your forehead, your cheeks, your eyelids; I shook your shoulders, calling, Paula, Paula. . . . And then, oh, Paula . . . ! and then you opened your eyes and looked at me!

"She has reacted well to the antibiotic. And she's not losing as much sodium. With luck, we can move her in a few more days," the physician on duty reported, without elaboration.

"She opened her eyes!"

"That doesn't mean anything, don't get your hopes up. Her level of consciousness is zero; she may hear a little, but she doesn't understand or recognize anything. I don't think she is suffering."

"Let's go have some hot chocolate and crullers to celebrate this splendid morning," my mother said, and we left the hospital, jubilant, threading our way through the filth.

You left the intensive care unit the same day the janitors' strike ended. While a team of people in rubber boots and gloves swabbed the floors with disinfectant, you were being wheeled on a cot, with Ernesto holding your hand, to a room in the Department of Neurology. Here there are six beds, all occupied, a lavatory, and two large windows that offer a glimpse of the end of winter; here is where you will stay until we can take you home. Now I can be with you all the time, but after forty-eight hours without leaving your side, I realized that my strength will not stand that pace and that it is more productive to hire someone to help. My mother and the nuns found a pair of nurses to look after you; the day nurse is a young, chubby, smiling girl who is constantly singing, and the night nurse is a taciturn and efficient woman in heavily starched white. Your mind is still somewhere in limbo; you open your eyes and look frightened, as if you were seeing ghosts. The neurologist is concerned, and after the Easter holidays he is going to perform various tests to check the state of your brain; they have prodigious machines capable of photographing one's most ancient memories. I try not to think of tomorrow. The future does not exist, the Indians of the Altiplano say, we can only be sure of the past—from which we draw experience and knowledge—and the present—a brief spark that at the instant it is born becomes yesterday. You have no control over your body; you cannot move yourself and you suffer violent spasms like electric shocks. In one way I am grateful for your state of complete innocence; it would be much worse if you understood how ill you are. By trial and error I am learning to care for you; at first the opening in your throat, the tubes and probes, horrified me, but I'm used to them now; I can bathe you and change your bedding without help. I have bought a white dress and nurses' shoes in order to blend in with the staff and avoid explanations. No one has ever heard of porphyria here and they believe you will never get well. "Your daughter is so pretty, poor child; pray God to take her quickly," patients who are still able to speak tell me. The atmosphere in this room is depressing; it reminds me of a place to warehouse the mad. One woman who is curled up like a snail never stops howling; she began to turn in upon herself two years ago and her merciless metamorphosis has advanced steadily ever since. Her husband comes in the evening after work; he washes her with a wet cloth, combs her hair, checks the restraints that confine her to her bed, and then sits down to observe her without a word to anyone. At the other end of the room, near a window, lies a stout country woman my age, jerking and thrashing. Elvira is mentally lucid, but has lost the meanings of words and command of her movements. She has clear ideas but cannot express them; she wants to ask for water and her lips form the word "train"; her hands and legs refuse to obey her, and she flounders about like a marionette with tangled cords. Her husband told me that when he came home from work one day he found her collapsed in a chair, babbling incoherently. He thought she was pretending to be drunk to entertain her grandchildren, but after hours went by and the children were sobbing with fear, he decided to bring her to Madrid. No one has been able to put a name to her illness. Every morning, professors and medical students pass through and examine her like some animal; they prick her with needles, ask her questions she cannot answer, and then leave, shrugging their shoulders. On weekends, her daughters and a stream of friends and neighbors file by to visit: she was the heart of her village. Her husband never budges from the chair beside her bed; there he spends the day and there he sleeps at night. He is indefatigable in his care for her, at the same time he scolds her, "Come on now, for Chrissakes, swallow the soup or I'll empty it over your head. Jesus God, this woman is a pain in the ass." This language is accompanied by loving solicitude and the tenderest of expressions. He confessed to me, blushing, that Elvira is the light of his life and without her nothing matters. Do you sense what is going on around you, Paula? I don't know whether you hear, whether you see, whether you understand any of the things happening in this madhouse, or even if you know me. You just stare toward your right, your wide eyes and dilated pupils fixed on the window where occasionally a pigeon alights. The doctors' pessimism and the sordidness of the ward are eating holes in my heart. Ernesto also looks very tired, but the one most affected is my mother.

One hundred days. It has been exactly one hundred days since you fell into your coma. My mother is drained; yesterday she could not get out of bed. She is so exhausted that finally she has bowed to our pressure to return to Chile. I bought her a ticket, and just a couple of hours ago took her to the plane. "Now, don't you dare die and make me the orphan of all orphans," I warned as we said goodbye. When I returned to the hotel, I found my bed turned back, a pot of lentil soup on the burner, and her prayer book left for company. And so that is the end of our honeymoon. Never before have we had so much time together; never, except when my children were babies, have I shared such a long and profound intimacy. With men I have loved, living together has always included elements of passion, flirtation, and modesty—or has degenerated into frank disgust. I didn't know how comfortable it is to share a space with another woman. I will miss her, but I need to be alone and gather my energy in silence: I am being deafened by hospital noises.

Ernesto's father is leaving soon, and I will miss him, too. I have spent hours in the company of this very manly man who takes a chair beside your bed to watch over you with uncommon delicacy and to divert me with his life's adventures. He lost his father and his uncles in the Spanish Civil War; of all his family, only the women and youngest children survived. Your husband's grandfather was executed against the wall of a church; during the confusion of those days, his wife, unaware that she was a widow, escaped from village to village with her three children, suffering hunger and terrible deprivations. She saved all three, and they grew up in Franco's Spain without modifying their strong Republican convictions. At eighteen, Ernesto's father was a young student; it was the height of General Franco's dictatorship, just when repression was at its worst. Like his brothers, he secretly belonged to the Communist Party. One day a female comrade fell into the hands of the police. He was immediately advised, and he told his mother and brothers goodbye and fled before the girl was forced to reveal his whereabouts. He first rambled through North Africa, but his steps led him to the New World, and finally to Venezuela; he worked there for more than thirty years, married, and had children. At Franco's death, he returned to his village in Cordoba in search of his past. He located some of his old comrades and from them found the address of the girl he had thought about every day for three decades. In a barren flat with stained walls, the woman was waiting, sitting by the window with her embroidery. He did not recognize her but she had not forgotten him, and held out her hands, thankful for that long overdue visit. That was when he learned that she had been tortured but had confessed nothing, and realized that his flight and his long exile had been unnecessary; the police had never been looking for him because no one had informed against him. It is too late now to think of changing things, the map of his destiny has already been drawn. He cannot return to Spain because his soul has been tanned like leather in the forests of the Amazon. During the countless hours we share in the hospital, he recounts, in the calmest of voices, incredible adventures: rivers wide as seas, peaks where no man had trod before, valleys where diamonds burst from the earth like seeds and serpents kill with the mere scent of their venom; he describes tribes wandering naked beneath centuries-old trees, Guajiro Indians who sell their wives and daughters like cattle; soldiers in the hire of drug traffickers; cattle rustlers who rape, kill, and burn with impunity. Then there was the day he went into the jungle with a group of laborers and a mule train; they were using their machetes to hack their way through the vegetation, until one of the men swung too wide and his machete slashed his leg to the bone. Blood gushed in torrents, despite a tourniquet and other measures to stop the flow. Then someone remembered the Indian who drove the mules—an ancient of days with a reputation for being a healer— and ran to get him from the end of the train. The Indian took his time coming, glanced at the leg, waved away the curious, and began his treatment with the parsimony of one who has often seen death. He fanned the mosquitoes away from the wound with his hat, soaked the leg in his spit, and traced a few crosses in the air, all the while chanting in some singsong jungle tongue. "And that stopped the hemorrhaging," Ernesto's father concluded in a casual tone. They bound up the frightful wound with a rag, tied the man onto an improvised travois and, without his losing another drop of blood, traveled with him several hours to the nearest first-aid station where his leg could be stitched and splinted. He is lame, but he has his leg. I told this story to the nuns who visit you every day and they were not particularly surprised; they are accustomed to miracles. If an Amazon Indian can staunch a stream of blood with saliva, just think, Paula, how much more science can do for you. I must get more help. Now that I am alone, the days are longer and the nights are darker. I have more than enough time to write, because once I have finished the rituals of your daily care, I have nothing more to do, except remember.

At the beginning of the sixties, my work had progressed from forestry statistics to a faltering beginning in journalism, which, in turn, and by pure chance, led to television. The rest of the world was already transmitting in color, but in Chile, the farthest corner of

the hemisphere, we were still in the first stages of experimental programs in black and white. The privileged owners of a television set
became the most influential persons in their district; neighbors, as if
hypnotized, clustered around the few existing sets to watch a
motionless geometric design on the screen and listen to elevator
music. They spent entire afternoons, openmouthed, eyes glazed,
awaiting some revelation that would change the course of their lives,
but nothing happened: just the square, the circle, and the same irritating melody. Eventually we moved from basic geometry to a few
hours of educational programming on the functioning of a motor,
the industrious character of the ant, and classes of first aid demonstrating mouth-to-mouth resuscitation on a pallid manikin. We
were also offered news, narrated as if on radio and without images,
and occasionally some silent film. For want of more interesting subjects, my boss in the FAO was assigned fifteen minutes to expound
on the problem of world hunger. It was the era of apocalyptic
prophesies: population growth was out of control, there was not
enough food to go around, the soil was exhausted, the planet would
perish in less than fifty years and the few survivors would be murdering each other for the last crumb of bread. The day of the program, my boss was indisposed and I was sent to the station to make
his excuses. "I'm very sorry," the producer said coldly, "but at three
o'clock this afternoon someone from your office must appear
before the camera, because that was our agreement and I have
nothing to fill that time." My feeling was that if the viewers could
tolerate the square and the circle, or Chaplin's *The Gold Rush* five
times a week, this emergency was not critical. I returned with a
piece of film edited with scissors and featuring a few feeble water
buffalo plowing a drought-parched paddy in some remote corner of
Asia. Since the documentary was in Portuguese, I invented a dramatic voice-over that more or less fit the sequence with the emaci-
ated beasts, and narrated it with such emphasis that no one was left
with any doubt about the imminent extinction of buffalo, rice, even
humankind itself. When the fifteen minutes was over, the producer,
with a sigh of resignation, asked me to come back every Wednesday
to campaign against hunger—the poor man was frantic to fill his
schedule. That was how I ended up in charge of a program for

which I had to do everything from the script to the design of the credits. Working in that station consisted of arriving on time, sitting before a red light, and talking into a void; I was never aware that on the other side of the light two million ears were awaiting my words and two million eyes judging my hairdo, and I was always amazed when strangers spoke to me on the street. The first time you saw me on the screen, Paula, you were a year and a half old, and the shock of seeing your mother's decapitated head peering through a pane of glass left you nearly catatonic. My in-laws had the only set within the radius of a kilometer, and every afternoon their living room was filled with viewers whom Granny treated like guests. She spent the morning baking cookies and turning the crank of an ice cream maker and nights washing plates and sweeping up the circus-level mess on her floors, with never a word of thanks for any of it. I became the most conspicuous person in the neighborhood; adults greeted me with respect and children pointed at me. I could have continued in that career the rest of my days, but finally the country tired of starving cattle and diseases of rice. When that happened, I was one of the few people around with television experience— rudimentary as it was—and could have undertaken a different program, but by then Michael had graduated and we both itched for adventure: we wanted to travel before we had more children. We obtained two scholarships and set off for Europe with you by the hand. You were nearly two years old and a complete lady in miniature.

Tío Ramón has not been the inspiration for any of the characters in my books; he is too decent and has too much common sense. Novels are made of the demented and the villainous, of people tortured by obsessions, of victims of the implacable mills of destiny. From the narrative point of view, an intelligent, good man like Tío Ramón is useless; on the other hand, as a grandfather he's perfect. I knew that the instant I handed him his first grandchild in the Geneva airport and watched tenderness surface from a secret wellspring hidden until then. He came to meet us wearing a large medal on a tricolor ribbon; he handed you a velvet box containing the keys to the city and welcomed you in the name of the Four Cantons, the Bank of

Switzerland, and the Calvinist Church. At that moment, I realized I truly loved my stepfather and, with a single stroke, the tormenting jealousy and rages of the past were erased. You were wearing the Sherlock Holmes hat and coat I had dreamed before you were born and that Mama Hilda, following my precise instructions, had stitched for you on her sewing machine. You spoke with propriety and behaved like a little lady, as your Granny had taught you. In Chile I had been working full time, and had little idea how to bring up children; it was very comfortable for me to delegate that responsibility, and now, in view of the splendid results, I realize that my mother-in-law did a much better job. Granny took it upon herself, among other tasks, to toilet train you. She bought two potties, a small one for you and a large one for her, and you both sat for hours in the living room, playing visitors, until you caught on. She had the only telephone in the neighborhood, and friends who came to make a call became accustomed to seeing that gentle English lady sitting opposite her granddaughter with her posterior bared to the world. It was Mama Hilda who discovered a way to get you to eat, because you had the appetite of a nightingale. She improvised a saddle that she strapped on her dog, a huge black beast with the stamina of a burro, and as you rode she followed with a spoon. In Europe, those two exemplary grandmothers were replaced by Tío Ramón, who convinced you that he was the world owner of Coca-Cola and that no one in all the universe and beyond could drink one without his personal authorization. You learned to call him on the telephone in French, interrupting sessions of the United Nations Council, to ask his permission to have a Coke. He also made you believe he was the owner of the zoo, the children's programs on television, and the famous fountain in Lake Geneva. Knowing the times the fountain was turned on, and trusting Swiss punctuality, he set his watch and then pretended to call the president of the republic to give the order by telephone; you watched out the window, and your face lighted with wonder when the water shot up from the lake like a majestic column rising toward the sky. He shared such surreal games with you that I came to fear for your mental health. He had a box containing six little dolls he called "Death Row Inmates," whose fate was to be executed at dawn the following morning.

Every night you presented yourself before that nonpareil executioner to plead for clemency, and always obtained a twenty-four-hour stay of sentence. He told you that he descended directly from Jesus Christ and, to prove that they both had the same last name, years later took you to the Catholic cemetery in Santiago to see the mausoleum of don Jesús Huidobro. He also assured you he was a prince, and that the day he was born people embraced each other in the street as church bells rang announcing the good news: *Ramón is born! Ramón is born.* He hung all the decorations he had received in his long diplomatic career around his neck and told you they were medals for heroism won in battles against the enemies of his kingdom. For years, Paula, you believed everything he told you.

That year we divided our time between Switzerland and Belgium, where Michael was studying engineering and I participated in a television course. In Brussels we lived in a tiny attic apartment above a barbershop. All the other renters were damsels with very short skirts, very low décolletages, a rainbow variety of wigs, and tiny, curly-haired dogs with bows around their necks. At any hour, we heard snatches of music, heavy breathing, and quarrels, as clients rushed in and out. The elevator opened directly into the single room of our floor, and when we forgot to shoot the bolt we sometimes awakened at midnight with a stranger by our bed asking for Pinky or Suzanne. My fellowship was part of a program for Congolese, to whom Belgium was indebted for many years of brutal colonization. I was the single exception, a light-skinned woman among thirty black males. After suffering a week of humiliations, I came to the conclusion that I was not willing to run such a gauntlet, and offered to withdraw, even though we would be badly strapped without the fellowship money. The director asked me to explain my sudden departure to the class, and I had no choice but to face that united front and in my lamentable French tell them that in my country men did not enter the women's bathroom unzipping their fly, did not shove women aside to go through a door first, did not knock each other down for a place at the table or to get on a bus, and that I felt badly mistreated and was leaving because I was not used to such foul behavior. A glacial silence greeted my peroration. After a long pause, one of them spoke to say that in his country no decent woman publicly exhibited her need to go to the bathroom, nor did she try to go through a door before the men but in fact walked several steps behind, and that his mother and his sisters never sat at the table with him, they ate what the men left. He added that they felt permanently insulted by me, that they had never seen a person with such bad manners, and, as I was a minority in the group, I would just have to make the most of it. "It is true that I am a minority in this course, but you are a minority in this country," I replied. "I am willing to make concessions, but you must do that, too, if you want to avoid problems here in Europe." It was a solution worthy of Solomon; we agreed upon certain basic rules, and I stayed on. They never wanted to sit with me at the table or on the bus, but they stopped bursting into the bathroom and physically shoving me. During that year, my feminism got lost in the shuffle: I walked a modest two meters behind my companions, never looked up or raised my voice, and was the last one through the door. Once, two of them came to our apartment to get some class notes and that same afternoon the concierge came to warn us that "people of color" were not welcome, and that she had made an exception in our case because though we were South American, we were not terribly dark-skinned. As a souvenir of my Belgian-African adventure, I have a photograph in which I appear in the center of my companions, my face like raw dough lost in a sea of thirty ebony visages. On our fellowships, Michael and I were paupers, but we were in our twenties, an age when poverty is fashionable. Many years later I returned to Belgium to accept a literary prize from the hands of King Baudouin. I was expecting a giant in a cape and crown, like the royal portraits, but found myself before a small, gentle, weary gentleman with a slight limp, whom I did not recognize. He asked me amiably whether I knew his country, and I told him about my time as a student, when we lived on such a tight budget that we ate nothing but fried potatoes and horse meat. He looked at me with dismay, and I was afraid I had offended him. "And do you like horse meat?" I asked, in an attempt to make amends.

Thanks to that diet, however, and other economies, we were able to travel from Andalusia to Oslo in a broken-down Volkswagen-cum-Gypsywagen that sneezed along the highway with all our

goods and chattel strapped to the roof. It served us with the loyalty
of a camel to the end of the trip, but when the moment came to
leave it behind, it was in such bad shape that we had to pay someone to haul it to the junkyard. For months we lived in a tent; you
didn't know there was any other way to live, Paula, and when we
went into a solid structure, you asked with amazement how they
folded the walls to load them onto a car. We poked through countless castles, cathedrals, and museums, carrying you in a backpack
and feeding you Coca-Cola and bananas. You had no toys, but you
entertained yourself imitating the tourist guides: at three you knew
the difference between Roman and Renaissance frescoes. In my
memory, the ruins, plazas, and palaces of all those cities blend
together; I'm not really sure whether I was in Florence or whether I
saw it on a postcard, whether we went to a bullfight or a horse race.
I cannot distinguish between the Côte d'Azur and the Costa Brava
and, in the stupefaction of exile from Chile, I lost the photographs
that prove I was ever in those places, and that piece of my past may
simply be a dream like so many that distort my reality. Part of the
confusion can be explained by my second pregnancy; it happened at
a most inopportune time, because with the bucking of the old VW
and the effort of setting up the tent and squatting to cook by a
campfire I was truly ill. Nicolás was conceived in a sleeping bag during the first glimmers of a cold spring, possibly in the Bois de
Boulogne, some thirty meters from homosexuals dressed as adolescent girls who sold themselves for ten dollars, and only a few steps
from a nearby tent that was the source of marijuana smoke and raucous jazz. With such antecedents, Nicolás should have been a wild
adventurer, but he turned out to be one of those calm souls who
inspire confidence at first sight. In the womb, he adjusted to circumstances as unobtrusively as one of the cells of my own body—
just as in a certain way he still is. Even in the best of cases, however,
a pregnancy is a major invasion, an amoeba growing in one's innards
and passing through multiple stages of evolution—fish, cockroach,
dinosaur, monkey—until it reaches human form. All during that
heroic tour through Europe, Nicolás journeyed quietly inside me,
but his presence inevitably created havoc with my thoughts. I lost
interest in the ruins of past civilizations, I was bored in museums, I

was carsick, and I lost my appetite. I suppose that explains why I can't remember the details of the trip.

We returned to Chile in the midst of the euphoria of the Christian Democrats, a party that promised reforms without drastic changes and had been elected with the support of the Right in order to prevent a possible triumph by Salvador Allende, whom many held to be Satan. The elections were tainted from the beginning by the campaign of terror the Right had been waging since the early years of the decade, when the Cuban Revolution had sent a surge of hope through all Latin America. Huge posters showed pregnant mothers defending their children against the menace of Russian soldiers. Nothing new under the sun: the same tactics had been used thirty years earlier during the time of the Popular Front, and soon would be employed against Allende in the elections of 1970. The Christian Democrats' politics of conciliation, backed by the North American copper companies, was destined to failure because it satisfied neither Left nor Right. Their agrarian project, which people called the "Flowerpot Reform," apportioned a few abandoned or poorly developed plots of land, but large holdings remained in the same old hands. Discontent spread, and within two years a large part of the population began to veer toward the Left; political parties that proposed true reforms joined together in a coalition and, to the surprise of the world in general, and to the United States in particular, Salvador Allende became the first Marxist president in history elected by popular vote. But I don't want to get ahead of myself. In 1966, the Christian Democrats were still celebrating their triumph in the parliamentary elections of the previous year, and there was talk that their party would govern the country for the next fifty years, that the Left had suffered an irreparable defeat, and that politically Allende was a dead duck. This was also the era of women who looked like undernourished orphans and wore dresses so short they barely covered their bottoms. There were a smattering of hippies in the most sophisticated neighborhoods of Santiago, in their Indian prints, necklaces, flowers, and long hair, but for anyone who had been in London and seen the druggies dancing half-naked in Trafalgar Square, Chilean hippies seemed rather pathetic. My life then was characterized by work and responsibilities; nothing was farther from my temperament than the bucolic indolence of the Flower Children. I did, however, immediately accept many of the external signs of that culture because I looked much better in long dresses, especially in the last months of pregnancy when I was absolutely round. I not only adopted flowers in my clothing, I painted them on the walls of our house and on our car—enormous yellow sunflowers and bright dahlias that scandalized my in-laws and our neighbors. Fortunately, Michael seemed not to notice; he was preoccupied with a new construction project and his long games of chess.

Nicolás made a difficult entry into the world; I was in labor for two days that are much more deeply engraved in my memory than all the year we traveled in Europe. I had the feeling I was falling off a precipice, gaining speed with every second, until a final tumultuous conclusion during which even my bones burst open as an uncontrollable earth force pushed the baby from my body. I had experienced nothing like that when you were born, Paula, because yours was a straightforward cesarean. There was nothing romantic about your brother's birth, only sweat and pain and loneliness. I had never heard that the father might participate in the process, and besides, Michael was not the ideal man for such events—he faints at the sight of a needle or blood. So I thought birth was a strictly individual affair, like death. I hadn't a clue that while I was suffering alone in my hospital room, other women of my generation were having their babies at home, accompanied by a midwife, their husband, friends, even a photographer, all smoking marijuana and listening to the Beatles.

Nicolás was born without a hair on his body but with a horn on his forehead and a purple arm. I was afraid that from having read so much science fiction I had brought to earth a creature from another planet, but the doctor assured me that your brother was indeed human. The unicorn effect was produced by the forceps they used to wrest him from me, and before long the purple faded from his arm. I remember him as a bald baby, but at some moment his papillary cells must have begun to function, because today he has thick eyebrows and a heavy head of wavy black hair. If you were jealous of your brother you never showed it, you were a second mother to him. The two of you shared a little room with storybook characters painted on the walls and a window where at night a sinister, shadowy dragon waved its terrifying claws at you. You came to my bed dragging the baby; you couldn't actually lift him but neither could you leave Nicolás alone at the mercy of the monster in the garden. Later, when he learned the fundamentals of fear, he slept with a hammer beneath his pillow to defend his sister. During the day, the dragon turned back into a sturdy cherry tree; its branches held swings and sheltered tree houses, and in the summer you and your brother always got stomach aches from the green fruit you fought the birds for. That tiny garden was a secure and enchanted world where you could set up a tent and sleep outside and play Indian, bury treasures, and raise worms. In an absurd pool at the back of the patio, you and Nicolás splashed with the neighborhood children and dogs. A wild grapevine grew on the roof, and you pressed the grapes and produced a wine no one could swallow. At Michael's parents' home a block away, you had an attic crammed with surprises, fruit trees, rolls freshly baked by a perfect grandmother, and a hole in the fence you could crawl through to run to your heart's content on the adjoining golf course. Nicolás and you grew up listening to Granny's English songs and my stories. Every night as I put you to bed, you gave me a subject or a first sentence, and in three seconds I would create a made-to-order story. Since then I have lost the knack of instant inspiration, but I hope it isn't dead and that in the future my grandchildren will revive it.

I HAVE HEARD IT SAID SO OFTEN THAT WE LIVE IN A MATRIARCHY IN Chile that I almost believe it. Even my grandfather and my stepfather, authoritarian gentlemen of the feudal school, have stated that without blushing. I don't know who invented the myth of the matriarchy nor how it has been perpetuated for more than a hundred years; perhaps some visitor from the past, one of those Danish geographers or merchants from Liverpool visiting our shores, noticed that Chilean women are stronger and more organized than the majority of men and frivolously concluded that they are in command, and from years of being repeated, the fallacy became dogma. If women have influence, it is only—and then only sometimes—within their home. Men control all the political and economic power, the culture and customs; they proclaim the laws and apply them as they wish, and when social pressures and the legal apparatus are not sufficient to subdue the most rebellious women, the Church steps in with its incontestable patriarchal seal. What is unforgivable, though, is that it is women who perpetuate and reinforce the system, continuing to raise arrogant sons and servile daughters. If they would agree to revise the standards, they could end machismo in one generation. For centuries, poverty has forced men to travel up and down the narrow length of Chile in search of a living; it is not rare that the same man who in winter scrabbles in the bowels of the mines in the north will, in summer, find himself picking fruit in the central valley or on a fishing boat in the south. The men come and go, but the women stay put; they are trees rooted in solid ground. Around them revolve their own children and others they have taken in; they care for the aged, the ill, the unfortunate—they are the axis of the community. In all social classes except the most privileged, abnegation and hard work are considered the supreme female virtues; a spirit of sacrifice is a question of honor: the more one suffers for family, the prouder one feels. Women are used to thinking of their mate as a foolish child whose every serious fault, from drunkenness to domestic violence, they forgive . . . *because he's a man.* In the sixties, a small group of young women who had had the good fortune to see the world beyond the Andes dared propose a challenge. As long as they dealt with vague complaints, no one paid any attention, but in 1967 the first feminist publication appeared, blasting the provincial stupor in which we were vegetating. The magazine was born as yet another whim of the owner of the most powerful publishing house in the nation, a millionaire whose intention was probably not to raise anyone's consciousness, nor anything mildly related to that, but to photograph androgynous adolescents for the fashion pages. He reserved for himself all dealings with the beautiful models, then looked within his social world for someone to do the rest of the work, and the choice fell to Delia Vergara, a recently graduated journalist whose aristocratic facade concealed a will of steel and a subversive intellect. This woman produced an elegant magazine with the same glamorous look and mindless trivia of so many other publications of that day—and today—but she allotted a portion of it for the promotion of her feminist ideals. She enlisted a pair of audacious women colleagues and created a style and a language that had never been seen in print in Chile. From the first issue, the magazine provoked heated polemics: the young welcomed it enthusiastically, while the most conservative segments of society rose up in defense of the morality, country, and tradition that surely would be endangered by equality between the sexes. By one of those strange twists of fate, Delia had been in Geneva and my mother had shown her one of my letters, which was how she knew of my existence. The tone of one or two of the paragraphs had intrigued her, and when she returned to Chile she looked me up and asked me to be a part of her enterprise. When we met, I had no job, I was about to give birth to Nicolás, and my lack of credentials was embarrassing: I had not attended the University, I had a head filled with fantasies, and, as a result of my nomadic school days, my writing was peppered with grammatic horrors. In spite of all that, Delia offered me a feature page with no conditions other than it be ironic, because in the midst of so many argumentative articles, she wanted something light. I accepted, without any idea of how difficult it is to be funny on demand. In private, we Chileans laugh easily and like to joke, but in public we are a people of serious simpletons paralyzed by fear of looking ridiculous. That worked in my favor because I had almost no competition. In my column, I treated males as troglodytes; I suppose that if any man had dared write with such insolence about the opposite sex he would have been lynched in a public plaza by a crowd of rampaging women, but no one took me seriously. When the first issues of the magazine were published with articles on contraceptives, divorce, abortion, suicide, and other unutterable subjects, the scandal was intense. The names of those of us who worked on the magazine traveled from mouth to mouth—sometimes with admiration, but usually with contempt. We put up with a lot of aggression and within a few years everyone except me—already married to a hybrid Englishman—ended up separated from Chilean husbands unable to bear their wives' assertiveness and celebrity.

I was only five when I had my first hint of the disadvantages of my gender. My mother and I were sitting on the gallery of my grandfather's house; she was teaching me to knit, while my brothers were playing in the poplar tree in the garden. My clumsy fingers fought to loop the wool between the needles, but I dropped stitches and tangled the yarn; I was sweating with concentration when my mother said to me, "Sit up straight, now, and keep your knees together like a lady." I threw the knitting as far as I could and at that instant decided I was going to be a man. I held firmly to that proposition until I was eleven, when my body began inexorably to change and I was betrayed by my hormones at the sight of my first love's monumental ears. Forty years had to go by before I accepted my condition and realized that, with twice the effort and half the recognition, I had achieved what some men sometimes achieve. Today, I wouldn't change places with anyone, but when I was young, daily injustices soured my life. It had nothing to do with Freudian envy—I can't think of any reason to covet that small and capricious masculine appendage, and if I had one I wouldn't know what to do with it. Delia lent me a stack of books by North American and European women writers and sent me off to read them in alphabetical order, to see whether they might sweep the romantic cobwebs from a brain poisoned by an overdose of fiction, and so, slowly, I discovered an articulate way of expressing the mute rage I had always felt. I became a formidable antagonist to Tío Ramón, who had to call upon his lowest oratorical tricks to hold his own with me; now it was I who composed statements on letterhead paper with three carbons, and he who refused to sign them.

One night Michael and I were invited to dinner in the home of a well-known Socialist politician who had made a career of fighting for justice and equality for the people. In his eyes, "the people" was composed solely of men; it had never occurred to him that women might be included. His wife held an executive position in a large corporation, and often appeared in the press as one of the few examples of the emancipated woman—I cannot fathom why she remained married to that protomacho. All the other guests were people important in politics or cultural affairs, and we, ten years younger, were very much out of place in that sophisticated gathering. At the table, someone complimented my humorous articles and asked whether I had never thought of writing something serious, and in a fit of inspiration I replied that what I really wanted to do was interview an unfaithful wife. An icy silence fell over the room; the shocked guests stared at their plates and no one said anything for several minutes. Finally, the lady of the house got up from the table and went into the kitchen to prepare coffee, and I followed, under the pretext of helping her. As we were arranging cups and saucers on a tray, she told me that if I promised to keep her secret and never, ever, reveal her identity, she would be happy to grant me that interview. The very next morning, recorder in hand, I went to her office, a sunny room in a glass and steel building in the heart of the city, where in her high executive position she reigned without female rival among a multitude of technocrats in gray suits and striped ties. She greeted me with no sign of anxiety—slim, elegant, wearing a short skirt and broad smile, and with several long gold chains accenting her Chanel suit—prepared to tell her story without the least shadow of conscience. The November issue of the magazine carried ten lines about the execution of Che Guevara, news that sent a seismic shock around the world, and four pages of my interview with the faithless wife that shattered the calm of Chilean society. In one week sales doubled, and I was signed on as a permanent member of the staff. Thousands of letters flooded the office, many from religious organizations and well-known hierarchs of the political Right unsettled by the detrimental public example of such a shameless hussy, but we also received letters from women confessing their own adventures. It is difficult today to imagine that something so banal could provoke that reaction; after all, infidelity is as old as the institution of matrimony. What no one could forgive was that the protagonist of the piece had the same motivations for adultery as a man: opportunity, boredom, dejection, flirtation, challenge, curiosity. The woman in my interview was not married to a brutal drunk or an invalid in a wheelchair; neither did she suffer the torment of impossible love. There was no tragedy in her life, she simply lacked compelling reasons to remain true to a husband who deceived her. Many people were horrified by the perfect organization of her setup: with two female friends, she rented a discreet apartment, kept it in impeccable condition, and had certain times during the week when she could take her lovers there. In that way, she was spared the danger of frequenting hotels where either of them might be recognized. It had not occurred to anyone that women could enjoy such comfort: a private apartment for affairs was the sole prerogative of males, there was even a French word for it: *garçonnière.* In my grandfather's generation, the practice was common among wealthy men, but now very few could afford that luxury and adulterers fornicated however and wherever they could, according to their means. In any case, there were more than enough rooms to rent for furtive assignations, and everyone knew their exact price and location.

Twenty years later, at some bend of my long peregrination, far from Chile in another corner of the world, I ran across the husband of the woman in the Chanel suit. He had been imprisoned and tortured during the early years of the military dictatorship and was scarred in both body and soul. He was living in exile, separated from his family, and his health was failing because he could not shake the prison cold that was devouring his bones. Even so, he had not lost his charm or his outrageous vanity. He scarcely remembered me; I stood out in his memory only because of the interview, which he had read with fascination.

"I was always crazy to know who that woman was," he said in a confidential tone. "I discussed it with all my friends. That was all anyone was talking about in Santiago. I would have given anything to have my little visit to that apartment—even better with her two friends. Forgive my lack of modesty, Isabel, but I think those three dames deserved to know what a real man is like."

"To tell you the truth, I think they did."

"So much time has gone by now, won't you tell me who she was?"

"No."

"At least tell me if I knew her!"

"Yes, you did . . . biblically."

My job on the magazine, and later in television, was an escape valve from the madness I inherited from my ancestors; without my work, the accumulated pressure would have landed me in a psychiatric ward. The prudish and moralistic atmosphere, the small-town mentality, and the rigidity of Chilean social norms at that time were overpowering. My grandfather soon adjusted to my public life and stopped throwing my articles into the trash; he never commented on them, but from time to time he asked me what Michael thought, and reminded me that I ought to be very grateful to have such a tolerant husband. He did not like my reputation as a feminist or my long dresses and antique hats, to say nothing of my Citroën painted like a shower curtain, but he forgave my extravagances because in real life I carried out my role as mother, wife, and housekeeper. Just for the fun of shocking everyone, I would have marched through the streets with a bra impaled on a broomstick—alone, of course, no one would have accompanied me—but in private life I had internalized the formulas for eternal domestic bliss. Every morning I served my husband his breakfast in bed, every evening I was waiting in full battle dress with his martini olive between my teeth, and every night I laid out the suit and shirt he would be wearing the next day; I shined his shoes, cut his hair and fingernails, and bought his clothes to save him the bother of trying them on, just as I did with my children. That was not only stupidity on my part, it was misdirected energy and excessive love.

I cultivated the external aspects of the hippies but in my actions lived like a worker ant, laboring twelve hours a day to pay the bills. The one time I tried marijuana—offered by a real hippie—I realized it was not for me. I smoked six joints in a row, and was rewarded not with the hallucinatory euphoria I had heard so much about but a headache: my pragmatic Basque genes are immune to the facile happiness of drugs.

I returned to television, this time with a feminist humor program, and collaborated on the only children's magazine in Chile, which I ended up directing after the founder died suddenly. For years I amused myself by interviewing murderers, seers, prostitutes, necrophiliacs, jugglers, quasi-saints who performed nebulous miracles, demented psychiatrists, and beggars with false stumps who rented babies to put a dent in charitable hearts. I wrote recipes invented on a moment's inspiration, and occasionally improvised a horoscope, guided by the birthdays of friends. Our astrologist lived in Peru and the mail was often delayed, or lost in the gullies of destiny. Once I called her to say that we had received the March horoscope but were missing February's, and she told me to publish the one we had, what was the problem? the order didn't change the outcome. After that, I began fabricating them myself, and had the same percentage of successes as she. The most difficult task was the lovelorn column, which I signed with the pseudonym Francisca Román. Where I lacked personal experience, I called on the inherited intuition of Memé and the counsel of Mama Hilda, who watched all the current soap operas and was a true expert in affairs of the heart. The archive of Francisca Román's letters could provide material for volumes of short stories—I wonder where those boxes of epistolary melodramas are now? I can't imagine how I had time for the house, the children, and my husband, but somehow I found it. In my free time, I made my clothes, wrote children's stories and plays, and exchanged a steady stream of letters with my mother. Michael, meantime, was always close at hand, celebrating the serene contentment into which we had settled with the ingenuous certainty that if we played by the rules, we would live happily ever after. He seemed to be in love, and I certainly was. He was a permissive, rather uninvolved father; at any rate, punishment and rewards were left to me, after all, children were supposed to be raised by their mothers. My feminism did not include sharing household duties, in fact, the idea never entered my mind; I thought liberation had to do with going out into the world and assuming male duties, not with delegating part of my load. The result was a terrible fatigue, as witnessed today by the millions of women of my generation who question feminist movements.

The furniture in our house tended to disappear and be replaced by questionable antiques from the Persian Market, where a Syrian merchant traded men's clothing for anything old. At the rate Michael's wardrobe was reduced, the house filled up with chipped chamber pots, treadle sewing machines, cart wheels, and gas streetlights. Michael's parents, alarmed by some of the characters who drifted in and out of our home, did everything possible to protect their grandchildren from potential dangers. My face on the television and my name in the magazine were open invitations to screwball characters like the post office employee who had a correspondence with Martians, or the girl who left her infant baby on my office desk. We kept the little girl with us for a while, and had decided to adopt her, but one evening when we returned home we discovered that her legitimate grandparents had taken her away with a police order. A miner from the north, a seer by trade who had lost his sanity from having prophesied so many catastrophes, slept on our living room sofa for two weeks, until the National Health Service strike was settled. The poor man had come to Santiago to be treated at the psychiatric hospital on the very day the strike began. Out of money and not knowing anyone, but with prophetic faculties intact, he was able to locate one of the few people in that hostile city willing to give him shelter. "That man has a screw loose, he could pull a knife and murder us all," a highly agitated Granny warned me. She collected her two grandchildren and had them sleep at her house as long as we had the seer, who, incidentally, turned out to be completely harmless and may even have saved our lives. He predicted that in a strong earthquake some of our walls would come down. Michael made a thorough inspection, reinforced certain points, and with the next minor quake only the patio wall collapsed, crushing our dahlias and the neighbor's rabbit.

Granny and Mama Hilda helped raise the children, Michael gave them stability and decency, the school instructed them, and the rest they acquired with their natural wit and talent. I merely tried to entertain them. You were a wise little girl, Paula. Even as a child, you wanted to educate people—your brother, the dogs, and your dolls all played the part of students. The time you had left from your teaching activities was divided among games with Granny, visiting residents of a neighborhood old folks' home, and sewing sessions with Mama Hilda—in spite of the exquisite embroidered batiste dresses my mother bought you in Switzerland, you always looked like an orphan in dresses you sewed for yourself. While my father-in-law spent his retirement years trying to resolve the squaring of the circle and other interminable mathematical problems, Granny was enjoying her brood in a true grandmotherly orgy; you climbed to the attic to play bandits, sneaked into the club to swim in the pool, and got decked out in my nightgowns to perform amateurish plays. In the company of that adorable woman, you, Paula, spent the summer baking cookies and the winter knitting striped mufflers for your friends in the geriatric home; later, after we left Chile, you wrote letters to each one of those great-grandparents you had adopted, until the last one died of loneliness. Those were the happiest and most secure years of our lives. Nicolás and you still treasure the happy memories that sustained you during the hard times when you begged and cried to go back to Chile. By then, though, we couldn't return. Granny was resting beneath a blanket of jasmine, her husband was lost in the labyrinths of senile dementia, our friends were dead or scattered around the world, and there was nowhere for us in our homeland. Only the house remained. It is still there, intact. Not long ago I went to visit it and was amazed by its size; it looked like a dollhouse with a moth-eaten wig for a roof.

Michael had commendable patience with me. He was not disturbed by the gossip or criticism I provoked, he never interfered in my projects, no matter how outlandish, and he defended me loyally even in my mistakes; our paths, nonetheless, were growing farther and farther apart. As I gravitated more toward feminists, bohemians, artists, and intellectuals, he devoted himself to his plans, his calculations, his building sites, and his chess and bridge games. He stayed very late at the office, because among Chilean professionals it is fashionable to work from sunup to sundown and never take a vacation; anything else is considered an indication of a bureaucratic mentality and leads to certain failure in the private sector. He was a good friend and a good lover, but I do not remember much about him; he is blurred in my memory like a badly focused photograph. We were brought up in the tradition that the husband provides for the family and the wife takes charge of home and children, but in our case it was not entirely that way. I began working before he did, and carried a large part of our expenses: his salary was earmarked for paying the mortgage on the house and making investments, and mine evaporated in day-to-day expenditures. Michael remained faithful to himself; he has changed very little over his life, but I offered too many surprises. I burned with restlessness, I saw injustices everywhere, I intended to transform the world, and I embraced so many different causes that I myself lost count and my children lived in a state of constant bewilderment. Ten years later, when we were established in Venezuela and my ideals had been crippled by the fortunes of exile, I asked the children—formed in the era of hippies and socialist dreams—how they wanted to live, and they both replied, in unison and without consultation, "like wealthy bourgeois."

Tío Ramón returned from Switzerland the same year my father died. My stepfather had slowly climbed the ladder of his diplomatic career and gained an important post in the chancellery. He took his grandchildren to the government palace, telling them it was his private residence, and seated them amid plush drapes and portraits of the Fathers of the Nation in the long ambassador's dining room, where white-gloved waiters served them orange juice. When you were seven, you had to write a composition at school on the theme of the family, and you wrote that your only interesting relative was Tío Ramón, prince and direct descendant of Jesus Christ, owner of a palace with uniformed servants and armed guards. Your teacher gave me the name of a child psychiatrist, but shortly afterward your reputation was saved. I was supposed to take you to the dentist but forgot, and you stood waiting for hours at the school door. The teacher tried unsuccessfully to locate either your father or me, and finally called Tío Ramón. "Tell Paula to stay right there, I will come get her immediately," he replied and, in fact, a half-hour later a presidential limousine with fluttering flags and an escort of two motorcycle policemen pulled up before the school. The chauffeur got out, hat in hand, opened the door of the backseat, and your grandfather emerged wearing a chestful of decorations and the black ceremonial cape that in a burst of poetic inspiration he had stopped by his house to pick up. You have forgotten that I left you waiting, Paula, but you will always remember that imperial entourage and the face of your teacher, who was so befuddled that she made a deep bow as she greeted your Tío Ramón.

My father died of a heart attack. There was no opportunity to hear the story of his great moments or of his misery because a sudden wave of blood flooded the deepest chambers of his heart and he lay dead in the street like a common beggar. He was taken by Public Assistance to the morgue, where an autopsy determined the cause of death. In going through his pockets the attendants found his papers, connected the name, and contacted me to identify the body. When they gave me the name, I never dreamed it was my father; I hadn't thought of him for years and there was no shadow of him in my life, not even bitterness at having been abandoned by him. Instead, I thought of my brother, whose second name is Tomás and who at the time was still somewhere with the mysterious sect of the Argentine Messiah. It had been months since we heard from him and, because of the family's natural bent for the tragic, we supposed the worst. My mother had futilely exhausted her energies in trying to locate him, and was inclined to believe rumors that her son had been enlisted by Cuban revolutionaries: the idea that he was following the footsteps of the dead Che Guevara was more palatable than thinking him hypnotized by a charlatan. Before leaving for the morgue, I called Tío Ramón at his office and stammered that my brother was dead. I reached that sinister building before he did and identified myself to an impassive official who led me to an icy room where a form covered in white lay on a bare cot. They turned back the sheet and I saw a pale, naked, heavyset man with a seam stitched from chin to pubis, a man to whom I felt not the remotest connection. Moments later, Tío Ramón arrived; he glanced at the body and informed us that the man was my father. I walked over to take another look, observing his features very carefully because I would never have an opportunity to see them again.

That day I learned of the existence of an older half-brother, the son of my father and a lover, who bore a remarkable resemblance to the boy in my mathematics class I had fallen in love with at fifteen. I also learned of three younger children my father had by a third woman, offspring to whom, ironically, he had given our names. Tío Ramón took charge of the funeral and of drafting a document in which we renounced any claims in favor of that other family. Juan and I immediately signed our names, and then falsified Pancho's signature to avoid unpleasant delays. The next day we walked behind the coffin of that stranger down a path in the General Cemetery; no one else attended the modest burial, my father left very few friends in this world. I have never again had contact with my half-brothers and -sisters. When I think of my father I can only see him lying motionless in the abysmal solitude of that frigid morgue.

My father's was not the first corpse I had seen so close. From a distance, I had glimpsed bodies in the street during the chaos of the war that shook Lebanon and during an uprising in Bolivia, but they seemed more like marionettes than people. I only remember Memé alive, and of my Uncle Pablo there was nothing left to see. The one true and present death in my childhood happened when I was eight, and the circumstances make it unforgettable. That night of December 25, 1950, I had lain awake for hours, wide-eyed in a darkness filled with the familiar sounds of the beach house. My brothers and my cousins occupied other cots in the same room, and through the cardboard thin walls I heard the night breathing in the next rooms, the constant humming of the refrigerator, and the stealthy scurrying of mice. Several times I wanted to get up and go out on the patio to cool off in the salt breeze, but I was discouraged by the thought of never-ending processions of blind cockroaches. Under a sheet damp with the eternal dew of the coast, I touched my body with amazement and terror, while images of that afternoon of revelations flashed like ragged clouds across the pale reflection of the moon in the window. I could still feel the fisherman's moist lips on my throat, his voice murmuring in my ear. From far away came the muted roar of the ocean, and every once in a while a car passed in the street, briefly lighting the slits in the shutters. In my chest I felt the vibrations of a campanile, the weight of a gravestone, a powerful claw creeping toward my throat, choking me. The Devil appears at night in the mirrors. . . . There was no one in the room with me; the only thing in the whole house was a flaking rectangle in the bathroom where my mother put on her lipstick, too high for me to see. But the Evil One not only inhabits mirrors, Margara had told me, he also roams in the darkness searching for human sin, and climbs inside perverse little girls to eat their entrails. I put my hand where the fisherman had put his, and immediately drew it back, frightened, confused by the mingling of repugnance and dark pleasure. I felt again his rough, strong fingers exploring my body, the rasp of his badly shaven cheeks, his smell, his weight, his obscenities in my ear. Surely the mark of sin was emblazoned on my forehead. How was it that no one had noticed? When I got back to the house, I had not dared look my mother or my grandfather in the eye; I had hidden from Margara and, pretending to have a stomach ache, had escaped early to bed, after taking a long shower and scrubbing all over with blue laundry soap, but nothing had removed the stains. Dirty . . . I would be dirty forever. . . . Even with all that, it never entered my head to disobey the fisherman's orders; the next day I would meet him again on the road with the geraniums and, as if in a trance, follow him into the woods, even if it cost my life. "If your grandfather finds out, he'll kill me," he had warned. My silence was sacred, his life was in my hands. The proximity of that second meeting filled me with terror, but also with fascination. What could there be beyond *sin*? The hours passed with excruciating slowness while I listened to the rhythmic breathing of my brothers and cousins and tried to calculate how long it was till dawn. With the first rays of the sun, I would be able to get out of bed and touch bare feet to the floor, because with the light the cockroaches went back to their corners. I was hungry; I thought of the jar of blancmange and cookies in the kitchen; I was cold and wrapped myself in the heavy blankets, but immediately began to rage with the heat of forbidden memories and delirium of anticipation.

Very early the next morning, while the family was still sleeping, I slipped out of bed, dressed, and went out to the patio; I circled around the house and went into the kitchen through the back door. The iron and copper pots hung on their hooks; live clams in a pail of salt water sat on the gray granite table beside a cloth sack with yesterday's bread. I couldn't open the jar of blancmange, but I cut off a chunk of cheese and a slice of quince paste and went outside to look at the sun, just rising over the hill like an incandescent orange. For no reason at all, I began walking toward the mouth of the river, the center of that small fishing village where it was still too early for any activity. I walked past the church, the post office, the general store, past the section of new houses, all exactly alike with their zinc roofs and wood terraces facing the sea, past the hotel where the young people went at night to dance to old rhythms because the new ones hadn't yet reached this backwater; I walked down the long market street where vegetables and fruit were sold, past the pharmacy, the Turk's dry goods store, the newspaper kiosk, the bar, and the billiard hall, still without seeing a soul. I came to the part of town where the fishing families lived, shanties with crude wood counters where seafood and fish were displayed, nets spread to dry like portentous spiderwebs, boots upside-down on the sand, waiting for their owners to recover sufficiently from the Christmas celebrations to go back out to sea. I heard voices, and saw people gathered near one of the farthest shacks, where the river empties into the sea. The sun was higher now and prickled hotly like ants on my shoulders. With the last bit of cheese and quince I reached the end of the street; cautiously I approached the small circle of people and tried to step through, but they pushed me back. At that moment, two policemen appeared on their bicycles; one blew his whistle and the other yelled, "Step aside, goddammit, we're the law." The circle parted briefly, and I saw the fisherman lying face up on the dark sand of the riverbed, his arms flung open in a cross, and wearing the same black trousers, the same white shirt, and the same rubber-soled shoes he had worn the day before when he took me into the woods. One of the policemen commented that he had received a blow on the head, and then I saw the dried blood on his ear and his neck. Something exploded in my chest, and my mouth was filled with the taste of bitter grapefruit; I bent over double, rocked by violent spasms. I dropped to my knees and vomited onto the sand a mixture of cheese, quince paste, and guilt. "What's that kid doing here?" someone said; I felt a hand on my arm but I jerked free and blindly began to run. I ran and I ran, with a piercing pain in my side and that bitter taste in my mouth, not stopping until I saw the red roof of my house, and then I collapsed at the edge of the street, a tiny ball beneath the bushes. Who had seen me in the woods with him? How did Tata find out? I couldn't think, the only thing I knew for sure was that he would

never again dive for sea urchins, that he lay dead on the sand, paying
for our mutual crime, that I was free and would not have to meet
him, and that he would never again take me to the forest. Much
later, I heard familiar sounds from the house: servants preparing
breakfast and the voices of my brothers and cousins. The milkman's
jenny went by with rattling milk cans, and the man who delivered
bread on his tricycle, and then Margara, grouching on her way to do
the shopping. I sneaked into the patio with the hydrangeas, washed
my face and hands in the stream from the hill, dabbed at my hair,
and went into the dining room, where my grandfather sat before his
newspaper and a steaming cup of *café con leche.* "Why are you looking at me like that?" he asked, smiling.

Two days later, when the coroner authorized it, the fisherman's
wake was held in his modest home. All the town, including summer
people, filed through to look at him; it wasn't often that anything
interesting happened and no one wanted to miss the novelty of a
murder, the only one anyone could remember in that resort town
since the crucified artist. Margara took me even though my mother
considered it a grisly spectacle, because Tata—who volunteered to
pay for the burial—declared that death is a natural phenomenon
and it is better to be exposed to it at a young age. At dusk, we
climbed the hill to the clapboard shack decorated with paper garlands, a Chilean flag, and humble bunches of flowers from gardens
along the coast. By then, the sound of tinny guitars was fading, and
the mourners, foggy from cheap wine, were dozing in rattan chairs
set in a circle around the coffin—a simple, unfinished pine box
lighted by four candles. The black-clad mother poked at the fire in a
wood stove where a sooty tea kettle was boiling, all the while muttering a stream of prayers interspersed with sobs and curses. The
neighbor women brought cups to serve tea, and the victim's
younger brothers, in their Sunday shoes and slicked-down hair, ran
around in the patio in a flurry of hens and dogs. A black beribboned
photograph of the fisherman from his days as a conscript stood on a
tottering chest of drawers. All through the night, family and friends
would take turns sitting with the corpse before it was lowered into
the ground, strumming badly tuned guitars, eating whatever the
women brought from their kitchens, and recalling the dead man in

the halting language of the drunk and the sorrowing. Margara moved forward, muttering under her breath and yanking my arm because I was hanging back. When we neared the coffin, she made me go up to it and pray an Our Father of farewell, because she believed that the souls of the murdered never find rest and come in the nighttime to punish the living. Laid out on a white sheet was the man whose hands had known my body three days earlier in the forest. I looked first with visceral fear, then with curiosity, searching for a resemblance, but could find none. That face was not the face of my sin, it was a pale mask with painted lips, brilliantined hair parted in the middle, a wad of cotton in each nostril, and a handkerchief tied around its head to keep the jaw from sagging.

Although the hospital is crowded with people in the afternoons, on Saturday and Sunday mornings it seems deserted. It is still dark when I get there, and I am so tired from the accumulated fatigue of the previous week that my purse is dragging the floor behind me. I walk through the endless, solitary corridors where even my heartbeats echo, and it seems I am walking the wrong way on a moving sidewalk. I am not moving forward, I am always in the same place, more and more exhausted. As I walk, I am whispering magic formulas of my own invention, and the closer I get to the building, to the long corridor of lost steps, to your room, to your bed, the more tightly my chest squeezes with anguish. You are like an overgrown baby, Paula. It is two weeks since you left the intensive care unit, and there is no change to speak of. You were tense after the move, as if you were frightened. Gradually, you have become more calm, but there is no indication of a consciousness, all you do is stare toward the window, absolutely motionless. I have not given up hope; I believe that in spite of the ominous prognosis you will come back to us, and even if you are not the brilliant and vivacious woman you were, you may be able to live an almost normal life and be happy, and I will be responsible for making it happen. Expenses have skyrocketed. I go to the bank and change money that flies from my wallet so quickly I don't even know where it goes, but I choose not to make an accounting, this is no time for prudence. I must find a physical therapist, because the hospital offers only minimal services;

from time to time two distracted girls show up—reluctantly—to move your arms and legs for ten minutes following some vague instructions from an energetic type with a mustache who seems to be their boss and who has seen you only once. There are too many patients and too few resources, so I exercise you myself. Four times a day I force you to move every part of your body. I begin with your toes, one by one, and work upward, slowly and firmly, because it isn't easy to loosen your fingers or bend your knees and elbows. I sit you up in the bed and pound your back to clear your lungs; I moisten the harsh hole in your throat with drops of water because the central heating dries the air, and to prevent deformation I place books at the soles of your feet and bind them with strips of bandage. I also separate your fingers with pieces of sponge rubber and try to keep your head straight with a collar improvised from a travel neck pillow and adhesive tape. These make-do measures are distressing, though, Paula. Soon I must get you where someone can help you, they say that rehabilitation works miracles. The neurologist asks me to be patient, tells me it is not possible to move you yet, much less take you halfway across the world in an airplane. I spend the day and much of the night in the hospital, and have become friends with the other patients in your room and their families. I give Elvira massages, and we are inventing a language of signs to communicate, since words betray her. I tell stories to the others, and in exchange they give me coffee from their thermoses and hefty ham sandwiches they bring from home. The snail-woman has been transferred to Room 0, she is nearing the end. Every day Elvira's husband tells me, "Your daughter is more alert," but I can read in his eyes that deep down he doesn't believe that. I have shown them photographs of your wedding and told them the story of your life. They know you very well by now, and some weep quietly when Ernesto comes and hugs you and whispers in your ear. Your husband is as tired as I am; he has dark circles under his eyes, and his clothes hang loose on him.

Willie came again from San Francisco. He tries to come often, to ease this long separation that seems to go on forever. When we made our commitment four years ago, we promised we would never be apart, but life has taken it upon itself to sabotage our plans. My husband is pure force, with as many virtues as he has defects; he swallows all the air around him and leaves me shaking, but it really does me good to be with him. Beside him, I sleep without pills, anesthetized by security and the warmth of his body. When I wake up, he brings me coffee in bed and makes me stay an hour longer, resting, while he goes to the hospital to relieve the night nurse. He sits in the waiting room in his faded blue jeans, work boots, black leather jacket, and a beret like the one my grandfather wore, which he bought in the Plaza Mayor. Despite his outfit, he looks like a Genoese sailor from centuries ago, and I expect someone to stop him in the street to ask him for navigational charts to the New World. He greets the patients in a Mexican-accented slang, and sits beside your bed to rub your hands and talk to you about what we will do when you come to California, while the other patients watch with amazement. Willie cannot hide his concern; in his role as a lawyer he has seen countless accident cases, and he has little hope that you will recover. He is preparing me for the worst.

"We will take care of her, many families do it, we aren't the only ones. Looking after Paula and loving her will give us new purpose, we'll learn a different form of happiness. We can go on with our lives and take Paula with us wherever we are. What's the problem?" he asks consolingly, with that generous and slightly ingenuous pragmatism that seduced me the moment we met.

"No!" I replied, not realizing I was shouting. "I won't listen to your dark predictions. Paula will get well!"

"You're obsessed. She's all you talk about, all you think about. You're falling off the edge so fast you can't stop yourself. You won't let me help you, you don't want to listen to reason. You must put some emotional distance between the two of you or you'll go nuts. And if you get sick, who will look after Paula? Please let me take care of you. . . ."

The healers come in the evenings; I don't know how they get in, but they are determined to bring you energy and health. In their everyday lives they are clerks, technicians, officials, ordinary people, but in their free time they study esoteric sciences and attempt to cure with the power of their convictions. They are sure they can charge the spent batteries of your sickly body, that your spirit is growing, renewing itself, and that from this immobility will emerge a different and better woman. They say I must not look at you with a mother's eyes, but with the golden eye, and then I will see you floating on another plane, imperturbable and indifferent to the terror and misery of this hospital room. They also, however, counsel me to be prepared, because if you have fulfilled your destiny in this world and are ready to continue the long voyage of the soul, you will not come back. They are part of a world organization and are in communication with other healers, so that they, too, will send you strength, just as the nuns are in contact with other congregations praying for you; they say that your recovery depends on your own will to live: the ultimate decision is in your hands. I don't dare tell any of this to my family in California, I know they would not look favorably on these spiritual physicians. Ernesto does not approve of their invasion, either; he does not want his wife to be a public spectacle, but I don't see how it can harm you, you're not even aware of them. The nuns participate in the ceremonies, too; they ring the Tibetan prayer bells, burn incense, and implore their Christian God and all the heavenly court, while the other patients watch the healing ceremonies with a certain reserve. Don't be afraid, Paula, they're not dancing with feathers pasted to their bodies or wringing roosters' necks to sprinkle you with blood, they merely fan you a little to remove any negative energy, then place their hands on your body, close their eyes, and concentrate. They ask me to help, to imagine a beam of light entering the top of my head, passing down through my body and coming out of my hands toward you, to visualize you healthy, and to stop crying, because sadness contaminates the air and perturbs the soul. I don't know whether any of this does any good, but one thing is sure: the spirit of the rest of us in the room has changed, we're happier. We have decided to control our sadness: we tune the radio to lively music, we share cookies, and we warn visitors not to come with long faces. The story hour has also been enlarged, now I'm not the only one telling, everyone is taking part. The most loquacious is Elvira's husband with a geyser of anecdotes; we take turns telling each other our lives, and when we run out of personal adventures, we begin to invent them, and from so much embroidering and giving free rein to our imaginations, we have perfected our form, and people come from other rooms to listen. In the bed where the snail-woman used to be, we have a new patient, a small dark girl covered with cuts and bruises, raped by four brutes in a park. Her belongings are marked with a red circle and the staff will not touch her without gloves, but we incorporate her into the strange family in this room, and wash her and feed her. At first, she thought she had awakened in an insane asylum, and covered her head with the sheet and shivered, but little by little, between the Tibetan bells, the radio music, and our baring our souls, she gained confidence and has begun to smile. She has become a friend of the nuns and the healers, and because she can't lift her head from her pillow, she asks me to read her gossip about movie stars and European royalty. Opposite Elvira now is a patient named Aurelia, who has been transferred here from the Department of Psychiatry; she suffers from convulsions and must have an operation for the brain tumor that causes them. At dawn on the day scheduled for her surgery, she carefully dressed and put on her makeup, told each of us goodbye with a warm hug, and left. "Good luck," "We'll be thinking about you," "Be of good cheer," we called as she went down the corridor. When they brought the bed to take her to the pavilion of torture she was gone; she had left the hospital and would not return until two days later, after the police had given up looking for her. A second day was set for the operation, and a second time they could not perform it, now because Aurelia had stuffed herself with half a *serrano* ham she had hidden in her purse and the anesthetist said he would be crazy to work with her under those conditions. Now the surgeon has gone off on his Easter vacation and who knows how long it will be until an operating room is available but, at least for the moment, our friend is safe. She attributes the source of her illness to the fact that her husband is "imminent"; from her gestures, I deduce she means "impotent." "It's *his* dinkus that doesn't work and *my* noodle they're going to split open," she laments with resignation. "If he could just do it, I'd be happy as a clam, and being sick would go right out of my mind. All the proof you need is that my spells began on our honeymoon, when old limp-wick was more interested in listening to boxing matches on the radio than in my nightgown with marabou trim."

Aurelia dances and sings flamenco; she speaks in rhymes and, unless I keep a close watch, she sprays you with her lilac perfume and paints your lips bright red. She makes fun of doctors, healers, and nuns alike, she thinks they are all a gang of butchers. "If your daughter hasn't been cured up till now by her mother's and her husband's love, then there's nothing to be done," she says. In the meantime, the police drop by to question the raped girl, and the way they treat her you would think she was the perpetrator, not the victim, of the crime. "What were you doing alone in that neighborhood at ten o'clock at night? Why didn't you scream? Were you on drugs? This is what happens when you go out looking for trouble, Missy, I don't know what you're complaining about." Aurelia is the only one with enough brass to take them on. She plants herself before them with her hands on her hips, and bawls them out. "Cut that crap, this isn't what you're paid to do. It's always us women who get the short end of the stick." "Keep out of this, now," they reply indignantly, "this doesn't have anything to do with you," but the rest of us applaud, because except for her seizures, Aurelia is amazingly lucid. She has three suitcases of flashy clothes under her bed, and changes several times a day; she piles on the makeup and whips her hair into a mousse of bleached curls. At the least provocation, she strips to show us her Renaissance flesh, and challenges us to guess her age and to look at her waist—the same measurement as before she was married. It runs in the family, she says, her mother was a beauty, too. And she adds with a touch of pique that her attributes don't do her much good since her husband is a eunuch. When he comes to visit, he sits dozing in a chair, bored, while she insults him and the rest of us make a tremendous effort to pretend we don't hear.

Willie is finding out where to take you, Paula—we need more science and fewer exorcisms—while I try to convince the doctors to let you leave and Ernesto to accept the necessity. He doesn't want to be separated from you, but there is no other alternative. This morning the two girls from rehabilitation came and for the first time decided to take you down to therapy on the ground floor. I was ready in my white uniform and went with them, pushing the wheelchair; there are so many people in this place, and everyone has seen me so long in the corridors, that no one doubts I'm a nurse. The head therapist needed only a superficial glance to decide he couldn't do anything for you: "Her level of consciousness is zero," he said, "she cannot obey instructions of any kind, and she has an open tracheotomy. I can't be responsible for a patient in that condition." That decided me to take you from this hospital and from Spain at the first possible moment, even though I can't imagine the trip. Even taking you a couple of floors on an elevator is a exercise that requires military strategy; a twenty-hour flight from Madrid to California is unimaginable, but I will find a way.

I obtained a wheelchair and with the help of Elvira's husband sat you in it, tied to the back with a twisted sheet because you crumple as if you had no bones. I took you to the chapel for a few minutes, and then out on the terrace. Aurelia, in the blue velvet robe that makes her look like a bird of paradise, went with me, and along the way made faces if anyone seemed too curious and stared at you. The truth is, Paula, you do look awful. I stopped the chair facing the park, among the dozens of pigeons that gather for bread crumbs. "I'm going to cheer Paula up a little," Aurelia said, and she began to sing and dance and twirl her hips with such gusto that we were soon surrounded with spectators. Suddenly, you opened your eyes, blinking at first, dazzled by the sunlight and fresh air you hadn't had in such a long time, and when finally your eyes focused you saw before you the novel spectacle of a plump middle-aged woman in blue dancing an impassioned flamenco in the midst of a whirlwind of startled pigeons. You raised your eyebrows with an expression of amazement, and I have no idea what passed through your mind, Paula; you began to cry with heartrending sadness, tears of impotence and fear. I hugged you, and explained everything that had happened, that for now you can't move but gradually you will recover, that you can't speak because you have a hole in your throat and the air doesn't reach your mouth, but when we close it you will be able to tell us everything, and that your task at this stage is just to breathe deeply. I told you that I love you, Paula, and will never leave you alone. After a while, you grew more calm. You never took your eyes from my face, and I think you recognized me, but maybe I imagined that. In the meantime, Aurelia suffered one of her attacks, and that was the end of our first adventure in the wheelchair. It is the neurologist's opinion that the crying doesn't mean anything. He can't understand why you continue in this static condition; he fears brain damage and told me that he has scheduled a series of tests for the beginning of next week. I don't want more examinations, I only want to wrap you in a blanket and run with you in my arms to the other side of the earth, where you have a family waiting for you.

THIS IMMOBILITY IS A STRANGE EXPERIENCE. THE DAYS ARE MEASURED grain by grain in an hourglass of patient sand, so slow the calendar does not record them. It seems I have been forever in this wintry city of churches, statues, and imperial avenues. All the resources of magic are futile, messages in bottles thrown into the sea with the hope they will be found on some distant shore and someone will come to rescue us—until now, however, there has been no answer. Through forty-nine years of a life of action and struggle, I have run after goals I can no longer recall, pursuing something nameless that was always a little farther on. Now I am forced to inaction and silence; no matter how much I run I get nowhere, and if I scream, no one hears. You, Paula, have given me this silence in which to examine my path through the world, to return to the true and the fantastic pasts, to recover memories others have forgotten, to remember what never happened and what still may happen. Absent, mute, paralyzed, you are my guide. Time moves so slowly. Or perhaps it doesn't move at all and it is we who pass through it. I have day after day to reflect, with nothing to do, only wait, while you lie in this mysterious state, like an insect in a cocoon. I ask myself what kind of butterfly will emerge when you awake. . . . I spend my hours by your side, writing. Elvira's husband brings me coffee and asks me why I put so much effort into this endless letter you cannot read. You will read it some day, I'm sure, and you will make fun of me in that teasing way you use to demolish my sentimentalism. Looking back, I view the totality of my fate and, with a little luck, I shall find meaning for the person I am. With a brutal expenditure of energy, I have been rowing upstream all my life. I am tired, I want to turn around, drop the oars, and let the current carry me gently toward the sea. My grandmother wrote in her notebooks to safeguard the fleeting fragments of the days and outwit loss of memory. I am trying to distract death. My thoughts swirl in inexhaustible eddies; you, on the other hand, are fixed in a static present, totally aloof from loss of the past or presages of the future. I am frightened. I have known fear before, but there was always an escape; even during the terror of the military coup there was the salvation of exile. Now I am in a blind alley with all doors closed to hope, and I don't know how to handle so much fear.

I imagine that you would prefer to hear about the happiest part of your childhood, the days when Granny was still alive, and your parents loved each other, and Chile was your country, but this notebook is coming to the seventies, when things began to change. I was very slow to realize that history had made such an abrupt about-face. In September 1970, Salvador Allende was elected president by a coalition of Marxists, Socialists, Communists, segments of the disillusioned middle class, and Christian radicals, all of whom grouped together under the emblem of the Popular Unity, determined to embark on a program of transition toward socialism without altering the nation's long bourgeois and democratic tradition. Despite evident contradictions in such a project, a wave of irrational hope mobilized many, many people in the society who had been waiting for the emergence of a New Man, a more generous, compassionate, and just individual motivated by high ideals. At the very instant Allende's triumph was proclaimed, his adversaries began to sabotage it, and the wheel of fortune took a tragic turn. The night of the election I did not go out in the street to celebrate with Allende's supporters, not wanting to offend my in-laws and my grandfather, who feared the rise in Chile of a new Stalin. Allende triumphed with his fourth candidacy, although there had been a widespread belief that he had used up his luck in the three earlier, failed campaigns. The Popular Unity doubted he could win, and came very close to choosing Pablo Neruda as its candidate. The poet had no political ambition, and he felt old and exhausted; he was interested only in his bride: poetry. Nevertheless, as a disciplined member of the

Communist Party, he was prepared to respect orders. When, after many internal discussions among party members, Salvador Allende finally was designated the official candidate, Neruda was the first to smile in relief and rush to congratulate him. The deep wound that split the country into irreconcilable factions began during that campaign, when families were divided, couples dissolved, and friendships lost. My father-in-law covered the walls of his house with rightist propaganda. We argued passionately, but stopped short of insults, because the affection we both felt for Granny and the children was stronger than our differences. At that time, Michael's father was still a handsome, healthy man, but the slow decline that would lead to the abyss of oblivion had already begun. He spent the mornings in bed wrapped up in his mathematics, and religiously followed the three soap operas that consumed a good part of the afternoon; sometimes he didn't dress at all, but wandered around in pajamas and slippers, waited on by his wife, who brought him his food on a tray. His obsession with washing his hands became uncontrollable: his skin was ulcerated and his elegant fingers like condor claws. He believed in his candidate's victory, but occasionally felt a twinge of doubt. In rhythm with the approaching elections, winter began to abate and spring burst into bud. Granny, busy in the kitchen with the first preserves of the season and with her grandchildren, did not participate in the political discussions but became very upset when she heard our heated voices. That year I became aware that my mother-in-law was secretly drinking, but she did it so discreetly no one else noticed.

On election day, those most surprised by their triumph were the winners; they honestly had not expected it. Behind the closed doors and windows of upper-class neighborhoods the defeated shuddered, convinced that the class hatred built up over centuries would cause mob violence, but that never happened, only peaceful demonstrations of rejoicing. A crowd chanting "The people, united, will never be defeated" marched through the streets waving banners and flags as the United States embassy staff met in emergency session. The North Americans had begun to conspire a year earlier, financing rightist extremists and trying to seduce certain generals sympathetic to a coup. In the barracks, a military in a state of alert awaited instructions. Tío Ramón and my mother were happy that Salvador Allende had won. Tata acknowledged his defeat, and, when Allende unexpectedly visited my parents' home that same night, he made an effort to greet him like the gentleman he was. The next day, as on any other day, I went to work; I found the building abuzz with contradictory rumors and the owner of the publishing house stealthily packing his cameras and readying his private plane to fly him, his family, and a major portion of his belongings out of the country, while a private sentry stood guard over his Italian racing car to prevent the supposedly inflamed rabble from defacing it. "We will carry on as if nothing has happened," Delia Vergara announced, using the same tone Miss St. John had employed years before in Lebanon when she decided to ignore the war. And so we did for the next three years. At dawn on the morning after the election, my father-in-law was one of the first in line at the bank to withdraw his money; he was planning to flee the country as soon as the Cuban hordes debarked or Soviet communists began executing Chilean citizens. "I'm not going anywhere, I'm staying here with my babies," Granny assured me, weeping behind her husband's back. The grandchildren had become her reason for living. But the moment for flight was postponed and the tickets lay on the mantelpiece, always at hand but never used, because none of the worst predictions ever came to pass: no one took the nation by assault, the borders remained open, there were no firing squads, as my father-in-law feared, and Granny stood firm that no Marxist would separate her from her grandchildren, certainly not one who had the same name as her daughter-in-law.

As there was no absolute majority, the congress was called on to decide the election. Until then, the rule of plurality had always been respected and the candidate who had one vote more than any other won, but, in this instance, the Popular Unity had awakened too much distrust. A long tradition, however, outweighed the fear of the parliamentarians and the power of the U.S. embassy, and after long deliberations by the congress—which was dominated by Christian Democrats—a document was drawn up demanding that Allende respect constitutional guarantees. He signed it and two months later, in a solemn ceremony, accepted the presidential sash. For the first time in history, a Marxist had been elected by democratic vote; the eyes of the world were on Chile. Pablo Neruda was appointed ambassador to France, where a year later he was informed he had won the Nobel Prize for Literature. When the aged King of Sweden handed him the gold medal, the poet dedicated it to all Chileans— "because my poetry belongs to my nation."

President Allende named Tío Ramón ambassador to Argentina, and so my mother became the administratrix of an enormous edifice on the one hill in Buenos Aires, with several grand salons, a dining room for forty-eight guests, two libraries, twenty-three bathrooms, and an indeterminate number of valuable rugs and artworks left from previous governments, a luxe difficult to reconcile with the Popular Unity, which aspired to an image of austerity and simplicity. There were so many service personnel—chauffeurs, cooks, waiters, chambermaids, and gardeners—that it took the acumen of a quartermaster to organize work and eating schedules. The kitchen functioned full-time, preparing cocktail parties, luncheons, ladies' teas, official banquets, and diets for my mother, who had developed stomach trouble from all her responsibilities. Although she barely tasted them, she invented recipes that made the embassy table famous. One of her triumphs was a turkey, presented intact, with feathers fanned from its rump and staring eyes; with the removal of four pins the skin peeled off like a dress to reveal moist meat and a body cavity stuffed with small birds that were in turn stuffed with almonds—a thousand light years from my Lebanese school lunches of slices of liver floating in tepid water. At one of those feasts, I met the most celebrated seer in Buenos Aires. She was sitting across the table from me, and never took her eyes off me until the meal was over. She must have been about sixty, aristocratic in appearance, and dressed in black in a somber and rather antiquated style. As we left the dining room she came up to me, saying she would like to talk with me in private; my mother introduced her as María Teresa Juárez, and accompanied us to a library. Without a word, the woman sat down on a sofa and pointed me to a place by her side; she took my hands, held them in hers for a few minutes that, not knowing what she intended, seemed very long, and finally made four predictions. I wrote them down at the time, and have never forgotten them: There will be a bloodbath in your country, You will be motionless or paralyzed for a long time, Your only path is writing, and One of your children will be known in many parts of the world. Which of them? my mother wanted to know. The seer asked to see their photographs, studied them for a few seconds, and then pointed to you, Paula. As the other three predictions have been fulfilled, I suppose the last will be too; that gives me hope that you will not die, since you haven't lived out your destiny. As soon as we leave this hospital, I intend to contact that lady, if she is still alive, and ask what she sees for you in the future.

Tío Ramón, enthusiastic about his mission in Argentina, opened the door of the embassy to politicians, intellectuals, press— anything and anybody that would contribute to Salvador Allende's project. Seconded by my mother, who demonstrated great fortitude, organization, and courage during those three years, he dedicated himself to normalizing the difficult relations between Chile and Argentina, two neighbors that had had considerable friction in the past and now had to overcome the suspicion inspired by the Chilean socialist experiment. In hours he stole from sleep, my stepfather examined the inventory and the nettlesome embassy accounts to assure that no funds were lost in excess or oversight. Every move of the Popular Unity was scrutinized by its political enemies, who were always on the lookout for the slightest excuse to denigrate its actions. His first surprise was the budget for security; he questioned his colleagues in the diplomatic corps and discovered that private bodyguards had become a real problem in Buenos Aires. What had begun as protection against kidnapping and assassinations had spiraled out of control, and by that time the guards numbered more than thirty thousand and were still growing. These private security forces constituted a true military unit, armed to the teeth, lacking ethics, superior officers, norms, or rules, and promoting terror to justify their own existence. It was an open secret that it was easy to kidnap or assassinate someone; all that was necessary was to meet the sum demanded by the guards and they would take on the task themselves. Tío Ramón, however, decided to take the risk, and fired his guards because he believed that the representative of a people's

government could not be surrounded by hired killers. Soon thereafter, a bomb exploded in the consulate that reduced lamps and
windows to a mountain of crystal dust and forever destroyed the
nerves of my mother's Swiss dog, but no one was wounded. To
smooth over the scandal, a press release was issued blaming the
incident on a faulty gas line. That was the first terrorist attempt my
parents confronted in Buenos Aires. Four years later, they would
have to slip away in the dead of night to save their skins. When they
accepted the post they had no concept of how much work was
required in that embassy, Chile's most important after Washington,
but they used experience accumulated through a lifetime of diplomatic service to fulfill their mission, and did it with such brilliance
that they would pay for it with many years of exile.

In the next three years, the government of the Popular Unity
nationalized Chile's natural resources—copper, iron, nitrates, coal—
which had been in foreign hands for years, refusing to pay even a
symbolic dollar of compensation. It dramatically expanded agrarian
reform, dividing among campesinos the large landholdings of the
old and powerful families, an act that unleashed unprecedented
hatred; it broke up monopolies that for decades had impeded competition in the marketplace and forced those companies to sell their
goods at a price within reach of most Chileans. Children were given
milk at school, clinics were organized in marginal neighborhoods,
and the incomes of the very poorest were raised to reasonable levels. These changes were cause for jubilant popular demonstrations
in support of the government; nevertheless, Allende's own supporters refused to face the fact that the reforms had to be paid for and
that the solution did not lie in printing more money. It was not long
before the onset of economic chaos and political violence. Outside
Chile, the changes were being followed with great interest, for here
was a small Latin American nation that had chosen the path of
peaceful revolution. Abroad, Allende had always enjoyed the image
of a progressive leader determined to improve the lot of workers
and to overcome economic and social injustices, but inside Chile
half the population detested him and the country was irreconcilably
divided. The United States, edgy about the possibility that Allende's

ideas might succeed and socialism spread irrevocably through the remainder of the continent, withdrew its credit and set up an economic blockade. Undermining from the Right, and errors by the Popular Unity itself, produced a crisis of never-before-seen proportions; inflation reached such astronomic numbers that it was impossible to know in the morning how much a liter of milk would cost by evening. There was paper money to burn, but very little to buy with it; long lines formed to buy essential products: oil, toothpaste, sugar, automobile tires. A black market was inevitable. For my birthday, my friends at work gave me two rolls of toilet paper and a can of condensed milk, the most coveted products of the moment. Like everybody in Chile, we were victims of anxiety about shortages. Sometimes we stood in line only out of fear of missing something, even if the reward was yellow shoe polish. A new occupation sprang up, hustlers who held your place in line, or bought products at the official price and then sold them for twice that amount. Nicolás became expert at getting cigarettes for Granny. My mother, through mysterious channels, sent me boxes of food from Buenos Aires, but her instructions were often garbled and we would receive a gallon of soy sauce or two dozen jars of pickled onions. In exchange we sent her grandchildren to her every two or three months. They traveled by themselves, with name and identification on signs around their necks. Tío Ramón convinced them that the magnificent embassy was his summer home, and if the children had ever had any doubt about their princely origins, it was thereby dissipated. To keep them from being bored, he gave them jobs in his office; the first wages of their lives were received from the hands of their formidable grandfather for services rendered as subsecretaries to the consulate's secretaries. That was also where they suffered through mumps and chicken pox, hiding in the twenty-three bathrooms so no one could take the stool sample needed for a medical examination.

We Chileans had always taken great pride in the fact that our chiefs of state had no bodyguards and that the courtyard of the Palacio de La Moneda was a public street. That all ended with Salvador Allende. Hatred had been aggravated to such a degree that associates feared for his life. His enemies were accumulating supplies to ambush him. This socialist president roared through the streets with twenty armed men in a flotilla of identical blue automobiles, none with distinctive markings, so that no one could know which one he was in. Before Allende, the president had lived in his own home, but Allende's house was small and did not lend itself to that role. So amid a barrage of hateful criticism, the government acquired a mansion in an upper-class neighborhood to serve as the official residence, and the Allende family was transported there with pre-Columbian ceramics, paintings collected over long years, works of art given by the artists themselves, inscribed first editions of books, and photographs recording important moments of Allende's political career. I had the opportunity to attend one or two gatherings in the new residence, where still the only topic of conversation was politics. When my parents came from Argentina, the president invited us to a summer house high in the hills near the capital, where he liked to spend weekends. After lunch we watched absurd cowboy movies, which he found relaxing. The bedrooms that opened onto the patio were occupied by a group of volunteer body-guards that Allende called "my personal friends" and whom his opposition qualified as terrorist guerrillas and murderers. Some of them were always around, alert, armed, and prepared to protect him with their own bodies. One of those days in the country, Allende tried to teach us to target shoot with a rifle given him by Fidel Castro, the same weapon found beside his body the day of the military coup. I, who had never held a gun in my hands, and had grown up on Tata's adage that "The Devil loads the charge in firearms," grabbed the rifle as if it were an umbrella and in clumsily shifting my grasp unwittingly pointed it at Allende's head. One of the guards immediately materialized out of thin air, jumped on me, and rolled me to the ground. That is one of the few memories I have of Allende during the three years of his government. I saw him less than I had before; I was not involved in politics and in fact continued to work at the publishing house he considered his worst enemy, without any idea of what was happening in the country.

Who was Salvador Allende? I don't really know, and it would be pretentious of me to offer a definitive portrait of him; it would take volumes, anyway, to describe his complex personality, the difficulty of his program, and the role he occupies in history. For years, I thought of him as just another uncle in a large family, the one representative on my father's side; it was only after his death and after leaving Chile that I became aware of his legendary dimensions. In private, he was a good friend to his friends and loyal to the point of imprudence; he could not conceive of betrayal and when he was betrayed found it nearly impossible to believe. I remember how quick he was with answers, and his sense of humor. He had been defeated in two campaigns but was still young when a journalist asked him what he would like to have engraved on his tombstone, and he replied instantly, *Here lies the future president of Chile.* In my view, his most outstanding characteristics were integrity, intuition, courage, and charisma: he followed his hunches, which rarely failed him, he did not turn away from risk, and he had the ability to captivate both masses and individuals. It was said that he could manipulate any situation to his advantage and that was why on the day of the coup the generals did not dare face him in person but chose to communicate by telephone and through messengers. He assumed the role of president with such dignity that it seemed arrogance; he had the bombastic gestures of a classical orator, and a characteristic way of walking with his chest out and holding himself very straight, almost on tiptoe, like a fighting cock. He slept very little at night, only three or four hours; you would see him at dawn reading or playing chess with his most faithful friends, but he could sleep for only a few minutes, usually in his automobile, and wake refreshed. He was a refined man, a lover of pedigreed dogs, objets d'art, elegant clothes, and strong women. He was very careful of his health, and prudent with food and alcohol. His enemies accused him of being a womanizer, and kept a close accounting of his bourgeois tastes, his lovers, his suede jackets, and silk neckties. Half the population feared he would lead the country into a Communist dictatorship and were ready to prevent that at any cost, while the other half celebrated the socialist experiment with murals of flowers and doves.

All this time, I was on another planet, doing my frivolous magazine articles and zany television programs, never suspecting the true proportions of the violence gestating in the shadows that finally would fall over all of us. In the midst of the national crisis, Delia, my boss at the magazine, sent me to interview Salvador Allende and ask what he thought about Christmas. We were readying the December issue some months in advance and in October it was not easy to approach a president who had urgent matters of state on his mind. I took advantage, however, of one of Allende's visits to my parents' home and timidly broached the subject to him. "Don't ask me bullshit like that, Isabel," was his bald reply. And so began and ended my career as a political correspondent. I continued to knock out homemade horoscopes, articles on interior decoration, gardens, and raising children, interviews with the odd and bizarre, the lovelorn column, and pieces on culture, art, and travel. Delia didn't trust me; she accused me of making up my interviews without ever leaving the house, and of putting my own opinions in the mouths of my subjects, and so she rarely gave me important assignments.

As problems of scarcities grew worse, the tension became unbearable and Granny began drinking more heavily. Following her husband's instructions, she joined her neighbors in the streets to protest food shortages in the traditional way: beating pots and pans. The men stayed out of sight while women marched with frying pans and cooking spoons in an apocalyptic clatter. That sound is unforgettable: it would begin with a solitary gong, then clanging was added from various other patios until the contagion spread and everyone got into the spirit; soon the women were out in the street and a deafening racket turned half the city into a living hell. Granny always tried to position herself at the head of a demonstration in order to prevent it from passing our house, where everyone knew one of the Allende family lived. Even so, in the eventuality that some bellicose ladies were moved to attack, the hose was always at the ready to dissuade them with streams of cold water. Ideological differences had not altered my camaraderie with my mother-in-law; we shared the children, the burdens of everyday life, our plans and hopes, and in our hearts we both thought nothing could separate us. To provide her a bit of independence, I opened a bank account in her name, but after three months had to close it because Granny never understood the mechanics of the transactions; she thought that as long as she had checks in the checkbook there was money in the account. She never wrote down what she spent, and in less than a week had used all her funds buying gifts for her grandchildren. Neither did politics alter the peace between Michael and me; we loved each other and were good companions.

It was then that my passion for theater began. Tío Ramón was named ambassador just at the time that kidnapping public figures became the vogue throughout Latin America. The possibility that it might happen to him served as inspiration for a play in which a group of guerrillas kidnaps a diplomat to exchange him for political prisoners. I dashed it off in a frenzy; I sat down at the typewriter and couldn't sleep or eat until I wrote the final word three days later. A prestigious theater company agreed to produce it, and so one night I found myself reading it with the actors, all of us sitting around a table on a cold, drafty, bare stage under a single lightbulb, wearing our overcoats and clutching thermos bottles with hot tea. Each actor read and analyzed his part, pointing out the whopping errors in the text. As the reading progressed, I slid farther and farther down in my chair, until I was barely visible above the table. At the end, thoroughly ashamed, I picked up the scripts and went home and rewrote the play from the first line, studying each character separately to give him or her coherence. The second version was better, but it lacked tension and a dramatic denouement. I attended all the rehearsals and incorporated most of the modifications suggested to me, and in so doing learned a few tricks that would prove to be helpful for my novels. Ten years later, when I was writing *The House of the Spirits,* I remembered those sessions around the table in the empty theater and tried to give each character a complete biography, a defined personality, and an individual voice—although, in the case of that book, the outrages of history and a tenacious lack of discipline on the part of the spirits undercut my intentions. The play, logically enough, was called *The Ambassador,* and I dedicated it to Tío Ramón, who did not get to see it because he was in Buenos Aires. It opened to good reviews but I could not take credit because it was actually the director and actors who made the work—only a few strands of my original idea survived. I do wonder sometimes whether it may not have saved my stepfather from being kidnapped, because, according to the law of probabilities, it was impossible that what I had written for the stage could happen in real life. It did not, I am sorry to say, protect another diplomat who was abducted in Uruguay and forced to undergo the ordeals I had imagined in the security of my home in Santiago. Now I am more careful about what I write, because I have found out that although something is not true today, it may be true tomorrow. A different theater company asked me for a play, and for them I wrote two musical comedies that we called *café-concierto* for lack of a better name, and they enjoyed an unexpected success. The second piece was memorable because it included a chorus of fat women to enliven the spectacle with singing and dancing. It was not easy to find attractive, over-weight soubrettes willing to make fools of themselves on the stage, so the director and I took up positions on a busy corner in the center of the city and stopped every fleshy prospect we saw go by to ask if she would like to be an actress. Many accepted enthusiastically, but as soon as they understood the demands of the work couldn't get away fast enough. It took several weeks to find six aspirants for the role. There was no space in the theater because of the current production, so we moved all the furniture out of our small living room and rehearsed there. We did have an out-of-tune piano which, in a flight of fancy, I had painted lime green and decorated with a courtesan reclining on a divan. The entire house shook with seismic shuddering when that monumental chorus minced as Greek vestal virgins, bopped to the rhythm of rock 'n' roll, flirted petti-coats in a frenetic cancan, and pirouetted on point to the chords of a *Swan Lake* that would have given Tchaikovsky a heart attack. Michael had to reinforce both the stage and the floor of our house to prevent their giving way beneath that pachydermal onslaught. The women, who had never had a day's physical exercise, began to shed pounds at an alarming rate, and to save that sensuous flesh from melting away, Granny fed them great pots of creamed noodles and apple tarts. For the opening of the play, we put up a sign in the foyer requesting that instead of sending the chorus girls flowers, please to order pizza. With these efforts, we were able to preserve the rounded hills and deep valleys of vast carnal topographies throughout two long years of arduous performances, including a national tour. Michael was enthusiastic about this artistic adventure, and attended so often that he knew the parts by heart and in an emergency could have replaced any of the actors, including the voluminous vestal virgins. You and Nicolás learned the songs, too, and ten years later, when I couldn't remember even the titles, you two could perform them from start to finish. My grandfather went several times, first out of a sense of family, and then for the pleasure, and every time the curtain fell he jumped to his feet with hurrahs and applause and flourishes of his cane. He fell in love with the chorus girls and offered long disquisitions on plumpness as an element of beauty and the sin against nature represented by the undernourished models in fashion magazines. His ideal of beauty was embodied in the owner of his liquor shop, with her Valkyrian breasts and epic buttocks and the good nature that prompted her to sell him gin disguised in bottles for mineral water. He dreamed of her on the sly, so Memé's vigilant ghost would not catch him in the act.

When Aurelia, the epileptic poet in your ward, dances in her disheveled boas and polka-dotted dresses, she reminds me of those massive ballerinas, and also of a personal adventure. Bedizened in her theatrical garb, Aurelia in middle age dances a meaner fandango than I ever did in my youth. One day an ad appeared in the newspaper offering work in a follies theater to young, tall, pretty girls. My boss at the magazine asked me to apply for the job, get behind the scenes, and write an article on the lives of those "pitiful women" as she, in her feminist rigor, classified them. I was nowhere close to meeting the minimal requirements, but this was one of those assignments no one else wanted to try. I didn't have the nerve to go alone, so I asked a good friend to go with me. We got all dolled up in the kinds of kinky clothes we supposed showgirls wore when not performing, and stuck a rhinestone brooch in my dog's topknot, a mutt we baptized Fifi for the occasion but whose real name was Dracula. When Michael saw how we were dressed, he decided we should not step outside the house without protection, and, since we didn't have anyone to leave the children with, they came along, too. The theater was in the center of the city; it was impossible to park anywhere near, and we had to walk several blocks. My friend and I took the lead—I with Dracula in my arms—and Michael, our knight in shining armor, brought up the rear with a child's hand in each of his. It was like parading through a bull ring: men charged appreciatively, suggesting a little tossing and goring, and shouting "Olé!", all of which we took as a good sign. There was a long line at the box office, only men, of course, most of them old, but also a few recruits on their day off, and a class of noisy adolescents in school uniform who naturally fell silent when they 'saw us. The porter, as decrepit as the rest of the place, led us up a rickety stairway to the second floor. Cued by the movies, we expected to see an obese gangster type with a ruby ring and chewed cigar, but instead, in the bare, empty, dust-covered loft, we were greeted by a woman in a drab overcoat, wool cap, and gloves with cut-off fingers, who might have been someone's aunt from the country. She was sitting in a pool of light, sewing on a sequined dress. A coal brazier at her feet was the only source of heat, and in another chair lay a hugely fat cat that stiffened like a porcupine when it saw Dracula. In one corner stood a full-length, triple-leaf mirror with a chipped frame, and from the ceiling hung large plastic bags containing the costumes for the extravaganza, incongruous, iridescent-feathered birds in that lugubrious barn.

"We came about the ad," my friend said, affecting a heavy accent from the docks district.

The good woman looked us over from head to toe, with a dubious glint in her eye: we didn't exactly fit her notion of showgirls. She asked whether we had experience in the trade, and my friend reeled off her résumé: Her name was Gladys, she was a beauty operator by day and singer by night; she had a good voice but didn't know how to dance, although she was willing to learn, it couldn't be all that hard. And before I could say a word on my own, she pointed to me and added that her friend here was named Salomé and was a follies star with a string of successes in Brazil, in particular, one act in which she appeared nude on stage, then Fifi, the trained dog, brought her clothes in his mouth and a burly mulatto put them on her. The black artist hadn't come, she said, because he was in the hospital, where he had recently been operated on for appendicitis.

By the time she finished her spiel, the woman had stopped sewing and was observing us openmouthed.

"Strip," she told us. I think she suspected something.

With that total lack of modesty slim people have, my friend wiggled out of her clothes, stepped into some high-heeled gold slippers, and paraded before the woman in the moss-colored overcoat. It was unbelievably cold. "OK, no boobs, but we stuff everything here. Now for Salomé," and aunty pointed a peremptory finger at me.

This was not a detail I had anticipated, but I didn't dare refuse. Shivering, I took off my clothes; my teeth were chattering, and I realized with horror that I was wearing woolen knickers Mama Hilda had knitted for me. Still holding the dog, who never stopped growling at the cat, I stuck my feet into the two-sizes-too-large gold shoes and began my promenade, shuffling my feet like a wounded duck. Suddenly the mirror caught my eye: in triplicate, from all angles, I saw myself in nothing but the shoes and Dracula. It was a humiliation I have not recovered from to this day.

"You're too short, but not bad otherwise. We can stick longer plumes on your head and put you in the front row and it won't be noticed. The dog and the exotic man we can do without, we have our own acts here. Come tomorrow and start rehearsing. The salary isn't great, but if you're nice to the gentlemen the tips are good."

Euphoric, we rejoined Michael and the children outside, unable to absorb the tremendous honor of having got the job on our first try. What we didn't know was that there was an ongoing shortage of chorus girls, and that the impresarios were desperate enough to hire a chimpanzee. Only a few days later, I found myself dressed in what chorus girls really wear, that is, a spangled G-string, an emerald in my navel, glittering pasties on my nipples, and an ostrich headdress heavy as a sack of concrete. Behind, nothing. I looked at myself in the mirror and realized the audience would welcome me with a hail of tomatoes; spectators paid to see firm, professional flesh, not a mother of two who lacked the natural attributes of the office. To top everything off, a team from National Television had come to film the spectacle that night; they were installing their cameras while the choreographer was trying to teach me how to walk down

a stairway between two rows of gold-painted, rippling-muscled
gladiators holding lighted torches.

"Keep your head up, lower your shoulders, and smile, woman!,
stop staring at the floor, and as you walk, cross one leg slightly in
front of the other. Smile, I tell you! And don't flap your arms
because in all those feathers you look like a broody hen. Watch out
for the torches and try not to burn up the plumes, they cost a fortune! Wag the ass, suck in the belly, *breathe.* If you don't breathe,
you'll pass out."

I tried to do everything he said, but he sighed and placed a lan-
gorous hand over his eyes, while the torches burned down and the
Romans stared at the ceiling with bored expressions. In a thought-
less moment, I peered through the curtain and got a glimpse of the
audience, a noisy mass of males impatient at being kept waiting fifteen minutes. I could not face them; I decided that death was
preferable and ran for the exit. The television camera that had
filmed me from the front during the rehearsal, descending the stairway lighted by the Olympic torches of the gilded athletes, later
filmed the image of a real chorus girl descending the same stairway,
shot from behind after the curtain was open and the crowd howling
with appreciation. They edited the film at the TV station, and I
appeared with my own head and shoulders but with the perfect
body of the nation's brightest follies star. The gossip filtered across
the Andes to the ears of my parents in Buenos Aires. The honorable
ambassador was forced to explain to the tabloid press that the
cousin of President Allende had not danced naked in a pornographic extravaganza, it was merely an unfortunate coincidence of
names. My father-in-law was waiting to watch his favorite evening
program when he saw me in the buff, and the shock literally took
his breath away. The other reporters at the women's magazine celebrated my, shall we say, exposé on the world of the chorus girl, but
the head of the firm, a devout Catholic and father of five children,
considered it a grave affront. Among other activities, I was the editor of the one magazine for children on the market, and in his view
the scandal offered a regrettable example to the young. He called
me into his office to ask whether it was true I had been brassy
enough to exhibit my bare backside to all the nation, and I had to

confess that, unfortunately, it was not *my* backside he'd seen but an editing trick. He looked me up and down and immediately took my word for it. The affair had no major consequences elsewhere. You and Nicolás went off to school with a chip on your shoulder, telling anyone who wanted to listen that the lady with the plumes was indeed your mother; that short-circuited any teasing and even led to my signing a few autographs. Michael shrugged his shoulders and made no comment to friends who were envious of his wife's spectacular body. More than one of them looked at me with a puzzled expression, unable to imagine how or why I hid beneath long hippie dresses the amazing physical attributes I had so generously revealed on the TV screen. I was keeping a prudent distance from Tata, until a couple of days later when he called me, choked with laughter, to say that the program had been almost as good as the wrestling matches in the Teatro Caupolicán, and wasn't it marvelous how everything looked much better on television than it did in real life? Unlike her husband, who refused to leave the house for a week or two, Granny boasted about my feat. In private, she confessed that when she saw me descending that stairway between two rows of aureate gladiators, she felt fulfilled, because that had always been her most secret fantasy. My mother-in-law had begun to change by then; she seemed agitated, and sometimes hugged her grandchildren with tears in her eyes, as if she had an intuition that a terrible shadow was threatening her precarious happiness. The tensions in the country had reached the stage of violence, and she, with the deep sensitivity of the truly innocent, could sense something momentous in the air. She was drinking cheap *pisco,* and hiding the bottles in strategic places. You, Paula, who loved her with infinite compassion, discovered the hiding places one by one and without a word carried off the empty bottles and buried them among the dahlias in the garden.

In the meantime, worn down by the pressures and work in the embassy, my mother had gone to a clinic in Romania where the renowned Dr. Aslan was working miracles with her geriatric pills. Mother spent a month in a convent cell, recovering from real and imaginary ills and reviewing in her memory old scars from the past.

The room next to hers was occupied by a charming Venezuelan who was moved by her tears and one day worked up the courage to knock at her door. "What's the matter, my dear?" he asked as he introduced himself. "There is nothing that can't be cured with a little music and a drop of rum." For the next weeks, like two elderly, hired mourners, dressed in the regulation bathrobe and slippers, they took up lawn chairs beneath the cloudy skies of Bucharest, and told the stories of their lives to one another, holding back nothing because they expected never to meet again. My mother shared her past, and he in turn confided his secrets; she showed him some of my letters and he offered photographs of his wife and his children, the one true passion of his life. At the end of the treatment, they met at the door of the hospital to say goodbye—my mother in her elegant travel outfit, rejuvenated by the prodigious art of Dr. Aslan, her green eyes washed by tears, and the Venezuelan caballero with his handsome suit and perfect smile—and very nearly did not recognize each other. Touched, he attempted to kiss the hand of that friend who had listened to his confessions, but she forestalled him by stepping closer and puting her arms around him. "I will never forget you," she told him. "If you ever need me, you have only to call," he replied. His name was Valentín Hernández; he was a powerful politician in his country, and a few years later when the winds of violence blew us in many directions he was essential to the future of our family.

My magazine and television reporting gave me a certain visibility; I was so often congratulated or insulted by people in the street that I came to think I was some kind of celebrity. During the winter of 1972, Pablo Neruda invited me to visit him at Isla Negra. The poet was not well; he had left his post at the embassy in Paris and returned to Chile and his coastal home to write his memoirs and his last poems facing the sea. I made meticulous preparations for that meeting; I bought a new recorder, wrote out lists of questions, I read two biographies and reread parts of his work—I even had the engine of my old Citroën checked so it would not fail me on such a delicate mission. The wind was whistling among the pines and eucalyptus, the sea was gray, and it was drizzling in that seaside town of

closed houses and empty streets. The poet lived in a labyrinth of
wood and stone, a capricious organism composed of added-on and
revamped rooms. A ship's bell, sculptures, and timbers from ship-
wrecks dominated the patio, and a bank of rocks offered a broad
vista of the beach and the tireless crashing of the Pacific Ocean. My
gaze was lost in a limitless expanse of dark water against a leaden
sky. Pure monotone of steel, gray upon gray, the landscape palpi-
tated. Pablo Neruda, with a poncho around his shoulders and a cap
crowning his great gargoyle head, welcomed me without formality.
He told me he enjoyed my humorous articles and sometimes pho-
tocopied them and sent them to friends. He was weak, but he found
the strength to lead me through the marvelous twists and turns of
that cave crammed with his trove of modest treasures and to show
me his collections of seashells, bottles, dolls, books, and paintings.
He was an inexhaustible collector: *I love all things, not only the grand
but the infinitely small: thimble, spurs, plates, flower vases. . . .* He also
liked his food. For lunch we had baked sea bass, that white, firm-
fleshed fish that is king of Chile's seas, and dry white wine. He
talked about the memoirs he was trying to write before death bilked
him of the opportunity, about my articles—he suggested compiling
them in a book—and about how he had discovered his figureheads
all over the world, those enormous wood carvings with a siren's
face and breasts that graced the prow of ancient ships. "These
maidens were born to live among the waves," he said, "they are
miserable on dry land, that's why I rescue them and set them facing
the sea." He talked for a long time about the political situation,
which caused him great agony, and his voice broke when he spoke
of his country's being divided into violent extremes. Rightist newspapers were publishing six-column headlines: CHILEANS, SAVE YOUR
HATRED, YOU'LL NEED IT!, inciting the military to take power and
Allende either to renounce the presidency or commit suicide, as
President Balmaceda had done in the past century to avoid a civil
war.

"They should be more careful about what they ask, they might
get it," the poet sighed.

"There will never be a military coup in Chile, don Pablo. Our
armed forces respect democracy," I said, trying to reassure him

with the oft-repeated clichés. After lunch it began to rain; the room darkened and the foreboding woman on the figurehead came alive, stepped from the wood, and greeted us with a shiver of naked breasts. I realized then that the poet was weary, that the wine had gone to my head, and that I must hurry.

"If you like, we can do the interview now," I suggested.

"Interview?"

"Well, that's why I'm here, isn't it?"

"Interview *me*? I'd never put myself through that," he laughed. "My dear child, you must be the worst journalist in the country. You are incapable of being objective, you place yourself at the center of everything you do, I suspect you're not beyond fibbing, and when you don't have news, you invent it. Why don't you write novels instead? In literature, those defects are virtues."

As I am telling you this, Aurelia is preparing to recite a poem she wrote especially for you, Paula. I asked her not to do it, because her poems demoralize me, but she insists. She has no confidence in the doctors, and doesn't think you will get well.

"You think they have all conspired to lie to me, Aurelia?"

"Ah, what an innocent you are. Don't you see that they always protect one another? They will never admit they blew it with your daughter, they're all rascals with the power of life and death in their hands. This is me talking, a woman who has lived from hospital to hospital. If you only knew the things I've seen. . . ."

Her strange poem is about a bird with petrified wings. It says you are already dead, and that you want to leave but can't because I am holding you back, that I am an anchor tied to your feet.

"Don't try so hard, Isabel. Can't you see you're really fighting against her? Paula isn't here anymore; look at her eyes, they're like black water. If she doesn't know her mother, it's because she's already gone. Accept it once and for all."

"Don't say that, Aurelia. . . ."

"Let her talk, the mad don't lie," Elvira's husband sighs.

What is there on the other side of life? Only night silence and solitude? What remains when there are no more desires or memories or hope? What is there in death? If I could be still, without speaking or thinking, without begging, crying, remembering, hop-

ing, if I could submerse myself in the most absolute silence, then
perhaps I could hear you, my dearest daughter.

AT THE BEGINNING OF 1973, CHILE WAS LIKE A NATION AT WAR, THE
hatred that had gestated in shadow day after day had been vented in
strikes, sabotage, and acts of terrorism for which extremists of the
Left and the Right both blamed the other. Peasant groups appropri-
ated private lands to build their own agrarian communities, workers
occupied factories and nationalized them, and representatives of the
Popular Unity seized control of banks, creating such a climate of
insecurity that it took no great effort for the political opposition to
sow panic. Allende's enemies perfected to a science their methods
for aggravating economic problems: they circulated rumors of bank
closings, inciting people to withdraw their money, they burned
crops and slaughtered cattle, they pulled essential articles from the
market—from truck tires to minuscule pieces of the most sophisticated electronic apparatus. Without needles or cotton, the hospitals
were paralyzed, without spare parts for their machines, factories
could not operate. An entire industry might be stymied for want of
a single part, leaving thousands of workers in the street. In response,
workers organized into committees, threw out their bosses, took
authority into their own hands and set up camps at the gate, watching day and night to prevent the owners from destroying their own
enterprises. Bank employees and public administrators also set up
guards to keep colleagues of the opposite stripe from jumbling files
in the archives, destroying documents, or placing bombs in the
restrooms. They lost precious hours in interminable meetings trying to reach collective decisions but, as everyone fought for the
chance to expound his own point of view on every insignificant
detail, they rarely reached an accord: what a supervisor normally
had decided in five minutes took the employees a week of Byzantine
discussions and democratic votes. On a larger scale, the same thing
was happening in the government; the parties of the Popular Unity
shared power by quotas, and decisions passed through so many fil-

ters that when finally something was approved it bore little, if any, resemblance to the original project. Allende had no majority in the congress, and his projects all crashed against the unyielding wall of the opposition. Chaos spread; Chile was living in a climate of insecurity and latent violence, and the heavy machinery of the government was grinding to a halt. At night, Santiago had the look of a city devastated by a cataclysm, the streets were dark and nearly empty because so few people dared go anywhere on foot and public transportation was crippled by strikes and gasoline rationing. The bonfires of the *compañeros,* as government backers were called, blazed in the city center as they mounted an all-night guard over buildings and streets. Brigades of youthful Communists painted propagandistic murals on walls and bands of extreme rightists drove through the streets in automobiles with dark tinted-glass windows, firing blindly. In areas where agrarian reform had been effected, the landowners plotted revenge, equipped with weapons that came as contraband across the long frontier of the Andean cordillera. Thousands of head of cattle were driven to Argentina through passes in the south, and others were slaughtered to prevent their reaching the market. At times the rivers ran red with blood and the current carried swollen cadavers of dairy cows and fattened hogs. The campesinos, who had lived for centuries obeying orders, joined together in cooperatives, but they lacked initiative, knowledge, and credit. They did not know how to use their freedom, and many secretly longed for the return of the *patrón,* that authoritative and frequently despised father who at least gave clear orders and in times of trouble protected them against natural disasters, crop blight, and epidemic disease among their animals. The *patrón* had friends and could get what was needed; in contrast, they did not have the courage to enter a bank and, even if they did, were unable to decipher the small print on the papers put before them for their signature. Neither could they understand what the devil the advisers sent by the government were mumbling about, with their big words and city way of talking, people with clean fingernails who didn't know which end of a plow was up and had never pulled a breech calf from a cow's rear. These country folk, however, did not hold back grain for the next planting, they butchered their breeding bulls, and lost the most crucial months of the summer arguing politics while ripe fruit fell from the trees and vegetables dried and withered in the field rows. As the last straw, the truck drivers went out on strike and there was no way to transport cargo from one end of the country to the other: some cities lacked food while in others produce and seafood lay rotting. Salvador Allende was hoarse from denouncing the sabotage, but no one listened to him, and he did not have enough people or suffi-cient power to deal with his enemies by force. He accused the North Americans of financing the strike; every truck driver was receiving fifty dollars a day not to work, so that there was no hope of resolving the conflict, and when he ordered out the army to impose order, they found that the engines had missing parts and they could not move the old tires blocking the highways; in addi-tion, the road was strewn with bent nails that blew out the tires of the military vehicles. A TV helicopter showed the ruin of useless iron rusting on asphalt highways. Shortages became a nightmare, but no one went hungry because people who could afford it bought in the black market, and the poor organized by barrios to obtain the essentials. The government pleaded for patience, and the minister of agriculture distributed pamphlets to teach citizens how to culti-vate vegetables on their balconies and in their bathtubs. Fearful that we wouldn't eat, I began to hoard food obtained with the cunning of a smuggler. I had previously joked with my mother-in-law, saying that if we can't get chicken we can eat noodles, and we'll be better off without sugar anyway, it will be good for our figures, but in the end I said the hell with scruples. Where once I had stood in line for hours to buy a kilo of meat of dubious origin, now the resellers brought the best cuts right to the house—of course, at ten times the official price. That solution was short-lived because it was too cynical to assail my children with lectures about socialist morality while serving black market pork chops for dinner.

Even with such grave problems, the people continued to cele-brate their victory, and when parliamentary elections were held in March, the Popular Unity increased its percentage of the vote. The Right realized then that tons of twisted nails on highways and the absence of poultry in the markets would not be enough to topple the Socialist government, and that realization drove them to the last phase of the conspiracy. From that moment, rumors began to circulate of a military coup. Most people had no idea what that meant; we had heard that in other countries on our continent soldiers seized power with boring regularity, and we boasted that nothing like that would ever happen in Chile: we had a solid democracy and we were not one of those Central American banana republics, or Argentina, where for fifty years every civilian government had been ended by a military takeover. We considered ourselves the Swiss of the continent. The chief of the armed forces, General Prats, advocated respecting the constitution and permitting Allende to serve out his term peacefully, but in June a faction of the army rebelled and rolled out into the streets in tanks. Prats tried to impose discipline, but by then the genie was out of the bottle. The parliament declared the government of the Popular Unity illegal, and the generals demanded the ouster of their commander in chief, although instead of showing their own faces they sent their wives to demonstrate in front of Prats's house in an embarrassing public spectacle. The general was forced to resign, and the president appointed Augusto Pinochet in his place, an obscure career officer whom no one had ever heard of until then but who was a very close friend of Prats, and who swore to remain loyal to the democracy. The country seemed nearly out of control, and Salvador Allende announced a plebiscite that would allow the voters to decide whether he should continue governing or resign and call new elections: the date was set for September 11. The example of the wives of the military acting in their husbands' stead was quickly imitated. My father-in-law, like many other men, sent Granny to the Military Academy to throw corn at the cadets, to see if they could stop behaving like hens and go out and defend their nation as they were sworn to do. He was so enthusiastic about the possibility of overturning socialism once and for all that he himself beat stewpans in his patio to back the neighbor women protesting in the street. Like most Chileans, he thought that the military respected the rule of law and would remove Allende from the presidency, restore order to a calamitous situation, rid the country of leftists and rebels, and immediately call a new election—and then, if everything turned out well, the pendulum would swing in the opposite direction and we would again have a conservative president. "Don't get your hopes up, even in the best of cases, we'll get a Christian Democrat," I warned him, knowing that his hatred of that party was greater than what he felt for the Communists. The idea that soldiers would not release the reins of power never occurred to my father-in-law, or anyone else—except those in on the secret of the conspiracy.

Celia and Nicolás have asked me to come home to California for the arrival of their baby in May. They want me to take part in the birth of my granddaughter; they say that after so many months of being exposed to death, pain, farewells, and tears, it will be a celebration to welcome this infant as her head thrusts into life. If the visions I have had in dreams come true, as they have at other times, she will be a dark-haired, likable little girl, with a will of her own. You must get better soon, Paula, so you can go home with me and be Andrea's godmother. Oh, Paula, why do I say things like that? You won't be able to do anything for a long time, we have years of patience and hard work and organization ahead. You will have to do the most difficult part, but I will be at your side to help you; you will not want for anything, you will be surrounded by peace and comfort, we will help you get well. I have been told that rehabilitation is very slow, and you may need it for the rest of your life, but it can work miracles. The porphyria specialist maintains that you will recover completely, but the neurologist has ordered a battery of examinations, which were begun yesterday. They have already done a very painful one to test your peripheral nerves. They rolled you through the maze of the hospital to another wing of the building; there they pricked your arms and legs with needles and then used electric stimuli to measure your reactions. We went through it together, you in the clouds of unconsciousness and I thinking of all the men and women and children in Chile who were tortured in a very similar way with electric prods. Each time the charge entered your body, I felt it in mine, exacerbated by terror. I tried to relax and breathe with you, at your rhythm, imitating what Celia and Nicolás do together in the natural childbirth classes; pain is inevitable in this life, but they say that it is almost always bearable if we do not put up resistance or add fear and anguish.

Celia had her first baby in Caracas, comatose with drugs and all alone because her husband was not allowed in the delivery room. The star of the event was neither she nor the baby, but the doctor, a high priest, masked and robed in white, who decided how and when he would officiate over these rites—he induced the birth on a convenient day of his calendar because he wanted to go to the beach for the weekend. That is also how it was when my children were born more than twenty years ago, apparently procedures have changed very little. Some months ago I took Celia for a walk in the forest and there among the tall sequoias and murmuring streams I delivered a sermon about the ancient art of midwives, natural child-birth, and the right to live to the fullest that unique experience in which the mother embodies the female life force in the universe. She listened quietly to my disquisition, from time to time casting an eloquent glance out of the corner of her eye: she judges me by my long dresses and the cushion for meditating I carry in my car, and believes I have become a New Age zealot. Before she met Nicolás, she belonged to a Catholic organization of the reactionary right; she was not permitted to smoke or wear trousers, what she read and what she saw at the movies was censored, contact with the opposite sex was reduced to a minimum, and every instant of her existence was regulated. In that sect, men must sleep on a board once a week to forestall carnal temptation, but women have their board every night, supposedly because of their more licentious nature. Celia learned to flagellate herself and wear a cilice with metal barbs made by La Candelaria nuns, disciplining herself out of love for her Creator and paying for sins, her own and those of others. Three years ago we could find little in common, grounded as she was in contempt for leftists, homosexuals, artists, and people of different races and social condition, but what saved us was a mutual empathy that overcame all these barriers. San Francisco took care of the rest. One by one her prejudices fell away, the hairshirt and scourge became part of the family lore, she undertook a reading program on politics and history and along the way turned her ideas inside out, she met homosexuals and recognized that they are not the devil incarnate, as she had been told, and she also came to accept my artist friends, even though some wear nose rings and green Mohawks. The racism

went in less than a week's time, as soon as she learned that in the
United States we are not whites but *Hispanics,* and occupy the lowest rung of the social ladder. I never try to force my ideas on her,
because she is a ferocious lioness who would not put up with prose-
lytizing, she merely follows the paths indicated by her instinct and
intelligence, but that day in the redwood forest I couldn't help
myself, and dusted off the best of the oratorical tricks I had learned
from Tío Ramón with the hope of convincing her we should seek
other less clinical and more humane methods for the upcoming
birth. When we got back home we found Nicolás waiting at the
door. "Tell your mother to explain all that stuff about the music of
the universe to you," this irreverent daughter-in-law said in passing
to her husband, and ever since, we have referred to Andrea's birth
as *The Music of the Universe.* In spite of her early skepticism, she and
Nicolás accepted my suggestion and now are planning to give birth
like Indians. Later I will have to convince you to do the same, Paula.
You are the star of this illness, you must give birth to your own
health, fearlessly and with great fortitude. Perhaps this is a creative
opportunity equivalent to Celia's having a baby: you can be born
into a new life through pain . . . cross a threshold . . . grow.

Yesterday, Ernesto and I were alone in a hospital elevator when a
nondescript woman got on, one of those beings with no outstanding
features, rather ageless and bland, a shadow. After a few seconds I
realized that my son-in-law had turned white; his eyes were
squeezed shut and he was gasping for breath, leaning against the elevator wall to keep from falling. I stepped toward him to help, and at
that instant the elevator stopped and the woman got off. We should
have ourselves, but Ernesto held me back, and the door closed. And
then I smelled your perfume, Paula, as clear and jolting as a scream,
and understood your husband's reaction. I pushed a button to stop
the car and we hung suspended between two floors, breathing the
last traces of the scent we knew so well, as tears coursed down
Ernesto's face. I don't know how long we were there before we
heard yelling and pounding from below; I pressed a different button
and we began to descend. We nearly fell out the door, Ernesto
stumbling and I supporting him, before the quizzical stares of the

people in the corridor. We went to the cafeteria and sat down, still trembling, before cups of hot chocolate.

"I'm half crazy," Ernesto told me. "I can't concentrate on my work. I see numbers on the computer screen and they look like Chinese; people talk to me and I don't answer; I'm so distracted that I don't know how they put up with me in the office, I'm making colossal errors. Paula feels so far away! If you only knew how much I love her and need her. . . . Life has no color without her, everything is gray. I live hoping the telephone will ring and it will be you and in an excited voice you tell me that Paula has awakened and is asking for me. When that moment comes I will be as happy as the day we met and instantly fell in love."

"You need to get this out of your system, Ernesto; the torment is too much to bear, you need to burn off some energy."

"I run, I lift weights, I practice my aikido. . . . Nothing helps. My love is like ice and fire."

"Forgive me for being so personal, but have you thought about taking some girl out . . . ?"

"I can't believe this is Paula's mother talking, Isabel! No, I can't touch another woman, I don't want anyone else. Without Paula, my life has no meaning. What does God want of me? Why is He torturing me like this? We made so many plans. . . . We talked about growing old together and making love until we were ninety, about all the places we would go, how we would be the center of a large family and our house would always be open to friends. Did you know that Paula wanted to found a home for the elderly poor? She wanted to devote to other old people all the care she wasn't able to give Granny."

"This is the worst thing that will ever happen to the two of you, Ernesto, but you will come through it."

"I'm just so tired. . . ."

One of the professors just came through here with a group of medical students. He doesn't know me, and because of my white gown and shoes I was able to stay while they examined you. I needed all the composure I learned with such difficulty in my school in Lebanon to maintain a neutral expression while they manipulated you so disrespectfully—as if you were already a cadaver—and talked about your case as if you couldn't hear. What they said was that, normally, recovery occurs in the first six months and you have been here four, that you are not going to evolve much more, that it is possible you will be in this state for years, that they cannot devote a hospital bed to an incurable patient, and that they will send you to an institution—I suppose they were referring to an asylum or a hospice. Don't believe any of it, Paula. If you understand what you hear, please forget all that. I will never abandon you; from here you will go to a rehabilitation clinic, and then home; I'm not going to let them go on tormenting you with electric needles and lapidary prognoses. Enough. Nor is it true there is no change in your condition; they don't see it because they're never here, but we who are always with you can chart your progress. Ernesto is sure you recognize him; he sits beside you, tries to get you to look at him, talks to you in a low voice, and I see how your expression changes. You are calmer, and sometimes you seem affected, you cry and move your lips as if you wanted to say something, or barely lift a hand, as if you wanted to caress him. The doctors don't believe that but they don't take time to observe you, all they see is a paralyzed and spastic woman who doesn't even blink when they yell her name. Despite the alarming slowness of this process, I know that little by little you are crawling out of the abyss where you have been lost for several months, and that one of these days you will connect with the present. I repeat that over and over, but sometimes I lose hope. Ernesto came upon me one day on the terrace, in deep thought.

"But think, carefully, what is the worst thing that can happen?"

"Not death, Ernesto, but for Paula to stay as she is."

"And do you think we will love her any less?"

As always, your husband is right. We are not going to love you less, only more; we'll get organized, we'll set up a hospital in our house, and when I'm not there your husband will take care of you, or your brother, or my grandchildren, we'll see, just don't worry, Paula.

At night when I reach the hotel I sink into the quiet and silence that is so indispensable for reconstituting the energy I use up in the noisy hospital. Many people visit the ward in the evening; it's hot and crowded, and some even have the nerve to smoke, without a thought for suffocating the patients. My hotel room has become a blessed refuge where I can order my thoughts, and write. Willie and Celia call me every day from California and my mother writes often, I have good company. If I could rest, I would feel stronger, but I sleep in fits and starts and often my torturous dreams are more vivid than reality. I wake a thousand times during the night, assaulted by nightmares and memories.

On September 11, 1973, at dawn, the navy rebelled, followed almost immediately by the army, the air corps, and finally the corps of *carabineros,* the Chilean police. Salvador Allende was instantly notified; he hurriedly dressed, said goodbye to his wife, and went to his office, prepared to live out his oath: "They will not take me alive from La Moneda." His daughters Isabel and a pregnant Tati rushed along with their father. The bad news spread like lightning, and ministers, secretaries, staff, trusted doctors, some newspapermen, and friends all came to the Palacio de La Moneda, a small multitude wandering through the rooms without knowing what to do, shaping battle plans and barricading doors with furniture according to confusing instructions from the president's bodyguards. Urgent voices suggested that the hour had come to call out the people in a huge manifestation in support of the government, but Allende realized that such a summons would result in thousands of deaths. In the meantime, he tried to dissuade the rebels through messengers and telephone calls, because none of their generals dared confront him in person. Then Allende's bodyguards received orders from their superiors to withdraw, because the police had joined in the coup; the president let them go but demanded they surrender their weapons. Now the Palacio was unguarded and the great wood doors with wrought-iron studs were closed from inside. Shortly after 9:00 A.M., Allende became aware that all his political skill would not be sufficient to change the tragic course of the day; the fact was that the band of loyalists locked inside the venerable colonial building were alone: no one would come to their rescue, the people were unarmed and without leaders. Allende ordered the women to leave, and his guards distributed weapons among the men, but very few knew how to use them. The news had reached Tío Ramón in the embassy in Buenos Aires, and he managed to speak by telephone with the president. Allende bid his old friend farewell: *"I shall not resign, I shall leave La Moneda only when my term is ended, as president, or when the people demand it—or dead."* As they spoke, military units throughout the nation were falling one by one into the hands of the instigators of the coup, and in those same barracks the purge was begun against any who remained faithful to the constitution: the first people shot that day were wearing uniforms. El Palacio was surrounded by soldiers and tanks; isolated shots were heard, and then a heavy shelling that penetrated the thick, centuries-old walls and set fire to furniture and drapes on the first floor. A helmeted Allende went out onto the balcony with a gun and fired off a couple of shots, but someone convinced him that exposing himself in that way was madness, and forced him to come back inside. A brief truce was arranged to remove the women, and at that time the president asked everyone to leave him and surrender, but few did so; the majority dug in on the second floor, as he embraced the six women still by his side and told them goodbye. His daughters did not want to leave him, but by then the outcome was clear and by their father's orders they were forcibly taken from the building. In all the confusion, they walked down the street without being stopped until an automobile picked them up and drove them to a safe haven. Tati never recovered from the pain of that separation and the death of her father, the man she loved most in life, and three years later, in exile in Cuba, she left her children in a friend's care and, without telling anyone goodbye, shot herself. The generals, who had not foreseen any resistance, did not know what to do; they did not want to make Allende a hero, so they offered him a plane and safe transport for him and his family. *"You have misjudged me, traitors,"* was his reply. They then announced an aerial bombardment. Time was short. For the last time, the president spoke to the people by means of the one radio station not in the hands of the mutinous military. His voice was deliberate and firm, his words so determined that his farewell did not resemble the last breath of a man about to die, but the dignified salute of a man taking his permanent place in history.

Assuredly, Radio Magellanes will be silenced, and the tranquil tone of my voice will no longer reach your ears. It does not matter. You will hear it still. I shall be with you always. At least you will remember me as an honorable man who was loyal to the loyalty of the workers. . . . Our opponents have the power, they can crush us, but social progress will not be stopped with crime or with force. History is ours, it is made by the people. . . . Workers of my nation, I have faith in Chile and in its destiny. Other men will surmount this gray and bitter moment in which treachery attempts to rule. You must never forget that—much sooner than later—the great avenue will open for a liberated people to pass through as they move toward constructing a better society. Viva Chile! Long live the people! Long live the workers!

Bomber planes flew like fatidic birds over the Palacio de La Moneda, dropping their bombs with such precision that they exploded through windows and in less than ten minutes set ablaze an entire wing of the building, while tanks lobbed tear gas canisters from the street. At the same time, other airplanes and tanks were attacking the official presidential home in an exclusive residential neighborhood. Smoke and fire engulfed the first floor of the palace, and began to invade the salons on the second floor where Salvador Allende and a few of his followers were still entrenched. There were bodies everywhere, many rapidly bleeding to death. The survivors, choked by smoke and tear gas, could not make themselves heard above the noise of the shelling, planes, and bombs. The army's assault troops stormed La Moneda through gaps burned by fire and shell, occupied the still blazing first floor, and with loudspeakers ordered the people above to exit the building by an external stone stairway. Allende realized that further resistance would end in a bloodbath and ordered his men to surrender, because they could better serve the people alive than dead. He said his final goodbyes with a firm handclasp, looking each man squarely in the eye. Then they emerged Indian file, with their arms above their heads. As they came out, the soldiers kicked them and beat them with the butts of their weapons and, once they were on the ground, continued to beat them until they were senseless, then dragged them into the street where they lay on the pavement while the voice of a crazed officer threatened to roll over them with the tanks. The president was left standing beside the torn and bloody Chilean flag in the ruined Red Salon, rifle in hand. Soldiers burst in with drawn weapons. The official version is that Allende placed the barrel of the rifle beneath his chin, pulled the trigger, and blew off his head.

That unforgettable Tuesday, I left my house for the office as I did every morning; Michael had also left and I suppose that a little later the children started off to school, bookbags on their backs, not knowing that classes had been suspended. After a few blocks, I noticed that the streets were nearly empty; I saw a few disconcerted housewives standing before closed bakeries and laborers with their lunchboxes walking to work because no buses were running; only military vehicles were in the streets, and my flower- and angel-painted car looked like a joke. No one stopped me. The car didn't have a radio to get the news but, even if it had, most information was already being censored. I thought about going by to say hello to Tata, maybe he would know what the devil was going on, but I didn't want to disturb him so early. I drove on toward the office, with the sensation that I was lost in the pages of one of the science fiction books I had loved so much as an adolescent: the city seemed congealed in a disaster from another planet. I found the door of the publishing house closed with a chain and padlock; through the glass, the concierge signaled me to go away, a detestable man who spied on all of us to report the slightest transgression. So this is a military coup, I thought, and turned around to go have a cup of coffee with Mama Hilda and talk over events. That was when I heard helicopters and, shortly after, the first planes roaring overhead at low altitude.

Mama Hilda was in her doorway, looking down the street with a gloomy face; as soon as she saw the gaudy car she knew so well, she ran to meet me with the bad news. She feared for her husband, a dedicated French teacher; he had gone to work very early and she had heard nothing from him since. We had coffee and toast as we tried to reach him by telephone, but no one was answering. I talked with Granny, who suspected nothing, and with the children, who were calmly playing; the situation did not seem too alarming, and it crossed my mind that I could spend the morning sewing with Mama Hilda, but she was uneasy. The school where her husband taught was in the very center of town, a few blocks from the Palacio de La Moneda, and on the only radio still reporting news, she had learned that that was the sector taken by the military. "They're shooting, they're killing people, they say not to go outside because of stray bullets. A friend called me who lives down there and she says she can see the dead and wounded, and trucks filled with people they've arrested. It seems there's a curfew, do you know what that is?" Mama Hilda stammered. No, I didn't know. Although her concern seemed exaggerated—after all, I had driven there without being bothered by anyone—I offered to go look for her husband. Forty minutes later, I parked in front of the school, went in the half-open door, but saw no one: the courtyards and schoolrooms were silent. An aged porter came shuffling out and pointed to the room where I could find my friend. The porter was incredulous: "How can this happen? The soldiers are rebelling!" In the classroom, I found Mama Hilda's husband sitting facing the blackboard; a pile of papers was stacked high on his desk, the radio was blaring, and he was sobbing, with his face in his hands. "Listen," he said. That is how I came to hear President Allende's last words. Later, we climbed to the top floor of the building and from there could see the roofs of La Moneda; we waited, without knowing why, because there wasn't any news being broadcast anymore, all the stations were transmitting military marches. When we saw the planes flying over, very low, heard the sound of the bombs, and watched a terrible column of smoke rise toward the sky, we felt as if we were trapped in a bad dream. We could not believe anyone would dare attack La Moneda, the heart of Chilean democracy. "What will happen to *compañero* Allende?" my friend wondered, his voice breaking. "He won't surrender," I replied. "Ever." At that moment, we finally understood the extent of the tragedy and the danger we ourselves were in. We left the porter, who refused to abandon his post, got into my car, and set off toward the residential area through the side streets, avoiding soldiers. I cannot explain how we reached his house without encountering any difficulty, or how I then drove all the way home—where Michael was waiting, nervously, and the children, happily, because of the unexpected vacation.

By midafternoon, I learned through a confidential telephone call that Salvador Allende was dead.

Telephone lines were overcrowded and international communications practically nonexistent, but I was able to call my parents in Buenos Aires to give them the terrible news. They had already heard, the censorship we were experiencing in Chile did not apply to the rest of the world. Tío Ramón lowered the flag to half-mast as a sign of mourning, and immediately presented his undeclinable resignation to the military junta. He and my mother made a rigorous inventory of all the public property in the residence, and two days later handed over the embassy. For them, that was the end of a thirty-nine-year diplomatic career. They were not willing to collaborate with the junta, they preferred uncertainty and anonymity. Tío Ramón was fifty-seven and my mother fifty-two; both were broken-hearted. Their country had succumbed to the insanity of violence, their family was scattered, their children far away, their friends dead or in exile. They were without employment and with few resources in a strange city where the horror of dictatorship and beginning phases of what would come to be called the "Dirty War" were already in the air. They said their goodbyes to the embassy staff, who showed them affection and respect till the last moment and, hand in hand, walked out with their heads high. In the gardens were throngs of people shouting the slogans of the Popular Unity, thousands of young and old, men, women, and children, weeping for the death of Salvador Allende and for their dreams of justice and freedom. Chile had become a symbol.

The terror began that same Tuesday at dawn, but some did not know it until several days later; others were slow to accept it and, despite all the evidence, a handful of the privileged were able to ignore it for seventeen years, and deny it even today. The four generals of the armed forces and the *carabineros* appeared on television, explaining the motives for the "Military Pronouncement," as they called the coup, while scores of corpses floated in the Mapocho River that runs right through the city, and thousands of prisoners were incarcerated in barracks, prisons, and new concentration camps set up all over the country within the space of a few days. The most violent of the generals of the junta appeared to be the one directing the air corps, the most insignificant, the head of the *carabineros,* the most colorless, a certain Augusto Pinochet, whose name few people had ever heard. No one suspected in that first public appearance that the man with the look of a genial grandfather would turn into the sinister figure in dark glasses, bemedaled chest, and Prussian emperor's cape later seen round the world in revealing photographs. The military junta imposed a curfew for many hours, only armed forces personnel could move through the streets. During that time, they searched all the government and public administration buildings, the banks, universities, industries, rural communities—entire towns—in search of adherents of the Popular Unity. Leftist politicians, reporters, intellectuals, and artists were arrested on the spot; labor leaders were shot without a hearing, and as there were not enough prisons to hold all those arrested they had to utilize schools and sports stadiums. We had no news at all; TV stations were transmitting animated cartoons and radios were broadcasting military marches; every so often, new edicts were issued outlining the orders of the day, and again on the screen we would see the four generals of the coup, with the escutcheon and flag of Chile as backdrop. They explained to the citizenry the overthrown government's Plan Z, which involved an interminable blacklist containing the names of thousands of persons they had planned to massacre within the next few days, an unprecedented genocide, but they, the generals, had stepped in to prevent it. They said that the nation had been in the hands of Soviet advisers and Cuban guerrillas, and that a drunken Allende had committed suicide not only out of shame for his own failure as leader but particularly because the valiant armed forces had uncovered his deposits of Russian armaments, his pantry full of chickens, his corruption, his thievery, and his bacchanals, as could be documented in a series of pornographic photographs that they, out of common decency, were not going to exhibit. Through press, radio, and television, they urged hundreds of persons to turn themselves in at the Ministry of Defense, and some unwary individuals did so in good faith, and paid for it dearly. My brother Pancho was among those listed, and was saved by the fact that he was on a diplomatic mission in Moscow, where he was marooned with his family for several years. The home of the president was taken by assault, after being bombed, and even the family's clothing was pillaged. As souvenirs, neighbors and soldiers took personal belongings, private papers, and artworks that the Allendes had collected all their lives. In workers' neighborhoods, the repression was merciless; in all of Chile there were summary executions, uncounted arrests, *desaparecidos* and tortured; there was nowhere to hide so many persecuted, nor ways to feed the thousands of families without work. How was it that suddenly so many informers, collaborators, torturers, and assassins sprang up? Perhaps they were always there and we simply failed to see them. Nor was it possible to explain the fierce hatred displayed by troops who themselves came from the lower social classes and now were martyrizing their brothers.

Salvador Allende's widow, daughters, and some of his closest colleagues took refuge in the Mexican embassy. The day after the coup, Tencha Allende, carrying a safe conduct and escorted by soldiers, went secretly to bury her husband in an unmarked grave. She was not allowed to view his body. With her daughters, she went into exile in Mexico, where they were received with honors by the president and generously sheltered by all the Mexican people. The discharged General Prats, who had refused to back the coup, was spirited out of Chile to Argentina in the dark of night because he had a solid following among the rank and file and it was feared he might lead a splinter group among the armed forces, even though in fact he had never remotely entertained that idea. In Buenos Aires, he lived a modest and retiring life; he had very few friends, among whom were my parents, he was separated from his daughters, and he feared for his life. A virtual prisoner in his apartment, he began quietly to write the bitter memories of those last days.

The day after the coup, a military order was issued to display a flag from every rooftop in celebration of the victory of the valiant soldiers who had so heroically defended Western-Christian civilization against the Communist conspiracy. A jeep stopped at our door to inquire why we had not complied with the order. Michael and I explained that I was a relative of Allende: "We're in mourning; if you want, we will fly the flag with a black band and at half-mast," we said. The officer stood thinking a moment, and as he had no instructions for such a contingency, left without further commentary. The denunciations had already begun, and we expected that at any moment there would be a call accusing us of who knows what crimes, but that did not happen; perhaps the affection everyone in the neighborhood felt for Granny saved us. Michael learned that a group of workers was trapped in one of the buildings he was constructing; they had not got out that morning and later could not leave because of the curfew, and were incommunicado and without food. We notified Granny, who crept across the street in a crouch to be with her grandchildren; we gathered provisions from our pantry and, as the radio had instructed for cases of emergency, left in our car, crawling at a snail's pace with windows open and holding a white flag on a stick. We were stopped five times, and each time Michael was ordered to get out; the banged-up Citroën was brusquely searched and we were permitted to continue. No one asked me anything, they didn't even look at me. I thought Memé's guardian spirit must have covered me with a mantle of invisibility. Later, however, I found out that it was an idiosyncrasy of the military that women don't count except as spoils of war. If they had examined my identification, and seen my name, we might never have delivered our basket of food. We had not felt any fear, because as yet we did not know the mechanisms of repression, and believed that to be safe from danger all we had to do was explain that we did not belong to any political party; we soon learned the truth, when the curfew was lifted and we could communicate with others.

At the publishing house, anyone who had actively participated in the Popular Unity was immediately dismissed; I remained, but under close observation. Delia Vergara, pale but firm, announced exactly what she had three years earlier: We shall go on working as usual. This time, nevertheless, was different. Several of her collaborators had disappeared, and the best journalist of the team was running around half-crazed trying to hide her brother. Three months later, she herself had to find asylum, and finally ended up in France, where she has lived for more than twenty years. The authorities called all the representatives of the press together to communicate the rules of strict censorship under which they were to operate; not only were some subjects forbidden, there were even dangerous words, such as *compañero,* which was expunged from the vocabulary, and others that were to be used with extreme caution, such as *people, union, community, justice, worker,* and many others identified with the lexicon of the Left. The word *democracy* could be used only when accompanied by an adjective: "conditional democracy," "authoritarian democracy," even "totalitarian democracy." My first direct contact with censorship came a week later, when the children's magazine I directed appeared on the stands with a cover illustration of four ferocious gorillas, accompanied by a long feature article inside. The armed forces took the cover as a direct reference to the four junta generals. We had prepared the color separations two months in advance, when the idea of a military coup was still quite remote; it was a freakish coincidence that the four gorillas appeared at just that time. The publisher, who had returned in his private plane as soon as the chaos of the first days died down a little, fired me and named another director, the same man who shortly afterward managed to convince the junta to revise all maps, reversing the continents so that the august fatherland would appear at the top of the page and not the very bottom, making south north and extending territorial seas to the shores of Africa. I lost my job as director, and soon would also lose my post on the women's magazine—as would the rest of the staff, because in the eyes of the military, feminism was as subversive as Marxism. Soldiers were cutting off women's pants legs in the street, because in their judgment only males could wear trousers; long hair on men was equated with homosexuality, and beards were shaved because it was feared a Communist might be hiding behind them. We had returned to the times of unquestionable male authority. Under the orders of a new director, the magazine made a sharp about-face and became an exact replica of dozens of other frivolous publications for women. The head of the firm returned to photographing his beautiful adolescent girls.

The military junta outlawed strikes and protests, it returned land to former landholders and mines to the North Americans, it opened the country to foreign business and capital, it sold millenary old-growth forests and fishing rights to Japanese companies, and established a system of fat commissions and corruption as the form of government. A new caste of young executives materialized, educated in the doctrines of pure capitalism, who rode around on chrome-plated motorcycles and managed the fate of the nation with merciless callousness. In the name of economic efficiency, the generals froze history; they opposed democracy as a "foreign ideology" and replaced it with a doctrine of "law and order." Chile was not an isolated case, for soon the long night of totalitarianism would spread across all Latin America.

PART TWO

May to December 1992

I AM NO LONGER WRITING SO WHEN MY DAUGHTER wakes up she will not feel so lost, because she is not going to wake up. These are pages Paula will never read. . . .

No! Why do I repeat what others say if I don't really believe it? Everyone has classified her case as hopeless. Brain damage, they say. . . . After looking at the most recent tests, the neurologist took me to his office and as gently as possible showed me the negatives on his view box, two large black rectangles on which the exceptional intelligence of my daughter was reduced to dark blobs. His pencil followed the convoluted paths of the brain, as he explained the terrible consequences of those shadows and lines.

"Paula has severe damage; there is nothing to be done, her mind is destroyed. We do not know when or how it happened; it could have been caused by lack of sodium, oxygen deprivation, overapplication of drugs, or it could simply be the devastating progress of the illness."

"Do you mean she will never be normal mentally?"

"It's a very bad prognosis; in the best of cases, she might reach the level of an infant."

"What does that mean?"

"I can't tell you at this stage, each case is different."

"Will she be able to talk?"

"I don't think so. And it seems probable that she will never walk, either. She will always be an invalid," he added, looking at me sadly over his eyeglasses.

"There is some mistake here. You must do the tests again!"

"I'm afraid this is the reality, Isabel."

"You don't know what you're saying! You never saw Paula when she was healthy, you don't have the vaguest idea what she's really like! She is *brilliant,* the most intelligent person in our family, always the first in everything she does. She has an indomitable spirit. Do you think she would give in? Never!"

"I am very sorry," he said quietly, taking my hands, but I no longer heard him. His voice was coming from very far away, as Paula's past flashed before me in rapid images. I saw her at every stage of her life: as a baby, naked and wide-eyed, looking at me with the same alert expression she had up till the last instant of her conscious life; taking her first steps with the intentness of a tiny schoolteacher; stealthily hiding her grandmother's sad bottles; at ten, dancing like a crazed marionette to music on the television; at fifteen, welcoming me with a forced hug and hard eyes when I came home after an abortive fling with a lover whose name I cannot remember; at her last high school party, with her hair to her waist, and later in her cap and gown. I saw her looking like a fairy princess in the snowy lace of her wedding dress, and in a blue cotton blouse and worn rabbit-fur slippers, bent over from pain and with her head on my knees, after she was struck by the illness. That evening, exactly four months and twenty-one days ago, we were still talking in terms of the flu, and I was discussing with Ernesto Paula's tendency to command our attention by exaggerating how she felt when she was sick. I saw her that fateful early morning when she began to die in my arms, vomiting blood. Those visions registered like jumbled snapshots superimposed on a slow and inexorably flowing time in which we all moved as sluggishly as if we were at the bottom of the sea, unable to spring like a tiger to stop the wheel of destiny whirling toward death. For nearly fifty years I have been a toreador taunting violence and pain with a red cape, secure in the protection of the good luck birthmark on my back—even though in my heart I suspected that one day I would feel the claws of misfortune raking my shoulder. But I never, ever, imagined that the blow would fall on one of my children. Again I heard the neurologist's voice: "She's not aware of anything; believe me, your daughter is not suffering."

"Oh, she's suffering, and she's afraid. I am going to take her home to California as quickly as possible."

"Here Paula's expenses are covered by the Spanish health care system; in the United States, the cost of medical care is sky-high. Besides, Isabel, the trip is very risky. Paula still is not retaining sodium well, her blood pressure and temperature are not stable, she has respiratory problems, it just isn't a good idea to move her at this time, she might not survive the trip. Here in Spain we have one or two institutions where she can be well looked after. She won't miss anyone. She has no sense of recognition, she doesn't even know where she is."

"Don't you understand that I will never leave her? Help me, Doctor, I don't care what it costs, I have to take her with me. . . ."

When I look back over the long trajectory of my life, I believe that the military coup in Chile was one of the dramatic turning points. A few years from now, I will perhaps remember yesterday as the second tragedy to put its stamp on my existence. I will never again be the person I was. I have been assured, again and again, that there is no cure for Paula, but I don't believe it. I am going to take her to the United States, they can help us there. Willie has found a place for Paula in a clinic; all that remains is to convince Ernesto to let me take her; he can't look after her by himself, and we will never put her in an institution. I will find some way to travel with Paula, she isn't the first gravely ill person to be moved. I will take her with me if I have to steal an airplane to do it.

The bay of San Francisco had never looked so beautiful; a thousand brightly colored sails were unfurled to celebrate the beginning of spring, people in shorts were jogging across the Golden Gate Bridge, and the mountains were vitally green because at last it had rained, after six years of drought. It had been too long since I had seen trees so luxuriant and skies so blue; nature was dressed for a party, in welcome, and the long winter of Madrid was behind us. Before we left the hospital, I took Paula to the chapel, dark and solitary as it almost always was but glowing with candles before the Virgin's altar in honor of Mother's Day. I placed Paula's wheelchair facing the wooden statue where my mother had wept so many tears during the hundred days of her grief, and lighted a candle in celebration of life. My mother always asked the Virgin to wrap Paula in her mantle and protect her from pain and sorrow and, if she planned to take her, at least not to let her suffer any longer. I asked the Goddess to help us reach California safe and sound, and to watch over us in this new phase we were entering and give us the strength to get through it. Paula, with her head bowed and her eyes fixed on the floor, painfully rigid, began to cry; her tears fell drop by drop, like the notes of a piano exercise. What had she understood? Sometimes I think she wants to tell me something . . . I think she may want to tell me goodbye. . . .

I went with Ernesto to pack her suitcase. Again inside the small, clean, precise apartment where they had been so happy for such a short time, I was, as always, struck by the Franciscan simplicity in which they lived. In Paula's twenty-eight years in this world, she had reached a maturity others never achieve; she knew how ephemeral life is and, because she was much more concerned about the restiveness of the soul, had removed herself from nearly everything material. "We go to our grave in a winding sheet, why do you bother?" Paula asked me once in a dress shop where I wanted to buy her three blouses. She had been tossing overboard the last vestiges of vanity and had no taste for adornment, for anything unnecessary or superfluous; in her clear view, there was space and patience only for the essentials. "I look everywhere for God but I can't find him," she told me shortly before she fell into the coma. Ernesto put some of her clothing in a bag, a few snapshots from their honeymoon in Scotland, her old rabbit-fur slippers, the silver sugar bowl she inherited from Granny, and the rag doll I had made for her when she was born, a moth-eaten relic now missing her yarn hair and one shoe-button eye, but a talisman Paula still dragged everywhere. We left in a basket the letters I had written over the years, letters that, like my mother, Paula bundled according to date.

I suggested throwing them out, but Ernesto said that one day she might ask for them. The apartment was swept clean, as if by a cold wind: on December 6, Paula had left there for the hospital, and never returned. Her vigilant spirit was present as we disposed of her few belongings and intruded upon her innermost privacy. Suddenly Ernesto was on his knees with his arms around my waist, shaking with the sobs he had held back these long months. I believe that, in that moment, he fathomed the depths of his tragedy and realized that his wife would never return to this Madrid apartment; she was now in a different dimension, leaving only the memory of the beauty and grace he had fallen in love with.

"Is it because we loved each other too much? Did Paula and I squander all the happiness we had a right to? Were we swallowed up by life? My love for her is unconditional, but it seems she doesn't need it anymore," he said.

"She needs it more than ever, Ernesto, but at this moment she needs me more because someone must take care of her."

"It isn't fair for you to bear that terrible responsibility alone. She's my wife. . . ."

"I won't be alone, I have the family. Besides, you can be there, too, you are always welcome in our house."

"But what will happen if I can't get a job in California? I can't live on your charity. But I can't be separated from her, either. . . ."

"Once Paula wrote me that when you came into her life everything changed, she felt complete. And she told me that sometimes when you were with other people, half dazed by the noise of several conversations, you had only to look at each other to know how much you were in love. Time stopped, and a magical space was carved out in which just the two of you existed. Maybe that's how it will be from now on: in spite of distance, the love you two share will be intact, in a separate compartment, beyond life and death."

At the last moment, before the door closed forever behind us, Ernesto gave me a wax-sealed envelope. It was in my daughter's unmistakable hand and it read, *To be opened after I die.*

"Months ago, in the middle of our honeymoon, Paula woke up screaming," Ernesto told me. "I don't know what it was she dreamed, but it must have been very disturbing because she couldn't get back to sleep. She wrote this letter and gave it to me. Do you think we should open it?"

"Paula isn't dead, Ernesto. . . ."

"Then you keep it. Every time I see the envelope, I feel a sharp pain here in my chest."

Goodbye to Madrid. . . . The corridor of lost steps, where I walked several times the distance around the globe, the hotel room, the pots of lentil soup, all left behind. For the last time, I hugged Elvira, Aurelia, and my other hospital friends, who cried as we left, the nuns, who gave me a rosary blessed by the pope, the healers, who came for the last time to apply the powers of their Tibetan bells, and the neurologist, the only doctor who stayed with me to the end, preparing Paula and obtaining signatures and permits so the airline would agree to transport her. I bought several first-class tickets, installed a stretcher, oxygen and other equipment, engaged a registered nurse, and took my daughter to the airport in an ambulance, where someone was waiting to drive us directly to the plane. Paula was sleeping, thanks to drops the doctor had given me at the last instant. I had combed her hair into the half ponytail she liked, tied with a scarf, and Ernesto and I had dressed her for the first time in long months; we chose one of my skirts and one of his jackets because when we looked in her closet there were only a couple of pairs of blue jeans, a blouse or two, and an overcoat, clothes too difficult to pull over her rigid body.

The trip between Madrid and San Francisco was a safari of more than twenty hours of nourishing an unconscious patient drop by drop, controlling her vital signs, and, when she grew restless, easing her into a merciful sopor with the miraculous drops. This all happened less than a week ago, but I have already forgotten the details. I barely remember that we were in Washington two hours, where an official from the Chilean embassy was waiting to facilitate our entry into the United States. The nurse and Ernesto tended Paula while I ran through the airport with the luggage and passports and permits, which the officials stamped without question after one glance at the pale and lifeless girl on the stretcher. In San Francisco, Willie was at the airport with another ambulance, and an hour later we were at the rehabilitation clinic where a team of doctors immediately evaluated

Paula, who had arrived bathed in cold sweat and with dangerously low blood pressure. Celia, Nicolás, and my grandson were waiting at the clinic door. Alejandro trotted toward me on his clumsy little legs with his arms out to me, but he must have felt the awful tension in the air because he stopped abruptly and backed away, frightened. Day after day, by telephone, Nicolás had been kept up to date on the details of Paula's illness, but he was not prepared for what he saw. He leaned over his sister and kissed her forehead; she opened her eyes and for a moment seemed to focus on who he was. "Paula, Paula!" he murmured, as tears ran down his cheeks. Celia, mute and terrified, protecting the baby in her womb with crossed arms, disappeared behind a column in the darkest corner of the room.

That night Ernesto stayed in the clinic, and I went home with Willie. I had not been there for months and I felt as if I were a stranger, as if I had never crossed that threshold before or seen that furniture or any of the things I had bought with such excitement. Everything was impeccable, and my husband had cut his best roses to fill the flower vases. I looked at our bed with the white batiste canopy and large embroidered pillows, the paintings I had taken everywhere with me for years, my clothes arranged by color in the closet, and it seemed very pretty but totally alien; my home was still the waiting room of the hospital, the hotel room, Paula's bare little apartment. I felt I had never been in this house and that my soul had been left behind in the corridor of lost steps and it would be a long time before I could find it. But then Willie put his arms around me, tight, and I sensed his warmth and his scent through the cloth of his shirt; I was wrapped in the unmistakable strength of his loyalty and I had a presentiment that the worst was over. From now on I would not be alone; beside him I would have the courage to meet all that fate had to offer.

Ernesto could stay in California only four days before he had to fly back to Spain to his job. He is negotiating a transfer to the United States so he can be close to Paula.

"Wait for me, my love. I will soon be back and then we'll never be apart again, I promise you. Be strong, don't give up," he said, as he kissed her goodbye.

Every morning, Paula is exercised and subjected to complicated tests, but in the afternoons there is free time for us to be with her. The doctors seem surprised by the excellent condition of her body; her skin is healthy, her body isn't deformed, and she hasn't lost the flexibility of her joints, despite the paralysis. The movements I had improvised are the same they employ, my braces contrived from books and elastic bandages are similar to those they build to order here, my thumping Paula's back to help her cough and the drops of water to moisten the tracheotomy serve the same purpose as their sophisticated respiratory machines. Paula has a bright private room with a window overlooking a patio filled with geraniums; we have hung family photographs on the walls and play soft music, and she has a television set with tapes of placid images of water and woods. Some of my friends brought Paula aromatic lotions, and in the morning we rub her with oil of rosemary to stimulate her, in the evening, lavender to make her drowsy, and, to refresh her, rose and chamomile. A man with large, magician's hands comes every day to give her Japanese massages, and she is tended by a team of six therapists; some work with her in the rehab room and others try to communicate by showing her boards with letters and drawings, playing different instruments, and even placing lemon or honey on her tongue to see if she reacts to the flavors. A porphyria specialist attends her, one of the few in existence, since no one is interested in this rare affliction. Some people know about it in passing because there was an English king who was thought to be mad but in fact suffered from porphyria. The doctor read the reports from the hospital in Spain, examined Paula, and determined that the brain damage is not a result of her illness but possibly an accident or error in her treatment.

Today we put Paula in a wheelchair, with cushions at her back, and took her outside to the clinic gardens. There a path winds through clumps of wild jasmine whose fragrance is as penetrating as Paula's lotions. Those flowers always remind me of Granny, and it's a strange coincidence that Paula is surrounded by them. We put a wide-brimmed straw hat and dark glasses on her to protect her from the sun, and dressed like that she looks nearly normal. Nicolás was pushing the chair, while Celia, who is very large now, and I, holding Alejandro, watched from a distance. Nicolás had cut some of the jasmine blossoms and placed them in his sister's hand, and was talking to her as if she could answer. I wonder what he was saying? I talk to her all the time myself, in case she has instants of lucidity and in one of those flashes we might succeed in reaching her. Early every morning, I repeat that this is summertime in California and she is with her family, and I tell her the date so she won't drift outside of time and space. At night I tell her that another day has passed, that it is time to dream, and I whisper into her ear one of those sweet English prayers Granny raised her on. I explain what has happened to her and that I am her mother and not to be afraid because she will come out of this stronger than ever, and that in the darkest moments, when all doors close to us and we feel trapped with no way out, there is always some unexpected opening toward escape. I remind her of the period of the terror in Chile and of the lonely years of exile, times that were also the most important in our lives because they gave us purpose and strength.

I, like thousands of other Chileans, have often asked myself whether I did the right thing in leaving my country during the dictatorship, whether I had the right to uproot my children and drag my husband to an uncertain future in a strange country, or whether it would have been better to stay where we were, trying to pass unnoticed—these are questions that cannot be answered. Events developed inexorably, as in Greek tragedies; disaster lay before my eyes, but I could not avoid taking the steps that led to it.

On September 23, 1973, twelve days after the military coup, Pablo Neruda died. He had been ill, and the sad events of those days ended his will to live. He lay dying in his bed at Isla Negra, staring, unseeing, at the waves crashing on the rocks beneath his window. Matilde, his wife, had erected a tight circle around Neruda to protect him from the news of what was happening, but somehow he learned of the thousands who were being arrested, tortured, and killed. "They mangled Victor Jara's hands, which was like killing a nightingale, and they say that he sang and sang, and that infuriated his torturers even more. What is happening," Neruda murmured, his eyes wild. "Everyone has gone mad." When he began to choke, he was taken by ambulance to a clinic in Santiago, while hundreds of telegrams from various world governments poured in offering political asylum to Chile's Nobel Laureate; some ambassadors went personally to persuade Neruda to leave, but he did not want to be away from his land in such cataclysmic times. "I cannot abandon my people, I cannot run away; promise me that you will stay, too," he asked of his wife, and she promised she would. The last words of this poet who had sung to life were: "They're going to shoot them, they're going to shoot them." The nurse administered a tranquilizer and he slipped into a deep sleep and never awakened. Death left upon his lips the ironic smile of his best days, when he disguised himself to entertain his friends. At that very moment, in a cell in the National Stadium, police were savagely torturing his driver to tear from him who knows what useless confession implicating the aged and peaceful poet. Neruda's wake was held in his blue house on San Cristobal Hill; it had been ransacked by troops and was in ruins: scattered everywhere were fragments of his ceramics, his bottles, his dolls, his clocks, his paintings—anything they could not take with them they broke and burned. Water and dirt streamed across the shards of glass covering the floor; as people walked over them, they made a sound like crunching bones. Matilde spent the night in the middle of the ruin, seated in a chair beside the coffin of the man who wrote her such incomparably beautiful love poems. She was accompanied by the few friends who dared defy the curfew and cross the ring the police had thrown around the house. Neruda was buried the next day in a borrowed grave, in a funeral bristling with the machine guns that bordered the streets through which the meager cortege passed. Few of his friends could be with him for his last journey, they were prisoners, or in hiding, or fearing reprisals. My coworkers from the magazine and I marched slowly behind the casket, carrying red carnations and shouting, "Pablo Neruda! Present, now and forever!" before the lines of red-eyed soldiers, all identical beneath their helmets, their faces camouflaged to conceal their identity and their weapons trembling in their hands. Halfway to the cemetery, someone shouted, "*Compañero* Salvador Allende!," and with a single voice we answered, "Present, now and forever!" Thus the burial of the poet also honored the death of the president, whose body lay in an unmarked tomb in a cemetery in a different city. "The dead cannot rest in an anonymous grave," an old man marching beside me said. When I got back home, I wrote my daily letter to my mother describing the funeral; she kept it with all the others, and eight years later gave it back to me and I was able to include it, almost word for word, in my first novel. I also told my grandfather, who listened, teeth clenched, to the end and then took my arms in an iron grip and shouted, Why the hell had I gone to the cemetery?, Didn't I know what was going on in Chile?, and Out of love for my children and respect for him—who couldn't take much more—to be careful. Wasn't it enough to appear on television with the name Allende? Why was I exposing myself like that? It was not incumbent on me to fight that fight.

"But evil is on the loose, Tata."

"What evil are you talking about! It's your imagination, the world has always been like this."

"Could it be we deny the existence of evil because we don't believe in the power of good?"

"Promise me that you'll keep your mouth shut and stay home," was his request.

"I can't promise that, Tata." And in fact, I couldn't, it was too late for such promises. Two days after the military coup, almost as soon as the curfew was lifted, I was, I don't know exactly how, swept into the network that immediately formed to help the persecuted. I first heard about a young leftist extremist who had to be hidden; he had escaped from an ambush with a bullet in his leg and his pursuers close upon his heels. He was able to hide in a friend's garage, where at midnight a sympathetic doctor extracted the bullet and bandaged the wound. His fever soared, despite antibiotics; he could not be kept any longer in the garage and it was impossible to think of taking him to a hospital, where he would automatically have been arrested. In his condition, he could not survive the difficult border crossing through the mountain passes to the south, where some were making their escape. His only hope was to find asylum, but only well-connected people, like politicians, journalists, intellectuals, and famous artists, were finding embassy doors opened to them; poor devils like him, and thousands of others, were left out in the cold. I was not at all sure what "asylum" meant, I had only heard it in our national anthem, which now sounded ironic—". . . *the country either will be free, or an asylum against oppression"*—but the situation seemed like something from a novel, and without really thinking about it, I offered to help him. I didn't stop to calculate the risk, because at that moment no one knew how terror operated, we were still acting under the principles of normality. I decided to take the direct approach, and drove to the Argentine embassy, parked my car as close by as possible, and walked to the gate with a pounding heart but firm stride. Through the iron grille I could see that the windows of the building had clothing hanging in them, and people looking out, shouting. The street was boiling with soldiers; I saw nests of machine guns and a small tank parked before the gate. The moment I approached, two guns were pointed at me. "What do you have to do to be granted asylum here?" I asked. "Your documents!" the soldiers barked in unison. I handed them my identification card and, one on each side of me, they led me to the guardhouse beside the gate, where I repeated my question to an officer, trying to hide the tremor in my voice. He looked at me with such amazement that we both smiled. "I'm here to prevent precisely that," he replied, studying the family name on my documents. After an eternity, he dismissed the soldiers and we were alone in the tiny gatehouse. "I've seen you on television. Ummm. . . , this must be for your program, of course," he said. He was pleasant, but categorical. As long as he was in charge, no one would be given asylum in this embassy; it wasn't like the Mexican embassy, where people wandered in any time they pleased, all they had to do was talk to the majordomo. I understood. The officer returned my papers, warned me to stay out of trouble, and we said goodbye with a handshake. I drove directly to the embassy of Mexico where hundreds had already been accepted, but Aztec hospitality stretched to include one more.

Then I learned that some of Santiago's poorer neighborhoods were under siege by the army; in others, the curfew was in force half the day, and many people were going hungry. Soldiers rolled in with tanks, surrounded the houses, and herded everyone outside. All males over fourteen were taken to the schoolyard or the soccer field—usually an empty lot with a few faint chalk lines—where, after the men were methodically beaten in view of the women and children, some were chosen by lot and taken away. A few returned, telling of nightmarish experiences and showing the scars of their torture. The mutilated bodies of others were thrown on garbage dumps at night, so everyone would learn the fate of subversives. In some areas, most of the men had disappeared, leaving family after family with no source of support. My role was to collect food and money for the church kitchens that provided warm meals to the youngest children. The sight of older brothers and sisters waiting outside with empty stomachs in the hope that a few pieces of bread would be left over is something forever engraved in my memory. I became very fastidious about soliciting help; friends learned to refuse me by telephone, and I think they hid when they saw me coming. Quietly, my grandfather gave me what he could, but he didn't want to know what I did with his money. He was frightened, and he barricaded himself in front of his television, tight within his four walls, but bad news seeped in through the windows and sprouted like moss in every corner; there was no way to avoid it. I don't know whether Tata's reason for being frightened was that he knew more than he confessed, or because eighty years of living had taught him the infinite possibilities of human wickedness. For me, it was a total surprise to discover that the world is violent and predatory and ruled by the implacable law of the survival of the fittest. Natural selection has not caused a flowering of intelligence or evolution of the spirit, at the first opportunity, we destroy one another like rats trapped in a too-small box.

I became acquainted with a segment of the Catholic community that in a way reconciled me with the Church from which I had parted company fifteen years before. Until then I had known only dogma, rites, guilt, and sin, the Vatican, which ruled the fate of millions of faithful throughout the world, and the official Church, almost always the advocate of the powerful, despite its social encyclicals. I had vaguely heard of liberation theology and the movement of worker priests, but I knew nothing of the militant Church, the thousands and thousands of Christians dedicated to serving those most in need with humility and anonymity. They formed a part of the only organization with the ability to help the victimized, the Vicaría de la Solidaridad, an entity created for that purpose by the cardinal during the first days of the dictatorship. For seventeen years, a large group of priests and nuns would risk their lives to save others and to report crimes. It was a priest who showed me the safest routes to political asylum. Some of the people I helped leap over a wall ended up in France, Germany, Canada, and the Scandinavian countries, all of which accepted hundreds of Chilean refugees. Once I had started down that road, it was impossible to turn back, because one case led to another and then another . . . and there I was, committed to various underground activities, hiding or transporting people, passing on for publication in Germany information others had obtained about the tortured or disappeared, and taping interviews with victims in order to establish a record of everything that happened in Chile, a task more than one journalist took on in those days. I could not suspect then that eight years later I would use that material to write two novels. At first I had no sense of the danger, and moved about in broad daylight, in the hubbub of the center of Santiago, in the warm summer and golden autumn. It was not until the middle of 1974 that I truly recognized the risks involved. I knew so little about the workings of terror that I was slow to perceive the warning signs: nothing indicated that a parallel world existed in the shadows, a cruel dimension of reality. I felt invulnerable. My motivations were not heroic, not in the least, merely compassion for such desperate people and, I have to admit it, the irresistible attraction of adventure. During moments of greatest danger I remembered the advice Tío Ramón gave me the night of my first party: *Remember that all the others are more afraid than you.*

In those uncertain times, people revealed their true faces. The most contentious political leaders were the first to subside into silence or to flee the country; in contrast, other people who had lived quiet, unassuming lives exhibited extraordinary valor. I had one good friend who was an out-of-work psychologist who earned his living as a photographer on our magazine, a gentle and somewhat naive man with whom we shared family Sundays with the children and whom I had never heard utter a word about politics. I called him Francisco, although that was not his name, and nine years later he served as model for the protagonist of *Of Love and Shadows*. He had contacts with religious groups because his brother was a worker priest and, through him, he learned of the atrocities committed throughout the country; more than once he put himself in danger to help others. During secret walks on San Cristobal Hill, where, we believed, no one could hear us, he used to pass on the news to me. Sometimes I worked with him, and other times I acted alone. I had devised a rather unimaginative system for the first meeting, generally the only meeting, with the person I was to help: we would agree on a time, I would drive very slowly around the Plaza Italia in my unmistakable vehicle until I picked up a quick signal, then slow down just long enough for someone to jump into the car. I never knew the names or stories behind those pale countenances and shaking hands, because our instructions were to exchange a minimum of words. I would be left with a kiss on the cheek and whispered thanks, and never know anything more of that person. It was more difficult when there were children. I know of one baby that to get past the guard at the gate and be reunited with its parents was smuggled into an embassy drugged with a sedative and hidden in the bottom of a basket of lettuce.

Michael knew about my activities and never objected, even when it came to hiding someone in the house. Serenely, he warned me of the dangers, somewhat amazed that so many assignments fell into my hands while he rarely knew anything that was going on. I don't know, I suppose my being a journalist had something to do with it; I was out in the streets talking to people, while he was always in the company of executives, the caste that benefited most from the dictatorship. I showed up one day at the restaurant where Michael always lunched with his associates in the construction company, to point out to them that they spent enough money on a single meal to feed twenty children for a month in the kitchen run by the priests, and then suggested that once a week they eat a sandwich in their office and give me the money they saved. My words were met with a stony silence, even the waiter stood frozen with his tray in his hand, and all eyes turned toward Michael; I expect they were wondering what kind of man this was who was unable to control his insolent wife. The president of the company removed his eyeglasses, slowly cleaned them with his napkin, and then wrote me a check for ten times the amount I had asked. Michael did not eat with them again, and with that gesture made his position clear. It was difficult for him, brought up as he was by strict and noble ideals, to believe the horror stories I told him or to conceive that we could all die, including our children, if any of the poor wretches who passed through our lives was arrested and confessed under torture to having been beneath our roof. We heard the most bloodcurdling rumors, but through some mysterious mechanism of the brain, which at times refuses to see the obvious, we dismissed them as exaggerations—until it was no longer possible to deny them. At night we would wake up sweating because a car had stopped outside during curfew, or because the telephone rang and no one was there, but the next morning the sun would rise, the children and the dog would crawl onto our bed, we would get up and make coffee, and life would start all over again, as if everything were normal. Months went by before the evidence was irrefutable and we were paralyzed by fear. How could everything change so suddenly and so completely? How could reality be so distorted? We were all accomplices, the entire society was mad. The devil in the mirror. . . . Sometimes, when I was alone in some secret place on the hill with time to think, I again saw the black waters of the mirrors of my childhood where Satan peered out at night, and as I leaned toward the glass, I realized, with horror, that the Evil One had my face. I was not unsullied, no one was: a monster crouched in each of us, every one of us had a dark and fiendish side. Given the conditions, could *I* torture and kill? Let us say, for example, that someone harmed my children. . . . What cruelty would I be capable of in that situation? The demons had escaped from the mirrors and were running loose through the world.

By the end of the next year, when the country was completely subjugated, a system of pure capitalism was initiated; because it favored only the executive class and workers lost all their rights, it had to be imposed by force. It did not follow the law of supply and demand, as the young ideologues of the Right claimed, because the work force was repressed and at the mercy of their employers. The social benefits people had obtained decades before were terminated, the right to hold meetings or strike was abolished, and labor leaders disappeared or were murdered with impunity. Businesses, caught up in a mad course of inhuman competition, demanded maximum productivity from their workers for minimum compensation. There were so many unemployed lining up at factory doors to find work that labor was available at near slave wages. No one dared protest, because in the best of circumstances a man could lose his job, but worse, he could be accused of being a Communist or a subversive and wind up in a cell tortured by the political police. An apparent economic miracle was created at great social cost; never before had Chile witnessed such a shameless exhibition of wealth, nor so many people living in extreme poverty. As an administrator, Michael had to dismiss hundreds of workers; he called them to his office by list to tell them that beginning the next day they were not to report to work, and to explain to them that in accord with the new rules they had lost their severance pay. He knew that each of those men had a family, and that it would be impossible for them to find another job; this dismissal was tantamount to an irrevocable sentence of misery. He started coming home demoralized and dejected; after a few months his shoulders sagged and his hair turned gray. One day he called a meeting of his associates to tell them that the situation was becoming obscene, that his foremen were earning the equivalent of three liters of milk per day. With laughter, they replied, "What matter? Those people don't drink milk, anyway." By that time, I had lost my position on both magazines and was taping my program in a studio under the surveillance of a guard with a machine gun. Censorship was not all that affected my work; I became aware that it was to the liking of the dictatorship that a member of the Allende family had a light comedy program on television—what better proof of normality in the nation? I resigned. I felt I was being watched, fear kept me awake nights, and I broke out in hives that I scratched till they bled. Many of my friends were leaving the country; some disappeared and were never mentioned again, as if they had never existed. One afternoon, an artist friend I hadn't seen in months visited me; once we were alone, he took off his shirt to show me scars that were not completely healed: his torturers had carved an "A" for Allende on his back. From Argentina, my mother implored me to be cautious and not do anything to provoke trouble. I could not forget the prophecies of María Teresa Juárez, the seer, and feared that, just as with the bloodbath she had foreseen, her prediction for me of immobility or paralysis might also come true. Didn't that in fact mean years in prison? I began to contemplate the possibility of leaving Chile, but did not dare speak of it aloud because it seemed that putting the thought into words could set in motion the gears of an irreversible mechanism of death and destruction. I went often to walk the paths on San Cristobal where I had played so many years ago on family picnics; I hid among the trees and screamed, with pain like a spear piercing my breast. Sometimes I packed food and a bottle of wine in a basket and went there with Francisco, who, using his knowledge of psychology, tried vainly to help me. Only with him could I talk about my clandestine activities, my fears, my unconfessable desire to escape. "You're crazy," he would tell me. "Anything is better than exile. How can you leave your home, your friends, your country?"

My children and Granny were the first to notice my state of mind. Paula, who was then a wise little girl of eleven, and Nicolás, who was three years younger, understood that all about them fear and poverty were spreading like a river overrunning its banks. They became silent and cautious. They had learned that the husband of one of their schoolteachers, a sculptor who before the coup had made a bust of Salvador Allende, had been arrested by three unidentified men who suddenly burst into his studio and hauled him away. No one knew where he was, and his wife didn't dare mention her trouble for fear of losing her job—we were still in the period when everyone thought that if someone disappeared, surely he was guilty. I don't know how my children learned of it, but that night they told me. They had gone to see their teacher, who lived a few blocks from our house, and found her bundled in shawls and sitting in the dark because she couldn't pay the electric bill or buy paraffin for the stoves. Her salary barely fed her three children, and she had had to take them out of school. "We want to give them our bicycles because they don't have money to take the bus," Paula informed me. They did and, from that day, Paula's mysterious activities increased; now she not only hid her grandmother's bottles and took gifts to her friends in the old people's home nearby, she also stowed jars of preserves and packages of rice in her bookbag for her teacher. Months later, when the sculptor returned home after surviving torture and prison, he created a Christ on the Cross in iron and bronze and gave it to our children. Ever since, it has hung beside Nicolás's bed.

My children never repeated what we talked about in the family, or mentioned the strangers who sometimes passed through the house. Nicolás began to wet his bed at night; he would wake up, humiliated, and come to my room with his head hanging and hug me, shivering. We should have given him more affection than ever, but Michael was depressed by the problems with his workers and I was running from one job to another, visiting the poor neighborhoods, and hiding people, all with my nerves rubbed raw. I don't think either of us provided the children the security or consolation they needed. In the meantime, Granny was being torn apart by opposing forces; on one side, her husband was boasting about the feats of the dictatorship and, on the other, we were telling her stories of repression. Her uneasiness turned into panic as her small world was threatened by hurricane-force winds. "Be careful," she would say from time to time, not sure herself what she meant, because her mind refused to accept the dangers her grandmotherly heart could sense. Granny's entire existence revolved around those two grandchildren. "Lies, it's all a pack of lies made up by the Soviets to run down Chile," my father-in-law told her any time she mentioned the terrible rumors contaminating the atmosphere. Just like my children, she learned not to voice her doubts and to avoid comments that might attract misfortune.

One year after the coup, the military junta ordered General Prats assassinated in Buenos Aires, because they believed that from there the former chief of the armed forces might head a rebellion of officers with democratic tendencies. They also feared that Prats was going to publish his memoirs revealing the treachery of the generals; by then, the official version of events of September 11 had been widely disseminated, justifying their actions and exalting the image of Pinochet to the point of heroism. Telephone messages and anonymous notes had warned General Prats that his life was in danger. Tío Ramón was also threatened because it was suspected that he had a copy of the general's memoirs, although he did not believe he was in actual peril. Prats, on the other hand, knew very well how his colleagues operated, and he was also aware that the death squadrons were beginning to operate in Argentina, maintaining with the Chilean dictatorship a horrendous traffic in bodies, prisoners, and documents of *desaparecidos*. Prats tried in vain to obtain a passport that would allow him to leave Argentina for Europe; Tío Ramón spoke with the Chilean ambassador, an old-time diplomat who had been his friend for many years, to plead with him to help the exiled general, but all he got were promises that were never fulfilled. Shortly before midnight on September 29, 1974, a bomb exploded in Prats's automobile as he arrived home after dining with my parents. The force of the explosion threw pieces of burning metal a hundred meters around; it dismembered the general, and his wife died in the blazing inferno. Minutes later, Chilean newspapermen congregated at the site of the tragedy, arriving before the Argentine police, as if they had been waiting just around the corner.

Tío Ramón called me at two in the morning to ask me to notify Prats's daughters and to tell me that he and my mother had left their house and were in hiding. The next day I flew to Buenos Aires on a strange mission, feeling as if I were blindfolded because I had no idea how I would find them. At the airport, a very tall man stepped forward to meet me and practically dragged me to a black car waiting at the gate. "Don't be afraid, I'm a friend," he said in a heavily German-accented Spanish, and there was such goodness in his blue eyes that I believed him. He was a Czechoslovakian representative to the United Nations who was plotting a way to get my parents to safer ground, somewhere where the long arm of terror could not reach them. He took me to an apartment in the center of the city, where I found them very calm, making plans for their escape. "You see now what those murderers are capable of, Isabel, please, you must leave Chile," my mother begged once more. We didn't have much time together, barely enough for them to tell me what happened and what to do with their things. That same day, their Czech friend managed to get them out of the country. We said goodbye with a desperate embrace, not knowing whether we would see each other again. "Keep writing me every day, and keep the letters until I have a place you can send them," my mother said at the last minute. Protected by the tall man with the compassionate eyes, I stayed in Buenos Aires to pack furniture, pay bills, release the apartment my parents had rented, and get the necessary papers to take back with me the Swiss dog that had been half crazed when the bomb exploded in the embassy. That pet became Granny's only companion when all the rest of us had to abandon her.

A few days later in Santiago, in the residence of the commander-in-chief where Prats and his family had lived until he was forced to resign, Pinochet's wife saw General Prats in broad daylight, sitting at the dining room table, his back to the window, illuminated by a timid spring sun. After her first shock, she realized that the vision was a result of a bad conscience, and gave it no further importance, but in the following weeks the ghost of the betrayed friend returned many times: it appeared, standing, in the salons, it walked loudly down the stairway, it peered through doorways, until its obstinate presence became intolerable. Pinochet had a gigantic bunker constructed, surrounded by a fortresslike wall capable of protecting him from enemies living and dead, but his security experts discovered that from the air it offered a perfect target for bombs. Then Pinochet had the walls of his bewitched house reinforced and the windows covered with armorplate; he doubled his armed guard, installed machine guns around the perimeter, and blocked off the street so no one could approach. I don't know how General Prats managed to filter through such fortifications.

By midyear of 1975, repression had been refined to perfection, and I fell victim to my own terror. I was afraid to use the telephone, I censored letters to my mother in case they were opened at the post office, and was careful about what I said even in the bosom of the family. Friends who had contact with the military had warned me that my name was on the blacklists, and soon after we received two death threats by telephone. I was aware that there were people who took pleasure from spreading panic, and perhaps I should not have listened to those anonymous voices, but after what had happened to General Prats and his wife, and my parents' miraculous escape, I didn't feel safe. One April afternoon, Michael and the children and I went to the airport to say goodbye to friends who, like so many others, had opted to leave. They had learned that Australia was offering land to new immigrants and had decided to test their luck as farmers. We were watching the departing plane when a woman who was a total stranger to me came up and asked, wasn't I the person on television? She insisted I go with her because she had something to tell me in private. Without giving me time to react, she pulled me into the restroom and once we were alone removed an envelope from her purse and handed it to me.

"Deliver this, it's a matter of life and death. I have to leave on the next plane; my contact didn't appear and I can't wait any longer," she said. She made me repeat the address twice, to be sure I had memorized it, and then ran away.

"Who was that?" Michael asked when he saw me come out of the restroom.

"I don't have any idea. She asked me to deliver this, she said it's very important."

"What is it? Why did you take it? It could be a trap. . . ."

All those questions, and others that occurred to us later, resulted in very little sleep that night. We didn't want to open the envelope because it was better not to know its contents, we were afraid to take it to the address the woman had given me, and neither could we bring ourselves to destroy it. During that long night I think that Michael realized that I didn't seek out problems, they found me. We could see finally how twisted reality had become when a request as simple as delivering a letter could cost us our lives, and when the subject of torture and death was now a part of our everyday conversation, something fully accepted. At dawn the next morning, we spread a map of the world on the dining room table to look for somewhere we might go. By then, half the population of Latin America was living under military dictatorships; using the pretext of combating Communism, the armed forces of several countries had been transformed into mercenaries for the privileged class and instruments of repression for the poor. In the next decade, military governments waged all-out war against their own peoples; millions of persons died, disappeared, and were exiled; never before on our continent had such a vast movement of human masses poured across borders. That morning, we discovered that there were very few democracies left in which to seek refuge, and that several of those—like Mexico, Costa Rica, and Colombia—

were no longer issuing visas for Chileans because too many had emigrated there in the last year and a half. As soon as the curfew was lifted, we left the children with Granny, gave instructions in case we did not return, and went to deliver the envelope to the indicated address. We rang the bell of an old house in the middle of town; a man dressed in blue jeans came to the door and, with great relief, we saw that he was wearing a clerical collar. We recognized his Belgian accent because we had lived in that country.

After fleeing Argentina, Tío Ramón and my mother found themselves with nowhere to go, and for months had to accept the hospitality of friends in foreign countries, unable to unpack their suitcases once and for all in a place of their own. About this time, my mother recalled the Venezuelan she had met in the geriatric clinic in Romania; following a hunch, she looked for the card she had kept all those years and called her friend in Caracas to tell him briefly what had happened. "Come on here, my dear, there's room for everyone," was Valentín Hernández's immediate response. That gave Michael and me the idea that we might move to Venezuela; from what we knew, it was a green and generous country where we could count on one friend and stay a while until the situation in Chile improved. We began to make plans: we would have to rent the house, sell the furniture, and find new jobs, but we rushed everything through in less than a week. That Wednesday, the children came home from school in abject terror; two strangers had cornered them in the street and then, after threatening them, gave them a message for me: "Tell that bitch of your mother that her days are numbered."

The next day I went to see my grandfather for the last time. I remember him always in the armchair I had bought him many years before at an auction, his mane like silver and his rustic cane in his hand. He must have been tall when he was young, because sitting down he still looked as if he were; with age, however, the pillars of his body had bowed and he had settled like a building with faulty foundations. I couldn't tell him goodbye; I didn't have the courage to say I was leaving, but I suppose he sensed it.

"Something has been worrying me for a long time, Tata. Did you ever kill a man?"

"Why are you asking me such a harebrained question?"

"Because you have a bad temper?" I hinted, thinking of the body of the fisherman lying face up on the sand, in those remote days when I was eight years old.

"You've never seen me with a weapon in my hands, have you? I have good reason not to trust them," he said. "When I was young I woke up one morning early when something hit the window of my room. I leaped out of bed, grabbed my revolver and, still half-asleep, pointed it out the window and fired. I came fully awake with the sound of the shot, and was horrified to realize I had tried to shoot some students coming home from a party. It was just one of them raking my shutter with his umbrella. Thank God, I didn't kill him, but I came within a hair of murdering an innocent man. Since then, my hunting rifles have been in the garage. I haven't used them for years."

It was true. Hanging from a bedpost was the sling Argentine gauchos use, two stone balls affixed to either end of a long strip of leather, which was what he kept at hand should anyone break into the house.

"And you never used those bolas or a club to kill anyone? Someone who insulted or harmed a member of your family?"

"I don't know what the devil you're talking about, Isabel. This country is filled with murderers, but I'm not one of them."

It was the first time he had referred to the situation we were living through in Chile; until then, he had limited himself to listening, tight-lipped and silent, to the stories I told him. He got to his feet with a small explosion of bones and curses; he could barely walk, but no one dared mention the possibility of a wheelchair. He motioned for me to follow him. Nothing had changed in his room since my grandmother died: black furniture arranged in the same positions, grandfather clock, the scent of the English soap he stored in his armoire. He opened his desk with the key he always carried in his jacket, looked through one of the drawers, and pulled out an antique biscuit tin and handed it to me.

"This was your grandmother's, now it's yours," he said, his voice breaking.

"I have to confess something, Tata. . . ."

"You're going to tell me you took Memé's silver mirror."

"How did you know it was me?"

"Because I saw you. I sleep very lightly. Now that you have the mirror you may as well have the rest. It's all that's left of Memé, but I don't need these things to remember her and I'd like for them to be in your hands, because when I die I don't want them thrown away."

"Don't think about dying, Tata."

"At my age, there's nothing else to think about. I know I will die alone, like a dog."

"I'll be with you."

"I hope you don't forget that you made me a promise. If you're thinking about going anywhere, remember that when the moment comes, you have to help me die with dignity."

"I haven't forgotten, Tata, don't worry."

The next day I flew to Venezuela, alone. I did not know I would never see my grandfather again. I went through the formalities at the airport with Memé's relics clutched to my chest. The biscuit tin contained the remnants of a crown of wax orange blossoms, a pair of child-size kid gloves the color of time, and a well-thumbed prayer book with mother-of-pearl covers. I also took with me a plastic bag with a handful of dirt from our garden, with the idea of planting forget-me-nots in another land. The official who checked my passport saw the frequent Argentine entrance and exit stamps and my newspaper pass and, as I assume he did not find my name on his list, let me leave. The plane climbed through a featherbed of clouds, and minutes later we crossed the snow-covered heights of the Andes. Those white peaks thrusting through winter clouds were the last image I had of my country. "I'll be back, I'll be back," I repeated like a prayer.

ANDREA, MY GRANDDAUGHTER, WAS BORN IN OUR TV ROOM, ON ONE of the first warm days of spring. Celia and Nicolás's apartment is on the third floor, and has no elevator, so it isn't practical in case of an emergency, and that's why they chose our ground floor as the place to bring the baby into the world, in a large, much lived-in room with windows opening onto the terrace; on clear days you can see the three Bay bridges and at night the lights of Berkeley twinkle from across the water. Celia has adjusted so well to the California lifestyle that she decided to carry *The Music of the Universe* to its ultimate conclusion, bypassing hospital and physicians to give birth among her family. Her first pains began at midnight; at dawn, her water burst and, soon after, she and Nicolás appeared at our house. They arrived with the dazed air of victims of a natural catastrophe, in bedroom slippers, carrying a worn black bag containing necessary belongings, and Alejandro, still half asleep and in his pajamas. He had no idea that within a few hours he would have to share his space with a little sister and that his totalitarian reign as only child and grandchild was about to end. Two hours later, the midwife arrived, a young woman willing to run the risk of working in private homes, driving a station wagon packed with the instruments of her trade and dressed like a hiker in shorts and Keds. She fit into the family routine so easily that soon she was in the kitchen helping Willie prepare breakfast. In the meantime, Celia was walking back and forth, leaning on Nicolás, never losing her calm, taking short breaths when she doubled over with pain, and resting when the small being in her womb gave her a brief respite. My daughter-in-law carries in her veins secret songs that mark the rhythm of her steps as she walks; during the contractions, she panted and rocked back and forth as if listening to an irresistible, internal Venezuelan drumbeat. Toward the end, I thought that occasionally she made fists of her hands and a flash of terror passed through her eyes, but immediately her husband made her look straight at him, and whispered something in the private code of husband and wife, and her tension eased. That was how time went by, vertiginously for me and all too slowly for the one bearing this ordeal without complaint, tranquilizer, or anesthesia. Nicolás supported her; my humble participation consisted of offering crushed ice and apple juice, and Willie's of entertaining Alejandro, while from a prudent distance the midwife followed developments without intervening. I couldn't help remember my own experience when Nicolás was born—so different from this. From the instant I crossed the threshold of the hospital, I lost my sense of identity and became a number, not someone with a name. They took my clothes, handed me a gown that opened in the back, and assigned me an isolated room where I was subjected to additional humiliations and then left alone. From time to time someone explored between my legs; my body had become a single throbbing, pain-filled cavern. I spent a day, a night, and a good part of the next day in labor, exhausted and frightened nearly to death, until finally someone announced that the big moment was approaching and I was taken to a delivery room. Flat on my back on a metal table, my bones turned to ash, blinded by lights, I gave myself to the suffering. I had nothing to do with anything now, the baby was struggling to come out and my hips opened to help without any intervention of will. Everything I had learned in manuals and courses was forgotten. There comes a moment when the journey begun cannot be halted; we roll toward a frontier, pass through a mysterious door, and wake on the other side in a different life: the child enters the world, and the mother a different state of consciousness, neither of the two will ever be the same. With Nicolás, I was initiated into the universe of woman, the previous cesarean had deprived me of the rite only female mammals share. The joyful process of engendering a child, the patience of gestation, the fortitude to bring it into life, and the feeling of profound amazement with which everything culminates can be compared only to creating a book. Children, like books, are voyages into one's inner self, during which body, mind, and soul shift course and turn toward the very center of existence.

The climate of tranquil joy that reigned in our house when Andrea was born bore no resemblance to my anguish in that delivery room twenty-five years earlier. By midafternoon, Celia made a sign; Nicolás helped her climb onto the bed and in less than a minute the apparatus and instruments the midwife carried in her station wagon materialized in the room. That girl in shorts seemed suddenly to mature; her tone of voice changed and millennia of female experience were reflected in her freckled face. "Wash your hands and be ready," she told me with a wink. "Now it's your turn to work." Celia put her arms around her husband, gritted her teeth, and pushed. And then, on a surging wave of blood, emerged a flattened, purplish face and a head covered with dark hair, which I held like a chalice with one hand while with the other I quickly unlooped the bluish cord wrapped around the baby's neck. With another brutal push from the mother, the rest of my granddaughter's body appeared, a blood-washed, fragile package: a most extraordinary gift. With a primeval sob, I felt in the core of my being the sacred experience of birth—the effort, the pain, the panic—and, gratefully, I marveled at my daughter-in-law's heroic courage and the prodigy of her solid body and noble spirit, designed for motherhood. Through a veil, I seemed to see a rapturous Nicolás, who took the baby from my hands and placed her on her mother's belly. Celia rose up from among her pillows, panting, dripping with sweat, transformed by inner light and, completely indifferent to the remainder of her body, which continued contracting and bleeding, she folded her arms about her daughter and welcomed her with a waterfall of words in a newly coined language, kissing and nuzzling her as every mammalian mother does, then offered the baby her breast in the most ancient gesture of humankind. Time congealed in the room, and the sun stopped above the roses on the terrace; the world was holding its breath to celebrate the miracle of that new life. The midwife handed me scissors; I cut the umbilical cord, and Andrea began a destiny separate from her mother's. Where did this small wonder come from? Where had she been before she was conceived in Celia's womb? I have a thousand questions to ask her, but I fear that by the time she can answer she will have forgotten what heaven was like. . . . Silence before being born, silence after death: life is nothing but noise between two unfathomable silences.

Paula spent a month in the rehabilitation clinic; they examined her inside and out and when they had finished gave us a devastating report. Michael had come from Chile, and Ernesto was there, too, on special leave from his job. He had succeeded in being transferred to New York, so that at least we were in the same country, six hours away in case of emergency and within easy reach by telephone any time we were overcome with sadness. He had not seen his wife since our nightmarish trip from Madrid and, in spite of my having kept him informed in minute detail, he was visibly affected when he found Paula looking so beautiful, and so much more absent. This man is like those trees that survive hurricane winds, he bends but doesn't break. He arrived with presents for Paula, rushed into her room, put his arms around her, and kissed her, murmuring how much he had missed her and how pretty she looked, as she stared staight ahead, her large eyes like a doll's, totally devoid of light. Later, Ernesto lay beside her to show her photographs from their honeymoon and recall happy times from last year; finally, they both slept, like any normal couple at siesta time. I pray he will meet some healthy woman with a gentle soul like Paula's, and be happy, far away from here; he should not be bound to someone so ill for the rest of his life, but it isn't time to talk about this yet, it's too soon. The physicians and therapists who treated Paula called the family together and gave us their verdict: her level of consciousness is nil, there have been no signs of change during these four weeks, they have not been able to establish communication with her, and it is realistic to expect that she will continue to deteriorate. She will never speak or be able to swallow, she will not be able to move of her own volition, and it is doubtful she will ever recognize anyone. Rehabilitation is out of the question, but she must have exercises to maintain flexibility. Their final recommendation was that we place her in an institution for people in her condition, because she will require permanent care and cannot be left alone, not even for a minute. A long silence followed the last words of the report. On the other side of the table sat Nicolás and Celia, holding their children, and Ernesto, with his head in his hands.

"It is important to decide what should be done in a case of pneumonia, say, or some serious infection. Will you opt for aggressive treatment?" asked one of the doctors.

None of us understood what he was saying.

"If massive doses of antibiotics are administered, or if she is placed in intensive care every time there is a crisis, she can live many more years. Without treatment, she will die sooner," he explained.

Ernesto lifted his head and our eyes met. I also looked at Nicolás and Celia and, without hesitating or consulting, each of the three made the same sign. "Paula will not be taken back to the intensive care unit, nor will we have her tortured with further blood transfusions, drugs, or painful tests. If her condition is serious, we will be at her side to help her die," I said, with a voice so firm I could not recognize it as mine.

Michael left the room, completely undone, and a few days later returned to Chile. In that instant it became clear that my daughter was being returned to my arms, and it would be I and I alone who assumed responsibility for her life and made decisions at the moment of her death. The two of us, together and alone, as on the day of her birth. I felt a wave of strength surge through my body like an electric current, and realized that the travails of my long road had been a cruel preparation for this test. I am not defeated, there is still much I can do. Western medicine is not the only alternative in these cases, I shall knock at other doors and resort to other methods, including the most improbable, to save my daughter. From the beginning, I planned to take Paula home, and so during the month she was in the clinic, I had watched how they cared for her and how they used the physiotherapy equipment. Within three days, I obtained everything we needed, including a hospital bed with a lift, and hired four women from Central America to help me with day and night shifts. I interviewed fifteen applicants and chose the four who seemed the most loving, because we have passed the stage for efficiency and are entering the stage of love. Each of the women carries the burden of a tragedy, but none has lost her motherly smile. One of them has knife scars on her arms and legs; her husband was murdered in El Salvador and she was left for dead in a pool of blood, with her three small children. Somehow, she dragged herself to where she could get help, and shortly afterward escaped the country, leaving her children with their grandmother. Another of the women is from Nicaragua; she has not seen her five children in many years but she is planning to bring them here, one by one; she works and saves every penny in order to be reunited with them one day. The first floor of our house had been turned into Paula's kingdom, but it is still the family room, too, where we have our television and music and the children's games. It was in this room that Andrea was born only a week ago, and her aunt will be living here for as long as she wants to remain in this world. Summer's geraniums are visible through the windows, and roses in wheelbarrows, loyal companions through many rough times. Nicolás painted the walls white, and we have surrounded Paula's bed with photographs of relatives and friends from happy years, and set her rag

doll on a shelf. There is no way to disguise the huge machines she
needs, but at least the room is more welcoming than the hospital
rooms where she has lived in recent months. On that sunny morning my daughter arrived in the ambulance, the house seemed to
open happily to welcome her. For the first half hour, everything was
activity, noise, and busyness, but suddenly everything had been
accomplished: Paula was installed in her bed and we began our routines; the family went their various ways, leaving the two of us alone,
and then I felt the silence and calm of the house in repose. I sat
beside Paula and took her hand as time ticked slowly by. As the
hours passed I watched the colors of the Bay change, and then the
sun was gone and June's late darkness began to fall. A large tortoiseshell cat I had never seen before jumped in through the open window, made a few turns around the room, familiarizing herself with
the layout, and then leapt onto the bed and lay at Paula's feet. She
likes cats, perhaps she called this one with her thoughts to keep her
company. The hectic pace of life has ended for me, I am moving to
Paula's rhythm, time is still on the clocks. Nothing to do. I have
days, weeks, years beside my daughter's bed, hours to spend without knowing what to expect. I do know that Paula will never be the
person she was before; her mind has gone God knows where, but
her body and her spirit are here. Paula's intelligence was her most
striking characteristic, it was at second glance that her goodness was
revealed; it is so hard for me to imagine that such a gifted brain is
reduced to a black cloud on an X-ray screen, that her bent for study,
her sense of humor, her memory for the smallest details are gone
forever. She is like a plant, the doctors said. The cat can entice me
to give her food and let her sleep on the bed, but Paula doesn't recognize me and cannot even squeeze my hand to indicate what she
wants. I have tried to teach her to blink, one for yes, two for no, but
it is a fruitless effort. At least she is here with me now, safe in this
house, with all of us protecting her. She will not be troubled again
with needles and probes; from now on, she will know only caresses,
music, and flowers. My task is to keep her body healthy and to prevent pain so that her spirit will have peace in which to fulfill the
remainder of its mission on earth. Silence. There are hours and
hours for doing nothing. I become aware of my body, of my breath-

ing, of the way my weight is distributed in the chair, of how my spinal column supports me and my muscles obey my desires. I decide I want a drink of water, and my arm moves to pick up the glass with the precise force and velocity; I drink, and I feel the movements of my tongue and lips, the fresh taste in my mouth, the cold liquid going down my throat. My poor daughter can do none of that; if she wants to drink she cannot ask, she must wait until someone else divines her need and comes to squirt water from a syringe into the tube in her stomach. She does not feel the relief of thirst satisfied, her lips are always dry; I can barely moisten them because if I wet them the liquid can go into her lungs. Stalled . . . the two of us are stalled within this brutal parenthesis. My friends have recommended a Dr. Cheri Forrester, who is experienced with terminal patients and known for her compassion; I called her and, to my surprise, she had read my books and will come to see Paula here in the house. She is a small and soft young woman with dark eyes and an intense expression, who said hello with a hug and listened with an open heart to my story of what has happened.

"What do you want me to do?" she asked finally, tears in her eyes.

"Help me keep Paula healthy and comfortable, help at the moment of her death, and help in seeking other avenues of treatment. I know that traditional doctors can't do anything for her, I'm going to try alternative medicine: healers, plants, homeopathy, everything I can find."

"That is just what I would do if she were my daughter, but you should set a time limit for these experiments. You can't live on wishful thinking, and things here don't come cheaply. Paula could remain in this condition for many years, so you must husband your strength and your resources with care."

"How long, then?"

"Let's say three months. If in that period of time there are no appreciable results, you stop trying."

"All right."

She introduced me to Dr. Miki Shima, a colorful Japanese acupuncturist whom I am saving to be a character in a novel, that is, if I ever write fiction again. The word spread quickly, and soon I had a parade of unconventional practitioners offering their services: one who sells magnetic mattresses for energy, a hypnotist who tapes stories from end to beginning and plays them to Paula on earphones, a holy woman from India who incarnates the Universal Mother, an Apache who combines the wisdom of his great-grandfathers with the power of crystals, and an astrologer who sees the future, but in visions so confused they can be interpreted in contradictory ways. I listen to all of them, at the same time trying not to disturb Paula's comfort. I also made a pilgrimage to a famous psychic in Utah, a man with dyed hair and an office filled with stuffed animals, who, without moving from his home, examined Paula with his third eye. He recommended a combination of powders and drops quite complicated to administer, but Nicolás, who is very skeptical about such things, compared the ingredients with a bottle of Centrum, an everyday multivitamin tablet, and found they were almost identical. None of these strange doctors has promised to restore my daughter's health, but perhaps they can improve the quality of her days and achieve some form of communication. The healers also offer me their prayers and natural remedies; one of them sent for holy water from a sacred spring in Mexico, and sprinkles it with such faith that maybe a miracle will happen. Dr. Shima comes each week and lifts our spirits; he examines Paula carefully, places his slender needles in her ears and feet, and prescribes homeopathic remedies. From time to time he strokes her hair as if she were his daughter, and his eyes fill with tears. "She's so pretty," he says. "If we can keep her healthy, maybe science will find a way to renew damaged cells, even transplant brains. Why not?" "No way, Doctor," I reply. "No one is going to conduct Frankenstein experiments on Paula." For me, he brought Oriental herbs which translate as, "For sadness provoked by grief or loss of love," and I suppose it is thanks to them that I continue to function with relative normality. Dr. Forrester observes all this with sadness. Maybe she also prays for a miracle. This kind woman has become a friend. She seems concerned about my health, too; she finds me depressed and drained, and has prescribed sleeping pills, warning me not to take more than one because they can be fatal.

It does me good to write, even though at times I can barely force myself to it because each word sears like a burn. These pages are an irreversible voyage through a long tunnel; I can't see an exit but I know there must be one. I can't go back, only continue to go forward, step by step, to the end. As I write, I look for a sign, hoping that Paula will break her implacable silence and answer somehow in these yellow pages—or perhaps I do it only to overcome my fear and to fix the fleeting images of an imperfect memory. It also helps to walk. A half-hour from our house there are hills and dense forests where I go to breathe deeply when I am choked by anguish or ground down by exhaustion. The landscape, green, humid, and rather somber, reminds me of the south of Chile: the same centuries-old trees, the sharp scent of eucalyptus, pine, and wild mint, the streams that turn to cascades in winter, the cries of birds and shrill of crickets. I have discovered a solitary place where verdant treetops form the high dome of a Gothic cathedral and a thread of water slips with its own music among the stones. I like to sit there, listening to the water and the rhythm of the blood in my veins, trying to breathe calmly and retreat within my own skin, but instead of finding peace, premonitions and memories thunder through my mind. In the most difficult moments of the past, I also sought solitude in a forest.

From the moment I crossed the cordillera that marks the boundary of Chile, everything began to go badly, and got progressively worse as the years went by. I did not know it yet, but I had begun to live the prophecy of the Argentine seer: many years of immobility. It was not to be within the walls of a cell or in a wheelchair, as my mother and I had conjectured, but in the isolation of exile. My roots were chopped off with a single whack and it would take six years to grow new ones nurtured in memory and in the books I would write. During that long period, frustration and silence were to be my prison. The first night in Caracas, sitting on a strange bed in a bare room, with the uninterrupted uproar from the street filtering through a small window, I took an accounting of what I had lost and contemplated the long road of obstacles and loneliness that lay ahead. The impact of arrival was that of having fallen onto a different planet. I had come from winter, the petrifying order of the dictatorship, and widespread poverty to a hot and anarchical country in the midst of a petroleum boom, an oil-rich society in which profligacy reached absurd limits: everything was flown in from Miami, even bread and eggs, because it was easier to import than to produce them. In the first newspaper that came into my hands, I read about a birthday party, complete with orchestra and champagne, held for some society woman's spoiled lapdog and attended by other pampered pooches in party togs. For me, raised in the sobriety of Tata's house, it was hard to believe such exhibitionism; with time, however, I not only got used to it, I learned to enjoy it. Love of revelry, the sense of living in the present, and the optimistic vision of the Venezuelans that at first terrified me later became the lessons I valued most from that period of my life. It took years to learn the rules of that society and to discover a way to slip over the rugged terrain of exile without creating too much friction, but when finally I succeeded, I felt freed of the back-bowing burdens I had carried in my own country. I lost my fear of appearing ridiculous, of social sanctions, of "coming down in the world," as my grandfather referred to poverty and my own hot blood. Sensuality ceased to be a defect that had to be hidden for the sake of gentility, and was accepted as a basic ingredient of my temperament and, later, my writing. In Venezuela, I cured myself of some ancient wounds, along with new animosities. I shed my old skin and met the world with my nerves laid bare until I grew another, tougher hide. In Venezuela, I educated my children, acquired both a daughter- and a son-in-law, wrote three books, and ended my marriage. When I think of the thirteen years I lived in Caracas, I feel a mixture of incredulity and lightheartedness. Five weeks after my arrival, when it was obvious that a return to Chile anytime soon would be impossible, Michael came and brought the children, leaving the house locked up with our belongings inside. He was not able to rent it because so many people were leaving the country that it made more sense to buy at a bargain price than to pay rent; furthermore, ours was a rustic cabin whose only value was sentimental. While it sat empty, the windows were broken out and the contents stolen, but we didn't know that until a year later, and by then it didn't matter. Those five weeks away from my children were a bad dream. I still remember with photographic clarity Paula's and Nicolás's faces when they got off the plane holding their father's hand and felt the hot and humid breath of that eternal summer. They were both wearing wool clothes; Paula had her rag doll under her arm and Nicolás was carrying the heavy iron Christ his teacher had given him. He looked smaller, and thin; I learned afterward that he had refused to eat in my absence. A few months later, thanks to visas obtained with the help of Valentín Hernández, who had never forgotten the promise he made my mother in the Romanian hospital, the entire family was reunited. My parents moved into an apartment two floors above our own, and, after complicated negotiations, my brother Pancho and his family were allowed to leave Moscow and join us in Venezuela. Juan also came, with the intention of staying, but he could not endure the heat and general commotion and so made arrangements to go to the United States on a student scholarship. Granny stayed in Chile, worn down by loneliness and sorrow; overnight, she lost the grandchildren she had raised and found herself facing an empty life of looking after an aged man who spent his days in bed watching television and a neurotic Swiss dog inherited from my mother. She began to drink more and more, and since the children were gone and she had no need to keep up appearances, she made no attempt to hide it. Bottles piled up in corners while her husband pretended not to see them. She practically stopped eating or sleeping; she spent her nights with a drink in her hand, rocking disconsolately in the chair where for years she had sung the children to sleep. Worms of sadness were eating away inside; the aquamarine of her eyes faded and her hair fell out in clumps; her skin grew thick and furrowed, like a turtle's. She stopped bathing and dressing, and wandered about in her robe and slippers, drying her tears on her sleeve. Two years later, Michael's sister, who lived in Uruguay, took her parents to live with her, but it was already too late to save Granny.

Caracas in 1975 was happy and chaotic, one of the world's most expensive cities. New buildings and broad highways were springing up everywhere and money was squandered in a surfeit of luxuries; there were bars, banks, restaurants, and hotels for love nests on every corner, and the streets were permanently clogged by the thousands of late-model automobiles that could not move in the pandemonium of the traffic. No one respected traffic lights, but they would stop dead on the freeway to let some distracted pedestrian cross. Money seemed to grow on trees; thick wads of bills changed hands with such speed that there was no time to count them. The men maintained several mistresses, the women went shopping in Miami every weekend, and children considered an annual trip to Disney World to be an innate right. Without money, you could do nothing, as I quickly learned after going to the bank to change the dollars I had bought in the black market in Chile and found to my horror that half were counterfeit. There were slums where people lived in misery, and regions where polluted water killed as many people as it had in the colonial era, but in the euphoria of easy wealth, no one remembered that. Political power was divided in a friendly manner between the two most powerful parties—the Left had been annulled and the guerrilla movement of the seventies, one of the most organized on the continent, defeated. Coming from Chile, it was refreshing to find that no one talked about politics or illness. The men, strutting with power and virility, wore ostentatious gold chains and rings, joked and spoke at a shout, and always had one eye on the women. Beside them, discreet Chileans with their high-pitched voices and delicate Spanish seemed like dolls on a wedding cake. The most beautiful women on the planet, the splendid product of many combined races, swayed their hips to a salsa rhythm, exhibiting exuberant bodies and winning every international beauty contest. The air vibrated, every opportunity was seized to break into song, radios blasted on the street, in cars, everywhere. Drums, four-string *cuatros,* guitars, singing, dancing, the country was one continuous fiesta on a petroleum binge. Immigrants came from the four cardinal points to this land to seek their fortunes—especially Colombians, who poured across the border by the millions to earn a living doing jobs no one else wanted. A foreigner was at first accepted only grudgingly, but soon the Venezuelans' natural generosity threw open the doors. The most disliked immigrants were from the Southern Cone—Argentines, Uruguayans, and Chileans—because they were primarily political refugees, intellectuals, technicians, and professionals who competed with Venezuelans at the higher echelons. I learned very quickly that when you emigrate, you lose the crutches that have been your support; you must begin from zero, because the past is erased with a single stroke and no one cares where you're from or what you did before. I met people who were truly eminent in their own country yet were unable to revalidate their professional licenses and ended up selling insurance door to door—also nobodies who invented diplomas and pedigrees and somehow fought their way to the top: everything depended on audacity and good connections. Anything could be had through a friend, or by paying the fee for corruption. A foreign professional could be granted a contract only through a Venezuelan associate who sponsored him and lent his name to the deal; otherwise, a newcomer had no chance at all. The going rate was fifty percent; one did the work and the other signed and collected his percentage up front, as soon as the first payments were made. Within a week of his arrival, a job came up for Michael in a broiling region in the eastern part of the country, an area just beginning to be developed because of the boundless treasure beneath the soil. All Venezuela was sitting on a sea of black gold; anywhere you buried a pick in the ground, a thick stream of oil shot up. The natural riches of that country are paradisaical; there are regions where nuggets of gold and raw diamonds are scattered across the earth like seeds. Everything grows in that climate; along the highways you see wild banana and pineapple trees, you toss a mango stone on the ground and within a few days have a tree—a flowering plant even budded on our television antenna. Nature there is still in a stage of innocence: warm beaches with white sand and matted trees, mountains with snowy peaks where lost ghosts of conquistadors still roam, vast lunar plains suddenly interrupted by prodigious *tepuys,* towering cylinders of live rock that look as if they were set there by giants from other planets, impenetrable jungles inhabited by ancient tribes that have yet to discover the Iron Age. Everything gives of itself unstintingly in that enchanted land. Michael became part of a gigantic project on one of the largest dams in the world, in a green and overgrown region of snakes, sweat, and crime. The men were housed in temporary camps, leaving their families in nearby cities, but my chances of finding work in that part of the country, or of finding good schools for the children, were nonexistent, so we three stayed in Caracas and Michael came to visit us every six or seven weeks. We lived in an apartment in the noisiest and most densely populated district of the city. For the children, who were used to walking to school, riding their bicycles, playing in their garden, and visiting Granny, it was hell; they couldn't go out alone because of the traffic and violence in the streets, they were bored to tears confined within four walls watching television, and every day they begged me, Please, could we go back to Chile? I did not help them bear the anguish of those early years; on the contrary, my bad humor rarefied the air we breathed. I could not find employment in any of the jobs I knew how to do, and past experience was less than useless—all doors were closed. I sent out hundreds of résumés, answered countless newspaper ads, and filled out a mountain of applications, all without a single bite; everything was left hanging while I awaited an answer that never came. I hadn't caught on that in Venezuela the word "no" is considered in bad taste. When I was told to "Come back tomorrow," my hopes were renewed; I failed to understand that postponement was an amiable form of rejection. From the modest celebrity I had enjoyed in Chile from my television and feminist reporting, I slumped to the anonymity and daily humiliation of a person looking for work. Thanks to a Chilean friend, I published a weekly humor column in a newspaper and continued to do so for several years just to keep a byline, but I was working for love of the art—the remuneration was equivalent to what I paid the taxi when I delivered the article. I did some translating, wrote some television scripts, and even a play. For some of my efforts, I was paid royally but the work never saw the light of day; in other cases, it was used but I never saw a cent of payment. Two floors above me, Tío Ramón dressed every morning in one of his ambassador suits and went out to look for work, but, unlike me, he never complained. His fall was more to be lamented than mine because he had risen higher, had lost more, was twenty-five years older, and must have had twice the dignity to be injured; even so, I never saw him depressed. On weekends, he organized trips to the beach with the children, veritable safaris that he tackled head on at the wheel of the car, with Caribbean music on the radio and a joke on his lips, sweating, scratching mosquito bites, and reminding us not to forget we were filthy rich, until finally we could take a dip in the warm turquoise ocean, elbow to elbow with hundreds of others with the same idea. Occasionally, on some blessed Wednesday, I would escape to the coast and enjoy a clean, empty beach, but such solitary excursions were filled with risks. In those times of loneliness and impotence, I more than ever needed some contact with nature—the peace of a forest, the silence of a mountain, the whisper of the sea—but women were not expected to go alone to the movies, much less somewhere in open country where anything could happen. I felt like a prisoner in the apartment, and in my own skin, just as my children did, but at least we were safe from the violence of the dictatorship, sheltered in the vastness of Venezuela. I had found a secure place to scatter the soil from my garden and plant forget-me-nots, but I didn't know that yet.

I awaited Michael's rare visits with impatience, but when finally we were together I felt inexplicably disillusioned. He arrived worn out from work and life in the camp; he was not the man I had invented in the suffocating nights of Caracas. In the following months and years, we ran out of words; it was all we could do to manage a neutral conversation sprinkled with commonplaces and polite phrases. I had the impulse to seize Michael by the shirt and shake him and scream at him, but I was inhibited by the rigorous sense of fairness instilled in my English schools and, instead, welcomed him with a tenderness that welled up spontaneously when I saw him but disappeared within minutes. The man had just spent weeks in the jungle working to support his family, he had left Chile, his friends, and the security of a good job to follow me in an unpredictable adventure, and I had no right to bother him with my heart's impatience. "It would be much healthier if you two would grab each other by the hair the way we do," was the comment of my mother and Tío Ramón, my only confidantes in that period, but it was impossible to confront a husband who offered no resistance; all Michael's aggression had sunk out of sight, converted into boredom in the cottony texture of our relationship. I tried to convince myself that despite the difficult circumstances nothing actually had changed between us. I did not succeed, but in trying I deceived Michael. If I had spoken frankly, the final disaster might have been avoided, but I lacked the courage to do it. I was burning with unanswered desires and worries; that was a time of several love affairs embarked upon to while away my loneliness. No one knew me, I owed no one explanations. I looked for release where I was least likely to find it, because in truth I am not cut out for sneaking around. I am very clumsy in the tangled stratagems of the lie; I left signs everywhere, but Michael was too decent to suspect that anyone could be untrue to him. I argued with myself in secret, and boiled with guilt, divided between disgust and rage against myself and resentment toward a remote husband floating imperturbably in a fog of ignorance— always pleasant and discreet, with unflagging equanimity, never asking for anything but expecting to be waited upon with a distant and vaguely grateful air. I needed an excuse to break off the marriage once and for all, but he never provided one—just the opposite, during those years his reputation for saintliness actually grew in the eyes of others. I suppose he was so absorbed in his work, and his need to have a home was so great, that he chose not to delve too deeply into my feelings or my activities. A chasm was widening beneath our feet but he did not want to see the signs and clung to his illusions to the last moment, when everything came crashing down with a roar. If he suspected anything, he may have attributed it to an existential crisis, thinking it would go away, like the twenty-four-hour flu. I realized only years later that blindness in the face of reality was the strongest facet of his character; I always assumed total responsibility for the failure of our love, that is, that I wasn't able to love him as much as he apparently loved me. I never asked myself whether he deserved more dedication, I only wondered why I couldn't give it. Our paths diverged; I was changing and drifting away from him and could do nothing to prevent it. While he was working in the exuberant vegetation and steamy humidity of a wild landscape, I was butting my head against the walls of the apartment in Caracas like a crazed rat, always looking south toward Chile and counting the days until our return. I never dreamed that the dictatorship would last seventeen years.

The man I fell in love with in 1978 was a musician, one more political refugee among the thousands from the south who flocked to Caracas in the decade of the seventies. He had escaped the death squads, leaving a wife and two children behind in Buenos Aires while he looked for a place to settle and find work, with a flute and a guitar as his only letter of introduction. I suppose that the love we shared caught him by surprise, when he least desired and needed it, just as it did me. A Chilean theater producer who lighted in Caracas, hoping to make a killing like so many attracted by the oil bonanza, got in touch with me and asked me to write a musical comedy on a local theme. It was an opportunity I couldn't pass up, I was out of a job and feeling desperate about how my small hoard of savings had evaporated. We needed a composer with experience in this type of show to write the songs, although I'm not sure why the producer preferred someone from the south to one of many excellent Venezuelan musicians. That was how, there beside a dusty baby grand piano, I came to meet the man who would be my lover. I remember very little about that first day; I did not feel comfortable with that arrogant and bad-humored Argentine, but I was impressed with his talent: with no effort at all, he incorporated my vague ideas into precise musical phrases, and he played any instrument by ear. To someone like myself, who can't sing "Happy Birthday," he seemed a genius. He was as slim and taut as a toreador, ironic and aggressive, with a Mephistophelian beard, cut rather short. He was as lonely and lost in Caracas as I, and I suppose that circumstance drew us together. A few days later, we went to a park, out of hearing of indiscreet ears, to go over the songs; he took his guitar and I brought a notebook and a picnic basket. That and other long musical sessions turned out to be pointless because, overnight, the producer vanished like smoke, leaving a theater under contract and nine people who never got paid. Some of us had wasted time and effort; others had invested money that disappeared without a trace—at least I was left with a memorable adventure. During that first outdoor repast, we shared the stories of our lives; I told him about the military coup and he brought me up to date on the horrors of the Dirty War and the reasons why he had to leave Argentina. The conversation ended, to my surprise, with my defending Venezuela against his criticisms, which were the very same I had made the day before. "If you don't like this country, why don't you go somewhere else? I for one am very grateful to be living with my family in this democracy; at least here they're not murdering people the way they are in Chile and Argentina," I said with an excess of passion. He burst out laughing, picked up his guitar, and began to strum a mocking tango. He made me feel like someone from the sticks, something that would happen many times in our relationship. He was one of those Buenos Aires night-owl intellectuals who frequent its old taverns and cafés, a part of the theater, music, and literary crowd, a voracious reader, a quarrelsome man with a quick answer for everything. He had seen the world and met famous people and was ferociously competitive, and I was seduced by his stories and his intelligence. In contrast, I doubt that I impressed him much at all; in his eyes, I was a thirty-five-year-old Chilean émigré who dressed like a hippie but had bourgeois mores. The one time I scored with him was when I told him that Che Guevara had dined at my parents' house in Geneva; from that moment on, he showed real interest in me. All my life, I have found that with most men that dinner with the heroic guerrilla of the Cuban Revolution acts as an irresistible aphrodisiac. Within a week, the summer rains had begun and our bucolic meetings in the park became far from private sessions in my house. One day he invited me to his apartment, a squalid, noisy room he rented by the week. We had coffee, he showed me photographs of his family, then one song led to another, and then another, until we ended up playing the flute in his bed. That is not one of the gross metaphors that horrify my mother, he did in fact treat me to a concert. I fell in love like a schoolgirl. After a month, the situation had become untenable; he announced that he was going to divorce his wife, and pressed me to leave everything and go with him to Spain, where other Argentine artists were already successfully established and friends and work were at his disposal. The rapidity with which he made those decisions seemed to me to be irrefutable proof of his love, until I later discovered that he was an unstable Gemini and that just as quickly as he was ready to fly with me to another continent, he could change his mind and return to the original status quo. Had I been a little more astute, or at least had I studied astrology when I was dashing off the magazine horoscopes in Chile, I would have observed his nature and acted more prudently but, as things turned out, I fell headfirst into a trivial melodrama that nearly cost me my children, even my life. I was in such a nervous state that I kept having automobile accidents; once I missed a red light, struck three moving vehicles, and was knocked unconscious for a few minutes. I felt stiff and sore when I came to—completely surrounded by coffins; helpful passersby had carried me into the nearest building, which happened to be a funeral parlor. In Caracas there was an unwritten code that replaced traffic laws; when you came to a corner, you looked at all the other drivers and in a split second decided who went first. The system was fair, and worked better than lights—I don't know whether it has changed, I suppose it's the same—but you have to be alert and know how to interpret the other drivers' expressions. In my emotional state, those signals, and others that allowed me to navigate in the world, were all mixed up. In the meantime, the atmosphere in my house was electric; the children could sense that the floor was moving beneath their feet and, for the first time, began to give me problems. Paula, who always had been a child too mature for her years, starting throwing the first tantrums of her life, slamming doors and locking herself in to cry for hours. Nicolás was acting like an outlaw at school, his grades were a disaster and he was bandages from head to foot: he cut himself, fell, split his head open, and broke bones with suspicious frequency. He discovered the joy of using his sling to catapult eggs against neighboring apartment buildings, as well as at pedestrians in the street below. Despite the fact that we were consuming ninety eggs a week, and that the wall of the building opposite us was one giant omelet baked hard by the tropical sun, I refused to accept the neighbors' accusations—until the day one of the projectiles was a direct hit on the head of a senator of the republic who happened to be passing beneath our windows. Had Tío Ramón not intervened with his diplomatic skills, they might have revoked our visas and thrown us out of the country. My parents, who suspected the reason for my nocturnal outings and prolonged absences, interrogated me until finally I confessed my illicit love. Mother took me aside to remind me that I had children to watch over and to point out the risks I was running, and also to tell me that, no matter what, I could count on her help if I needed it. Tío Ramón also led me aside to advise me to be more discreet—"You don't have to marry your lovers"—and to say that whatever my decision might be, he would stand by me. "You are coming with me to Spain right now or we will never see each other again," the man with the flute threatened between two impassioned arpeggios, and as I could not make up my mind, he packed up his instruments and left. Within twenty-four hours, the urgent telephone calls from Madrid began; I was on edge during the day and awake most of the night. Between the children's problems, automobile repairs, and peremptory amorous demands, I lost track of the days and was taken by surprise when Michael arrived for his visit.

That night I tried to speak with my husband and explain what was happening but before I could get a word out, he announced an upcoming business trip to Europe and invited me to go with him while my parents took care of the children for a week. "You must keep the family together, lovers come and go without leaving scars; go to Europe with Michael, it will be good for you two to be alone," my mother advised. "Don't ever admit an infidelity, even if you're caught in bed, because you'll never be forgiven for it," was Tío Ramón's counsel. So we went to Paris, and while Michael was working I sat in the sidewalk cafés along the Champs-Élysées to think about the soap opera I was swallowed up in, tortured by the choice between memories of a flute on hot, rainy tropical afternoons and the natural pinpricks of guilt, wishing a lightning bolt would flash from the heavens and put a drastic end to my doubts. I saw the faces of Paula and Nicolás on every child walking by; of one thing I was sure: I could not be separated from my children. "You don't have to leave them, bring them along," came the persuasive voice of my lover, who had obtained the name of the hotel where I was staying and kept calling from Madrid. I decided I would never forgive myself if I did not give love a chance—possibly my last, since I thought that at thirty-six I was on the verge of decrepitude. Michael returned to Venezuela and I, using the excuse that I needed to be alone for a few days, took the train to Spain.

That clandestine honeymoon—strolling arm in arm through cobbled streets, eating by candlelight in ancient taverns, sleeping in each other's arms, celebrating the incredible fortune of having stumbled upon this love unique in all the universe—lasted exactly three days, the time it took Michael to come looking for me. When I saw him, pale and flustered, and he took me in his arms, the more than twenty years we had shared fell over me like an inescapable cloak. I realized that I felt great affection for this prudent man who offered faithful love and represented stability and hearth. Our relationship lacked passion, but it was harmonious and secure. I did not feel strong enough to face a divorce or to create further problems for my children, they had enough with being immigrants. I said goodbye to my forbidden love among the trees in El Retiro park, which was coming alive after a long winter, and took the plane to Caracas. "The past doesn't matter, it will all work out, we will never mention this again," said Michael, and he was true to his word. In the months that followed, I tried several times to talk with him but it was impossible, we always ended up skirting the issue. My infidelity remained unresolved, an unconfessable dream hovering like a cloud above our heads; had it not been for the persistent calls from Madrid, I would have thought that the whole matter was another invention of my fevered imagination. During his visits, Michael was seeking peace and rest; he needed desperately to believe that nothing had changed in his orderly existence and that his wife had completely recovered from her mad escapade. Betrayal had no place in Michael's mental processes. He did not understand the nuances of what had happened, but assumed that if I had come back to him it was because I no longer loved the other man; he believed that our marriage could be the same as it had been, and that silence would heal the wounds. It was not the same, however, something had broken, something we would never be able to repair. I would lock myself in the bathroom and cry my heart out, while in the bedroom Michael pretended to read the newspaper so he wouldn't have to ask the reason for my tears. I had another serious car accident, but this time, a fraction of a second before the impact, I was aware that it was the accelerator I had jammed to the floorboard, not the brake.

Granny began to die the day she was separated from her two grandchildren; the agony lasted three long years. Doctors blamed alcohol; they said she had destroyed her liver—she was bloated and her skin was a dirty color—but the truth was that she was dying of grief. The moment came when she lost all sense of time and place, and days lasted two hours and nights did not exist; she stayed close beside the door, waiting for the children, and she never slept because she heard their voices calling her. She lost interest in her house, closed her kitchen, and never again flooded the neighborhood with the aroma of cinnamon cookies; she stopped cleaning inside or watering her garden; the dahlias languished and worms infested the plum trees heavy with rotted, unpicked fruit. My mother's Swiss dog, now with Granny, lay down in a corner to die inch by inch, like her new mistress. My father-in-law spent that winter in bed, nursing an imaginary cold because he could not face his fear of life without his Young Lady, he thought that by ignoring the facts he could change reality. The neighbors, who thought of Granny as the community's fairy godmother, at first took turns calling on her and keeping her occupied, but eventually they began to avoid her. That gentlewoman with the celestial blue eyes, impeccable in her flowered cotton dresses, forever busy with the delicacies of a kitchen where the door was always open to the neighborhood children, rapidly turned into a balding old crone who babbled incoherently and asked anyone she saw if they had seen her grandchildren. When she could no longer find her way around her own house, and looked at her husband as if she didn't know who he was, Michael's sister had to intervene. She had gone to visit her parents and found them living in a pigsty; no one had cleaned in months and garbage and empty bottles were piled high; decay had definitively taken over the house and the soul of its inhabitants. Frightened, she realized that the situation had gone too far; it was no longer a question of mopping floors, picking up, and hiring someone to look after the old people, as she had thought, she would have to take them with her. She sold some of the furniture, stored the rest in the attic, closed up the house, and set off for Montevideo with her parents. In the confusion of the last hour, the dog sneaked away and no one ever saw her again. Before a week had gone by, Michael's sister notified us in Caracas that Granny had used up her last ounce of strength, was too weak to get out of bed, and had been taken to the hospital. Michael was at a critical stage in his work; the jungle was devouring the construction site, the rain and swollen rivers had swept away the dams, and the next day crocodiles were swimming in excavations dug for the foundations. Once again, I left the children with my parents, and flew to say my farewells to Granny.

Uruguay during that period was a country for sale. Using the pretext of eliminating the guerrillas, the military dictatorship had established the dungeon, torture, and summary execution as a style of governing. Thousands of people disappeared or were killed; almost a third of the population emigrated, escaping from the horror of the times, while the military and a handful of their cronies grew rich on the spoils. Since people leaving the country could not take much with them, they were forced to sell their belongings; signs for sales and auctions went up on every block, and property, furniture, cars, and works of art were sold at bargain prices. Collectors from the rest of the continent gathered like piranhas to snap up antiques. On a gray August dawn, the dead of winter in the Southern Cone, the taxi bore me from the airport to the hospital through silent streets where half of the houses stood empty. I left my suitcase in the porter's lodge, climbed two flights of stairs, and ran into a night-duty nurse who led me to Granny's room. I didn't recognize her; in those three years she had metamorphosed into a small lizard, but then she opened her eyes and through the clouds I glimpsed a spark of turquoise. As I fell to my knees beside the bed, she murmured, "Hello, dear, how are my children?" but before she could hear the answer, a wave of blood washed her into unconsciousness and she never waked again. I sat beside her, waiting for daylight, listening to the gurgling of the tubes suctioning her stomach and breathing air into her lungs, remembering the happy and the tragic years we had shared, and treasuring her unconditional affection. "Let go, Granny, don't fight and suffer any longer, please, go quickly," I begged her, while I stroked her hands and kissed her feverish forehead. With the sunlight, I remembered Michael, and called to tell him to take the first plane and join his father and sister, for he should not be absent in this crisis.

Dear, sweet Granny hung on patiently until the next day, so her son could see her alive for a few minutes. We were both beside her bed when she stopped breathing. Michael went out to console his sister, and I stayed to help the nurse bathe my mother-in-law, giving back to her in death the infinite care she had lavished on my children in life, and as I sponged her body and smoothed the few remaining hairs on her skull and sprayed her with cologne and dressed her in a clean gown her daughter had brought, I told her about Paula and Nicolás, about our life in Caracas, about how much we had missed her and how much I had needed her in this hapless stage of my life when our home was being lashed by adverse winds. The next day we left Granny in an English cemetery beneath a blanket of jasmine, in the precise place she would have chosen to rest. I went with Michael's family to pay our last respects, and was amazed to see them without tears or emotion, restrained by that refined sobriety Anglo-Saxons exhibit when they bury their dead. Someone read the ritual words, but they didn't register because all I could hear was Granny's voice humming her grandmotherly songs. Each of us dropped a flower and a handful of dirt on the coffin, hugged one another in silence, and slowly walked away. Now she was alone, dreaming in a garden. And ever since, anytime I smell jasmine, Granny appears.

When we got back to the house, my father-in-law went to wash his hands while his daughter prepared afternoon tea. In a few minutes, he came to the dining room, still in his dark suit, with his hair slicked down and a rosebud in his lapel, handsome and young looking; he pushed back the chair with his elbows to avoid touching it with his fingers, and sat down.

"And where is my Young Lady?" he asked, surprised not to see his wife.

"She isn't with us any longer, Papa," said his daughter, and we all looked at each other, alarmed.

"Tell her tea is served and we're waiting for her."

That was our notice that time had stopped for him and that he had not absorbed the fact that his wife was dead. He lived with that delusion for the rest of his days. He had been oblivious during the funeral, as if he were attending the burial of a distant relative, and from that instant on had retreated into his memories; a curtain of senility dropped before his eyes and he never again connected with reality. The only woman he had ever loved was beside him, forever young and happy, and he forgot that he had left Chile and lost everything he owned. For the next ten years, until he died in a nursing home, shrunken to the size of a child, he was convinced he was in his house beside the golf course, that Granny was in the kitchen making plum jelly, and that at bedtime they would sleep in the same bed they had every night for forty-seven years.

The moment had come to talk with Michael about things too long unspoken, he could not continue to dwell comfortably in a fantasy the way his father did. The following day, on a rainy afternoon, bundled up in wool ponchos and mufflers, we went for a walk on the beach. I don't remember the exact moment I had finally accepted the idea that I must leave him, perhaps it had been as I watched Granny die, or when we filed out of the cemetery, leaving her beneath the jasmine, or maybe I had decided weeks before. Neither do I remember how I told Michael that I was not going back to Caracas with him, that I was going to Spain to try my luck, and taking the children with me. I told him I knew how difficult it would be for them, and that I was very sorry there was no way to prevent this new hardship, but the young have to follow their mother's destiny. I chose my words carefully, weighing them so as to inflict the least pain, bowed by my sense of guilt and by the compassion I felt for Michael: within a few hours this man had lost his mother, his father, and now his wife. He replied that I was totally out of my mind and incapable of making decisions, so he would make them for me in order to protect me and protect our children. I could go to Spain, if that was what I wanted, and this time he would not come looking for me, nor would he do anything to stop me—but he would never let me take Paula and Nicolás. In addition, I was not, he said, entitled to any of our savings, because by abandoning our home, I forfeited all my rights. He begged me to reconsider, and promised that if I gave up this insane idea, he would forgive everything, we would wipe the slate clean and begin with a fresh start. Only then did I realize that I had worked for twenty years and had nothing to show for it since the returns for my efforts had been absorbed in day-to-day expenses; Michael, on the other hand, had wisely invested his earnings and the few assets we had were in his name. Without money to support the children, I could never take them with me—even if their father allowed them to go. It was a calm discussion that lasted barely twenty minutes, without raised voices, and ended with a sincere farewell embrace.

"Don't say anything bad about me to Paula and Nicolás," I asked.

"I will never speak ill of you. Remember that all three of us love you very much and will be waiting for you."

"I'll come for them as soon as I get a job."

"I will not give them to you. You may see them whenever you wish, but if you leave now you lose them forever."

"We'll see about that. . . ."

In my heart, I was not too alarmed; I felt sure that Michael would have to cave in eventually because he hadn't the faintest idea what taking care of youngsters involved and until then had fulfilled his fatherly duties from a comfortable distance. His job was a real sticking point: he could not take the children to that half-tamed part of the country where he spent most of his time, but neither could he leave them alone in Caracas. I was sure that before a month had passed he would be desperate and begging me to take charge of them.

I left the funereal winter of Montevideo to land the next day in the boiling August of Madrid, prepared to live out my love to its ultimate consequences. From the romantic illusion I had invented in our clandestine rendezvous and hasty letters, I fell into the sordid reality of a poverty that nights and days of inexhaustible embraces could not mitigate. We rented a small, dark apartment in one of dozens of identical red brick buildings in a working-class district on the outskirts of the city. There was no touch of green, not a single tree grew there; all you could see were dirt patios, playing fields, cement, asphalt, and brick. That ugliness was like a slap in the face. "You're a spoiled bourgeois brat," my lover laughed, smiling between kisses, but underneath the joviality his reproach was serious. In the flea market, we acquired a bed, a table, three chairs, and a few plates and saucepans that a huge, nasty-tempered man delivered in his broken-down van. On an irresistible whim, I also bought a flower vase, although there was never money to buy flowers to put in it. Every morning we went out to look for work, and every evening we returned, exhausted and empty-handed. His friends avoided us, promises dissolved like salt in water, doors were slammed in our faces, no one responded to our applications, and money seemed to melt away. I saw my daughter and son in every child playing in the street; being separated from them pained me physically, and I came to believe that the constant burning in my stomach was either an ulcer or cancer. There were times I had to choose between having bread or buying stamps for a letter to my mother, and those days I fasted. I tried to write a musical comedy with my lover, but the congenial complicity of our picnics in the park and afternoons beside the dusty piano in the Caracas theater had dissipated: our anxiety was coming between us, our differences became more and more pronounced, our defects were magnified. We never spoke of Paula and Nicolás, because any time they were mentioned the breach between us widened; I moped and he was sulky. The most superficial incidents became fuel for a fight; our reconciliations were true tourneys of passion that left us half stupefied. And so three months went by. During that time I had found neither employment nor friends; my last savings were gone, and so was my passion for a man who surely deserved better. It must have been hell to live with my anguish over my absent children, the way I raced to the mailbox, and my trips at night to the airport, where an ingenious Chilean knew how to connect cables to the telephone to make free international calls. There behind the backs of the police, all of us penniless refugees from South America—*sudacas,* they called us with scorn—gathered to talk to our families on the other side of the world. That was how I found out that Michael had gone back to his job and the children were alone, watched over by my parents from their apartment two floors above ours, that Paula had assumed the household duties and care of her brother with the iron discipline of a sergeant, and that Nicolás had broken an arm and was growing thinner by the day because he didn't want to eat. In the meantime, my love was unraveling, destroyed by poverty and nostalgia. I had soon discovered that the man I had fallen in love with became demoralized when faced with everyday problems, and fell into depressions or fits of frenetic humor. I could not imagine Paula and Nicolás with such a stepfather, and that is why when Michael finally recognized that he could not care for them and was ready to turn them over to me, I knew I had touched bottom and could not continue to deceive myself with fairy tales. I had followed the flutist in a hypnotic trance, like the mice of Hamelin, but I could not drag Paula and Nicolás into a similar fate. That night, in the bright light of reason, I examined my countless errors of recent years, from the absurd risks I had taken at the height of the dictatorship that finally forced me to leave Chile to the polite silences that separated me and Michael, and the injudicious way I had fled my house without offering an explanation or facing the basic consequences of a divorce. That night my youth ended and I entered a new phase of my life. Enough, I said. At five o'clock in the morning, I went to the airport, managed to put through a free call, and spoke with Tío Ramón, asking him to send money for my plane ticket. I told my lover goodbye, knowing I would never see him again, and eleven hours later I landed in Venezuela, defeated, without luggage, and with no plan but to put my arms around my children and never let them go again. Michael was waiting at the airport. He greeted me with a chaste kiss on the forehead and tear-filled eyes; he said emotionally that everything that had happened was his responsibility for not having taken better care of me, and asked me out of consideration for the years we had shared and my love for the family to give him another chance and begin all over again. "I need time," I replied, defeated by his nobility and furious without knowing why. In silence, he drove up the hill toward Caracas and as we reached the house announced that he would give me all the time I desired, that he was leaving for his job in the jungle and occasions to see each other would be few.

Today is my birthday, I have lived half a century. Maybe this evening friends will come by to visit; here, people drop in without prior warning, ours is an open house where the living and the dead go hand in hand. We bought it several years ago, when Willie and I realized that our love at first sight was not giving any signs of diminishing and we needed a place larger than his own. When we first saw it, it seemed it had been waiting for us—more accurately, had been calling to us. It had a weary air: the paint was peeling from the wood, it needed many repairs, and it was dark inside, but it had a spectacular view of the Bay and a benevolent soul. We were told that the former owner had died here a few months before, and we thought she must have been happy within these walls because her memory still lingered in the rooms. We signed within half an hour, without bargaining, and in recent years it has become a sanctuary for an Anglo-Latin tribe where words in Spanish and English echo back and forth, something spicy is always simmering on the stove, and at mealtimes we have many guests around the table. The rooms stretch and multiply to accommodate new arrivals: grandparents, grandchildren, Willie's children, and now Paula, this girl who is slowly turning into an angel. A colony of skunks dwells in the foundations, and every evening the mysterious tortoiseshell cat appears—apparently it has adopted us. Several days ago, she deposited on my daughter's bed a newly killed, still bleeding, bird with blue wings; I suspect that is her way of repaying our kindnesses. In the last four years, the house has been transformed with large skylights to let in the sun and the stars, white rugs and walls, Mexican floor tiles, and a small garden. We contracted with a crew of Chinese workmen to build a storage space, but they didn't understand English, confused our instructions and, by the time we realized it, had added to the ground floor two rooms, a bath, and a strange area that ended up as Willie's workshop. In the basement I have hidden sinister surprises for the grandchildren: a plaster skeleton, treasure maps, and trunks filled with pirate disguises and fake jewels. I have the hope that a scary cellar will act as a stimulus to their imaginations, as my grandfather's did for mine. At night, the house shudders, moans, and yawns, and I have the feeling that memories of people who have lived here, the characters that escape from books and dreams, the gentle ghost of the former owner, and Paula's soul, which at times is freed from the painful bonds of its body, all roam through the rooms. Houses need births and deaths to become homes. Today is a day of celebration; we will have a birthday cake and Willie will come home from the office laden with shopping bags and ready to devote the afternoon to planting his rosebushes in terra firma. That is his gift to me. Those poor plants in wine barrels symbolized the nomadic life of their owner, who always left one door open to escape should life turn a drab antbrown. That was how it was with all his previous relationships, they reached a point at which he packed his clothes and left, wheeling his barrels to a different destination. "I think we will be here for a long while, it's time now to plant my roses in the garden," he told me yesterday. I like this man from a different race who walks with long strides, laughs explosively, speaks with a booming voice, annihilates his chicken at dinner with a few slashes of his knife, and cooks without any fuss—so different from other men I have loved. I celebrate his bursts of masculine energy because he compensates for them with a boundless reserve of gentleness, which he can summon at any moment. He has survived great misfortune without being tainted with cynicism and can today give himself without qualification to our late-blooming love and to this Latin tribe in which he now occupies a central position. Later, the rest of the family will gather; Celia and Nicolás will settle in to watch television while Paula drowses in her chair. We will fill the plastic pool on the terrace for Alejandro, who now feels at ease with his silent aunt, and he can splash around. I think today will be another peaceful Sunday.

I am fifty years old, I have entered the last half of my life but I feel as strong as when I was twenty, my body has not failed me yet. *Vieja,* old lady . . . , that's what Paula affectionately called me. Now the word frightens me a little, it suggests someone with warts and varicose veins. In other cultures, elderly women dress in black, tie a kerchief around their heads, grow a mustache, and retire from worldly strife to devote themselves to piety, lamenting their dead, and tending their grandchildren, but here in the United States women go to grotesque lengths to look eternally healthy and happy. I have a fan of fine wrinkles at the corners of my eyes, like tiny scars of past laughter and tears; I look like the photograph of my clairvoyant grandmother, the same expression of intensity tinged with sadness. I am losing hair at my temples. A week after Paula fell ill I found bare spots round as coins; they say they are caused by grief and will grow back, but I honestly don't care. I had to cut Paula's long hair and now she has the head of a boy; she looks much younger, a child again. I wonder how much longer I will live, and why. Time and circumstances have placed me beside this wheelchair to watch over my daughter. I am her guardian, and my family's. . . . I am quickly learning the advantages of disengagement. Will I write

again? Every stage of the road is different, and maybe the one having to do with literature is behind me. I will know in a few months,
next January 8, when I sit down at my typewriter to begin another
novel and test the presence or the silence of the spirits. Recently, I
have been empty, my inspiration has dried up, but it is also possible
that stories are creatures with their own lives and that they exist in
the shadows of some mysterious dimension; in that case, it will be a
question of opening so they may enter, sink into me, and grow until
they are ready to emerge transformed into language. They do not
belong to me, they are not my creations, but, if I succeed in breaking down the wall of anguish in which I am enclosed, I can again
serve them as medium. If that doesn't happen, I will have to find a
new calling. Ever since Paula became ill, a dark curtain has separated me from the fantasy world in which I used to move so freely;
reality has become intractable. Today's experiences are tomorrow's
recollections; I have never before lacked for dramatic events to feed
my memories, and it was from them all my stories were born. Eva
Luna says at the end of my third book: *I also try to live my life as I
would like it . . . like a novel.* I don't know whether my road has been
extraordinary or whether I have written these books out of a banal
existence, but only adventures, love, happiness, and suffering are
stored in my memory; the petty happenings of everyday life have
disappeared. When I look back, it seems to me that I was the protagonist of a melodrama; now, in contrast, everything is suspended,
I have nothing to tell, the present has the brutal certainty of tragedy.
I close my eyes and before me rises the painful image of my daughter in her wheelchair, her eyes staring toward the sea, her gaze
focused beyond the horizon where death begins.

What will happen with this great empty space that I am today?
What will fill me now that not a whiff of ambition remains, no project, nothing of myself? The force of the suction will reduce me to a
black hole, and I will disappear. To die. . . . The idea of leaving the
body is fascinating. I do not want to go on living and die inside; if I
am to continue in this world I must plan the years I have left. Perhaps
old age is a new beginning, maybe we can return to the magic time of
infancy, to that time before linear thought and prejudices when we
perceived the universe with the exalted senses of the mad and were

free to believe the unbelievable and to explore worlds that later, in the age of reason, vanished. I have very little to lose now, nothing to defend; could this be freedom at last? I have the idea that we grand-mothers are meant to play the part of protective witches; we must watch over younger women, children, community, and also, why not?, this mistreated planet, the victim of such unrelenting desecration. I would like to fly on a broomstick and dance in the moonlight with other pagan witches in the forest, invoking earth forces and howling demons; I want to become a wise old crone, to learn ancient spells and healers' secrets. It is no small thing, this design of mine. Witches, like saints, are solitary stars that shine with a light of their own; they depend on nothing and no one, which is why they have no fear and can plunge blindly into the abyss with the assurance that instead of crashing to earth, they will fly back out. They can change into birds and see the world from above, or worms to see it from within, they can inhabit other dimensions and travel to other galaxies, they are navigators on an infinite ocean of consciousness and cognition.

WHEN I DEFINITIVELY RENOUNCED MY CARNAL PASSION FOR THE indecisive Argentine musician, there lay before my eyes a boundless desert of boredom and loneliness. I was thirty-seven years old, and, confusing love in general with a lover in particular, I had decided to cure myself forever of the vice of infatuation, which had, after all, brought me nothing but complications. Fortunately, I did not entirely succeed; the inclination lay dormant, like a seed crushed beneath two meters of polar ice that stubbornly bursts through with the first warm breeze. After I returned to Caracas to be with my husband, my lover persisted for some time, more as a duty than out of any other reason, I think. The telephone would ring, I would hear the characteristic click of international calls and hang up with-out answering. With the same determination, I tore up his letters without opening them, until finally the flutist's attempts at commu-nication ended. Fifteen years have gone by, and if you had told me then that the day would come when I would forget him, I would not have believed it; I was sure I had shared one of those rare heroic love affairs that because of its tragic ending constitutes the stuff of opera. Now I have a more modest vision, and hope simply that if at one of the turns of the road I meet him again, I will at least recognize him. That thwarted relationship was an open wound for more than two years; I was literally sick from love, but no one knew it—not even my mother, who watched me closely. Some mornings, crushed by frustration, I could not find the strength to get out of bed, and some nights I was wrung out by memories and raging desires that—like my grandfather—I battled with icy showers. In a fever to sweep away the past, I tore up the scores of the pied piper's songs and my play, an act that has occasioned regret, because they may have had some merit. I cured myself with the thickheaded remedy Michael had suggested: I buried love in the quicksand of silence. I did not mention what had happened for several years, until it had stopped paining me, and my resolve to eliminate the memory of even the good caresses was so extreme that I went too far, and have an alarming hiatus in my memory that has swallowed not only the misery of that time but also a large part of the happiness.

That adventure brought back to me the first lesson of my childhood, one I can't believe I forgot—that there is no freedom without financial independence. During the years of my marriage, I had unknowingly placed myself in the same vulnerable position my mother had been in when she was dependent on my grandfather's charity. As a child, I had promised myself that would never happen to me, I was determined to be strong and productive like the patriarch of the family, so I would not have to ask anything of anyone, and I had achieved the first part but, instead of managing the money I earned, I had, out of laziness, entrusted it to the care of a husband whose saintly reputation seemed to me a sufficient guarantee. That sensible and practical man, who had perfect control over his emotions and was apparently incapable of committing an unfair or dishonorable act, seemed more qualified than I to look after my interests. I can't imagine where I got such an idea. In the turbulence of the life we shared, and because of my own talent for extravagance, I lost everything. When I went back to my husband, I decided that my first step in this new phase would be to find a steady job, save everything I could, and change the rules of our domestic finances so that his income was earmarked for household expenses and mine went into savings. It was not my plan to accumulate money for a divorce; there was no need, in fact, for cynical stratagems, because once the troubador had disappeared into the sunset, the husband's wrath subsided, and he would undoubtedly have negotiated a separation on fairer terms than those he had laid down on the wintry beach in Montevideo. I stayed with Michael for nine years, acting with absolute good faith, believing that with luck and dedication we could fulfill the promise of forever-after we had made at the altar. Notwithstanding, the very fiber of our alliance was rent, for reasons that had little to do with my infidelity and much more with old accounts, as I discovered later. In our reconciliations, the two children tipped the scale, as well as half a lifetime invested in our relationship and the calm affection and common interests that united us. I did not take into account my passions, which finally were stronger than those prudent objectives. For a very long time, I felt sincere affection for my husband; I am sorry that the quality of the last years eroded the good memories of our youthful days.

Michael went off to the remote province where crocodiles dozed in the holes for the foundations with the aim of finishing the job and looking for work that demanded less sacrifice, and I stayed with the children, who had changed greatly in my absence; they seemed totally adjusted to their new country, and no longer talked about going back to Chile. In those three months, Paula had left childhood behind and become a beautiful young girl obsessed with learning: she got the best grades in her class, studied guitar without the least aptitude for it, and, after mastering English, began on French and Italian with the aid of records and dictionaries. Meanwhile, Nicolás had grown a span, and materialized one day with his pants' legs at midcalf, his sleeves halfway up his arms, and with the self-same bearing as his grandfather and father. He had recent stitches on his head, several scars, and the secret ambition to scale the tallest skyscraper in Caracas without ropes. He dragged around huge metal drums he used for storing human and assorted animal feces, a disagreeable task for his class in natural science. He intended to demonstrate that those fetid gases could be used as an

energy source and that through a process of recycling it was feasible
to use excrement as a cooking fuel instead of washing it out to sea
through sewers. Paula, who had learned to drive, ferried him
around to stables, henhouses, and friends' bathrooms to collect the
raw material for his experiment, which he stored in the house
under the always present danger that heat would cause the gases to
explode and coat the entire neighborhood with shit. The camaraderie of their childhood had been transformed into a solid complicity that bound them together till Paula's last day of consciousness. That pair of slender adolescents tacitly understood my determination to bury that painful episode in our lives. I suppose that my
having betrayed them left deep scars and who knows how much
resentment against me, but neither of them mentioned what had
happened until several years later when finally we sat down to talk
about it and discovered, to our amusement, that no one remembered the details and that all of us had forgotten the name of the
lover who came so close to being their stepfather.

As so often happens when one follows the road indicated in the
book of destinies, a series of coincidences helped me put my plans
into practice. For three years, I had not made any friends or found
work in Venezuela, but the minute I focused all my energy on the
task of adapting and surviving, I succeeded in less than a week. My
mother's tarot cards, which previously had predicted the classic
intervention of a dark-skinned man with a mustache—I took that
to be a reference to the flutist—again made a revelation, this time
announcing a blond woman. In fact, only a few days after my return
to Caracas, Marilena, a teacher with golden hair, came into my life
to offer me employment. She owned an institute that specialized in
art and classes for children with learning disabilities. While her
mother, an energetic Spanish lady, acted as secretary and oversaw
the business side of the academy, Marilena taught ten hours a day
and devoted another ten to researching the ambitious methods with
which she hoped to change the education system in Venezuela and,
why think small?, the world. My job consisted of helping her super-
vise the teachers and organize the classes, attracting students
through an advertising campaign, and maintaining good relations

with the parents. We became very good friends. She was a woman as bright as her hair of gold, pragmatic and direct, who forced me to accept harsh reality when I strayed into sentimental muddles or patriotic nostalgia, and who ripped out by the root any thought of self-pity on my part. With her I shared secrets, learned a new occupation, and shook off the depression that had paralyzed me for so long. She taught me the codes and subtle keys of Caracas society, which until then I had not understood because I was applying Chilean criteria, and within a couple of years I fit in so well that all I lacked was a Caribbean accent. One day in the bottom of a suitcase, I found a small plastic bag containing a handful of soil and remembered that I had brought it from Chile with the idea of planting in it the best seeds of memory, but had not done so because I hadn't meant to stay; instead, I had kept looking toward the south, hoping the dictatorship would fall and I could go home. I decided that I had waited long enough, and in a quiet, very personal, ceremony I mixed Venezuelan earth with the dirt from my old garden, filled a flowerpot, and planted a forget-me-not. The spindly plant that came up was ill-suited for that climate, and promptly died, probably of sunstroke; after a while I replaced it with a rambunctious tropical plant that grew with the voraciousness of an octopus.

My children adapted, too. Paula fell in love with a young man of Sicilian origin, a first-generation immigrant like herself, still faithful to the traditions of his homeland. His father, who had made a fortune in construction materials, was waiting for Paula to finish school—since that was what she wanted—and learn to cook before celebrating the marriage. I was dead set against it, even though in my heart I couldn't help but like that generous young man and his enchanting clan, a large, cheerful family without metaphysical or intellectual pretensions, who gathered every day to celebrate life with succulent feasts of the best of Italian cuisine. The swain was the oldest son and grandson, a tall, muscular, blond young man with the temperament of a Polynesian, who spent all his time in placid diversions involving his yacht, his beach house, his collection of automobiles, and innocent partying. My sole objection to this potential son-in-law was that he had no job and hadn't finished his education; his father provided him a generous allowance and had promised him a furnished house when he married

Paula. One day he confronted me, pale and trembling but with a steady voice, to tell me that we should stop beating around the bush and call a spade a spade: he was tired of my specious questions. He explained that, in his eyes, work was a necessity, not a virtue, and if you could eat without having to get a job, only an imbecile would have difficulty choosing. He could not understand our compulsion for sacrifice and toil; he wondered why, if we were "filthy rich" as Tío Ramón was always proclaiming, we would get up every morning at dawn and labor twelve hours. Obviously, in our view, that was the only measure of integrity. I confess that he shook the stoic scale of values I inherited from my grandfather, and ever since I have confronted work with a slightly more playful spirit. The marriage was postponed, because when Paula graduated from school she announced she wasn't ready for pots and pans and intended to study psychology. Her sweetheart had to accept her plan, first, because she didn't consult him about it, and second, because it was a profession that would better prepare her for bringing up the half-dozen children he planned to have. It was, however, too much for him to digest when she enrolled in a seminar on sexuality and then—lugging a case filled with eye-opening accoutrements—she went around measuring penises and orgasms. I had to agree that this was not the best idea; after all, we weren't in Sweden and people were clearly not going to approve of that specialty, but I didn't offer an opinion because Paula would have nailed me with the very feminist arguments I had instilled in her from early childhood. I did venture that she should be discreet, because if she acquired a reputation as a sexologist no one would have the nerve to take her out—men fear comparisons—but she withered me with one professional glance and that was the end of the conversation. Toward the end of the seminar, I had to make a trip to Holland, and Paula asked me to bring back certain didactic materials difficult to obtain in Venezuela. Which was how I found myself one night in the most sordid streets of Amsterdam, poking through X-rated shops for the artifacts on her list: telescoping rubber cocks, dolls with authentic orifices, and videos featuring imaginative combinations of women and spirited paraplegics or libidinous dogs. The blush on my cheeks when I bought these treasures could not compare with how red in the face I was in the Caracas airport when the customs officials opened my suitcase and fingered those outré objects before the mocking regard of the other passengers, especially when I explained they were not for my own personal use but my daughter's. That marked the end of Paula's engagement to the Sicilian with the gentle heart. Over time, he settled down, finished school, started working in his father's firm, married, and had a child, but he never forgot his first love. Ever since he learned of Paula's illness, he has called from time to time to offer his support, as do a half-dozen other men who weep when I give them the bad news. I have no idea who these strangers are, what role they played in my daughter's life, or what deep imprint she left on their souls. Paula planted vigorous seeds as she passed through the lives of others, I have seen the fruit during these eternal months of agony. Everywhere she went, she left friends and love. Persons of all ages and conditions communicate with me to ask about her; they cannot believe that such misfortune has befallen her.

In the meantime, Nicolás was climbing the most rugged peaks in the Andes, exploring submarine caves to photograph sharks, and breaking bones with such regularity that every time the phone rang I began to tremble. If there was no real reason for me to worry, he found ways to invent them, with the same ingenuity he had employed in his experiment with natural gases. One evening I came home from the office and found the house dark and apparently empty. I could see a light at the end of the hall, and so I walked toward it, calling, absentmindedly, until suddenly in the frame of the bathroom door I saw my son with a rope around his neck. There was enough light for me to see the protruding tongue and rolled back eyes of a hanged man before I dropped to the floor like a stone. I did not lose consciousness but I could not move, I was like a block of ice. When Nicolás saw my reaction, he unbuckled the harness from which he was so skillfully suspended and rushed to comfort me, showering me with repentant kisses and swearing he would never give me such a scare again. His good intentions lasted about two weeks, until he discovered the way to submerse himself in the bathtub and breathe through a fine glass straw so I would find him drowned, and then the next time, when he appeared with one arm in a sling and a patch over one eye. According to Paula's psychology manuals, his accidents revealed a hidden suicidal tendency and his desire to torture me with heart-stopping jokes was motivated by unexpressed anger, but, for the peace of mind of all, we concluded that textbooks can be mistaken. Nicolás was a little rough as a boy but not a suicidal maniac, and his affection for me was so obvious that my mother had diagnosed an Oedipus complex. Time proved our theory. When he was seventeen, my son woke up one morning a man; he put his experimental drums, nooses, mountain-climbing gear, harpoons for killing sharks, and first-aid kit into a box at the back of the garage, and declared that he was thinking of taking up computers. Now when I see him, with his serene intellectual expression and a child in each arm, I ask myself if I didn't dream that terrifying vision of him swinging from a home-rigged gallows.

During that period, Michael completed his work in the jungle and moved back to the capital with the idea of setting up his own construction business. Slowly and cautiously, we were mending the torn fabric of our relationship, until it became so amiable and harmonious that to others we seemed very much in love. My salary supported us for a time while Michael looked for contracts in an explosively expanding Caracas where every day they were cutting down trees, leveling hills, and demolishing houses to build, seemingly overnight, new skyscrapers and highways. The status of my blonde friend's academy was so precarious that we sometimes had to draw on her mother's pension or our savings to cover expenses at the end of the month. Throngs of students flocked in just before final exams when their parents suspected they were not going to pass their courses; with special tutoring they caught up, but instead of continuing their classes to correct the source of their problem, they disappeared as soon as they passed their tests. For several months our receipts had been very erratic, and the institute was barely surviving; we were anxiously approaching January, when we would have to enroll enough children to keep our frail vessel afloat. By December, the situation was critical. Marilena's mother and I, who performed all the administrative chores, went over the accounts time and again, trying fruitlessly to make the negative numbers balance. We were engrossed in this task when the cleaning woman happened by our desk, an affectionate Colombian who often treated us to her delicious flan. When she saw us desperately juggling figures, she asked with sincere interest what the problem was, and we told her our difficulties.

"Well, in the evenings, I work at this funeral home, and when we're running short on clients we wash the place down with *Quitalapava,*" she said.

"What's that?"

"Why, a spell. You have to do a good cleaning. First, you wash the floors from the back toward the door, to get the bad luck out, and then from the door back in, to summon the spirits of light and consent."

"And then?"

"And then the dead begin to pile in."

"We don't need any corpses here, we need children."

"Same thing, *Quitalapava* works for any business."

We gave her some money, and the next day she came in with a gasoline can filled with a stinking, suspicious-looking liquid; in the bottom was a milky, yellowish sediment, then a layer of some gurgling broth, all topped with something like crankcase oil. We had to stir it up before we used it, and cover our noses with handkerchiefs because the smell was enough to knock us out. "I hope my daughter doesn't find out about this," sighed Marilena's mother, who was nearly seventy but had lost none of the vitality and good humor that led her to leave her native Valencia thirty years before to follow an unfaithful husband to the New World, confront him for living with a concubine, demand a divorce, and immediately forget him. Captivated by that lavish country in which she felt free for the first time in her life, she and her daughter stayed on and, with tenacity and ingenuity, did very well. This remarkable woman and I scrubbed the floor on our hands and knees, murmuring the ritual words and smothering our giggles, because if we openly made fun the whole enterprise would have been shot to hell: seriousness and good faith are required if you want sorcery to work. We invested two days in that labor, and were rewarded with sprained backs and raw knees, and no matter how wide we opened the windows and doors we could not get the stink out, but it was worth it all: the first week of January there was a long line of parents at our door, with children in hand. In view of such spectacular results, I was struck with the idea of using what was left in the can to improve Michael's luck, and so one night I scrubbed his office exactly the way we had at the academy. I heard no results for several days, except comments about a strange odor. I consulted with our cleaning woman, who assured me that the *empavado* was my husband himself, and that the way to resolve that would be to take him to the Montaña Sagrada for a cleansing ceremony, advice that lay far outside the range of possibility. A man like Michael, the end product of a British education, a career in engineering, and the vice of chess, would never lower himself to magic ceremonies. I kept thinking, however, about the logic of witchcraft, and concluded that if the miraculous liquid worked for scrubbing floors, there was no reason it shouldn't be effective on a human being. The next morning when Michael was in the shower, I sneaked up behind him and doused him with the dregs from the can. He howled with surprise, and after only a few minutes turned the color of a lobster; he also lost a few clumps of hair, but exactly two weeks later he acquired a Venezuelan partner and a fabulous contract.

My friend Marilena never learned the reason for the extraordinary bonanza that year, but she doubted it would last; she was tired of struggling with the budget and was contemplating the possibility of a change. In discussing the matter, the idea arose—inspired, surely, by effluvia from the spell still lurking in the cracks of the floorboards—of transforming the institute into a school where she could make serious application of her first-rate educational theories to solving learning problems and, in the process, eliminate the traumas to our account books. That was the beginning of a solid enterprise that within a few years became one of the most respected schools in Caracas.

I have a lot of time for meditating in this California autumn. I must get used to my daughter as she is and not remember her as the charming, happy girl she was; neither should I lose myself in pessimistic visions of the future but take each day as it comes, without expecting miracles. Paula depends on me for her survival, she is my baby again, as she was at birth: for her, both the celebrations and stresses of living are past. I position her chair on the terrace facing San Francisco Bay and Willie's rosebushes, laden with blossoms since he took them from the wine barrels to sink their roots in terra firma. Sometimes my daughter opens her eyes and stares at the iridescent surface of the water; I step into her line of vision but she doesn't see me, her pupils are like bottomless wells. I can communicate with her only at night when she comes to visit me in dreams. I sleep fitfully, and often wake with the certainty that she is calling me. I jump out of bed and run to her room, where almost always something is wrong: her temperature or her blood pressure has shot up, she is sweating or she is cold, she is lying in an awkward position and her muscles are cramping. The woman who stays with her at night tends to fall asleep when the Spanish-language television programs are over. Those times, I lie down with Paula and cradle her on my breast as well as I can, since she is larger than I am, while I pray that she may find peace, that she rest in the serenity of the mystics, that she inhabit a paradise of harmony and silence, that she meet the God she sought so avidly in her brief span. I seek inspiration to divine her needs and to help keep her comfortable so her spirit can travel without disturbance to the place of encounters. What must she be feeling? Sometimes she is frightened, trembling, her eyes wide and staring, as if she were seeing visions from Hell; other times she is far away, motionless, as if she had already left everything behind. Life is a miracle, and for her it ended abruptly, without time to say goodbye or settle accounts, at the moment of vertiginous, youthful momentum. She was cut off just as she was beginning to wonder about the meaning of things, and left me the charge of finding the answer. Sometimes I spend the night wandering through the house, like the mysterious skunks in the basement that creep up to eat the cat's food, or my grandmother's ghost that escapes from her mirror to chat with me. When Paula is asleep, I go back to my bed and put my arm around Willie with my eyes fixed on the green numerals of the clock; the hours pass, inexorable, eating up the present—now is the future. I should take Dr. Forrester's pills; I don't know why I hoard them like a treasure, hidden in the basket with my mother's letters. Some early mornings I watch the sun come up through the large windows in Paula's room; with each dawn the world is created anew, the sky is streaked with shades of orange and night's haze rises from the water, veiling the landscape in misty lace, like a delicate Japanese screen. I am a raft without a rudder, adrift on a sea of pain. During these long months I have been peeling away like an onion, layer after layer, changing; I am not the same woman, my daughter has given me the opportunity to look inside myself and discover interior spaces—empty, dark, strangely peaceful—I had never explored before. These are holy places, and to reach them I must travel a narrow road blocked with many obstacles, vanquish the beasts of imagination that jump out in my path. When terror paralyzes me, I close my eyes and give myself to it with the sensation of sinking into storm-tossed waters, pounded by the fury of the waves. For a few instants that are a true eternity, I think I am dying, but little by little I comprehend that, despite everything, I am still alive because in the ferocious whirlpool there is a merciful shaft through which I can breathe. Unresisting, I let myself be dragged down, and gradually the fear recedes. I float into an underwater cave, and rest there for a while, safe from the dragons of despair. Raw and bleeding inside, I cry without tears, as animals may cry, but then the sun comes up and the cat comes to ask for her breakfast, and I hear Willie's footsteps in the kitchen, and the odor of coffee spreads through the house. Another day is beginning, a day like any other day.

NEW YEAR'S, 1981. THAT DAY BROUGHT HOME THE FACT THAT SOON I would be forty and had not until then done anything truly significant. Forty! That was the beginning of the end, and I did not have to stretch too much to imagine myself sitting in a rocking chair knitting socks. When I was a lonely and very angry child living in my grandfather's house, I dreamed of heroic exploits: I would be a famous actress and, instead of buying fur coats and jewels, I would give all my money to an orphanage; I would discover a vaccine against broken bones; I would stick my finger in a dike to save another Dutch village and . . . wait a minute! I mean, be a second Dutch boy with my thumb in the dike. I wanted to be Tom Sawyer, or the Black Pirate, or Sandokán, and after I had read Shakespeare and incorporated tragedy into my repertoire, I wanted to be one of those magnificent characters who, after living life to the full, dies in the last act. The idea of becoming an anonymous nun came to me much later. In that period of my life, I felt different from my brothers, and other children. I never saw the world as they did; to me, things and people tended to become transparent, and dreams and stories in books were more real than reality. At times I had moments of terrifying lucidity and believed that I could divine the future and the remote past, long before I was born; it was as if all times were occurring simultaneously in one space, and suddenly, through a small window that opened for a fraction of a second, I traveled to other dimensions. In my adolescence, I would have given anything to belong to the boisterous clique that danced to rock 'n' roll and smoked behind adults' backs, but I didn't try, because I knew I wasn't one of them. The sense of loneliness that had plagued me since childhood became even more acute, but I consoled myself with the vague hope that I was cut out for a special destiny that someday would be revealed to me. Later, I threw myself into the routines of matrimony and motherhood, in which the unhappiness and solitude of my early youth receded and my plans for greatness were forgotten. My work as a journalist, my involvement in theater and television, kept me busy; I did not again think in terms of destiny until the military coup brought me to a brutal confrontation with reality and forced me to take a new direction. Those years of self-imposed exile in Venezuela could be summarized in a single word that for me had the weight of a curse: mediocrity. At forty, it was a little late for surprises, my time was quickly running out and I was sure of nothing but the unsatisfactory quality of my life, and boredom, but pride prevented me from admitting it. I assured my mother—the only person interested in knowing—that everything was going well in my tidy little life; with stoic discipline, I had recovered from my thwarted love, I had a secure job, for the first time I was saving money, my husband seemed still to love me, and my family was back on the normal track. I even dressed like an inoffensive schoolteacher—what more could anyone ask? Not a trace remained of the fringed shawls, long skirts, and flowers in my hair, but sometimes, when I was alone, I took them from the bottom of a suitcase and tried them on for a few minutes before the mirror. I was choking in my role as a sensible bourgeois woman, consumed by the desires of my youth, but I had no right to complain; I had risked everything once, had lost, and fate had given me a second chance, I should be grateful for my good fortune. "It's a miracle what you've pulled off, Isabel, I never thought you would be able to put your marriage and your life back together," my mother told me one day with a sigh that was not relief, and in a tone that to me sounded ironic. She may have been the only person to sense the contents of my Pandora's box, but she didn't dare lift the lid. That New Year's in 1981, while everyone was celebrating with champagne and fireworks were bursting outside to announce the new year, I made a vow to master my ennui and humbly resign myself to the mundane existence lived by almost everyone else. I decided that it was not difficult to sacrifice love if I had the noble companionship of my husband, and that steady employment at the school was preferable to the risks of journalism or the theater, and that I ought to plan to stay indefinitely in Venezuela instead of sighing over an idealized country that lay at the far end of the planet. Those were reasonable resolutions, and anyway, after twenty or thirty years, when my passions had dried up, when I couldn't remember even the bad taste of failed love and boredom, I could enjoy a tranquil retirement from the sale of shares I was accumulating in Marilena's business. The plan was entirely rational—and it lasted not quite a week. On January 8, someone called from Santiago saying that my grandfather was very ill; that news canceled all my promises of good behavior and launched me in an unexpected direction. Tata was now nearly one hundred years old; he had the skeleton of a bird, was a semi-invalid, and sad, but perfectly lucid. Once he had read the last word of the *Encyclopædia Britannica* and memorized the huge dictionary of the Spanish Royal Academy, and when he lost all interest in the vicarious disasters of his soap operas, he knew it was time to die, and wanted to do it with dignity. Dressed in his threadbare black suit and with his cane between his knees, he settled himself in his armchair and, in view of the fact that his granddaughter had failed him so badly, summoned the ghost of my grandmother to help him at that critical time. Through the years, we had kept in touch by means of my steady stream of letters and his sporadic replies. I decided to write him one last time, to tell him he could go in peace because I would never forget him and planned to bequeath his memory to my children and my children's children. To prove it, I began the letter with an anecdote about my great-aunt Rosa, my grandfather's first sweetheart, a young girl of almost supernatural beauty who had died in mysterious circumstances shortly before they were to marry, poisoned either by error or malice, and whose soft sepia-tone photograph always sat on the piano in Tata's house, smiling with unalterable beauty. Years later, Tata married Rosa's younger sister, my grandmother. From the first lines I wrote, other wills took control of my letter, leading me far away from the uncertain story of the family to explore the more secure world of fiction. During the journey, my motives became muddled, and the limits between truth and invention blurred: as the characters came to life, they were more demanding than my own children. With my head in limbo, I worked a double schedule at the school, from seven in the morning to seven at night, committing catastrophic errors. I don't know how I avoided wrecking the operation; I kept only half an eye on the accounts, the teachers, the students, and the classes, while all my real attention was centered on the canvas bag in which I carried the pages I churned out at night. My body functioned like an automaton, while my mind was lost in that world being born word by word. I reached home as it was growing dark, ate dinner with the family, took a shower, and then sat down in the kitchen or dining room before a small portable typewriter until fatigue forced me to bed. I wrote without effort, without thinking, because my clairvoyant grandmother was dictating to me. At six in the morning, I had to get up to go to work, but those few hours of sleep were sufficient; I went about in a trance, I had energy to burn, as if I had a lighted flame inside me. The family heard the clacking of the keys and saw me with my head in the clouds, but no one asked a single question; they may have guessed I didn't have an answer, that in fact I wasn't sure what I was doing, because although my intention to write my grandfather a letter had quickly faded, I could not admit that I had launched into a novel, that idea seemed presumptuous. I had spent more than twenty years on the periphery of literature— journalism, short stories, theater, television scripts, hundreds of letters—without daring to confess my true calling. I would have to publish three novels translated into several languages before I put down "writer" as my profession when I filled out a form. I carried my papers everywhere out of fear they would be lost, or that the house would burn down; I was as solicitous of that ribbon-tied pile of pages as I would be with a newborn baby. One day, when the bag had become very heavy, I counted five hundred pages that were whited out so many times with correction fluid that some were stiff as cardboard; others were stained with soup, or had glued-in sections that unfolded like maps—O blessed computer, that today allows me to make clean corrections! But now I had no one to send that long, long letter to, my grandfather had departed this earth. When we received the news of his death, I felt a kind of happiness, since that was what he had wanted for years, and I continued to write with even more confidence because that splendid old man had at last joined Memé, and both were reading over my shoulder. My grandmother's fantasies and Tata's sly laugh accompanied me every night. The epilogue was the most difficult part; I wrote it many times, without finding the tone I wanted: it seemed sentimental, or sounded like a sermon or a political tract. I knew what I wanted to tell but didn't know how to express it, until once again ghosts came to my aid. One night I dreamed that my grandfather was lying in his bed with his eyes closed, just as he was that early morning in my childhood when I crept into his room to steal the silver mirror. In the dream, I lifted the sheet and saw he was dressed in mourning, complete with necktie and shoes, and realized he was dead. I sat down by his side, there amidst the black furniture, to read him the book I had just written, and as my voice narrated the story the furniture turned blond again, blue veils fluttered over the bed, and the sun came in through the window. I awakened, startled, at three in the morning with the solution. Alba, the granddaughter, is writing the story of her family beside the body of her grandfather, Esteban Trueba, who is to be buried the next morning. I went into the kitchen, sat down at the typewriter, and in less than two hours, without a pause, wrote the ten pages of the epilogue. They say a book is never finished; instead, the author just gives up. In this case, my grandparents, perhaps bothered by seeing their memories betrayed, forced me to put the words "The End." I had written my first book. I did not know those pages would change my life, but I felt that a long period of paralysis and muteness had ended.

I bound up the pages in the same ribbon I had used for a year and shyly handed it to my mother, who returned it after a few days, horrified, asking me how I dared reveal our family secrets and describe my father as a degenerate—even naming him by name. Actually, I had given the French count in my story a name chosen at random: Bilbaire. I suppose I had heard it somewhere, stored it in some forgotten compartment, and when I created the character bestowed it on him without the least awareness of having used my paternal grandmother's surname. With that reaction from my mother came certain suspicions about my father that had tormented my childhood. To please her, though, I agreed to the change and, after much searching, found a French patronymic with one fewer letter that would fit easily into the same space: I could paint over "Bilbaire" with the correction fluid and type in "Satigny," a task that took several days, revising page by page, rolling each page into the portable and consoling myself as I did this dog work with the thought that Cervantes wrote *Don Quijote* with a quill pen, by candlelight, in prison, and with his one remaining hand. After I changed the name, my mother enthusiastically entered into the game of fiction, participated in choosing the title *The House of the Spirits,* and offered stupendous ideas, including some for the controversial count. It was my mother, who has a morbid imagination, who had the idea that among the scabrous photographs the count collected was one of "a stuffed llama riding atop the lame servant girl." Ever since, my mother has been my editor, the only person who corrects my books, because someone with the capacity to create something so twisted deserves all my confidence. It was also she who insisted I publish the book; she contacted Argentine, Chilean, and Venezuelan publishers, sent letters right and left, and never lost hope, even though no one offered to read the manuscript, or even replied. One day we were given the name of a person in Spain who might help us. I didn't know such people as literary agents existed, in fact, like most normal human beings, I had never read a page of literary criticism, and could not have imagined that books are analyzed in universities with the same intensity accorded stars in the firmament. Had I known, it would never have occurred to me to try to publish that pile of pages defaced with soup and correction fluid that the mailman dutifully placed on the desk of Carmen Balcells in Barcelona. That magnificent Catalan, doting mother to nearly all the great Latin American writers of the last three decades, took the trouble to read my book and within a few weeks called to tell me that she would like to be my agent, and also to warn me that even though my novel wasn't bad, that didn't mean very much— anyone can succeed with a first book, only the second would prove I was a writer. Six months later, I was invited to Spain for the publication of the novel. The day before I left, my mother entertained the family with a dinner to celebrate the occasion. As dessert was served, Tío Ramón handed me a package; I opened it, and there before my awestruck eyes was the first copy of my book, straight from the presses, which he had obtained with the sleight of hand of a veteran dealmaker, importuning editors, mobilizing ambassadors on two continents, and utilizing the diplomatic pouch to get it to me in time. It is impossible to describe my feelings at that moment; all I can say is that I have never experienced it with any of my other books, or their translations into languages I thought were dead, or adaptations to film or stage: that copy of *The House of the Spirits,* with its rose-colored border and image of a woman with green hair, touched my deepest emotions. I left for Madrid with the book in my arms, easily visible to any who might wish to look, and accompanied by Michael, who was as proud of my feat as my mother was. They went into bookstores to ask if they had my book, and created a scene if they said "no" and another if they said "yes," but this time because they had not sold them all. Carmen Balcells had met us at the airport enveloped in a purple fur coat and, around her neck, a mauve silk muffler that dragged the ground behind her like the fading tail of a comet; she opened her arms wide and at that instant became my guardian angel. She threw a party to present me to the Spanish intelligentsia, but I was so frightened I spent a good part of the evening hiding in the bathroom. That night in her house I saw for the first and last time two pounds of Iranian caviar with soup spoons at the disposal of the guests, a pharaonic extravagance totally unjustified since, however you looked at it, I was a flea, and she had no way to foresee the providential trajectory that novel would trace—she must have been swayed by the illustrious name of Allende, along with my provincial appearance. I still remember the first question I was asked in an interview conducted by the most renowned literary critic of the moment: "Can you explain the cyclical structure of your novel?" My expression must have been totally bovine, because I hadn't any idea what he was talking about. In my vocabulary, only buildings had "structure," and the only "cyclical" I was familiar with referred to the moon or menstruation. Shortly thereafter, the best publishing houses in Europe, from Finland to Greece, bought the translation rights and the book shot off on its meteoric career. One of those rare miracles had happened that every author dreams of, but I did not absorb the scandalous success until a year and a half later when I was about to finish a second novel, just to prove to Carmen Balcells that I was a writer and demonstrate that the caviar had not been a total waste.

I continued to work twelve hours a day at the school, not daring to resign because Michael's million-dollar contract, won in part through the cleaning woman's liquid magic, had gone up in smoke. Through one of those coincidences so precise that they seem metaphors, his job had crashed to the ground the very day my book was launched in Madrid. When we got off the airplane in the Caracas airport, Michael's associate met us with the bad news; the joy of my triumph was erased, replaced by the dark clouds of his misfortune. Accusations of corruption and bribes in the bank financing the job had forced legal intervention; payments were frozen and the project was paralyzed. The most prudent course would have been to close the office immediately and try to liquidate what we could, but Michael believed the bank was too powerful, and, because political interests were involved, the legal battle would go on forever; he thought that if he could keep his head above water for a while, everything would settle down and the contract would come back to him. In the meantime, his associate, a little more shrewd about how the game was played, disappeared with his own part of the money, leaving Michael without work and up to his neck in a sinkhole of debts.

Problems finally consumed Michael, but he refused to admit his downfall or his depression until the day he fainted. Paula and Nicolás carried him to his bed and I tried to revive him by slapping his face and pouring water over him, as I had seen in the movies. Later, the doctor diagnosed high blood sugar and commented, amused, that diabetes is not usually cured with buckets of cold water. Michael fainted so frequently that we all became accustomed to it. We had never heard the word porphyria, and no one attributed his symptoms to that rare metabolic disorder; three years would go by before a niece fell ill and after months of exhaustive tests doctors in a North American clinic diagnosed the illness and said the whole family should be tested. That was how we discovered that Michael, Paula, and Nicolás all were affected by that condition. By then, our marriage was like a glass bubble we were taking great precautions not to shatter; we treated each other with ceremonious courtesy and made obstinate efforts to stay together, despite the fact that every day our paths grew farther apart. We had respect and affection for one another, but the relationship weighed on me like lead; in my nightmares, I walked across a desert pulling a cart, and with every step my feet and the wheels sank into the sand. In that loveless period, I found escape in writing. While my first novel was making its way through Europe, I was still typing every night in the kitchen of our house in Caracas, but I had updated myself, now I worked on an electric typewriter. I began *Of Love and Shadows* on January 8, 1983, because that day had brought me luck with *The House of the Spirits,* thus initiating a tradition I honor to this day and don't dare change; I always write the first line of my books on that date. When that time comes, I try to be alone and silent for several hours; I need a lot of time to rid my mind of the noise outside and to cleanse my memory of life's confusion. I light candles to summon the muses and guardian spirits, I place flowers on my desk to intimidate tedium and the complete works of Pablo Neruda beneath the computer with the hope they will inspire me by osmosis—if computers can be infected with a virus, there's no reason they shouldn't be refreshed by a breath of poetry. In a secret ceremony, I prepare my mind and soul to receive the first sentence in a trance, so the door may open slightly and allow me to peer through and

perceive the hazy outlines of the story waiting for me. In the following months, I will cross that threshold to explore those spaces and,
little by little, if I am lucky, the characters will come alive, become
more precise and more real, and reveal the narrative to me as we go
along. I don't know how or why I write; my books are not born in
my mind, they gestate in my womb and are capricious creatures
with their own lives, always ready to subvert me. I do not determine
the subject, the subject chooses me, my work consists simply of
providing enough time, solitude, and discipline for the book to
write itself. That is what happened with my second novel. In 1978,
in the area of Lonquén, some fifty kilometers from Santiago, they
found the bodies of fifteen campesinos murdered by the government and hidden in abandoned lime kilns. The Catholic Church
reported the discovery and the scandal exploded before authorities
could muffle it; it was the first time the bodies of *desaparecidos* had
been found, and the wavering finger of Chilean justice had no
choice but to point to the armed forces. Several *carabineros* were
accused, tried, and found guilty of murder in the first degree—and
immediately set free by General Pinochet under a decree of
amnesty. The news was published around the world, which was how
I learned of it in Caracas. By then, thousands of people had disappeared in many parts of the continent, Chile was not an exception.
In Argentina, the mothers of the *desaparecidos* marched in the Plaza
de Mayo carrying photographs of their missing children and grandchildren; in Uruguay, the names of prisoners far exceeded physical
bodies that could be counted. What happened in Lonquén was like
a knife in my belly, I felt the pain for years. Five men from the same
family, the Maureiras, had died, murdered by *carabineros*. Sometimes
I would be driving down the highway and suddenly be assaulted by
the disturbing vision of the Maureira women searching for their
men, years of asking their futile questions in prisons and concentration camps and hospitals and barracks, like the thousands and thousands of other persons in other places trying to find their loved
ones. In Lonquén, the women were more fortunate than most; at
least they knew their men had been murdered, and they could cry
and pray for them—although not bury them, because the military
later scattered the remains and dynamited the lime kilns to prevent

their becoming a site for pilgrimages and worship. One day those women walked up and down a row of rough-hewn tables, sorting through a pitiful array—keys, a comb, a shred of blue sweater, a lock of hair, or a few teeth—and said, This is my husband, This is my brother, This is my son. Every time I thought of them, I was transported with implacable clarity to the times I lived in Chile under the heavy mantle of terror: censorship and self-censorship, denunciations, curfew, soldiers with faces camouflaged so they couldn't be recognized, political police cars with tinted glass windows, arrests in the street, homes, offices, my racing to help fugitives find asylum in some embassy, sleepless nights when we had someone hidden in our home, the clumsy schemes to slip information out of the country or bring money in to aid families of the imprisoned. For my second novel, I didn't have to think of a subject, the women of the Maureira family, the mothers of the Plaza de Mayo, and millions of other victims pursued me, obliging me to write. The story of the deaths at Lonquén had lain in my heart since 1978; I had kept every press clipping that came into my hands without knowing exactly why, since at that time I had no inkling that my steps were leading toward literature. So by 1983, I had at my disposal a thick folder of information, and knew where to find other facts; my job consisted of weaving those threads into a single cord. I was relying on my friend Francisco in Chile, whom I meant to use as model for the protagonist, a family of Spanish Republican refugees on whom to pattern the Leals, and a couple of women I had worked with on the women's magazine in Santiago as inspiration for the character of Irene. I drew Gustavo Morante, Irene's fiancé, from a Chilean army officer who followed me to San Cristobal Hill one noontime in the autumn of 1974. I was sitting under a tree with my mother's Swiss dog, which I used to take for walks, looking down on Santiago from the heights, when an automobile stopped a few meters away and a man in uniform got out and walked toward me. I froze with panic; for a split second I considered running, but instantly knew the futility of trying to escape and simply waited, shivering and speechless. To my surprise, the officer did not bark an order to me but removed his cap, apologized for disturbing me, and asked if he could sit down. I still was unable to speak a word, but since arrests were always made by several men it calmed me to see that he was alone. He was about thirty, tall and handsome, with a rather naive, unlined face. I noticed his distress as soon as he spoke. He told me he knew who I was; he had read some of my articles, and hadn't liked them, but he enjoyed my programs on television. He had often watched me climb the hill and had followed me that day because he had something he wanted to tell me. He said that he came from a very religious family; he was a devout Catholic and as a young man had contemplated entering the seminary, but had gone to the military academy to please his father. He soon discovered he liked that profession, and with time the army had become his true home. "I am prepared to die for my country," he said, "but I didn't know how difficult it is to kill for it." And then, after a very long pause, he described the first detail he had commanded, how he was assigned to execute a political prisoner who had been so badly tortured he couldn't stand and had to be tied in a chair, how in a frosty courtyard at five in the morning he gave the order to fire, and how when the sound of the shots faded he realized the man was still alive and staring tranquilly into his eyes, because he was beyond fear.

"I had to approach the prisoner, put my pistol to his temple, and press the trigger. The blood splattered my uniform. It's something I can't tear from my soul. I can't sleep, I am haunted by the memory."

"Why are you telling me this?" I asked.

"Because it isn't enough to have told my confessor, I want to share it with someone who may be able to make use of it. Not all the military are murderers, as is being said; many of us have a conscience." He stood, saluted me with a slight bow, put on his cap, and left.

Months later, another man, this one in civilian clothes, told me something similar. "Soldiers shoot at the legs to force the officers to fire the *coup de grace* and stain themselves with blood, too," he said. I jotted down those memories and for nine years kept them at the bottom of a drawer, until I used them in *Of Love and Shadows*. Some critics considered the book sentimental, and too political; for me, it is filled with magic because it revealed to me the strange powers of fiction. In the slow and silent process of writing, I enter a different state of consciousness in which sometimes I can draw back a veil and see the invisible, the world of my grandmother's three-legged table. It is not necessary to mention all the premonitions and coincidences recorded in those pages, one will suffice. Although I had abundant information, there were large lacunae in the story, because many of the military trials were conducted in secret and what was published was distorted by censorship. In addition, I was far from the scene and could not go to Chile to interrogate the involved parties as I would have done under other circumstances. My years as a journalist had taught me that it is in personal interviews that one obtains the keys, motives, and emotions of a story, no research in a library can replace the firsthand information derived from a face-to-face conversation. During those warm Caracas nights, I wrote the novel from the material in my file of clippings, a few books, some tapes from Amnesty International, and the inexhaustible voices of the women of the *desaparecidos* speaking to me across distance and time. Even with all that, I had to call upon my imagination to fill in blanks. After she read the original, my mother objected to one part that to her seemed absolutely improbable: the protagonists, at night and during curfew, go by motorcycle to a mine sealed off by the military; they find a break in the fence and enter an area that is off-limits, dig into the mouth of the mine with picks and shovels, find the remains of the murdered, photograph them, return with the proof, and deliver it to the cardinal, who finally orders the tomb opened. "That's impossible," she said. "No one would dare run such risks at the height of the dictatorship." "I can't think of any other way to resolve the plot, just think of it as literary license," I replied. The book was published in 1984. Four years later, the list of exiles who could not return to Chile was abolished and for the first time I felt free to go back to my country to vote in a plebiscite that finally unseated Pinochet. One night the doorbell rang in my mother's house in Santiago and a man insisted in talking with me in private. In a corner of the terrace, he told me he was a priest, that he had learned in the sanctity of the confessional about bodies buried in Lonquén, had gone there on his motorcycle during curfew, had opened a sealed mine with pick and shovel, had photographed the remains and taken the proof to the

cardinal, who ordered a group of priests, newspapermen, and diplomats to open the clandestine tomb.

"No one has any knowledge of this except the cardinal and
myself. If my participation in that matter had been known, I'm sure
I wouldn't be here talking with you, I would be among the disappeared. How did you learn?" he asked.

"The dead told me," I replied, but he did not believe me.

Of Love and Shadows also brought Willie into my life, and for that
I am grateful.

My first two novels were slow to cross the Atlantic, but finally they
arrived in Caracas bookstores, some people read them, a couple of
favorable reviews were published, and the quality of my life
changed. Circles I had not had access to opened to me, I met interesting people, I was invited by various print media to collaborate,
and I was called by television producers who wanted to roll out the
red carpet for me, but by then I knew how uncertain promises can
be and chose not to leave my secure position at the school. One day
at the theater, a man with a soft voice and careful pronunciation
came up to me to congratulate me on my first novel; he said it had
touched him deeply: among other reasons, because he and his family had lived in Chile during the government of Salvador Allende and
had witnessed the military coup. Later, I found out he had been
imprisoned during those first days of indiscriminate brutality,
because his neighbors, not recognizing his accent, had thought he
was a Cuban agent and had informed on him. That was the beginning of my friendship with Ildemaro, the most significant of my life,
a combination of good humor and rigorous lectures. I learned a lot
under his tutelage; he guided my reading, revised some of my writing, and argued politics with me. When I think of him, I seem to
see his finger pointed toward me as he instructs me on the work of
Benedetti or clears the fog from my brain with an erudite sermon
on socialism. That is not the only image, however; I also remember
him weak with laughter or red with embarrassment when we punc-
tured his solemnity with jokes. We incorporated him, his wife, his
three children, and even a grandmother into our family and for the
first time in many years again felt the warmth of being a tribe; we

reinstated our Sunday dinners, our children thought of themselves
as cousins, and we all had keys to both houses. Ildemaro, who is a
physician but has a greater calling for the arts, provided us with
tickets to a multitude of functions we attended because we didn't
want to offend him. At first, Paula was the only one with sufficient
courage to laugh at the sacred cows of art in his presence, but soon
the rest of us followed her example, and we ended by organizing an
informal theater troupe with the aim of parodying our friend's cultural events and intellectual disquisitions. He, however, quickly
found a clever way to undercut our scheme: he became the most
active member of the company. Under his direction, we mounted
spectacles that transcended the limits of our long-suffering circle
of friends, as, for instance, a lecture on jealousy that featured a
machine of our own invention to measure "the level of the jealousy
factor" in victims of that scourge. One psychiatric association—I
can't remember whether Jungian or Lacanian—took us seriously;
we were invited to perform a demonstration, and one night found
ourselves in the headquarters of the institute with our preposterous
satire. Our Jealousy Machine consisted of a black box with erratic
needles indicating measurements and capriciously blinking lights
connected by cables to a helmet on Paula's head, who valiantly
enacted the role of guinea pig while Nicolás manipulated the controls. The psychiatrists listened, amazed, and took notes; some
seemed somewhat perplexed, but in general they were satisfied, and
the next day a scholarly review of the program appeared in the
newspaper. Paula survived the Jealousy Machine and became so
fond of Ildemaro that she made him the recipient of her most intimate confidences and to please him accepted the starring role in all
the company's productions. Now Ildemaro calls me frequently
about Paula; he listens to my report without interrupting and tries
to give me encouragement—but not hope, because he has none
himself. There was nothing back then to indicate that it would be
my daughter's fate to suffer this calamity; she was a beautiful,
twenty-year-old student, brilliant and happy, who had no qualms
about playing the fool on stage if Ildemaro requested it. Our indefatigable Mama Hilda, who had left Chile and followed our family
into exile, and who lived half her life in our house, kept a perma-

nent sewing operation going in the dining room, where we made
our costumes and sets. Michael participated with good humor, even
though his health and enthusiasm tended to flag. Nicolás, who suffers from stage fright and empathetic shyness, was in charge of the
technical production—light, sound, and special effects—and in that
way could remain behind the curtains. Little by little, most of our
friends were drawn into the troupe and there was no one left as
audience, but rehearsing the works was so entertaining for actors
and musicians that no one cared if we performed to an empty
house. Our home was filled with people, noise, and laughter; finally
we had an extended family and felt comfortable in this new country.

The same was not true of my parents, however. Tío Ramón saw
himself approaching seventy and wanted to go back to Chile to die,
as he announced with certain drama, eliciting belly laughs from all
of us who know him to be immortal. Two months later, we watched
him pack his suitcases and, shortly after, he left with my mother to
return to a country where they had not set foot in many years and
where the perennial general continued to govern. I felt like an
orphan, and I was afraid for them; I had a foreboding that we would
never live in the same city again and readied myself to resume the
old routine of the daily letters. As a send-off, we gave a large party
with Chilean wines and dishes and presented the last performance
of the theater company. Using song and dance, actors and puppets,
we narrated the torturous life and illegal loves of my mother and
Tío Ramón, played by Paula and Ildemaro—outfitted with diabolical false eyebrows. This time we did have a public, because nearly all
the good friends who had been so hospitable to my parents in that
warm country attended. In a place of honor was Valentín Hernández, whose generous visas opened the doors to us. It was the last
time we saw him, because shortly afterward he died of a sudden illness, leaving behind a grief-stricken wife and descendants. He was
one of those loving and watchful patriarchs who gather all his loved
ones beneath his protective cloak. It was not easy for him to die
because he did not want to go while his family was exposed to the
gales of these terrifying modern times and, in his heart of hearts, he
may have dreamed of taking them with him. One year later, his
widow convened her daughter, son-in-law, and grandchild to com-

memorate her husband's death in a happy way, as he would have wished, by taking them for a vacation. Their plane crashed, and few were left of that family to weep for the missing.

In September 1987, my third novel, *Eva Luna*, was published in Spain; this one was written in the full light of day on a computer in the large studio of a new house. The two preceding books had convinced my agent that I intended to take literature seriously, and me that it was reasonable to risk leaving my job to devote myself to writing, even though my husband had not emerged from bankruptcy and we still had unpaid debts. I sold my shares in the school and we bought a large house perched on a hillside—a little ramshackle, it's true, but Michael remodeled it, making it into a sunny refuge with room to spare for visitors, relatives, and friends, and for Mama Hilda to install herself comfortably in a sewing room and me in an office. In the foundations of the house, midpoint on the hill, was a bright and well-ventilated cellar, so large we planted in the middle of a tropical garden the vine that replaced the forget-me-nots of my nostalgia. The walls were lined with bookshelves, filled to overflowing, and right in the middle of the room I set a large table, the only piece of furniture. That was a period of great change. Paula and Nicolás, now independent and ambitious young adults, were attending the university; they were on their own now, and it was obvious they did not need me, but the complicity among the three of us was immutable. After her love affair with the young Sicilian, Paula became more serious about her studies in psychology and sexuality. Her chestnut hair fell to her waist; she did not use makeup and her long white cotton skirts and sandals accentuated her virginal appearance. She did volunteer work in the roughest slums, places even the police didn't venture after sunset. By then, violence and crime had skyrocketed in Caracas; our house had been broken into several times and there were horrible rumors of children kidnapped in shopping centers in order to harvest their corneas and sell them to eye banks, of women raped in parking lots, of people murdered simply to steal a watch. Paula would go off in her little car, carrying a bag of books, and I would be sick with apprehension. I begged her a thousand times not to go into those parts of the city, but she didn't listen because she felt she was protected by her good intentions and her belief that everyone knew who she was. Paula had a mature mind, but had not outgrown girlish emotions; the same woman who in the airplane memorized the map of a city she had never visited, rented a car at the airport, and drove straight to the hotel, or who in four hours could put together a course on literature that I used for university lectures, fainted when she was vaccinated and was nearly traumatized in vampire movies. She practiced her psychology tests on Nicolás and me, and confirmed that her brother has an IQ approaching genius and, in contrast, that her mother suffers severe retardation. She tested me again and again, but the results never varied, they always produced an embarrassing intellectual coefficient. Happily, she never experimented on us with the paraphernalia from the seminar on sexuality.

With *Eva Luna,* I was finally aware that my path was literary, and for the first time dared say, "I am a writer." When I sat down to begin that book, I did not do so as I had with the two earlier ones, filled with excuses and doubts, but in full control of my will and even with a certain measure of arrogance. "I am going to write a novel," I said aloud. Then I turned on the computer and without a second thought launched into the first sentence: *My name is Eva, which means "life"* . . .

MY MOTHER HAS COME TO CALIFORNIA FOR A VISIT. I NEARLY DID NOT recognize her at the airport: a small elderly woman in black, a porcelain great-grandmother, with a quavering voice and a face ravaged by sorrow and the fatigue of the twenty-hour flight from Santiago. She began crying as she hugged me, and continued to cry all the way to the house, but, once there, she went straight to a bathroom, took a shower, dressed in cheerful colors, and came downstairs with a smile to say hello to Paula. Even expecting to find her worse, she was shocked when she saw her; Mother still has a vivid memory of her favorite granddaughter as she used to be. One of Paula's caregivers tried to console her: "She is in limbo, *Doñita,* with all the babies who died without being baptized and the souls rescued from purgatory." "What a waste, my God, what a waste!" my mother kept repeating, but never near Paula, because she thinks she may be able to hear. "Don't project your anxiety and wishes on her, Madame," advised Dr. Shima. "Your granddaughter's former life is ended; she is living now in a different state of consciousness." As could have been foreseen, my mother was taken with Dr. Shima. He is an ageless man with a timeworn body, young face and hands, and a thick head of dark hair; he uses suspenders and wears his pants up beneath his armpits. He walks with a slight limp and laughs with the malicious expression of a child caught with his hand in the cookie jar. Both of them pray for Paula, she with her Christian faith, and he with his Buddhist. In my mother's case, it is the triumph of hope over experience, because for seventeen years she prayed for General Pinochet to pass on to his reward, and not only is he in good health, he still has the frying pan by the handle. "God is slow, but He will come through," she replies when she is reminded of this. "I assure you that Pinochet is headed for the grave." As are we all, from the moment we are born, dying a little every day. In the afternoons, this ironic grandmother sits down with her knitting beside her grand-daughter's bed and talks to her with no thought for the sidereal silence into which her words fall. She chats about the past and recounts the latest gossip, comments on her own life, and some-times, a little out of tune, sings a hymn to the Virgin Mary, the only song she can remember all the way through. She thinks that from her bed, Paula works subtle miracles, obliges us to grow, and teaches us the paths of compassion and wisdom. She suffers for Paula and suffers for me, two pains that cannot be avoided.

"Where was my daughter before I brought her into the world? Where will she go when she dies?"

"Paula is already in God. God is *what binds,* what holds together the fabric of life . . . what you call love," my mother replied.

Ernesto is here, taking advantage of a week's vacation. He still maintains the illusion that his wife will recover sufficiently for him to have a life with her, even if very limited. He used to think a higher power would intervene and suddenly, with a long yawn, she would awake, grope for his hand, and in a voice rusty with disuse ask what happened. "Doctors are wrong all the time," he told me, "and they know very little about the brain." Now, however, he did not rush in impetuously to see her, but cautiously, as if afraid. We had taken special pains with Paula's hair and dressed her in the clothes he brought her on his last visit. He put his arms around her with great tenderness, as her caregiver scurried toward the kitchen, teary-eyed, and my mother and I sought refuge on the terrace. For the first few days, he spent hours scrutinizing Paula's reactions, looking for some spark of intelligence, but gradually he stopped; we watched him slump, shrink, until the optimistic aura of his arrival darkened into the penumbra that envelops us all. I tried to suggest that now Paula is not his wife but his spiritual sister and that he must not feel he is bound to her, but he looked at me as if he were hearing a sacrilege. The last night he broke down and realized finally that no miracle is going to give him back his eternal bride and that, however much he looked, he would find nothing in the unfathomable abyss of her empty eyes. He woke up terrified from a nightmare and came in the dark to my room, shaking and wet with sweat and tears, to tell me the dream.

"I dreamed that Paula was climbing a long extension ladder, and when she got to the top she leaped off into emptiness before I could stop her. I was desperate. Then I saw her lying on a table, and for a long time she lay there, unchanged, while my life went on. Then she began to lose her hair, and weight, until she suddenly sat up and tried to tell me something but I interrupted her to reproach her for having abandoned me. She went back to sleep on the table, wasting away, without completely dying. Finally, I realized that the only way I could help her would be to destroy her body, so I took her in my arms and placed her on a fire. Her body turned to ashes, which I scattered in a garden. Then her ghost came to say goodbye to the family, and last, she turned to me to tell me she loved me, and immediately began to fade away. . . ."

"Let her go, Ernesto," I begged him.

"Can you do that? If you let her go, then I will, too," he answered.

It came to me how for countless centuries women have lost their children, how it is humanity's most ancient and inevitable sorrow. I am not alone, most mothers know this pain, it breaks their heart but they go on living because they must protect and love those who are left. Only a group of privileged women—in very recent times and in advanced countries where health care is available to all who can afford it—can hope that all their children will live to be adults. Death is always hovering nearby. Ernesto and I went to Paula's room, closed the door, and, just the two of us, proceeded to improvise a brief ritual of parting. We told Paula how much we loved her, we reviewed the wonderful years we had lived together and assured her she would always be in our memories. We promised her we would be with her until her last moment in this world and that we would find her again in another, because in fact we would not be separated. "Die now, my love," Ernesto pleaded, on his knees beside her bed. "Yes, Paula, go now," I added in silence, because my voice failed me.

Willie insists that I talk and walk in my sleep, but that isn't true. At night I wander barefoot and silent through the house so I won't disturb the spirits or the skunks that slip upstairs to devour the cat's food. Sometimes we meet face to face, and they raise their beautiful striped tails, like furry peacocks, and stare at me, their noses quivering, but they must have become accustomed to my presence, because until now they have never shot their ominous spray inside the house, only in the basement. I don't walk in my sleep, I walk in my sorrow. "Take a pill and try to rest a few hours," Willie begs me, exhausted. "You need to see a psychiatrist, you're obsessed, and from thinking about Paula so much, you're seeing visions." He maintains that my daughter does not come to our room at night, that it's impossible, she can't move, and I'm just having nightmares like so many dreams that seem more true than reality. But who knows . . . maybe there are other means of spiritual communication besides dreams, and, incapacitated though she is, Paula has found a way to talk to me. My senses have been sharpened so that I perceive the invisible, but I am not mad. Dr. Shima comes by often, and he tells me that Paula has become his guide. The three months have passed, and the psychics, hypnotists, seers, and mediums have all gone; now only Dr. Forrester and Dr. Shima are attending my daughter. Sometimes he merely meditates a few minutes beside her; other times he examines her meticulously, uses his needles to relieve the pain in her bones, administers Chinese medications, then shares a cup of tea with me where we can talk freely without being over-heard. I had the courage to tell him that Paula comes to visit me at night and he didn't find it strange, he said she also talks to him.

"How does she do that, Doctor?"

"I wake in the early morning to the sound of her voice."

"How do you know it's hers? You've never heard her. . . ."

"Sometimes I see her clearly. She points out places where she has pain, suggests changes in the medicines, asks me to help her mother in this ordeal—she knows how much you are suffering. Paula is very tired and wants to go, but her body is strong and she may live a long time."

"How much longer, Dr. Shima?"

From his magic case, he took out a velvet bag containing his I Ching sticks, concentrated on a secret prayer, shook them, and threw them on the table.

"Seven. . . ."

"Seven years?"

"Or months or weeks, I don't know, the I Ching is very vague. . . ."

Before he left, he gave me some mysterious herbs; he believes that anxiety runs down the body's and the mind's defenses, and that there is a direct relationship between cancer and sorrow. Dr. For-rester also prescribed something for depression. This extraordinary woman is full of compassion; she has nothing of the usual cynicism that most doctors have. I have the bottle put away in the basket with my mother's letters, hidden beside the sleeping pills, because I have decided not to seek relief in drugs; this is a road I must travel bleed-ing. Images of Celia giving birth come back to me often; I see her sweating, ripped by her pains, biting her lips, progressing step by step through that long travail without the aid of tranquilizers, serene and conscious, helping her daughter into life. I see her in her climac-tic effort, open as a wound, as Andrea's head emerges; I hear her tri-umphal shout and Nicolás's sob, and again experience our blessing in the holy quiet of this room where now Paula is sleeping. My daugh-ter's strange illness may be like that birth; I must grit my teeth and have courage, knowing that this torment will not be forever, that one day it will end. And how? It can only end with death. . . . I hope that Willie will have the patience to wait for me because it may be a long while, perhaps the seven years of the I Ching. It isn't easy to keep love alive in these conditions, everything conspires against intimacy; I am always weary in body and my soul is not in me. Willie doesn't know how he can help me, and I don't know what to ask of him; he doesn't dare press any harder for fear of alienating me, yet, at the same time, he doesn't want to abandon me. In his pragmatic mind, the most reasonable move would be to put Paula in a hospital and try to get on with our lives, but he never mentions that possibility because he knows it would drive an irrevocable wedge between us. "I wish I could take your burden and carry it myself, my shoulders are broader," he says hopelessly, but he already has enough with his own problems. My daughter is gently failing in my arms, but his is killing herself with drugs in the back alleys across the Bay; she could die even before mine, of an overdose, the slash of a knife, or AIDS. His older son wanders like a homeless man through the streets, stealing and trafficking. If the telephone rings at night, Willie leaps out of bed with the latent foreboding that the body of his daughter is lying in some ditch by the port, or that the voice of a policeman will inform him of some new crime committed by his son. He lives under shadows from the past, and frequently something leaps out to rip and claw him, but now not even the worst news crushes him; he is dropped to his knees, but the next day he is on his feet again. I often ask myself how I wound up in this melodrama. My mother attributes it to my taste for truculent stories, and believes that is the principal ingredient in my feelings for Willie, and that another woman with more common sense would have bolted at the sight of such calamity. When I met Willie, he made no attempt to hide the fact that his life was in chaos; I knew from the beginning about his delinquent children, his debts, and the complications in his past, but in the impetuous arrogance of new love, I decided there were no obstacles we could not overcome.

It is difficult to imagine two men more different than Michael and Willie. By the middle of 1987, my marriage had nowhere to go; tedium was absolute and to avoid waking at the same hour in the same bed I went back to my old habit of writing at night. Depressed, out of work, and stuck in the house, Michael was going through a bad time. To escape his constant presence, I sometimes fled and lost myself in the jungle of Caracas expressways. Fighting the traffic, I resolved many scenes in *Eva Luna,* and ideas came to me for other stories. On one memorable jag, trapped for a couple of hours in my car in heat like molten lead, I wrote "Two Words" at one stretch, on the backs of my checks, a kind of allegory about the hallucinatory power of narration and language that then became the key for a collection of short stories. Although for the first time I felt secure in the strange craft of writing—with my two earlier books, I had the feeling I had accidentally landed in a slippery mud pit—*Eva Luna* insisted on writing itself. I had no control over that fractious story; I had no idea where it was going or how to end it. I was ready to massacre all the characters in a hail of bullets to get out of the mess and be rid of them. As the last straw, halfway through I was left without a male protagonist. I had planned everything for Eva and Huberto Naranjo, two poor, streetwise, orphaned children who grew up in parallel circumstances, to fall in love. Midbook, the expected encounter took place, but, when finally they embraced, it turned out that the only thing that interested him were his revolutionary activities; he was, besides, a terribly clumsy lover. Eva deserved more; that was what she let me know and there was no way to convince her of the contrary. I found myself on a dead-end street with a frustrated heroine tapping her foot while the hero sitting on her bed cleaned his rifle. About that time, I had to go to Germany on a book tour. I landed in Frankfurt, and from there traveled across the rest of the country by car, driven by an impatient chauffeur who flew along frosty autobahns at suicidal speeds. One night in a northern city, a man came up after my talk and invited me to have a beer, because, he said, he had a story for me. Sitting in a small café where we could scarcely see each other's faces through the gloom and cigarette smoke, as rain poured down outside, this stranger told me about his past. His father had been an officer in the Nazi army, a cruel man who mistreated his wife and children and who in the war had been given the opportunity to satisfy his most brutal instincts. He told me about his retarded younger sister, and how his father, steeped in pride of race, had never accepted her but forced her to live like an animal, silent, huddling under a white cloth—covered table so he wouldn't have to see her. I wrote all that, and a lot more he gave me that night as a gift, on a paper napkin. Before we said good night, I asked whether it was mine to use, and he said yes, that was why he had told me. When I returned to Caracas, I fed the paper napkin into the computer and out came Rolf Carlé, head to toe, an Austrian photographer who became the novel's protagonist and replaced Huberto Naranjo in the heart of Eva Luna.

One of those warm June mornings in Caracas when storms gather early over the hills, Michael came down to my studio in the cellar to bring the mail. I was lost in the Amazon jungle with Eva Luna, Rolf Carlé, and their companions in adventure, and at the sound of the door, I looked up and saw an unknown figure crossing the bare room, a tall, slim man with a gray beard and eyeglasses, bowed shoulders, and an opaque aura of fragility and melancholy. It was several seconds before I recognized my husband and realized what strangers we had become. I searched my memory for the embers of the carefree love of our twenties, but could not find even ashes, only the weight of dissatisfaction and ennui. I had a vision of an arid future, growing old day by day beside a man I no longer admired or desired, and I felt a howl of rebellion rising from deep inside me. At that instant, the words that with fierce discipline I had left unspoken for years tumbled out in a voice I could not recognize as my own.

"I can't take any more, I want a separation," I said, not daring to meet his eyes, and, as I spoke the words, that vague, flogged beast of burden pain I had carried for years lifted from my shoulders.

"I have noticed how distant you've been for some time. I guess you don't love me any longer and we should consider a separation," he stammered.

"There isn't much to consider, Michael. It's been said now, so the best thing is to do it today."

And we did. We called the children, explained that we had stopped loving each other like married people, although our friendship remained intact, and we asked their help in setting out the practical details of breaking up our home. Nicolás turned red, as he always does when he is trying to control a strong emotion, and Paula burst into tears out of compassion for her father, whom she always protected. Later, I found out that they weren't surprised, they had been expecting something like this for a long time. Michael seemed paralyzed, but I was infused with manic energy; I began to pull dishes from the kitchen, clothes from the closets, books from the shelves, and then ran out to buy pots and pans, a coffee pot, a shower curtain, lamps, food, and even plants, to set up a separate household. With the excess energy, I began putting together pieces of cloth in the sewing room to make a quilt, which I have today as a souvenir of those frenetic hours that determined the second half of my life. The children divided up our belongings, wrote a simple, one-page agreement, and the four of us signed it without ceremony or witnesses. Then Paula found an apartment for her father, and Nicolás got a truck to transport half our belongings. Within a few hours, we undid twenty-nine years of love and twenty-five years of marriage with no slamming doors, recriminations, or lawyers, only a few inevitable tears, because in spite of everything we had affection for one another and I believe that in a certain way we still do. That night, the storm broke that had been building up all day, one of those infamous thunder-and lightning tropical downpours that turn Caracas into a disaster zone: storm sewers back up, streets flood, traffic forms a series of gigantic serpents of stalled automobiles, and mud slides wipe out whole slums on the hillsides. When finally the truck of our divorce pulled away, followed by the children on their way to install their father in his new home, and I was alone in the house, I threw open the windows and doors to let the wind and rain blow in to sweep away the past; I began to dance and whirl like a maddened dervish, weeping with sadness for what was lost and laughing with relief for what was gained, while crickets and tree frogs sang outside, and inside the torrential rain streamed across the floor and the gale blew dead leaves and bird feathers in a whirlwind of farewells and freedom.

I was forty-four; I supposed that from then on my fate would be to grow old alone, and intended to be dignified doing it. I called Tío Ramón and asked him to oversee the matrimonial annulment in Chile, a simple procedure if the couple is in agreement, if you have money for a lawyer, and if you know a couple of friends willing to commit perjury. Running away from explanations, and to outwit my sense of guilt, I accepted a series of lectures that took me from Iceland to Puerto Rico, passing through a dozen North American cities. In that variety of climates, I needed all the clothes I had but decided to carry only what was indispensable; my looks were far from my mind, I felt bogged down, with no hope of reprieve, in a passionless maturity, so it was a happy surprise to find that, if a woman is available, there is no shortage of men. I wrote a document, with three copies, retracting the one I had signed in Bolivia in which I had said that because of Tío Ramón I would never meet any men, and sent it to Chile by certified mail. Sometimes it's fair to offer your arm to be twisted. . . . Those two months, I took pleasure from the embrace of a polar bear of a poet in Reykjavík, the company of a young mulatto in the torrid nights of San Juan, and a scattering of other memorable encounters. I am tempted to invent wild erotic rites to adorn my memoirs, as I suppose others do, but in these pages I am trying to be honest. At moments, I felt I touched a lover's soul, and even dreamed of the possibility of a deeper relationship, but the next day I took another plane, and my enthusiasm dissolved among the clouds. Weary of fleeting kisses, I decided the last week to concentrate on my work, after all, lots of people live a chaste existence. I could never have guessed that at the end of that numbing journey Willie was waiting for me and my life would be forever changed; my premonitions failed me miserably.

In a city in northern California where I gave my last lecture, it befell me to live one of those overblown love affairs that serve as fodder for the romances I translated in my youth. Willie had read *Of Love and Shadows;* he had suffered for the characters and thought that in that book he had found the kind of love he wished for but had never experienced. I suspect he hadn't known where to look; even then he was placing ads in the personal columns to find someone, as he candidly told me on our first date. Some of the responses are still rattling around in a drawer somewhere, among them, the dazzling photograph of a woman wearing nothing but a boa—a boa *constrictor!*—and with no comment but her telephone number beneath the photo. Despite the snake, or perhaps because of it, Willie didn't mind giving up a couple of hours to meet me. One of the women professors from the university introduced him to me as the last heterosexual bachelor in San Francisco. After I spoke, I dined with a group around a table in an Italian restaurant; Willie sat facing me, with a glass of white wine in his hand, saying nothing. I admit that I felt a certain curiosity about this Irish-looking North American lawyer with an aristocratic appearance and silk tie who spoke Spanish like a Mexican *bandido* and had a tattoo on his left hand. There was a full moon, and the velvety voice of Frank Sinatra was crooning "Strangers in the Night" as our ravioli was served. This is the kind of detail that is forbidden in literature; in a book, no one would dare combine a full moon with Frank Sinatra. The problem with fiction is that it must seem credible, while reality seldom is. I can't explain what attracted Willie, who has a past filled with tall blondes. As for me, I was drawn by his story. And also, why not say it?, by his blend of refinement and roughness, strength of character, and an intimate gentleness that I sensed thanks to my mania for observing people to use later in my writing. At first, he didn't have much to say; he limited himself to watching me from across the table with an indecipherable expression. After the salad, I asked him to tell me the story of his life, a trick that saves me the effort of making conversation: the man queried expounds while my mind wanders through other worlds. In this case, however, I did not have to feign interest; as soon as he began to speak, I realized I had stumbled upon one of those rare gems treasured by storytellers: this man's life was a novel. The samples he had revealed during that hour or two awakened my greed; that night in the hotel I couldn't sleep, I needed to know more. Luck was with me, and the next day Willie located me in San Francisco, the last stop on my tour, to invite me to view the Bay from a mountainside and have dinner at his house. I imagined a romantic date in a modern apartment with a view of the Golden Gate Bridge, a cactus beside the door, champagne and smoked salmon, but there was nothing of that sort: his house and his life resembled the scene following a shipwreck. He picked me up in one of those sports cars with barely enough room for two, where you ride with your knees clamped to your ears and your rear scraping the asphalt; it was embellished with dog hair, crushed soft drink cans, fossilized french fries, and toy guns. The drive to the top of the mountain and the majestic spectacle of the

Bay impressed me, but I didn't expect to remember it very long; I've seen too many vistas and I had no thought of returning to the western United States. We descended along a curving highway bordered with large trees; a concerto was playing on the radio, and I had the sensation of having lived that moment before, of having been in that place many times, of belonging there. Later, I knew why: the north of California looks like Chile, the same rough coastline, hills, vegetation, birds, even the cloud formations in the sky.

Willie's one-story house, a washed-out gray with a flat roof, was on the water. Its one charm was a ruined dock with a sailboat that had become a nest for gulls. Willie's son Harleigh came out to meet us, a ten-year-old so hyperactive he seemed crazed; he stuck out his tongue at me while he kicked the doors and shot rubber projectiles from a cannon. On a shelf I saw ugly crystal and porcelain bibelots but almost no furniture, except in the dining room. Willie explained that the Christmas tree had burned and scorched all the furnishings, and then I noticed there were still ornaments hanging from the ceiling, with ten months' accumulation of cobwebs. I offered to help my host get dinner, but I felt lost in that kitchen crammed with appliances and toys. Willie introduced me to the other inhabitants of the house: his older son—who by a strange coincidence was born the same day of the same year as Paula—so drugged-out he could scarcely hold his head up, his companion, a young girl in the same straits, an exiled Bulgarian with his young daughter—they had come for one night and had settled in to live— and Jason, the stepson Willie had taken in after divorcing his mother, the only one with whom I could establish human communication. Later, I became aware of the existence of a daughter far gone in heroin and prostitution, whom I have seen only in jail or the hospital, where she frequently ends up. Three gray mice with chewed, bloody tails languished in a cage and several fish floated belly-up in a cloudy aquarium; there was also a monster of a dog that urinated in the living room and then happily trotted off to romp in the ocean—he would return at dessert time dragging the rotted corpse of some huge bird. I was ready to make a run for the hotel, but curiosity was stronger than panic, and I stayed. While the Bulgarian watched a football game on television with his little girl

asleep on his knees, and the drug addicts snored in their particular
paradise, Willie set to work: he cooked, threw loads of clothes into
the washing machine, fed the numerous beasts, patiently listened to
a surreal story Jason had just written and wanted to read aloud, and
prepared the bath for his younger son, who at ten was incapable of
doing it himself. I had never seen a father doing a mother's work,
and was moved much more than I wanted to admit. I felt divided
between a healthy aversion toward this unhinged family and a dangerous fascination for that man playing the maternal role. It may be
that I began mentally to write *The Infinite Plan* that night. The next
day, Willie called again; our mutual attraction was evident but we
were aware it had no future because, in addition to the obvious
drawbacks—children, pets, language, cultural differences, and
lifestyles—we lived ten hours apart by jet. Even so, I decided to
postpone my vow of chastity and spend one night with him, knowing it would be goodbye forever the next morning, as in a bad flick.
We would not be able to carry out this plan in the privacy of my
hotel, it had to be his house because he didn't dare leave his
younger son in the care of the Bulgarian, the drug addicts, or the
young intellectual. I arrived with my beat-up suitcase at that strange
dwelling where animal fug was mixed with salt air and perfume
from the seventeen rosebushes planted in wine barrels, with the
thought that I might live one unforgettable night—in any case, I
had nothing to lose. "Don't be surprised if Harleigh has a jealous
fit, I never invite women friends home," Willie warned me, and I
sighed with relief, because at least I wouldn't find the boa constrictor rolled up in the bath towels, but the child accepted me without
a second glance. When he heard my accent, he had confused me
with one of a long line of frightened Latin housekeepers who had
lasted no longer than the first cleanup. By the time he found out I
was sharing his father's bed, it was already too late, I had come to
stay. That night, Willie and I made love notwithstanding the exas-
perating child kicking the door, the howling dog, and the quarrels
among the remaining boys. His room was the one refuge in that
house; through the window, the stars and the ruined boat at the
dock created an illusion of peace. Beside the large bed, I saw a
wooden chest, a lamp, and a clock; farther away, a stereo. Expensive

shirts and suits hung in the closet and in the impeccable bathroom I found the same English soap my grandfather always used. I held it to my nose, incredulous; I hadn't smelled that mixture of lavender and Creolin for twenty years, and the crafty image of that unforgettable old man smiled at me from the mirror. It's fascinating to observe the personal belongings of a man one is beginning to love, how they reveal his habits and his secrets. I turned back the bed and felt the white sheets and spartan duvet, I read the titles of the books piled on the floor, I poked through the bottles in the medicine cabinet and, apart from antihistamines and pills to worm the dog, found no medicines; I smelled clothing that had no hint of tobacco or perfume, and within a few minutes I knew a lot about this man. I felt like an interloper in this world with no hint of femininity, everything was simple, practical, and manly. I also felt safe. That austere room invited me to make a clean beginning, far from Michael, Venezuela, and the past. To me, Willie represented a new destiny in another language and a different country; it was like being born again, I could invent a fresh version of myself only for this man. I sat at the foot of the bed, very still, like an alert animal, with my antenna tuned in all directions, examining with my five senses and my intuition the signals in this alien space, registering the most imperceptible signs, the subtle information of walls, furniture, objects. This tidy room canceled the terrible impression of the rest of the house; I realized that there was a part of Willie's soul that longed for order and refinement. Now that we have shared a life for several years, everything has my seal on it, but I have not forgotten who he was then. Sometimes I close my eyes, concentrate, and am again in that room and see Willie before I came to him. I like to remember the smell of his body before I had touched it, before we melded and shared the same odor. That brief time by myself in Willie's bedroom, while he struggled with Harleigh, was decisive; in those minutes, I was prepared to give myself without reserve to the experience of a new love. Something essential had changed, although I did not yet know it. For nine years, ever since those unsettling times in Madrid, I had reined in my passions. The debacle of the troubador with the magic flute had taught me elementary lessons of caution. I hadn't lacked for lovers, it's true, but until that

night in Willie's house I had not opened my heart to give and take
without holding back; one part of me had always been on guard,
and even in the intimate and special encounters that inspired the
erotic scenes of my novels, I had protected my heart. Before Willie
closed the door and we were alone and put our arms around each
other—first with caution and then with a strange passion that
streaked through us like lightning—I sensed that this was not to be
a transitory adventure. That night we made love slowly, serenely,
exploring maps and highways as if we had all the time in the world
for our journey, speaking softly in an impossible patois of English
and Spanish that ever since has been our private Esperanto, telling
each other snippets of the past in pauses in between caresses, totally
indifferent to the beating at the door and barking of the dog. At
some moment there was silence, because I remember clearly the
murmurs of love, each word, each sigh. Through the large window
spilled a faint glow from the distant lights of the Bay. Accustomed to
torrid Venezuela, I shivered with cold in that unheated room, even
after I put on Willie's cashmere sweater that hung to my knees,
wrapping me in an embrace scented with English soap. Throughout
our lives, we had been accumulating experiences that perhaps
helped us to know each other and to develop the necessary instincts
to divine the other's wishes, but even had we behaved with the
clumsiness of cubs, I think that night would have been decisive for
each of us. What was new for him? For me? I don't know, but I like
to think we were destined to meet, recognize each other, and fall in
love. Or perhaps the difference was that we charted a course
between two equally powerful currents: passion and tenderness. I
was not concerned with my own desire; my body moved without
impatience, without seeking an orgasm, with the tranquil confidence that everything would be fine. I surprised myself with tear-
filled eyes, eased by sudden emotion, caressing Willie, grateful, and
calm. I wanted to stay with him, and I wasn't frightened by his children, nor by fear of leaving my world to adopt a new country. I felt
that our love could renew us, return a certain innocence to us, wash
away the past, illuminate the dark corners of our lives. We slept in a
tangle of arms and legs, soundly, as if we had been together always,
exactly as we have every night from then on.

My plane to Caracas left very early; it was still dark when we were awakened by the alarm clock. While I showered, dizzy with exhaustion and unforgettable impressions, Willie brewed a pot of strong coffee that had the virtue of bringing me back to reality. I took my leave of the room that for a few hours had served as a temple, with the strange suspicion that before long I would see it again. On the way to the airport, as the dawn began to break, Willie hinted with inexplicable timidity that *he liked me.*

"That doesn't mean very much. I need to know whether what happened last night is an invention of a confused mind or whether in fact you love me and we have some sort of commitment."

So great was his surprise that he had to pull over and stop the car; I didn't know that you never say the word "commitment" to a North American bachelor.

"But we've just met, and you live on another continent!"

"Is it the distance that worries you?"

"I'll come to Venezuela to visit in December, and we can talk then."

"This is October, between now and December, I could be dead."

"Are you ill?"

"No, but you never know. . . . Look, Willie, I'm too old to wait around. Tell me right now whether we can give this love a chance, or if it would be better to forget the whole thing."

Pale, he started the motor again, and we drove the rest of the way in silence. His goodbye kiss was prudent, and he repeated that he would come see me during the holidays at the end of the year. The minute the plane took off, I tried very seriously to forget him, but obviously it didn't work, because as soon as we landed in Caracas, Nicolás noticed something.

"What is it, Mama? You seem strange."

"I'm worn out, Nicolás, I've been traveling for two months. I need to rest and get a change of clothes and get my hair cut."

"I think it's more than that."

"Maybe I'm in love. . . ."

"At your age?" He laughed out loud. "Who with?"

I wasn't sure of Willie's last name, but I had his telephone number and address and—at the suggestion of my son, who had the idea I should spend a week in California to get the gringo out of my mind—I sent him by express mail a two-column contract: one outlining my demands and the other listing what I was prepared to offer in a relationship. The first was longer than the second and included several key points—such as fidelity, because experience had taught me that unfaithfulness is destructive and tiring—and other less essential requirements such as reserving the right to decorate our house in my taste. The contract was based on good faith: neither of us would ever intentionally do anything to wound the other; if hurt was inflicted, it would be by error, not malice. Willie was so amused that he forgot his juristic caution, signed in the spirit of prolonging the joke, and sent it back by return mail. With that, I packed a bag containing a few clothes and the assorted fetishes I always carry with me, and asked my son to take me to the airport. "See you soon, Mama. You'll be back in a few days with your tail tucked between your legs," was his mocking farewell. From Virginia, where she was working on a master's degree, Paula expressed her doubts about this adventure by telephone.

"I know you, *vieja,* you're going to get yourself in a terrible jam. Nicolás is wrong, you won't be over it in a week. If you're going to visit that man, it's because you're prepared to stay with him. Go easy, because if you do, you're sunk, you'll have to take on all his problems." But it was too late for judicious warnings.

The beginning was a nightmare. I had always thought of the United States as my personal enemy because of its disastrous policy toward Latin America and its participation in Chile's military coup. I would have to live in this empire and travel it from end to end to understand its complexity, know it, and learn to love it. I had not used my English in more than twenty years; I could barely decipher the menu in a restaurant, I didn't understand the news on television, or the jokes, much less the language of Willie's boys. The first time we went to the movies and I found myself sitting in the dark beside a lover wearing a checked shirt and cowboy boots and holding a liter of soda and bucket of popcorn in his lap, while on the screen a madman ripped a girl's breasts with an ice pick, I thought I had come to the end of my rope. I talked with Paula that night, as I often did. Instead of repeating her warning, she reminded me of the deep emotions that had bound me to Willie from the start and advised me not to waste energy on small things but to concentrate on real problems. In truth, there were matters much more grave than cowboy boots or a tub of popcorn, from doing battle with the bizarre people invading us to adapting to the style and rhythm of a man who had lived eight years as a bachelor and whose lowest priority in the world was a bossy woman in his life. I began by buying new sheets and burning his in a bonfire on the patio, a symbolic ceremony intended to fix forever in his mind the idea of monogamy. "What's that woman doing?" asked Jason, half-asphyxiated by the smoke. "Don't worry, it must be a custom of the natives of her country," Harleigh calmed him. I immediately threw myself into cleaning and straightening up with such fervor that in a careless moment I threw away all of Willie's tools. He was close to a volcanic eruption, but then remembered the basic point in our contract: it had not been intentional on my part, but a blunder. The broom also swept before it the old Christmas ornaments, the collections of crystal figurines, and the photographs of long-legged lovers, along with four boxes of pistols, machine guns, bazookas, and cannons belonging to Harleigh that were replaced by books and educational toys. The dying fish exited down the drain and I let the mice out of their cage—the poor creatures were leading a miserable existence, anyway, with nothing to do but chew each other's tails. I explained to Harleigh that the unhappy rodents would find more satisfying activities in our neighbors' gardens, but three days later we heard a faint scratching at the door and when we opened it saw one of them with its innards spilling out, staring up with feverish eyes and begging to come in with expiring squeaks. Willie picked up the mouse and cuddled it, and for the next few weeks we slept with it in our room, treating it with antibiotics and creams to grow new skin, until it recovered. When the Bulgarian got wind of the new order, he decamped, looking for a more stable environment, and, after stealing his father's car, Willie's older son and his sweetheart also disappeared. Jason, who had spent the last year resting by day and partying by night, had no recourse but to get up early, take a shower, clean his room, and go off to school, muttering under his breath. Harleigh was the only one who accepted my presence and tolerated the new rules with good humor, because for the first time he felt secure and attended; he was so happy that with time he even forgave the mysterious disappearance of his pets and arsenal of weapons. Until then, he had never known any kind of limits, he behaved like a small savage, quite capable of breaking out glass with his fists in one of his attacks of rebellion. So deep was the empty place in his heart that in exchange for enough affection and joshing to fill it, he was willing to adopt the alien stepmother who had turned his house upside down and stolen from him a large part of his father's attention. More than four years of experience in the school in Caracas where we dealt with difficult children were not much help with Harleigh; his problems confounded the most expert, and his need to create a disturbance the most patient, but, by good fortune, the kind of kidding mutual liking we shared was a lot like affection, and helped us get along.

"I don't have to love you," he had said with a defiant face a week after we met, when he saw that it wasn't going to be easy to get rid of me.

"Neither do I. We can make an effort and try to love each other, or just treat each other with good manners. Which do you prefer?"

"Let's try to love each other."

"Good, and if that doesn't work, we can always fall back on respect."

The boy lived up to his word. For years, he tested my nerves with unflinching tenacity, but he also climbed into my bed to read stories, dedicated his best drawings to me, and even in his worst fits never forgot our pact of mutual respect. He, like Jason, came to be another son in my life. Now they are two strapping young men— one attending the university and the other finishing school after having overcome childhood traumas—whom I still have to hassle about taking out the garbage and making their beds, but we are good friends and can laugh about the fearsome pitched battles of the past. There were occasions when I felt defeated before the con- frontation began, and others when I was so tired I looked for reasons not to go home. At those moments, I remembered Tío Ramón's favorite phrase, *Remember that all the others are more afraid than you,* and I returned to the fray. I lost every battle with them but, miraculously, I think I am winning the war.

I was not yet settled in when I was offered a contract at the University of California to teach writing to a group of aspiring young authors. How can you teach someone to tell a story? Paula, by telephone, gave me the key, with a heavy dose of irony: tell them to write a bad book, that's easy, anyone can do it. And that's what we did. Each of the students set aside his or her secret dream of producing the Great American Novel and enthusiastically and fearlessly waded into the writing. Along the way, we adjusted, corrected, cut, and polished and, after many discussions and much laughter, out came their opuses, one of which was published with much ballyhoo by a major New York firm. Since then, any time I fall into a period of doubt, I tell myself I am going to write a bad book, and the panic passes. I moved a table into Willie's room, and there by the window I sat and wrote on a pad of yellow, lined paper like the one I am using now to put down these recollections. From time left over from classes, reading student work, driving back and forth to Berkeley, household chores, and Harleigh's problems, from that first convulsive year of life in the U.S., almost without my realizing, came several stories with a Caribbean flavor published shortly after as *The Stories of Eva Luna.* They were gifts from a different dimension; each one came to me whole as an apple, from the first to the last sentence, just as "Two Words" had been manifest in a traffic jam in Caracas. A novel is a long, drawn-out project in which endurance and discipline count most. It is like embroidering a complex needlepoint with many-colored floss; it is worked on the wrong side, patiently, stitch by stitch, taking care to see that the knots are not visible and following a vague design that can be appreciated only at the end when the last thread is in place and the tapestry is turned to the right side to judge the completed effect. With a little luck, the charm of the whole masks the defects and flaws in the execution. In a short story, on the other hand, everything is readily perceived; nothing can be left out, nothing can be added. There is a precise amount of space and limited time, and if the narrative is reworked too much, it loses that gust of freshness that lifts the reader. Writing a short story is like shooting an arrow: it requires the instinct, practice, and precision of a good archer—strength to pull the bow, an eye for distance and velocity, and good luck—to hit the bull's-eye. A novel is achieved with hard work, the short story with inspiration. For me the genre is as difficult as poetry, and I don't think I will attempt it again, unless, like *The Stories of Eva Luna,* fictions rain on me from the heavens. Once more it was proved to me that time alone with my writing is magical, the hour of sorcery, my only salvation when everything around me threatens to come crashing down.

The last piece of that collection, "And of Clay Are We Created," is based on a tragedy that occurred in Colombia in 1985, when the violent eruption of the volcano Nevado Ruiz produced an avalanche of melted snow that flowed down the mountainside and completely buried a village. Thousands perished, but the world remembers the catastrophe specifically because of Omaira Sánchez, a thirteen-year-old girl who was trapped in the mud from the slide. For three days, she died an anguishingly slow death before photographers, journalists, and television cameras flown in by helicopter. Her eyes staring from the television screen have haunted me ever since. I still have her photograph on my desk; again and again I studied it, trying to comprehend the meaning of her martyrdom. Three years after the event, in California, I tried to exorcise that nightmare by telling her story. I wanted to describe the torment of that poor child buried alive, but, as I was writing it, I realized that was not the core of the story. I gave it a different turn and tried to narrate from the point of view of the man who stayed by the young girl's side those three days, but when I finished that version, I understood I still hadn't captured the essence. The real story is about a woman—and I am that woman—who watches the televised struggle of the man holding the girl. It is about my feelings and the inevitable changes I experienced while witnessing the agony of that child. Once the collection of stories was published, I thought Omaira was out of my life, but I soon learned that was not the case; she is a dogged angel who will not let me forget her. When Paula fell into a coma and became a prisoner in her bed, inert, dying slowly before the helpless gaze of all around her,

I remembered the face of Omaira Sánchez. My daughter was trapped in her body, as the girl had been trapped in mud. Only then did I understand why I had thought about her all those years, and finally could decipher the message in those intense black eyes: patience, courage, resignation, dignity in the face of death. If I write something, I fear it will happen, and if I love too much, I fear I will lose that person; nevertheless, I cannot stop writing or loving. . . .

Given that the devastating fury of my broom had not fully penetrated the levels of chaos in that household, I convinced Willie that it would be easier to move than to clean, and that is how we came to live in this house of the spirits. That was the year Paula met Ernesto, and they moved in together for a time in Virginia, while Nicolás, alone in the large house in Caracas, complained that we had abandoned him. Before long, Celia appeared in his life to reveal to him certain mysteries, and in the euphoria of recently discovered love his sister and his mother were relegated to the background. We talked by telephone in complicated three-way conversations to tell each other our latest adventures and to comment ecstatically on the amazing coincidence of all three of us having fallen in love at the same time. As soon as Paula finished her studies, she and Ernesto would move to Spain, where they would begin the second phase of their life together. Nicolás explained to us that his sweetheart belonged to the most reactionary wing of the Catholic Church; there was no question of sleeping under the same roof before they married, and so they planned to wed as soon as possible. It seemed difficult to understand what he could have in common with a girl whose ideas were so different from his own, but he replied circumspectly that Celia was sensational in all other ways and, if we did not press her, he was sure her religious fanaticism would ebb. Once again, time proved him right. My son's unbeatable strategy is to plant his feet firmly, play out a lot of rope, and wait, thus avoiding useless confrontations. He wins by outwaiting his opposition. When he was four years old and I was trying to teach him to make his bed, he replied in his semi-baby talk that he was willing to do any domestic chore except that one. It was useless to try to force him; first he bribed Paula and then he begged Granny, who sneaked in through a window to help him until I surprised her, precipitating the only fight we ever had. I thought that Nicolás's stubbornness could not last forever, but for twenty-two years he slept on the floor with the dogs, like a beggar. Now that he had a sweetheart, the problem of the bed was out of my hands. While he was falling in love with Celia and studying computer science at the university, he learned karate and kung fu in order to defend himself in an emergency, because the criminals in Caracas had singled out our house and had broken and entered in broad daylight, perhaps with the blessing of the police.

Through our unabating correspondence, my mother was up to date on the details of my adventure in the United States, but, even so, she was shocked when she arrived to visit my new home. To make a good impression, I had starched tablecloths, hidden dog stains under potted plants, and made Harleigh swear to behave like a human being and his father not to curse in Spanish in my mother's presence. Willie not only cleaned up his language, he put away the cowboy boots and went to a dermatologist to have the tattoo on his hand erased with a laser, but left the skull on his arm because only I see it. My mother was the first to speak the word "marriage," as she had been years before with Michael. "How long do you intend to be his concubine? If you're going to live in this combat zone, at least get married, that way, no one can talk, and you will be eligible for a decent visa—or," she asked in the tone of voice I know so well, "do you plan to be an illegal alien all your life?" Her suggestion caused an outburst of enthusiasm from Harleigh, who by then was accustomed to having me around, and a panic attack in Willie, who had two divorces behind him and a string of unsuccessful love affairs. He told me he needed time to think it over, which seemed reasonable to me. I said he could have twenty-four hours, or I was going back to Venezuela. We got married.

In the meantime, in Chile, my parents were preparing to vote in the plebiscite that would decide the fate of the dictatorship. One of the clauses of the constitution Pinochet had drawn up to legitimize his tenure as president stipulated that in 1988 he would consult the people to determine whether his government was to continue and, should it be rejected, call democratic elections for the following year:

the general could not conceive of being caught in a trap of his own devising. The military, ready to perpetuate themselves in power, had not recognized how much discontent had intensified in those years or that people had learned hard lessons, and organized. Pinochet orchestrated a massive propaganda campaign; in contrast, the opposition was limited to fifteen minutes of television time a day—at eleven o'clock at night when it was presumed that everyone would be sleeping. Instants before the appointed hour, three million alarm clocks rang and Chileans rubbed the sleep from their eyes to watch that fabulous quarter hour in which popular ingenuity approached the level of genius. The *NO* campaign was characterized by humor, youth, and the spirit of reconciliation and hope. The campaign of the *SI* party was a botch of military hymns, threats, addresses by the general, posed amid patriotic emblems, and clips from old documentaries showing people standing in line during the days of the Popular Unity. If there were still any undecided voters, the sparkle of the *NO*s overcame the irritating weightiness of the *SI*s, and Pinochet lost the plebiscite. That year, after thirteen years of absence, Willie and I landed in Santiago on a glorious sunny day. I was immediately encircled by a group of *carabineros* and again felt the bite of terror, but then, to my amazement, I realized that they were not there to carry me off to prison but to protect me from the rush of a small crowd that had come to welcome me. As they called my name, I thought they had confused me with my cousin Isabel, Salvador Allende's daughter, but several people stepped forward with books to be signed. My first novel had defied censorship by circulating from hand to hand in photocopies until it became *persona grata* in the bookstores; as a result, it probably attracted benevolent readers who read it out of pure contrariness. Later, I learned that a journalist friend of mine had broadcast my arrival on the radio, turning the discreet visit I had planned into news. As a joke, he also announced that I had married a Texas oil millionaire, according me a prestige impossible to obtain through mere literature. I cannot describe the emotion I felt when we crossed the majestic peaks of the cordillera of the Andes and I stepped onto the soil of my homeland, breathed the warm valley air, heard the accent of our Spanish, and in Immigration received the solemn greeting, almost like an admonition, typical of our public officials. I was so weak in the knees, I had to lean on Willie as we passed through customs and saw my parents and Mama Hilda, waiting with open arms. That return is the perfect metaphor for my life. I had fled from my country, frightened and alone, one wintry, cloudy late afternoon, and returned, triumphant, on my husband's arm one splendid summer morning. My life is one of contrasts, I have learned to see both sides of the coin. At moments of greatest success, I do not lose sight of the pain awaiting me down the road, and when I am sunk in despair, I wait for the sun I know will rise farther along. On that first trip, I had a warm but timid welcome because the fist of the dictatorship still had a tight grip. I went to Isla Negra to visit Pablo Neruda's house, abandoned for many years, where the ghost of the old poet still sits facing the sea writing his immortal poems, and where the wind rings the large ship's bell to summon the gulls. On the wooden fence that surrounds the property are hundreds of messages, many written in pencil over faded traces of others erased by the caprices of weather, and some carved into wood eaten by the salt air, messages of hope for the prophet-bard who still lives in the hearts of his people. I looked up my women friends, and saw Francisco again, who had changed very little during those thirteen years. Together we climbed San Cristobal Hill to look down on the world from above and remember the period when we went there to escape everyday brutality and to share a love so chaste we never dared put it into words. I visited Michael, now remarried and the grandfather of a new family, installed in the house his father built, living exactly the life he had planned in his youth, as if losses, betrayals, exile, and other misfortunes were but a parenthesis in the perfect organization of his destiny. He welcomed me as a friend; we walked through the streets of our old neighborhood and rang the bell of the house where Paula and Nicolás grew up, looking insignificant now in its straw wig, the cherry tree still beside the window. A smiling woman opened the door and good-naturedly listened to our sentimental explanations and then let us come in and go through the whole house. On the floor were other children's toys and on the walls, photographs of other faces, but our memories lingered in the air. Everything looked smaller, with that soft sepia patina of nearly forgotten memories. Outside, I said goodbye to Michael, and, as soon as he was out of sight, burst into inconsolable sobs. I was crying for those perfect times of our early youth, when we truly loved one another and thought it would be forever, when our children were small and we believed we could protect them from all harm. What happened to us? Perhaps we are in this world to search for love, find it and lose it, again and again. With each love, we are born anew, and with each love that ends we collect a new wound. I am covered with proud scars.

One year later, I returned to vote in the first election since the military coup. Once he had lost the plebiscite, and was caught up in the snare of his own constitution, Pinochet had to call elections. He comported himself with the assurance of a victor, never imagining he could be defeated, because on his side he had the monolithic unity of the armed forces, the support of the most powerful economic sectors, a multimillion-dollar propaganda campaign, and the fear many had of freedom. Also in his favor was the history of irreconcilable differences among the political parties, a past of such rancor and unpaid accounts that it seemed impossible they could reach an accord. Rejection of the dictatorship, however, outweighed ideological differences; an agreement was made among parties opposing the government, and in 1989 their candidate won the election, making him the first legitimate president since Salvador Allende. Pinochet was forced to hand over the presidential sash and seat and take one pace backward, but he did not retire completely, his sword hung suspended above the heads of all Chileans. The country awakened from a lethargy of nearly seventeen years and took the first step in a transitional democracy in which for eight more years General Pinochet continued as commander in chief of the armed forces; a part of the Congress and all the Supreme Court had been designated by him, and the military and economic structures remained intact. There would be no justice for crimes committed, the perpetrators were protected by a decree of amnesty they had declared on their own behalf. "I will not allow anyone to harm a hair on any soldier's head," threatened Pinochet, and the country observed his conditions in silence, fearing another coup. The victims of the repression, the Maureiras and thousands of others, had to postpone their mourning and wait. Perhaps justice and truth might have helped bind up Chile's deep wounds, but the arrogance of the mili-

tary impeded that. Democracy would crawl forward at the slow and
zigzagging pace of the crab.

PAULA CAME TO MY ROOM AGAIN LAST NIGHT. I HEARD HER ENTER WITH
her light step and the striking grace that was hers before the ravages
of her illness; in her nightgown and slippers, she climbed onto my
bed and sat at my feet and talked to me in the voice she used to
exchange confidences. "Listen, Mama, wake up. I don't want you to
think you're dreaming. I've come to ask for your help. . . . I want to
die and I can't. I see a radiant path before me, but I can't take that
first step, something is holding me. All that's left in my bed is my
suffering body, degenerating by the day; I perish with thirst and cry
out for peace, but no one hears me. I am so tired! Why is this happening? You, Mama, who are always talking about your *friendly spirits*,
ask them what my mission is, what I have to do. I suppose there is
nothing to fear, death is just a threshold, like birth. I'm sorry I can't
keep my memory, but I have been detaching myself from it, anyway;
when I go I will go naked. The only recollection I'm taking with me
is of the loved ones I leave behind; I will always be with you in some
way. Do you remember the last thing I was able to whisper to you
before I slipped into this long night? 'I love you, Mama,' that's what
I said. I'm telling you again, now, and I will tell you in dreams every
night of your life. The only thing holding me back a little is having
to go alone; if you took my hand it would be easier to cross to the
other side—the infinite loneliness of death frightens me. Help me
one more time, Mama. You've fought like a lioness to save me, but
reality is overpowering you. It's all useless now; give up, stop the
doctors and medicines and prayers, because nothing will make me
healthy again, there will be no miracle, no one can change the
course of my destiny and I don't want it anyway; I have lived my
time and I want to say goodbye. Everyone in the family understands
that but you; I am eager to be free, you're the only one who hasn't
accepted the fact that I will never be as I was before. Look at my
wasted body, think of how my soul wants to escape and the terrible

bonds holding it back. Oh, *vieja,* this is so hard for me, and I know it is for you, too. What can we do? In Chile, my grandparents are praying for me and my father is clinging to the poetic recollection of a spectral daughter, while on the other side of this country Ernesto is floating in a sea of ambiguity, still unaware that he has lost me forever. Actually, he is already a widower, but he can't weep for me or love another woman as long as my body is breathing here in your house. In our brief time together, we were very happy; I am leaving him so many good memories that he won't have years enough to exhaust them. Tell him I will never forsake him, he will never be alone; I will be his guardian angel, as I will be yours. The twenty-eight years you and I shared were happy, too; don't torture yourself thinking about what could have been, things you wish you had done differently, omissions, mistakes. . . . Get all that out of your head! After I die, we will stay in contact the way you do with your grand-parents and Granny; I will be in you as a constant, soft presence, I will come when you call, communication will be easier when you don't have the misery of my sick body before you and you can see me as I was in the good days. Do you remember that time we danced the *paso doble* in the streets of Toledo, leaping over puddles and laughing in the rain beneath our black umbrella? And the star-tled faces of the Japanese tourists taking pictures of us? That's how I want you to see me from now on: two best friends, two happy women defying the rain. Yes, I had a good life. . . . It's so hard to let go of the world! But I can't bear the misery of the seven years Dr. Shima predicted; my brother knows that, and he is the only one with enough courage to set me free. I would do the same for him. Nicolás has never forgotten our old complicity, and he has clear ideas and a serene heart. Do you remember how he defended me from the shadows of the dragon at the window? You can't imagine how much mischief we hid from you, how we fooled you to protect each other, how many times you punished one for something the other had done, without our ever telling. I don't expect you to help me die, no one can ask that of you, only that you not hold me back any longer. Give Nicolás a chance. How can he give me a hand if you never leave me alone? Please don't grieve, Mama. . . ."

"Wake up, you're crying in your sleep!" I hear Willie's voice coming from a great distance, and, without opening my eyes, I try to sink farther into the darkness so my daughter will not disappear: this may be her last visit, I may never hear her voice again. "Wake up, wake up, it's a nightmare. . . ." My husband is shaking me. "Wait for me, Paula! I want to go with you!" I scream, and then he turns on the light and tries to put his arms around me, but I push him away brusquely because she is smiling at me from the doorway, lifting one hand to wave goodbye before vanishing down the hallway, her white nightgown floating like wings and her bare feet barely brushing the carpet. Beside my bed are her rabbit fur slippers.

Juan came to participate in a two-week theological seminar. He was very busy analyzing God's motives, but he found a way to spend hours with me and with Paula. Ever since giving up his Marxist convictions to devote himself to divine studies, something I cannot put my finger on has changed in his person: the slightly tilted head, the slower gestures, the more compassionate gaze, the more restrained vocabulary—now he doesn't end each sentence with a swear word, as he used to. During this visit I plan to shake that air of solemnity a little; it would be too much if religion killed his sense of humor. My brother describes himself in his role as pastor as a *manager of suffering;* his hours are eaten up with consoling and trying to help people who have no hope, in administering the scarce resources available for the dying, the drug addicts, the prostitutes, the abandoned children, and other wrecks in the multitudinous Court of Miracles that makes up humanity. His heart cannot stretch far enough to embrace so much pain. Since he lives in the most conservative area of the United States, to him California seems like a land of weirdos. By chance, he witnessed a gay parade, an exuberant Dionysian carnival, and then in Berkeley he attended frenzied demonstrations for and against abortion, political wrangles on the university campus, and a convention of street evangelists shouting their doctrines amid beggars and aging hippies, the last remnants of the sixties, still with their shell necklaces and flowers painted on their cheeks. Horrified, Juan learned that at the seminary courses are offered in *The Theology of the Hula Hoop* and *How to Earn a Living Making Fun of the Bible*. Every time this beloved brother comes, we mourn Paula's fortune, finding some remote corner of the house where no one can see us, but we also laugh as we did when we were young, when we were discovering the world and thought we were invincible. I can tell him even the most secret things. I listen to his counsel as I rattle pans in the kitchen to cook up new vegetarian dishes for him—a pointless labor since he barely pecks at his food: his nourishment is ideas and books. He spends long hours alone with Paula, I think, praying. He no longer wagers she will get well; he says that the presence of her spirit in the house is very strong, that she is clearing spiritual paths to us and sweeping our lives clean of trivia, leaving only the essential. In her wheelchair, vacant-eyed, motionless, pale, she is an angel opening doors to the divine so we may glimpse its immensity.

"Paula is getting ready to leave the world. She is exhausted, Juan."

"What do you plan to do?"

"I would help her die if I knew how."

"Don't even think of it! You would carry a burden of guilt for the rest of your days."

"But I will feel even more guilty if I leave her in this martyrdom. . . . What will happen if I die before she does? Imagine that I'm gone, who would take care of her?"

"That moment hasn't come, you gain nothing by getting ahead of yourself. Life and death have their time. God never sends us suffering without the strength to bear it."

"You're preaching at me, Juan, like a priest. . . ."

"Paula doesn't belong to you. You should not prolong her life artificially, but neither should you shorten it."

"How far does 'artificial' go? Have you seen the hospital I have downstairs? I control every function of her body; I measure every drop of water that goes into her system, and there are a dozen bottles and syringes on her table. And since she can't swallow for herself, if I don't feed her through that tube in her stomach, she will die of hunger within a week."

"Would you be able to withhold food from her?"

"No, never. But if I knew how to speed up her death without pain, I think I would do it. If I don't, sooner or later Nicolás will, and it isn't fair for him to take on that responsibility. I have a handful of sleeping pills I've been keeping for months, but I don't know if they're enough."

"Oh, Isabel. . . . How much can you suffer?"

"I don't know. I think I'm at the end of my strength. If only I could give her my life and die in her place. I'm lost, I don't know who I am, I try to remember who I was once but I find only disguises, masks, projections, the confused images of a woman I can't recognize. Am I the feminist I thought I was, or the frivolous girl who appeared on television wearing nothing but ostrich feathers? The obsessive mother, the unfaithful wife, the fearless adventurer, or the cowardly woman? Am I the person who helped political fugitives find asylum or the one who ran away because she couldn't handle fear? Too many contradictions. . . ."

"You're all of them, and also the samurai who is battling death."

"Was battling, Juan. I've lost."

Difficult times. Weeks of such anxiety that I don't want to see anyone; I can barely speak or eat or sleep; I write for hours on end. I keep losing weight. Until now, I was so busy fighting Paula's illness that I could deceive myself, imagine that I could win this battle of Titans, but now that I know Paula is going, my efforts are absurd. She is worn out; that's what she tells me in dreams at night and when I wake at dawn and when I am walking in the forest and the breeze carries her words to me. On the surface, everything seems more or less the same—except for those urgent messages, her everweaker voice asking for help. I am not the only one who hears it, the women who help me care for her are beginning to say their adieus. The masseuse decided it was not worthwhile to continue her sessions because, as she said, "Our girl is not responding." The physiotherapist called, stammering, tongue-tied with apologies, until finally he confessed that Paula's incurable illness was affecting his energy. The dental hygienist came, a young woman Paula's age, with the same long hair and thick eyebrows, so much like her they could pass for sisters. Every two weeks, she cleans Paula's teeth with great delicacy, so she won't hurt her, then hurries away without letting me see her face, trying to hide her emotions. She refuses to charge anything; up till now, there's been no opportunity for her to hand me a bill. We work together, because Paula becomes rigid when anyone tries to touch her face; only I can open her mouth and brush her teeth. This visit I noticed the hygienist was worried; no matter how carefully I do the daily cleaning, there are problems with Paula's gums. Dr. Shima often comes by on the way from work and brings me messages from his I Ching sticks. We stand close to the bed, talking about the soul and accepting death. "When she leaves us, I will feel a great void," he says. "I'm used to Paula now, she's very important in my life." Dr. Forrester seems uneasy, too. After her last examination, she was silent for a long time while she thought over her diagnosis, and finally she said that from a clinical point of view little had changed; nevertheless, she said, Paula seems less and less with us: she sleeps too much, her eyes are glassy, she doesn't react to noises anymore, her cerebral functions are diminished. But in spite of everything, she is more beautiful: her hands and ankles are finer, her neck longer, her pale cheeks dramatically emphasize her long black eyelashes. Her face has an angelic expression, as if finally she had obliterated all doubt and found the divine fount she had sought so resolutely. She is so different from me! I can't recognize anything of me in her. Or of my mother or my grandmother—except the large, dark, slightly melancholy eyes. Who is this daughter of mine? What accident of chromosomes navigating from one generation to the next in the most recondite spaces of the blood and hope determined this girl?

Nicolás and Celia keep us company; we spend much of the day in Paula's room, closed now against the cold. In the summer, the children played on the terrace in their plastic pool littered with dead mosquitoes and bits of soupy cookies while our invalid rested beneath a parasol, but now that autumn is gone and winter is beginning, the house has drawn into itself and we all gather in Paula's room. Celia is a consummate ally, generous and stable; she has been acting as my assistant for several months. I don't have the heart to work, and without her I would be crushed beneath a mountain of paper. She usually has a child in her arms or dangling on a hip, and her blouse unbuttoned to nurse Andrea. This granddaughter of mine is always happy; she plays by herself and falls asleep on the floor sucking the corner of a diaper, so quiet that we forget where we put her and, unless we're careful, could step on her. As soon as I learn to live with sadness, I will take on my grandmotherly duties. I will think up stories for the children, bake cookies, make puppets and colorful costumes to fill the theater trunk. I need Granny; if she were here she would be nearly eighty, a slightly dotty and eccentric old lady with only a handful of hair on her head, but with her talent for raising children intact.

It seems this year will never end, yet I don't know where all the hours and days have gone. I need time. Time to clear away confusion, heal wounds, and renew myself. What will I be like at sixty? Not one cell of the girl I was remains in the woman I am today, only memory, enduring and persevering. How long will it take to travel through this dark tunnel? How long to get back on my feet?

I keep Paula's letter in the same tin box that contains Memé's relics. I take it out sometimes, reverently, like a holy object, imagining that it contains the explanation I long for, tempted to read it but also paralyzed by superstitious fear. I ask myself why a young, healthy, deeply in love woman in the middle of her honeymoon would write a letter to be opened after her death? What did she see in her nightmares? What mysteries lie hidden in the life of my daughter? Sorting through old snapshots, I see her again fresh and vital, always with an arm around her husband, her brother, or her friends; in all of them, except her wedding pictures, she is in blue jeans and a simple blouse, her hair tied with a kerchief, without adornment. That is how I must remember her, but that smiling girl has been replaced by a melancholy figure submersed in solitude and silence. "Let's open the letter," Celia urged for the thousandth time. In the last few days, I have been unable to communicate with Paula; she is not visiting me now. Before, the minute I stepped through the door I perceived her thirst, her muscle cramps, the variations in her blood pressure and temperature, but now I can't sense her needs in advance. "All right, let's open it," I agreed finally. I went to get the box; shakily, I broke the wax seal, opened the envelope, and took out two pages written in Paula's precise hand, and read aloud. Her clear words came to us from another time.

I do not want to remain trapped in my body. Freed from it, I will be

*closer to those I love, no matter if they are at the four corners of the planet. It
is difficult to express the love I leave behind, the depths of the feelings that join
me to Ernesto, to my parents, to my brother, to my grandparents. I know you
will remember me, and as long as you do, I will be with you. I want to be cre-
mated and have my ashes scattered outdoors. I do not want a tombstone with
my name anywhere, I prefer to live in the hearts of those I love, and to return
to the earth. I have a savings account; use it to help children who need to go to
school or to eat. Divide my things among any who want a keepsake—actually,
there is very little. Please don't be sad, I am still with you, except I am closer
than I was before. In another time, we will be reunited in spirit, but for now
we will be together as long as you remember me. Ernesto. . . . I have loved you
deeply and still do; you are an extraordinary man and I don't doubt that you
can be happy after I am gone. Mama, Papa, Nico, Grandmother, Tío Ramón;
you are the best family I could ever have had. Don't forget me, and . . . let's
see a smile on those faces! Remember that we spirits can best help, accompany,
and protect, those who are happy. I love you dearly.*
    Paula.

Winter is back and it won't stop raining; it's cold, and you are worse
every day. Forgive me for having made you wait so long, Paula. . . .
I've been too slow, but now I have no doubt, your letter is so revealing!
Count on me, I promise I will help you, just give me a little more
time. I sit beside you in the quiet of your room in this winter that will
be eternal for me, the two of us alone, just as we have been so often
over these months, and I open myself to pain without offering any
resistance. I rest my head on your chest and feel the irregular beat of
your heart, the warmth of your skin, the slow rhythm of your breathing;
I close my eyes and for a few instants imagine that you are simply
sleeping. But sorrow explodes within me with the fury of a sudden
storm and I feel your nightgown grow damp with my tears while a
visceral moan born in the depths of the earth rises through my body
like a spear and fills my mouth. They assure me you are not suffering.
How do they know? It may be that in the end you have become
accustomed to the iron armor of paralysis, and have forgotten the
taste of a peach or the simple pleasure of running your fingers
through your hair, but your soul is trapped and yearns to be free.
There is no respite from this obsession; I know that I have failed in

the most important challenge of my life. Enough! Just look at the ruins of what is left of you, Paula . . . dear God! This is the premonition you had on your honeymoon, and why you wrote the letter. "Paula is already a saint, she is in heaven and suffering has washed away all her sins," says Inés, your scarred Salvadoran nurse who spoils you like a baby. How lovingly we care for you! You are never alone, day or night; every half-hour we move you, to maintain what little flexibility you have left; we monitor every drop of water and every gram of food; you receive your medicines on a precise schedule; before we dress you we bathe you and massage you with lotion to keep your skin healthy. "It's incredible what you've been able to do; she wouldn't do this well in any hospital," says Dr. Forrester. "She can live seven years," Dr. Shima predicts. For what? You are like the fairy-tale Sleeping Beauty in her glass coffin, except that no prince will come to save you with a kiss; no one can wake you from this final dream. Your only exit, Paula, is death. Now I can dare think it, say it to you, and write it in my yellow pad. I call upon my sturdy grandfather and my clairvoyant grandmother to help you cross the threshold and be born on the other side; I especially summon Granny, your grandmother with the transparent eyes, the one who died of sorrow when she had to be separated from you. I call her to come with her golden scissors to cut the strong thread that keeps you tied to your body. Her photo—when she is still young, with the hint of a smile and liquid eyes—is near your bed, as are those of all your guiding spirits. Come, Granny, come for your granddaughter, I plead, but I fear that neither she nor any other shade will come to lift this chalice of anguish from me. I will be alone beside you to take you by the hand to the very doorway to death, and, if I can, I will cross through with you.

Can I live in your stead? Carry you in my body so you can recover the fifty or sixty years stolen from you? I don't mean remember you, but live your life, be you, let you love and feel and breathe in me, let my gestures be yours, my voice your voice. Let me be erased, dissolved, so that you take possession of my body, oh, Paula, so that your inexhaustible and joyful goodness may completely replace my lifelong fears, my paltry ambitions, my depleted vanity. To vent my suffering, I want to scream to my last breath, rend my clothing, pull out my hair, smear myself with ashes, but I have lived half a century under rules of proper behavior; I am an expert in suppressing wrath and bearing pain, so I have no voice for screaming. Maybe the doctors are mistaken and the machines lie, maybe you are not entirely unconscious and you are aware of my state of mind; I must not distress you with my weeping. I am drowning in choked-back grief. I go outside on the terrace where there is not enough air to feed my sobs or enough rain to cry my tears. I get into my car and drive away from the town toward the hills; almost blindly, I reach the forest where I go to walk, the haven where I so often come to be alone and think. I plunge into the woods along paths made rough with winter's debris. I run, tripping over branches and rocks, pushing through the saturated greenery of this vast bosky space, so like the forests of my childhood, the ones I crossed through on muleback, following behind my grandfather. My feet are heavy with mud and my clothes are dripping and my soul is bleeding, and as it grows dark, and when finally I can go no farther after walking and stumbling and slipping and getting up to flounder on, I drop to my knees, tear my blouse, ripping off buttons, and with my arms opened into a cross and my breast naked, I scream your name, Paula. The rain is a mantle of dark crystal and somber clouds lower among the black treetops and the wind bites at my breasts, turns my bones to ice, scrubs me clean inside with its swirling, wintry tatters. I bury my hands in the muck, claw out wet clods of dirt, and rub them on my face and mouth, I chew lumps of saline mud, I gulp the acid odor of humus and medicinal aroma of eucalyptus. "Earth, welcome my daughter, receive her, take her to your bosom; Mother Goddess Earth, help us," I beg Her, and moan into the night falling around me, calling you, calling you. Far in the distance, a flock of wild ducks passes, and they carry your name to the south. Paula . . . Paula . . .

EPILOGUE

Christmas 1992

NEAR DAWN ON SUNDAY, DECEMBER 6, AFTER A miraculous night in which the veils that conceal reality were parted, Paula died. It was at four in the morning. Her life ended without struggle, anxiety, or pain; in her passing there was only the absolute peace and love of those of us who were with her. She died in my arms, surrounded by her family, the thoughts of those absent, and the spirits of her ancestors who had come to her aid. She died with the same perfect grace that characterized all the acts of her life.

For some time, I had sensed the end. I knew with the same irrefutable certainty with which I awakened one morning in 1963 knowing that, only a few hours before, a daughter had been conceived in my womb. Death came with a light step. Paula's senses had been closing down, one by one, during the previous weeks; I think she could not hear any longer, her eyes were almost always closed, and she did not react when we touched or moved her. Inexorably, she was drifting away. I wrote a letter to my brother describing the symptoms imperceptible to others but evident to me, looking ahead with a strange mixture of anguish and relief. Juan answered with a single sentence: I am praying for her and for you. To lose Paula was unbearable torment, but it would be worse to watch her slowly agonize through the seven years foreseen by the I Ching sticks. That Saturday, Inés came early and we prepared the basins of water to bathe Paula and wash her hair; we set out her clothes for the day, and changed her sheets, as we did each morning. As we began to remove her nightgown, we noticed she was deep in an abnormal sopor, like a swoon, lifeless, and wearing the expression of a child, as if she had returned to the innocent age when she used to cut flowers in Granny's garden. I knew then that she was ready for her last adventure and, in one blessed instant, the confusion and terror of this year of affliction vanished, giving way to a diaphanous tranquillity. "Do you mind, Inés, I want to be alone with her," I asked. Inés threw herself on Paula and kissed her. "Take my sins with you, and try to find forgiveness for me up there," she pleaded, and she did not want to leave until I assured her that Paula had heard her and would serve as her messenger. I went to advise my mother, who hurriedly dressed and came down to Paula's room. The three of us were alone, accompanied by the cat, crouched in a corner with her inscrutable amber pupils fixed on the bed, waiting. Willie was doing the marketing and Celia and Nicolás never come on Saturdays, that's the day they clean their apartment, so I calculated we had several hours to say our farewells without interruptions. My daughter-in-law, however, woke that morning with a presentiment and, without a word of explanation, left her husband to the household chores, picked up her two children, and came to see us. She found my mother on one side of the bed and me on the other, silently caressing Paula. She says that the minute she entered the room, she noticed how still the air was, and what a delicate light enveloped us, and she realized that the moment we most feared and, at the same time, desired had come. She sat down with us while Alejandro played with his toy cars on the wheelchair and Andrea dozed on the rug, clutching her security blanket. A couple of hours later, Willie and Nicolás arrived; they, too, needed no explanation. They lighted a fire in the fireplace and put on Paula's favorite music: Mozart and Vivaldi concertos and Chopin nocturnes. We must call Ernesto, they decided, but his telephone in New York didn't answer and they concluded he was still on his return flight from China and could not be located. The petals from Willie's last roses were beginning to fall on the night table among the medicine bottles and syringes. Nicolás went out to buy flowers, and shortly after returned with armfuls of the flowers Paula had chosen for her wedding: the smell of tuberose and iris spread softly through the house while the hours, each slower than the last, became tangled in the clocks.

At midafternoon, Dr. Forrester came by and confirmed that something had changed in her patient's condition. She did not detect any fever or signs of pain, Paula's lungs were clear, and neither was this a new onslaught of porphyria, but the complex mechanism of her body was barely functioning. "It seems to be a cerebral hemorrhage," she said, and suggested calling a nurse to bring oxygen to the house, in view of the fact that we had agreed from the beginning we would never take her back to a hospital, but I vetoed that. There was no need to discuss it; everyone in the family had concurred that we would not prolong her agony, only make her comfortable. Unobtrusively, the doctor sat down near the fireplace to wait, she, too, caught up in the magic of that unique time. She would spend all night with us, not as a physician, but as the friend she had become. How simple life is, when all is said and done. . . . In this year of torment, I had gradually been letting go: first I said goodbye to Paula's intelligence, then to her vitality and her company, now, finally, I had to part with her body. I had lost everything, and my daughter was leaving me, but the one essential thing remained: love. In the end, all I have left is the love I give her.

I watched the sky grow dark beyond the large windows. At that hour, the view from the hill where we live is extraordinary; the water of the Bay is like phosphorescent steel as the landscape turns to a fresco of shadows and lights. As night approached, the exhausted children fell asleep on the floor, covered with a blanket, and Willie busied himself in the kitchen preparing something to eat; we had only recently realized that none of us had eaten all day. He came back after a while with a tray and a bottle of champagne we had saved all year for the moment when Paula waked again in this world. I couldn't eat, but I toasted my daughter so she would awake happy in another life. We lighted candles, and Celia picked up her guitar and sang Paula's songs; she has a deep, warm voice that seems to issue from the earth itself, and her sister-in-law loved to hear her. "Sing just for me," she would coax Celia, "sing low." A wondrous lucidity allowed me to live those hours fully, with penetrating intuition and all five senses alert, as well as others whose existence I hadn't been aware of. The warm glow of the candles illuminated my daughter—silken skin, crystal bones, the shadows of her eyelashes—now sleeping forever. Transported by the intensity of our feeling for Paula, and the loving comradeship women share during the fundamental rituals of life, my mother, Celia, and I improvised the last ceremonies: we sponged Paula's body, anointed her skin with cologne, dressed her in warm clothing so she wouldn't feel cold, put the rabbit fur slippers on her feet, and combed her hair. Celia placed photographs of Alejandro and Andrea in her hands: "Look out for them," she asked. I wrote our names on a piece of paper, brought my grandmother's bridal orange blossoms and one of Granny's silver teaspoons, and placed all of them on Paula's breast for her to take as a remembrance, along with my grandmother's silver mirror, because I reasoned that if it had protected me for fifty years, surely it would safeguard Paula during that last crossing. Now Paula was opal, alabaster, translucent . . . and so cold! The cold of death comes from within, like a blazing, internal bonfire; when I kissed her, ice lingered on my lips like a burn. Gathered around her bed, we looked through old photographs and remembered the happiest times of the past, from the first dream in which Paula revealed herself to me, long before she was born, to her comic fit of jealousy when Celia and Nicolás were married. We celebrated the gifts she had given us in life, and all of us said goodbye and prayed in our own way. As the hours went by, something solemn and sacred filled the room, just as on the occasion of Andrea's birth. The two moments are much alike: birth and death are made of the same fabric. The air became more and more still; we moved slowly, in order not to disturb our hearts' repose. We were filled with Paula's spirit, as if we were all one being and there was no separation among us: life and death were joined. For a few hours, we experienced that reality the soul knows, absent time or space.

I slipped into bed beside my daughter, cradling her against my bosom, as ' had when she was young. Celia removed the cat, and arranged the two sleeping children so their bodies would warm their aunt's feet. Nicolás took his sister's hand; Willie and my mother sat on either side, surrounded by ethereal beings, by murmurs and tenuous fragrances from the past, by ghosts and apparitions, by friends and relatives, living and dead. All during the slow night, we waited, remembering the difficult moments, but especially the happy ones, telling stories, crying a little and smiling a lot, honoring the light of Paula as she sank deeper and deeper into the final sleep, her breast barely rising at slower and slower intervals. Her mission in this world was to unite all those who passed through her life, and that night we all felt sheltered beneath her starry wings, immersed in that pure silence where perhaps angels reign. Voices became murmurs, the shape of objects and the faces of our family began to fade, silhouettes fused and blended; suddenly I realized that others were among us. Granny was there in her percale dress and marmalade-stained apron, with her fresh scent of plums and large blue eyes. Tata, with his Basque beret and rustic cane was sitting in a chair near the bed. Beside him, I saw a small, slender woman with Gypsy features, who smiled at me when our glances met: Memé, I suppose, but I didn't dare speak to her for fear she would shimmer and vanish like a mirage. In other corners of the room, I thought I saw Mama Hilda with her knitting in her hands, my brother Juan, praying beside the nuns and children from Paula's school in Madrid, my father-in-law, still young, and a court of kindly old people from the geriatric home Paula used to visit in her childhood. Only a while later, the unmistakable hand of Tío Ramón fell on my shoulder, and I clearly heard Michael's voice; to my right, I saw Ildemaro, looking at Paula with the tenderness he reserved just for her. I felt Ernesto's presence materializing through the windowpane; he was barefoot, dressed in aikido attire, a solid figure that crossed the room without touching the floor and leaned over the bed to kiss his wife on the lips. "Soon, my beautiful girl; wait for me on the other side," he said, and removed the cross he always wore and placed it around her neck. Then I handed him the wedding ring I had worn for exactly one year, and he slipped it on Paula's finger, as he had the day they were married. Then I was again in the portentous dream I had in Spain, in the silo-shaped tower filled with doves, but now my daughter wasn't twelve, she was twenty-eight years young; she was not wearing her checked overcoat but a white tunic, and her hair was not pulled back into a ponytail but hanging loose to her shoulders. She began to rise, and I with her, clinging to the cloth of her dress. Again I heard Memé's voice: *No one can go with her, she has drunk the potion of death.* . . . But I pushed upward with my last strength and grasped her hand, determined not to let go, and when we reached the top of the tower I saw the roof open and we ascended together. Outside, it was already dawn; the sky was streaked with gold and the countryside beneath our feet gleamed, washed by a recent rain. We flew over valleys and hills, and finally descended into a forest of ancient redwoods, where a breeze rustled among the branches and a bold bird defied winter with its solitary song. Paula pointed to the stream; I saw fresh roses lying along its banks and a white powder of calcined bones on the bottom, and I heard the music of thousands of voices whispering among the trees. I felt myself sinking into that cool water, and knew that the voyage through pain was ending in an absolute void. As I dissolved, I had the revelation that the void was filled with everything the universe holds. Nothing and everything, at once. Sacramental light and unfathomable darkness. I am the void, I am everything that exists, I am in every leaf of the forest, in every drop of the dew, in every particle of ash carried by the stream, I am Paula and I am also Isabel, I am nothing and all other things in this life and other lives, immortal.

Godspeed, Paula, woman.

Welcome, Paula, spirit.